Penguin Edu

Intelligence and Ability

Edited by Stephen Wiseman

General Editor

B. M. Foss

Advisory Board

Michael Argyle
Dalbir Bindra
P. C. Dodwell
G. A. Foulds
Max Hamilton
Marie Jahoda
Harry Kay
S. G. M. Lee
W. M. O'Neil
K. H. Pribram
R. L. Reid
Roger Russell
Jane Stewart
Anne Tresiman
P. E. Vernon
Peter B. Warr
George Westby

Intelligence and Ability

Selected Readings
Second Edition

Edited by Stephen Wiseman

Penguin Books

Penguin Books Ltd, Harmondsworth,
Middlesex, England
Penguin Books Inc, 7110 Ambassador Road,
Baltimore, Md 21207, USA
Penguin Books Australia Ltd,
Ringwood, Victoria, Australia

First published 1967
Reprinted 1968
Second edition 1973
This selection copyright © the Estate of Stephen Wiseman 1967, 1973
Introduction and notes copyright © the Estate of Stephen Wiseman 1967, 1973
Copyright acknowledgement for items in this volume will be found on page 377

Made and printed in Great Britain by
Richard Clay (The Chaucer Press) Ltd,
Bungay, Suffolk
Set in Monotype Times

Contents

Preface 7

Introduction 9

Editor's Acknowledgements 19

Part One
The Pioneers 21

1 F. Galton (1892)
Classification of men according to their natural gifts 25

2 C. Spearman (1904)
'General intelligence'; objectively determined and measured 37

3 T. L. Kelley (1928)
The boundaries of mental life 63

4 G. Thomson (1936)
Intelligence and civilization 83

Part Two
Structure of the Mind 99

5 P. E. Vernon (1950)
The hierarchy of ability 101

6 C. Burt (1949)
The structure of the mind 115

7 J. P. Guilford (1959)
Three faces of intellect 141

Part Three
Nature v. Nurture 161

8 D. O. Hebb (1949)
The growth and decline of intelligence 165

9 C. Burt (1955)
The evidence for the concept of intelligence 182

Part Four
Theory v. Practice   205

10 R. B. Cattell (1967)
*The theory of fluid and crystallized general intelligence
checks at the five to six year old level*   209

11 A. R. Jensen (1969)
Intelligence, learning ability and socio-economic status   230

12 H. J. Eysenck (1967)
*Intelligence assessment: a theoretical and experimental
approach*   244

Part Five
Cross-Cultural Studies   269

13 A. R. Jensen (1969)
How much can we boost IQ and scholastic achievement   273

14 G. S. Lesser, G. Feifer and D. H. Clark (1965)
*Mental abilities of children from different social-class and
cultural groups*   279

15 P. E. Vernon (1969)
Types of social structure and values   292

Part Six
Wider Implications   311

16 G. A. Ferguson (1954)
Learning and human ability   313

17 J. McV. Hunt (1961)
Intelligence and experience   333

Acknowledgements   377
Author Index   378
Subject Index   382

Preface

Stephen Wiseman died before he could put the finishing touches to the second edition of this book. The task of dotting the *i*s and crossing the *t*s was left. Even this was simplified by the meticulous efforts of his personal secretary, Mrs Jean Day, who organized and typed his manuscript amendments for this edition. Apart from this preface, the introduction to Part Five part of the acknowledgements, and the provision of detailed references, this second edition is as Stephen Wiseman planned it. The restructuring of the book followed his reassessment of the priorities within the permitted size of this volume and took into account the comments on the first edition made by his colleagues and by the teachers and student teachers who read his book.

Dr Wiseman was looking forward to his retirement in 1973 as an opportunity to write extensively and thus his death in 1971 was a tragedy for British education, as we have lost the volumes that would have appeared. He was a great educator. His northern social conscience had been integrated by years in the classroom and the university lecture hall, as well as by the daily graft of research. He was one of the few men in education who could keep his head above the clouds to see the way ahead and yet keep his feet on the ground, so that he was firmly in touch with the realities of the day. Such men are few and far between.

K. B. Start

Introduction

This book deals with man's intellectual powers, their nature, form and structure. This is an area of psychology that has received much attention from the research workers, and the gains have been considerable. The great number of investigations made in the inter-war years into the range of individual differences among children, for example, extended significantly the boundaries of our factual knowledge, permitted new insights and fostered a developing theory of human abilities. We began to know (or to feel that we knew) much more about the *cognitive* aspects of the mind than about the *affective* or *conative*. This tripartite division, so useful as a means of structuring the complexities of the relatively new subject of psychology, came to be a handicap as well as a help, since it encouraged the erection of walls and the creation of water-tight compartments. It is clear, now, that it is not only unrealistic but misleading to think of man's intellectual gifts and capabilities purely in cognitive terms. The effect of motivation, for example, can make nonsense of predictions of the potentiality of children based solely on measures of cognitive ability. Some of the Readings collected here exemplify this danger; others suggest the interconnections between emotion, will and intellectual function. For the student, however, it is important to emphasize the need to relate the contents of this volume to those others dealing with personality and emotional development.

One of the advantages claimed for the study of history is that it enables us to understand more clearly the complexities lying behind the problems of our modern age, and that a realization of some of the sources of these may enable us to avoid at least some of the mistakes we might otherwise make. That is one of the justifications for adopting a strongly historical approach to the selection of readings in this volume. Although a great deal of research has been done in the cognitive field, we are far from achieving a clearly defined and generally accepted theoretical structure for it. Controversies still abound – and some are major controversies which must be resolved before significant progress can be made. A knowledge of the paths leading up to the positions occupied by the major contestants is a necessary preliminary for the student wishing to make an intelligent appraisal of differing schools of thought.

Perhaps there is another – though doubtless less powerful – reason for an historical approach. I must confess to a certain degree of chauvinism here. We must undoubtedly acknowledge our great indebtedness to America for the massive scale of her research effort in psychology, and not least in the cognitive field. The development of psychology must have been very much slower and more hesitant without this powerful attack. But we must also recognize that the foundations on which it was built were – to a very considerable extent – British. A book of readings such as this which did not start with Galton, and which did not include contributions from such pioneers and innovators as Spearman, Burt, Thomson and Vernon would indeed be a lop-sided and misleading production. Since, in the nature of things, our university and college libraries carry ever-increasing proportions of American textbooks in psychology and educational psychology, it is all the more important to emphasize this country's fundamental contributors. I believe that this is not mere chauvinism, but a necessary process in understanding some of the basic conflicts already mentioned. There are both American and British schools of thought in the cognitive field, and particularly so in theories of the structure of abilities. Eventually they will come together: but this will happen later rather than sooner if the peculiarly British contributions receive less than their deserved share of attention. If I were to hazard a prediction (and 'hazard' is the right word here) I would guess that the final solution – if there is to be one – will lie nearer the British than the American line of thought.

Since I have mentioned chauvinism in connection with American contributions, perhaps this is an appropriate place to enter an apology for the omission of any contribution from a very famous Frenchman, Binet. No doubt my overall choice of papers will be criticized from many points of view – inevitably so, I feel, since such a selection must be a highly personal one in the end, and is unlikely to please anyone completely – but perhaps this omission will attract more criticism than any other. I can, and must, of course, plead lack of space, but this is not a wholly satisfying answer. Binet's contribution was considerable, but it was a contribution to measurement rather than to theory. To him we owe the concept of *mental age*, which at a stroke cut through the major difficulties of measurement, and permitted a comparison of child with child, and of normal with abnormal. The fact that Binet's original test, even if many times revised, is still in use in nearly every country in the world, is sufficient testimony to the value of his work. Without it the development of theory would have been a great deal slower, but he himself was relatively unconcerned with theory: he saw himself as a practitioner endeavouring to solve immediate problems:

... let us recall to mind precisely the limits of the problem for which we are seeking a solution. Our aim is, when a child is put before us, to take the measurement of his intellectual powers, in order to establish whether he is normal or if he is retarded. For this purpose we have to study his present condition, and this condition alone. We have to concern ourselves neither with his past nor his future; as a result we shall neglect entirely his etiology, and notably we shall make no distinction between acquired idiocy and congenital idiocy; and this is all the more reason why we should set aside absolutely all the considerations of pathological anatomy which might explain his intellectual deficiency. So much for the past. As for the future, we shall observe the same restraint; we shall not seek in any way to establish or to prepare a prognosis and we leave the question of whether his backwardness is curable or not, capable of improvement or not, entirely unanswered. We shall confine ourselves to gathering together the truth on his present condition (Binet and Simon, 1905).[1]

This quotation from Binet reminds us that the study of man's abilities has important and immediate relevance to practical problems of the modern world as well as being of concern to the theoretician. This was well exemplified in the First World War, when the Americans, with their characteristic genius for applied science, produced the 'Army Alpha' intelligence test for use in selection for, and within, the armed forces. This was the world's first large-scale 'group test' (in contrast to the individual test of Binet), and it was a triumphant success. Crude though it was by modern standards, the test was found to predict 'trainability' to a remarkable extent, and it gave American psychologists a clearly recognized place among the applied scientists, as well as providing the theoreticians with a mass of data that were to occupy them for many years. By the time the Second World War was upon us, the value of tests of ability and aptitude was clearly recognized, and psychologists were recruited as personnel selection officers in both Britain and America. Probably a state of war presents the most favourable conditions for the use of psychological tests. Speed is

1. I am indebted to my colleague, Mr Asher Cashdan, for drawing my attention to this passage, and to Miss Anne Wallace for the translation.

essential in the allocation of men to jobs, and in selecting recruits for training in specialist duties, many of which are highly technical. Any rapid method of selection which will yield predictions of success better than chance is recognized as worth while, even though it may be known that more traditional methods – which take much more time – can achieve a higher degree of accuracy.[2]

Leaving aside the wartime applications of mental measurement, there is no doubt that the field which has seen the greatest application is that of educational psychology. This has been so, not only because the study of children permits us to investigate the development of abilities, but also because children in school provide the psychologist with convenient, captive subjects. This was recognized even by Galton.[3] The years between the wars saw an immense amount of work devoted to the investigation of individual differences among children, and this, together with the development of new and powerful statistical techniques, particularly factor analysis, permitted the slow emergence of a coherent theory of the structure of human abilities. This is not to say that a complete and final pattern has now emerged. There are still major controversies and disagreements, and there are still significant differences between the views of most British and most American psychologists. But these differences are coming to be seen as mainly differences in techniques of analysis: the end products show considerable similarities, and the two major schools have certainly drawn closer together in the last decade.

Binet's work began from the problems created in the Parisian school system by the existence of dull and backward pupils. These problems are major ones for the teacher, so it is not surprising that much of the work of mental measurement among schoolchildren has been focused on the diagnosis of backwardness. The success of the concept of 'mental age' in the measurement of intelligence led to the production of standardized tests of educational attainments. The teacher was now provided with accurate measuring instruments which would yield, for each of his pupils,

2. It is also true, of course, that research in personnel selection has often shown some traditional methods of selection – possessing high prestige – to be relatively worthless.

3. 'The subject of character deserves more statistical investigation than it has yet received, and none have a better chance of doing it well than schoolmasters; their opportunities are indeed most enviable. It would be necessary to approach the subject wholly without prejudice, as a pure matter of observation, just as if the children were the fauna and flora of hitherto undescribed species in an entirely new land.' (Galton, 1907.)

a reading age, a spelling age, an arithmetic age and so on. Burt was the outstanding British pioneer in this, and many hundreds of teachers have used his *Handbook of Tests*, reprinted from his major classic *Mental and Scholastic Tests* (1921; 4th edn, 1962). The teacher could now estimate, with a considerable degree of accuracy, the *degree* of backwardness of each of his pupils, and also its *extent*. He was able to draw a profile of educational attainments, and base his remedial work on this. For the first time the school was provided with the tools with which comprehensive educational guidance could be undertaken. It is, perhaps, understandable that the emphasis in all this work was on backwardness, which to the teacher is an inescapable problem. The psychologists' investigation of individual differences revealed the great range of ability to be found in any representative group of children. The distribution curve was roughly symmetrical, ranging from the very bright. In a random sample of ten-year-olds one might expect mental ages to range from five to fifteen. Few individual teachers, perhaps, are faced with quite such a wide range of ability, but differences in mental age of five or six years between brightest and dullest are by no means uncommon in primary-school classes. The teacher is clearly aware of the difficulties of dealing with the dullest – but the challenge of the brightest is equally demanding, and far less often recognized. The fact that the very able pupil can cope with ease with the normal demands made upon him by the school often blinds us to the fact that we are grossly negligent in omitting to provide him with the material he needs for the full development of his considerable potential. This lack of balance is – slowly – being redressed, and a few more educationists and educational psychologists on both sides of the Atlantic are now beginning to concern themselves with the bright child and the brilliant child. Terman and his co-workers[4] had less impact upon American policy than did the psychological shock of the first Russian sputnik.

The assimilation of mental tests into the professional armoury of the teacher brought its hazards as well as its opportunities. This is inevitable, perhaps, when new techniques and new instruments are placed at the disposal of the practitioner, and it is not surprising that some of the limitations of the tests were ignored by

4. Terman's follow-up (1925–59) of 1000 gifted children is a unique study. The first volume appeared in 1925 and has been followed by four other volumes. The last, *The Gifted Group in Mid-Life*, was published in 1959.

their more enthusiastic devotees, or that the interpretations of test results were often too facile and oversimplified. The psychologists themselves were not wholly free from blame; they were often guilty of oversimplification when they addressed themselves to teachers. The major problem arose over the question of the educational and psychological significance of mental age, or of IQ, and the confusion between the theoretical concept and the actual, measured result. Much of the experimental work in the first three decades of the century went to show that the Intelligence Quotient (the ratio of mental age to chronological age) tended to remain constant – at least up to the age of fifteen or sixteen. Such a finding is, of course, consonant with the theory that intelligence, as measured by the tests, is a constant power, unaffected by environmental forces such as education. Spearman's theory of the 'general factor', g, gave support to such a view: 'Every mind tends to keep its total simultaneous cognitive output constant in quantity, however varying in quality. . . . Every manifestation (of this quantitative principle) is superposed upon, as its ultimate basis, certain primordial but variable individual potencies.' (Spearman, 1923.) The emergence of g from the hierarchy of intercorrelations of tests of educational abilities and aptitudes seemed to correspond to the concept of 'intelligence' handed down from Plato, Aristotle and Cicero: that basic, innate power of the mind, any deficiency in which no efforts of school or church can overcome. And so the way seemed clear for the teacher in his interpretation of the test results of his pupils. If he were faced with a boy having a mental age of eight, and if the boy's educational age matched this, then all was well. The fact that the boy's chronological age happened to be, say, ten, was relatively unimportant. He was retarded by two years, but this was because he was *dull*, and the fact that mental age and educational age coincided 'proved' that he was not *backward*. This was, of course, a most comforting doctrine for the teacher, absolving him from any effort to provide remedial measures. The fact that the teacher was equating the theoretical concept of intelligence as purely innate with the *measurement* obtained from an inevitably fallible test was very frequently forgotten: and psychologists themselves were not noticeably vehement in their protestations.

For, of course, the psychologists themselves were far from agreed as to how near the Platonic concept was the measured IQ. This is not surprising. The heredity–environment debate has a very long history. As I have said elsewhere, it is for education and educationists a fundamental problem, but it is equally fundamental for the philosopher and the politician. Even to pose the question has been dangerous in certain periods of our history; to give a particular answer has been to invite imprisonment, torture and death. This is because of the entanglement of the problem with the question of authority – divine or secular. Speculation about it has been regarded as heretical and treasonable, directed against the power of the church or the state, whenever this power has been in the hands of an hereditary elite. The witch-doctor, the prince-bishop, the baron, the emperor have all proclaimed the power of inborn factors; the reformer, the republican, the radical, the revolutionary have emphasized the equality of man and the potentiality of education, training and a favourable environment. It is, therefore, a social and political question first, and an educational question second. (Wiseman, 1964.)

Research between the wars failed to obtain a clear-cut answer to the question. For many children, the IQ was demonstrably constant, within the limits of the error of measurement. But with dramatic environmental differences the influence of quality of education and of background on measured IQ was clearly evident. Gordon's research in 1923 on canal boat children gave a typical result, showing that for such children, leading a nomadic life with little or no schooling, IQ fell with age. The average IQ of the youngest child in canal boat families was 90; of the oldest, 60. Tests which we standardized on children of normal home backgrounds and of normal school experience are clearly inappropriate – in the standards they set for children such as those tested by Gordon. We are now much more aware of the limitations of our measuring instruments, and accept the impossibility of devising intelligence tests which are completely culture-free. The new generation of teachers is – or ought to be – warned against the dangerous assumption that a mental age derived from an intelligence test can be regarded as a 'ceiling' above which the pupil cannot hope to rise.

But this is not to say that all controversy is silent in the nature–nurture battle. Human nature being what it is, this is unlikely to happen for a very long time. Burt, in his 1955 paper (a revised version of which appears in Part Three), commented that 'an excessive emphasis on heredity has now been succeeded by an equally excessive emphasis on environment', a tendency which is part of the present accent on sociology and sociological explanation. For the student this is a difficult field, since he approaches the evidence with a 'mental set' produced by his own philosophy and political convictions, which in turn have been affected by his upbringing and the attitudinal forces of home, school and neighbourhood. And he must not be so naïve as to suppose that his 'elders and betters' – and the writers of the books and papers containing the evidence – are immune from such forces. He needs to be aware of Pastore's work (1949), which concerned biologists and geneticists, their views on the environment–heredity problem, and the relationship between these views and their political beliefs. His conclusion was that such beliefs were significant determinants of the position they adopted in the controversy, and influenced the formulation of their hypotheses, their methodology, their conclusions and their views on the implications of these conclusions for the organization of society.

Amid these readings on intelligence and ability the reader will find very few references to *aptitudes*. This reflects the real situation. In the twenties and thirties, some psychologists believed that it would prove possible to identify and isolate many separate 'aptitudes', which would be of the very greatest help in vocational guidance and selection. This hope has proved a vain one. It is true that the vocational psychologist has a fairly impressive battery of tests to call on, but when these are looked at more closely they will be found to contain measures of motivation, interest and attitude, as important determinants of aptitude; measures of intelligence, both verbal and non-verbal; measures of 'group factors' such as v or n or k. There are unlikely to be separate tests of aptitude for engineering, or for dentistry, or for architecture. The notion that for any individual there is one 'perfect' occupation or vocation, for which his abilities and aptitudes fit him uniquely, is no longer held (if, indeed, it ever was). What matters is first, the level of general, cognitive ability; second, the pattern of group factors. These together will indicate to the psychologist a group of many occupations which are 'possible'. The choice between these will depend mainly upon interest and motivation. It is true that the test battery of the American vocational psychologist will appear somewhat different from that of the British. Thurstone's view of man possessing an assortment of many 'primary abilities' will be reflected in the tests he employs. But the second-order factors lying behind this assortment of tests brings the end-result very close indeed to that achieved by the British psychologist who bases his technique on the hierarchical structure described by Burt and by Vernon in Part Two.

The time-span of the Readings reprinted in this book is close on a hundred years. How much progress have we made? A re-reading of the contribution from that hereditary genius Francis Galton makes one feel that we have done little more than validate and systematize the flashes of insight which he then produced. The final section of the book, however, begins to draw together the results of an impressive volume of research and inquiry in the cognitive field, and shows the first movement towards an integration of two major sectors of psychological theory: learning theory and man's abilities and aptitudes. Once a firm integration of these two streams of research is achieved a new era will have dawned for the educational psychologist and the vocational psychologist. Meanwhile the study of intelligence, ability and aptitude will continue to fascinate the theoretician and the applied psychologist alike, and there is unlikely to be any slackening in our research effort. There are few who underrate the importance of the task in terms of its potentiality for the progress of mankind and the achievement of equality of opportunity. It is fitting to end this introduction with a quotation from the introduction to Galton's *Hereditary Genius*, a quotation which retains its full force and relevance nearly a century after it was first written:

I wish again to emphasize the fact that the improvement of the natural gifts of future generations of the human race is largely, though indirectly, under our control. We may not be able to originate, but we can guide. . . . It is earnestly to be hoped that inquiries will be increasingly directed into historical facts, with a view of estimating the possible effects of reasonable political action in the future, in gradually raising the present miserably low standard of the human race to one in which the Utopias in the dreamland of philanthropists may become practical possibilities. (Galton, 1892.)

References

BINET, A. and SIMON, R. (1905) *L' Année Psychologique*, vol. 2.
BURT, C. (1921), *Handbook of Tests*, King.
GALTON, F. (1907), *Inquiries Into Human Faculty*, Everyman.
GALTON, F. (1892), *Hereditary Genius*, 2nd edn, Macmillan.
PASTORE, N. (1949), *The Nature – Nurture Controversy*, Cambridge University Press.
SPEARMAN, C. (1923), *The Nature of Intelligence and the Principles of Cognition*, Methuen.
TERMAN, L. M. (1925–59), *Genetic Studies of Genius*, Stanford University Press.
WISEMAN, S. (1964), *Education and Environment*, Manchester University Press.

Editor's Acknowledgements

First edition

While I must accept sole responsibility for the choice of Readings reprinted in this volume, I must acknowledge my indebtedness to the many friends and colleagues who assisted me by discussion, and by suggestions for inclusions. It will be obvious to them that I did not always act on their advice: nevertheless, they had considerable influence on the final shape of the book. Among these helpers I am particularly indebted to Mr L. B. Birch, Sir Cyril Burt, Mr T. Fitzpatrick, Mr T. H. B. Hollins, Mr D. McMahon, Professor P. H. Taylor and Professor F. W. Warburton. And most of all I must express my gratitude to Mrs Sybil Shields who undertook the arduous work of typing, copying, collating and generally organizing the material for publication.

Stephen Wiseman

Second edition

In preparing this second edition, Dr Wiseman consulted many of his friends and colleagues. Having sought this guidance he would have, as usual, been most grateful for their comments and suggestions, but reserved to himself responsibility for any inadequacies the reader may find, as was his way.

K. B. Start

Part One
The Pioneers

Galton can fairly be described as the father of experimental
educational psychology. The first of our Readings is taken from
his famous book *Hereditary Genius*, and from this short extract
some of the author's many gifts may be apparent. His
outstanding characteristic was, perhaps, an intensely inquiring
mind, one that was for ever producing questions and probing at
problems. But he was not content with arm-chair philosophizing
and speculation: his approach was empirical; he sought facts to
satisfy his questions. He believed in *measurement* as one of the
basic necessities, from which facts could be produced, and hence
theories evolved. Once his measurements were obtained –
anthropometric measurements, for example, or measurements
of human mental ability – he found it necessary to devise
techniques of analysis of the data. He invented *correlation*, one
of the experimental psychologists' most important tools:
Pearson polished the tool, but Galton designed the prototype.
And in the extract printed here the reader will discern, in Galton's
'classification', the fundamental first steps towards the concept
of standardized scores. Galton was a polymath – a geographer
and an explorer before he was an anthropometrician – and he
also had no doubts about the scientist's responsibilities to society.
The following quotation from the introduction to *Hereditary
Genius*, with its insistence on our duty to humanity, is
characteristic of the man:

I shall show that social agencies of an ordinary character whose
influences are little suspected are at this moment working towards
the degradation of human nature and that others are working towards
its improvement. I conclude that each generation has enormous power
over the natural gifts of those that follow, and maintain that it is a
duty we owe to humanity to investigate the range of that power, and
to exercise it in such a way that, without being unwise towards ourselves,
it shall be advantageous to future inhabitants of the Earth.

It is, perhaps, a sobering thought that this could well be written again today, one hundred years later. The second of the pioneers to appear in this first section is Charles Spearman, army officer turned psychologist. There is no doubt about his being a true pioneer. The contribution printed here is an extract from a famous paper published in 1904. This was a work of great significance: it forms the foundation of an impressive edifice of experimental work; it was the basis of an elaborate and highly significant theory of the organization of man's abilities; and from this paper developed the statistical techniques from which factor analysis developed. This was the opening statement of a debate which has long continued: 'general' v. 'specific' traits, the existence of group factors, the existence of 'general intelligence' itself. Throughout this book will be found references to Spearman and his theories, and for this reason alone it seemed imperative to include at least extracts from this historic paper.

The third paper comes from an American, to underline the interest and energy which emanated from the USA in response to the stimulus of Galton and Spearman. T. L. Kelley is one of the giants of the American scene. This extract is from *Crossroads in the Mind of Man*, a highly significant book, and one which gives the first sign of a major breakaway of the American theorists from the Spearman model. Here we see the emergence of the concept of *group factors*, and a closely reasoned argument questioning Spearman's theories.

The final contributor represented here – Thomson – ranks with Spearman and Burt as one of the great formative influences on British psychology and psychometrics. It would be unthinkable to produce a book of Readings on intelligence and ability which did not include something from his pen. The choice was not easy, but the lecture text finally chosen is one which seems to me to be particularly appropriate. First, it begins by indicating – all too briefly – one of the main forces guiding the direction of his researches and writings: his passionate desire to ensure adequate educational opportunity for the less privileged child. Thomson's own experience as a scholarship boy from a humble home was something that he never forgot. His experience as Professor of Education at Durham University and as a member of the Northumberland Education Committee during the years of the Depression, when the north-east became one of the black spots of the nation, was undoubtedly another major influence. And when he moved to Edinburgh he set up this country's first educational test bureau, at Moray House, as part of his campaign for improving the accuracy and validity of educational selection. But the lecture reproduced here shows him as someone much more than a mere test technician and statistician: he was a philosopher as well as a psychologist. Those who knew him remember him with deep affection, for he was a man of great compassion and deep sympathy as well as of incisive intellect: and something of these qualities is revealed in this lecture.

1 F. Galton

Classification of Men According to their Natural Gifts

Excerpts from F. Galton, *Hereditary Genius*, Macmillan, 2nd edn, 1892, chapter 3, pp. 14–36.

I have no patience with the hypothesis occasionally expressed, and often implied, especially in tales written to teach children to be good, that babies are born pretty much alike, and that the sole agencies in creating differences between boy and boy, and man and man, are steady application and moral effort. It is in the most unqualified manner that I object to pretensions of natural equality. The experiences of the nursery, the school, the university, and of professional careers, are a chain of proofs to the contrary. I acknowledge freely the great power of education and social influences in developing the active powers of the mind, just as I acknowledge the effect of use in developing the muscles of a blacksmith's arm, and no further. Let the blacksmith labour as he will, he will find there are certain feats beyond his power that are well within the strength of a man of herculean make, even although the latter may have led a sedentary life. Some years ago, the Highlanders held a grand gathering in Holland Park, where they challenged all England to compete with them in their games of strength. The challenge was accepted, and the well-trained men of the hills were beaten in the foot-race by a youth who was stated to be a pure Cockney, the clerk of a London banker.

Everybody who has trained himself to physical exercises discovers the extent of his muscular powers to a nicety. When he begins to walk, to row, to use the dumb bells, or to run, he finds to his great delight that his thews strengthen, and his endurance of fatigue increases day after day. So long as he is a novice, he perhaps flatters himself there is hardly an assignable limit to the education of his muscles; but the daily gain is soon discovered to diminish, and at last it vanishes altogether. His maximum performance becomes a rigidly determinate quantity. He learns to an inch how high or how far he can jump, when he has attained the highest state of training. He learns to half a pound the force he can exert on the dynamometer, by compressing it. He can strike a blow against the machine used to measure impact, and drive its index to a certain graduation, but no further. So it is in running, in rowing, in walking, and in every other form of physical exertion. There is a definite limit to the muscular powers of every man, which he cannot by any education or exertion overpass.

This is precisely analogous to the experience that every student has had of the working of his mental powers. The eager boy, when he first goes to school and confronts intellectual difficulties, is astonished at his progress. He glories in his newly developed mental grip and growing capacity for application, and, it may be, fondly believes it to be within his reach to become one of the heroes who have left their mark upon the history of the world. The years go by; he competes in the examinations of school and college, over and over again with his fellows, and soon finds his place among them. He knows he can beat such and such of his competitors, that there are some with whom he runs on equal terms, and others whose intellectual feats he cannot even approach. Probably his vanity still continues to tempt him, by whispering in a new strain. It tells him that classics, mathematics, and other subjects taught in universities are mere scholastic specialities, and no test of the more valuable intellectual powers. It reminds him of numerous instances of persons who had been unsuccessful in the competitions of youth, but who had shown powers in after-life that made them the foremost men of their age. Accordingly, with newly furbished hopes, and with all the ambition of twenty-two years of age, he leaves his University and enters a larger field of competition. The same kind of experience awaits him here that he has already gone through. Opportunities occur – they occur to every man – and he finds himself incapable of grasping them. He tries, and is tried in many things. In a few years more, unless he is incurably blinded by self-conceit, he learns precisely of what performances he is capable, and what other enterprises lie beyond his compass. When he reaches mature life, he is confident only within certain limits, and knows, or ought to know, himself just as he is probably judged of by the world, with all his unmistakable weakness and all his undeniable strength. He is no longer tormented into hopeless efforts by the fallacious promptings of overweening vanity, but he limits his undertakings to matters below the level of his reach, and finds true moral repose in an honest conviction that he is engaged in as much good work as his nature has rendered him capable of performing.

There can hardly be a surer evidence of the enormous difference between the intellectual capacity of men than the prodigious differences in the numbers of marks obtained by those who gain mathematical honours at Cambridge [. . .]

The mathematical powers of the last man on the list of honours, which are so low when compared with those of a senior wrangler, are mediocre, or even above mediocrity, when compared with the gifts of Englishmen generally. Though the examination places 100 honours men above him, it puts no less than 300 'poll men' below him. Even if we go so far as to allow that 200 out of the 300 refuse to work hard enough to get honours, there will remain 100 who, even if they worked hard, could not get them. Every tutor knows how difficult it is to drive abstract conceptions, even of the simplest kind, into the brains of most people – how feeble and hesitating is their mental grasp – how easily their brains are mazed – how incapable they are of precision and soundness of knowledge. It often occurs to persons familiar with some scientific subject to hear men and women of mediocre gifts relate to one another what they have picked up about it from some lecture – say at the Royal Institution, where they have sat for an hour listening with delighted attention to an admirably lucid account, illustrated by experiments of the most perfect and beautiful character, in all of which they expressed themselves intensely gratified and highly instructed. It is positively painful to hear what they say. Their recollections seem to be a mere chaos of mist and misapprehension, to which some sort of shape and organization has been given by the action of their own pure fancy, altogether alien to what the lecturer intended to convey. The average mental grasp even of what is called a well-educated audience will be found to be ludicrously small when rigorously tested.

In stating the differences between man and man, let it not be supposed for a moment that mathematicians are necessarily one-sided in their natural gifts. There are numerous instances of the reverse, of whom the following will be found, as instances of hereditary genius, in the appendix to my chapter on 'Science'. I would especially name Leibnitz, as being universally gifted; but Ampère, Arago, Condorcet, and D'Alembert were all of them very far more than mere mathematicians. Nay, since the range of examination at Cambridge is so extended as to include other subjects besides mathematics, the differences of ability between the highest and the lowest of the successful candidates is yet more glaring than what I have already described. We still find, on the one hand, mediocre men, whose whole energies are absorbed in getting their 237 marks for mathematics; and, on the other hand, some few senior wranglers who are at the same time high classical scholars and much more besides. Cambridge has afforded such instances. Its list of classical honours is comparatively of recent date, but other evidence is obtainable from earlier times of their occurrence. Thus, Dr George Butler, the Head Master of Harrow for very many years, including the period when Byron was a school boy (father of the present Head Master, and of other sons, two of whom are also head masters of great public schools), must have obtained that classical office on account of his eminent classical ability; but Dr Butler was also senior wrangler in 1794, the year when Lord Chancellor Lyndhurst was second. Both Dr Kaye, the late Bishop of Lincoln, and Sir E. Alderson, the late judge, were the senior wranglers and the first classical prizemen of their respective years. Since 1824, when the classical tripos was first established, the late Mr Goulburn (son of the Right Hon. H. Goulburn, Chancellor of the Exchequer) was second wrangler in 1835, and senior classic of the same year, But in more recent times, the necessary labour of preparation, in order to acquire the highest mathematical places, has become so enormous that there has been a wider differentiation of studies. There is no longer *time* for a man to acquire the necessary knowledge to succeed to the first place in more than one subject. There are, therefore, no instances of a man being absolutely first in both examinations, but a few can be found of high eminence in both classics and mathematics, as a reference to the lists published in the *Cambridge Calendar* will show. The best of these more recent degrees appear to be that of Dr Barry, late Principal of Cheltenham, and now Principal of King's College, London (the son of the eminent architect, Sir Charles Barry, and brother of Mr Edward Barry, who succeeded his father as architect). He was fourth wrangler and seventh classic of his year.

In whatever way we may test ability, we arrive at equally enormous intellectual differences. Lord Macaulay [. . .] had one of the most tenacious of memories. He was able to recall many pages of hundreds of volumes by various authors, which he had acquired by simply reading them over. An average man could not certainly carry in his memory one thirty-second – ay, or one hundredth – part as much as Lord Macaulay. The father of Seneca had one of the greatest memories on record in ancient times [. . .] Porson, the Greek scholar, was remarkable for this gift, and, I may add, the 'Porson memory' was hereditary in that family. In statesman-ship, generalship, literature, science, poetry, art, just the same enormous differences are found between man and man; and numerous instances recorded in this book will show in how small degree eminence, either in these or any other class of intellectual powers, can be considered as due to purely special powers. They are rather to be considered in those instances as the result of concentrated efforts made by men who are widely gifted. People lay too much stress on apparent specialities, thinking over-rashly that, because a man is devoted to some particular pursuit, he could not possibly have succeeded in anything else. They might just as well say that, because a youth had fallen desperately in love with a brunette, he could not possibly have fallen in love with a blonde. He may or may not have more natural liking for the former type of beauty than the latter, but it is as probable as not that the affair was mainly or wholly due to a general amorous-ness of disposition. It is just the same with special pursuits. A gifted man is often capricious and fickle before he selects his occupation, but when it has been chosen, he devotes himself to it with a truly passionate ardour. After a man of genius has selected his hobby, and so adapted himself to it as to seem unfitted for any other occupation in life, and to be possessed of but one special aptitude, I often notice, with admiration, how well he bears him-self when circumstances suddenly thrust him into a strange posi-tion. He will display an insight into new conditions, and a power of dealing with them, with which even his most intimate friends were unprepared to accredit him. Many a presumptuous fool has mistaken indifference and neglect for incapacity; and in trying to throw a man of genius on ground where he was unprepared for attack, has himself received a most severe and unexpected fall. I am sure that no one who has the privilege of mixing in the society of the abler men of any great capital, or who is acquainted with the biographies of the heroes of history, can doubt the existence of grand human animals, of natures pre-eminently noble, of indivi-duals born to be kings of men. I have been conscious of no slight misgiving that I was committing a kind of sacrilege whenever, in the preparation of materials for this book, I had occasion to take the measurement of modern intellects vastly superior to my own, or to criticize the genius of the most magnificent historical speci-mens of our race. It was a process that constantly recalled to me a once familiar sentiment in bygone days of African travel, when I used to take altitudes of the huge cliffs that domineered above me as I travelled along their bases, or to map the mountainous land-marks of unvisited tribes, that loomed in faint grandeur beyond my actual horizon.

I have not cared to occupy myself much with people whose gifts are below the average, but they would be an interesting study. The number of idiots and imbeciles among the twenty million inhabitants of England and Wales is approximately estimated at 50,000, or as 1 in 400. Dr Seguin, a great French authority on these matters, states that more than thirty per cent of idiots and imbeciles, put under suitable instruction, have been taught to conform to social and moral law, and rendered capable of order, of good feeling, and of working like *the third* of an average man. He says that more than forty per cent have become capable of the ordinary transactions of life, under friendly control; of under-standing moral and social abstractions, and of working like *two-thirds* of a man. And, lastly, that from twenty-five to thirty per cent come nearer and nearer to the standard of manhood, till some of them will defy the scrutiny of good judges, when com-pared with ordinary young men and women. In the order next above idiots and imbeciles are a large number of milder cases scattered among private families and kept out of sight, the existence of whom is, however, well known to relatives and friends; they are too silly to take a part in general society, but are easily amused with some trivial, harmless occupation. Then comes a class of whom the Lord Dundreary of the famous play may be considered a representative; and so, proceeding through succes-sive grades, we gradually ascend to mediocrity. I know two good instances of hereditary silliness short of imbecility, and have reason to believe I could easily obtain a large number of similar facts.

To conclude, the range of mental power between – I will not say the highest Caucasian and the lowest savage – but between the greatest and least of English intellects, is enormous. There is a continuity of natural ability reaching from one knows not what height, and descending to one can hardly say what depth. I pro-pose in this chapter to range men according to their natural abili-ties, putting them into classes separated by equal degrees of merit, and to show the relative number of individuals included in the several classes. Perhaps some person might be inclined to make an offhand guess that the number of men included in the several classes would be pretty equal. If he thinks so, I can assure him he is most egregiously mistaken.

The method I shall employ for discovering all this is an application of the very curious theoretical law of 'deviation from an average'. First, I will explain the law, and then I will show that the production of natural intellectual gifts comes justly within its scope.

The law is an exceedingly general one. M. Quételet, the Astronomer-Royal of Belgium, and the greatest authority on vital and social statistics, has largely used it in his inquiries. He has also constructed numerical tables, by which the necessary calculations can be easily made, whenever it is desired to have recourse to the law. Those who wish to learn more than I have space to relate should consult his work, which is a very readable octavo volume, and deserves to be far better known to statisticians than it appears to be. Its title is *Letters on Probabilities*, translated by Downes, Layton and Co., London, 1849.

So much has been published in recent years about statistical deductions, that I am sure the reader will be prepared to assent freely to the following hypothetical case: Suppose a large island inhabited by a single race, who intermarried freely, and who had lived for many generations under constant conditions; then the average *height* of the male adults of that population would undoubtedly be the same year after year. Also – still arguing from the experience of modern statistics, which are found to give constant results in far less carefully guarded examples – we should undoubtedly find, year after year, the same proportion maintained between the number of men of different heights. I mean, if the average stature was found to be sixty-six inches, and if it was also found in any one year that 100 per million exceeded seventy-eight inches, the same proportion of 100 per million would be closely maintained in all other years. An equal constancy of proportion would be maintained between any other limits of height we pleased to specify, as between seventy-one and seventy-two inches; between seventy-two and seventy-three inches; and so on. Statistical experiences are so invariably confirmatory of what I have stated would probably be the case as to make it unnecessary to describe analogous instances. Now, at this point, the law of deviation from an average steps in. It shows that the number per million whose heights range between seventy-one and seventy-two inches (or between any other limits we please to name) can be *predicted* from the previous datum of the average, and of any one other fact, such as that of 100 per million exceeding seventy-eight inches.

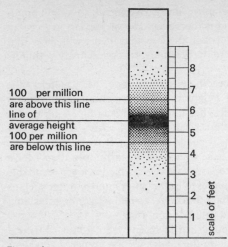

100 per million
are above this line
line of
average height
100 per million
are below this line

8
7
6
5
4
3
2
1

scale of feet

Figure 1

Figure 1 will make this more intelligible. Suppose a million of the men to stand in turns, with their backs against a vertical board of sufficient height, and their heights to be dotted off upon it. The board would then present the appearance shown in the diagram. The line of average height is that which divides the dots into two equal parts, and stands, in the case we have assumed, at the height of sixty-six inches. The dots will be found to be ranged so symmetrically on either side of the line of average, that the lower half of the diagram will be almost a precise reflection of the upper. Next, let a hundred dots be counted from above downwards, and let a line be drawn below them. According to the conditions, this line will stand at the height of seventy-eight inches. Using the data afforded by these two lines, it is possible, by the help of the law of deviation from an average, to reproduce, with extraordinary closeness, the entire system of dots on the board.

M. Quételet gives tables in which the uppermost line, instead of cutting off 100 in a million, cuts off only one in a million. He divided the intervals between that line and the line of average into eighty equal divisions, and gave the number of dots that fall within each of those divisions. It is easy, by the help of his tables, to calculate what would occur under any other system of classification we pleased to adopt.

This law of deviation from an average is perfectly general in its application. Thus, if the marks had been made by bullets fired at a horizontal line stretched in front of the target, they would have been distributed according to the same law. Wherever there is a large number of similar events, each due to the resultant influences of the same variable conditions, two effects will follow. First, the average value of those events will be constant; and, secondly, the deviations of the several events from the average will be governed by this law (which is, in principle, the same as that which governs runs of luck at a gaming-table).

The nature of the conditions affecting the several events must, I say, be the same. It clearly would not be proper to combine the heights of men belonging to two dissimilar races, in the expectation that the compound results would be governed by the same constants. A union of two dissimilar systems of dots would produce the same kind of confusion as if half of the bullets fired at a target have been directed to one mark, and the other half to another mark. Nay, an examination of the dots would show to a person, ignorant of what had occurred, that such had been the case, and it would be possible, by aid of the law, to disentangle two or any moderate number of superimposed series of marks. The law may, therefore, be used as a most trustworthy criterion, whether or no the events of which an average has been taken are due to the same or to dissimilar classes of conditions.

I selected the hypothetical case of a race of men living on an island and freely intermarrying, to ensure the conditions under which they were all supposed to live being uniform in character. It will now be my aim to show there is sufficient uniformity in the inhabitants of the British Isles to bring them fairly within the grasp of this law [. . .]

I argue from the results obtained from Frenchmen and from Scotchmen that, if we had measurements of the adult males in the British Isles, we should find those measurements to range in close accordance with the law of deviation from an average, although our population is as much mingled as I described that of Scotland to have been, and although Ireland is mainly peopled with Celts. Now, if this be the case with stature, then it will be true as regards every other physical feature – as circumference of head, size of brain, weight of grey matter, number of brain fibres, etc.; and thence, by a step on which no physiologist will hesitate, as regards mental capacity.

This is what I am driving at – that analogy clearly shows there must be a fairly constant average mental capacity in the inhabitants of the British Isles, and that the deviations from that average

– upwards towards genius, and downwards towards stupidity –
must follow the law that governs deviations from all true averages
[. . .]

The number of grades into which we may divide ability is purely a matter of option. We may consult our convenience by sorting
Englishmen into a few large classes, or into many small ones. I
will select a system of classification that shall be easily comparable
with the numbers of eminent men, as determined in the previous
chapter. We have seen that 250 men per million become eminent;
accordingly, I have so contrived the classes in Table 1 that
the two highests, F and G, together with X (which includes
all cases beyond G, and which are unclassed), shall amount to
about that number – namely to 248 per million.

It will, I trust, be clearly understood that the numbers of men
in the several classes in my table depend on no uncertain hypothesis. They are determined by the assured law of deviations from
an average. It is an absolute fact that if we pick out of each million
the one man who is naturally the ablest, and also the one man
who is the most stupid, and divide the remaining 999,998 men
into fourteen classes, the average ability in each being separated
from that of its neighbours by *equal grades*, then the number in
each of those classes will, on the average of many millions, be as
it is stated in the table. The table may be applied to special, just
as truly as to general ability. It would be true for every examination that brought out natural gifts, whether held in painting,
in music, or in statesmanship. The proportions between the
different classes would be identical in all these cases, although the
classes would be made up of different individuals, according as
the examination differed in its purport.

It will be seen (*see* Table 1) that more than half of each million
is contained in the two mediocre classes a and A; the four mediocre classes a, b, A, B, contain more than four-fifths, and the six
mediocre classes more than nineteen-twentieths of the entire
population. Thus, the rarity of commanding ability, and the vast
abundance of mediocrity, is no accident, but follows of necessity,
from the very nature of these things.

The meaning of the word 'mediocrity' admits of little doubt.
It defines the standard of intellectual power found in most provincial gatherings, because the attractions of a more stirring life
in the metropolis and elsewhere are apt to draw away the abler
classes of men, and the silly and the imbecile do not take a part in
the gatherings. Hence, the residuum that forms the bulk of the

Table 1 Classification of men according to their natural gifts

| Grades of natural ability, separated by equal intervals | | Numbers of men comprised in the several grades of natural ability, whether in respect to their general powers, or to special aptitudes | | | | | | | |
| Below average | Above average | Proportionate, viz. one in | In each million of the same age | In total male population of the United Kingdom, say 15 millions, of the undermentioned ages: | | | | | |
				20–30	30–40	40–50	50–60	60–70	70–80
a	A	4	256,791	641,000	495,000	391,000	268,000	171,000	77,000
b	B	6	161,279	409,000	312,000	246,000	168,000	107,000	48,000
c	C	16	63,563	161,000	123,000	97,000	66,000	42,000	19,000
d	D	64	15,696	39,800	30,300	23,900	16,400	10,400	4700
e	E	413	2423	6100	4700	3700	2520	1600	729
f	F	4300	233	590	450	355	243	155	70
g	G	79,000	14	35	27	21	15	9	4
x all grades below g	X all grades above G	1,000,000	1	3	2	2	2	—	—
On either side of average			500,000	1,268,000	964,000	761,000	521,000	332,000	149,000
Total, both sides			1,000,000	2,536,000	1,928,000	1,522,000	1,042,000	664,000	298,000

The proportions of men living at different ages are calculated from the proportions that are true for England and Wales. (Census 1861, Appendix, p. 107.)

Example: The class F contains 1 in every 4300 men. In other words, there are 233 of that class in each million of men. The same is true of class f. In the whole United Kingdom there are 590 men of class F (and the same number of f) between the ages of 20 and 30; 450 between the ages of 30 and 40; and so on.

general society of small provincial places is commonly very pure in its mediocrity.

The class C possesses abilities a trifle higher than those commonly possessed by the foreman of an ordinary jury. D includes the mass of men who obtain the ordinary prizes of life. E is a stage higher. Then we reach F, the lowest of those yet superior classes of intellect, with which this volume is chiefly concerned.

On descending the scale, we find by the time we have reached f, that we are already among the idiots and imbeciles. We have seen [. . .] that there are 400 idiots and imbeciles to every million of persons living in this country; but that 30 per cent of their number appear to be light cases, to whom the name of idiot is inappropriate. There will remain 280 true idiots and imbeciles to every million of our population. This ratio coincides very closely with the requirements of class f. No doubt a certain proportion of them are idiotic owing to some fortuitous cause, which may interfere with the working of a naturally good brain, much as a bit of dirt may cause a first-rate chronometer to keep worse time than an ordinary watch. But I presume, from the usual smallness of head and absence of disease among these persons, that the proportion of accidental idiots cannot be very large.

Hence we arrive at the undeniable, but unexpected conclusion, that eminently gifted men are raised as much above mediocrity as idiots are depressed below it; a fact that is calculated to considerably enlarge our ideas of the enormous differences of intellectual gifts between man and man.

I presume the class F of dogs, and others of the more intelligent sort of animals, is nearly commensurate with the f of the human race, in respect to memory and powers of reason. Certainly the class G of such animals is far superior to the g of human kind.

2 C. Spearman

'General Intelligence':
Objectively Determined and Measured

Excerpts from C. Spearman, '"General intelligence": objectively
determined and measured', *American Journal of Psychology*, vol. 115, 1904,
pp. 201–92.

Today it is difficult to realize that only as recently as 1879 Wundt
first obtained from the authorities of Leipzig University one little
room for the then novel purpose of a 'psychological laboratory'.

In twenty-four years, not only has this modest beginning
expanded into a suite of apartments admirably equipped with
elaborate apparatus and thronged with students from the most
distant quarters of the globe, but all over Germany and in almost
every other civilized country have sprung up a host of similar
institutions, each endeavoring to outbid the rest in perfection.
The brief space of time has sufficed for Experimental Psychology
to become a firmly established science, everywhere drawing to
itself the most vigorous energies and keenest intellects.

But in spite of such a brilliant career, strangely enough this new
branch of investigation still meets with resolute, wide-spread, and
even increasing opposition. Nor are its enemies at all confined to
belated conservatives or crotchety reactionaries; they are rather
to be found among the most youthful schools of thought; their
strength may be in some measure estimated from the very elaborate apology which one of the best-known experimental psychologists has lately found himself called upon to utter on behalf
of his profession.

And, indeed, when we without bias consider the whole actual
fruit so far gathered from this science – which at the outset seemed
to promise an almost unlimited harvest – we can scarcely avoid a
feeling of great disappointment. Take for an example Education.
This is the line of practical inquiry that more than all others has
absorbed the energy and talent of the younger workers and that
appears to offer a peculiarly favorable field for such methods. Yet
at this moment, notwithstanding all the laborious experiments
and profuse literature on the subject, few competent and unprejudiced judges will venture to assert that much unequivocal
information of capital importance has hitherto thus come to light.

Nor have the results been more tangible in Psychiatry or in any other department of applied psychology.

Those, then, who have the highest opinion concerning the potentialities of this new science, will feel most bound to critically examine it for any points of structural incompleteness [. . .]

The present article, therefore, advocates a 'Correlational Psychology', for the purpose of positively determining all psychical tendencies, and in particular those which connect together the so-called 'mental tests' with psychical activities of greater generality and interest. These will usually belong to that important class of tendencies produced by community of organism, whereby sufficiently similar acts are almost always performed by any one person in much the same manner; if, for example, he once proves good at discriminating two musical tones, he may be expected to manifest this talent on any subsequent occasion, and even in another portion of the scale.

For finding out the classes and limits of these individual functions, modern psychology seems to have mainly contented itself with borrowing statements from the discredited 'faculties' of the older school and then correcting and expanding such data by inward illumination. The following work is an attempt at the more fatiguing procedure of eliciting verifiable facts; the good intention and the difficulty of such an enterprise may, perhaps, be allowed to palliate the shortcomings in its execution [. . .]

In the first place, only one out of them all (Wissler at Columbia) attains to the first fundamental requisite of correlation, namely, a *precise quantitative expression.* Many writers, indeed, have been at great trouble and have compiled elaborate numerical tables, even bewilderingly so; but nowhere do we find this mass of data focused to a single exact result. In consequence, not only has comparison always been impossible between one experiment and another, but the experimenters themselves have proved quite unable to correctly estimate even their own results; some have conceived their work to prove that correspondence was absent when it really existed to a very considerable amount; whereas others have held up as a large correlation what in reality is insignificantly small. Later on, we shall come upon examples of both kinds of bias. With this requisite is closely bound up another one no less fundamental, namely, that the ultimate result should not be presented in some form specially devised to demonstrate the compiler's theory, but rather should be a perfectly impartial representation of the *whole* of the relations elicited by the experiments.

Next, with the same exception as before, not one has calculated the 'probable error'; hence, they have had no means whatever of judging how much of their results was merely due to *accidental coincidence*. This applies not only to the experiments executed with comparatively few subjects, but even to those upon the most extensive scale recorded. The danger of being misled by combinations due to pure chance does, indeed, depend greatly upon the number of cases observed, but in still larger degree upon the manner in which the data are calculated and presented.

Thirdly, in no case has there been any clear explicit definition of the problem to be resolved. A correspondence is ordinarily expressed in such a general way as neither admits of practical ascertainment nor even possesses any great theoretical significance; for a scientific investigation to be either possible or desirable, we must needs restrict it by a large number of qualifications. Having done so, any influence included (or excluded) in contravention of our definition must be considered as an *irrelevant and falsifying factor*. Now, in many of the experiments that we have been discussing, even in those upon a quite small scale, the authors have tried to kill as many birds as possible with one stone and have sought after the greatest – instead of the least – diversity; they have purposely thrown together subjects of all sorts and ages, and thus have gone out of their way to invite fallacious elements into their work. But in any case, even with the best of intentions, these irrelevant factors could not possibly be adequately obviated, until some method had been discovered for *exactly measuring* them and their effect upon the correlation; this, to the best of my knowledge, has never been done. As will presently be seen, the disturbance is frequently sufficient to so entirely transform the apparent correlation, that the latter becomes little or no evidence as to the quantity or even direction of the real correspondence.

Lastly, no investigator seems to have taken into any consideration another very large source of fallacy and one that is inevitably present in every work, namely, the *errors of observation*. For, having executed our experiment and calculated the correlation, we must then remember that the latter does not represent the mathematical relation between the two sets of real objects compared, but only between the two sets of measurements which we have derived from the former by more or less fallible processes.

The result actually obtained in any laboratory test must necessarily have in every case been perturbed by various contingencies which have nothing to do with the subject's real general capacity; a simple proof is the fact that the repetition of an experiment will always produce a value somewhat different from before. The same is no less true as regards more practical appraisements, for the lad confidently pronounced by his teacher to be 'dull' may eventually turn out to have quite the average share of brains. These unavoidable discrepancies have always been ignored, apparently on some tacit assumption that they will act impartially, half of them tending to enhance the apparent correlation and half to reduce it; in this way, it is supposed, the result must in the long run become more and more nearly true. Such is, however, not at all the case; these errors of observation do not tend to wholly compensate one another, but only partially so; every time, they leave a certain balance *against the correlation*, which is in no way affected by the number of cases assembled, but solely by the size of the mean error of observation. The amount of consequent falsification is in physical inquiry often unimportant, but in psychology it is usually large enough to completely vitiate the conclusion. This falsifying influence has in many of the above experiments, especially the more extensive ones, occurred in exaggerated form; for even those experimenters who are most careful in the ordinary routine of the laboratory have yet allowed themselves to be seduced by the special difficulties attending this sort of work; urged on the one hand by the craving after an imposing array of cases – somewhat *ad captandum vulgus* – and sternly restricted on the other side by various personal considerations (such as restiveness and fatiguability of the youthful subjects, fear of deranging school hours, etc.) they have too often fallen into almost incredibly hurried and inadequate methods of testing. Here, again, mere goodness of intention will not avail beyond a very limited extent, for the most painstaking work is far from entitling us to assume that the observational fallacy has been reduced to insignificant dimensions; we can have no satisfactory guarantee, until some method has been devised of precisely measuring the disturbance, and this does not seem to have ever been attempted. [. . .]

The present undertaking, therefore, has only ventured once more to approach the problem, because believing to have elaborated a new and reasonably complete methodological procedure, such as appears capable of at last bringing light upon this and innumerable other important regions hitherto inexplorable. [. . .]

As regards the delicate matter of estimating 'Intelligence', the guiding principle has been not to make any *a priori* assumptions as to what kind of mental activity may be thus termed with greatest propriety. Provisionally, at any rate, the aim was empirically to examine all the various abilities having any *prima facie* claims to such title, ascertaining their relations to one another and to other functions.

Four such different kinds of Intelligence have been introduced into the present work. First, there is that revealed in the ordinary classification according to school order (based here upon examinations). This clearly represents *Present Efficiency* in such matters as Latin, Greek, Mathematics, etc. Examples of this kind will be found in experimental series 3 and 4.

The next sort of Intelligence derives from the same school order but so modified as to exclude all influence of Age. Such a corrected order may be provisionally accepted as representing, not Proficiency, but *Native Capacity*. It has been arrived at by taking the difference between each boy's rank in school and his rank in age. For obvious reasons, it has been preferred to consider the absolute and not the relative differences; a boy, for instance, who was twentieth by examination and twenty-second by age would be placed just above one who was fifteenth by examination and sixteenth by age, the former being two places and the latter only one better than would have been expected with greatest probability.

The resulting order is clearly but a first approximation, to which we may apply any number of further corrections. For our present purpose, the following has appeared the most that can be practically required (and even this makes no appreciable change in the final values obtained). Evidently, the top boy is prevented from proving his full capabilities by want of competitors; let us suppose that he happens also to be the oldest; then, on our method above, he will seem no better than a boy of middle age and at the same time of middle-school order; but the latter will in reality always be found below many younger than himself, compensating this by being also above about an equal number of older ones; now, our top boy has not let himself be surpassed by a single one of his juniors, and therefore would certainly have gone above a great many of his seniors, had the school included such. The top boy's true position may be roughly estimated by making him an extra allowance of a number of places equal to the general mean deviation of actual from average rank (which in this case comes to five places); clearly, also, such allowance may with equal right be claimed by the top boy, even if he does not happen to be the oldest; further, the same correction is applicable in slighter degree to the second boy, in still slighter to the third, and so on in a rapidly diminishing curve up to the centre of the school. For practical purposes, it has seemed sufficient to allow the next four boys, 4, 3, 2, and 1 places respectively; naturally, the whole of this correction must be repeated inversely for the bottom end of the school. Though this explanation is rather complicated, the correction is very easily carried out and, as stated, its effect is hardly appreciable.

The third kind of Intelligence is that represented and measurable by the general impression produced upon other people. This forms the basis of the common broad assortment of the children by their teachers into 'bright', 'average', 'dull' respectively; and with such an assortment I have had to content myself for the elder children in the second series of experiments, while for those under seven years of age, I have not obtained any intellective grading at all.[1] But for the more important series 1, a list of relative rank was procured of satisfactory completeness. It may be noted that teachers, if directly asked for such a detailed list, frequently begin by asserting it to be impracticable. It will be generally found, however, that if they be merely requested to pick out the brightest pupil of all, they can do so without any great trouble; and when they are next requested to select the brightest of the remainder, they are still able to perform the desired feat; and so on, until the classification is complete.

The fourth and last sort of Intelligence which has here been estimated is that known as *common sense*. To this end, the oldest of the children of series 1 was interviewed and interrogated concerning her comrades in precisely the manner described above, except that the criterion was not to be 'brightness at school work' but 'sharpness and common sense out of school'; and she seemed to have no great difficulty in forming her judgments concerning the others, having, indeed, known them all her life. As a check, and in order to eliminate undue partialities, it had been arranged that, as she left the house, the second oldest child should enter it and thus be able to give an as far as possible independent list, since neither had beforehand had any idea of what was wanted. Finally, a similar list was obtained from the rector's wife, who also had always lived in this village; but her graduation is unfortunately incomplete and therefore unusable, for she professed

1. The day after these experiments I left the neighborhood of the school.

inability to pronounce verdict upon some few children who had not come much under her notice; as far as it went, it appeared perfectly homologous with the other two lists.

Procedure in deducing results

1. *Method of correlation.* So far this chapter has been occupied with obtaining estimates as to the reagents' respective abilities in the several sensory and intellective functions. This is an operation requiring the fullest use of psychological insight; and, therefore, based on the long preliminary investigation previously described, every effort has been made to ferret out and evade all circumstances tending to make our little sample of facts appreciably misrepresentative of the real general relations or psychologically superficial and misleading. But the next portion of our problem is of a very definite objective nature; we wish to ascertain how far the observed ranks in the several abilities tend to correspond with one another; this, it is believed, is no longer a task to be effected by exertions of psychological ingenuity; instead of constructing complex arbitrary tables and plausible but more or less fanciful explanatory stories, we now are in need of such a procedure as will impartially utilize all our information in the *demonstrably most complete manner* and will focus it to a plain quantitative value; for the moment, psychology has to give way to mathematics.

Accordingly, all the more important correlations in the present work have been worked out by the best method hitherto evolved, that of 'product moments', as Pearson terms it; only instead of using the actual measurements obtained for the reagents' respective thresholds, the change had been made of employing the numbers denoting their relative ranks; a full explanation of the advantages of this modification may be found in the article specially devoted to the topic (the chief being a reduction of the probable error equivalent to doubling the quantity of cases observed). Merely subsidiary results have often been reckoned by the much more convenient method of 'rank differences', while a few correlations were for various reasons not amenable to either of these more exact methods, and therefore had to be worked out by Pearson's auxiliary method or mine of 'class averages' (the latter has generally been preferred, on account of its smaller probable error). All these are but different ways of more or less closely arriving at the same measure of correlation, and thus all the results can be freely compared with one another.

The method of 'product moments', though sometimes involving lengthy calculations, is so simple a principle that it can be worked by any moderately intelligent schoolboy. Explanation and illustration are given in the above article; here, nothing more than the general formula can be stated, which is as follows:

$$r = \frac{Sxy}{\sqrt{Sx^2 \cdot Sy^2}}$$

where $x =$ any individual deviation from the general median as regards one of the compared characteristics,

$y =$ the deviation of the same individual as regards the other characteristic,

$Sxy =$ the sum of such products for all the individuals,

$Sx^2 =$ the sum of the squares of all the various values of x,

$Sy^2 =$ the same for y,

and $r =$ the required correlation.

2. *Elimination of observational errors*. This necessitates a further mathematical operation, which, however, is very brief and does not involve anything more than elementary arithmetic. There are two formulae, one theoretical and the other empirical:

$$r_{pq} = \frac{r_{p'q'}}{\sqrt{r_{p'1p'2} \cdot r_{q'1q'2}}} \qquad 1$$

and $$r_{pq} = \frac{\sqrt[4]{mn \cdot r_{p''q''}} - r_{p'q'}}{\sqrt[4]{mn} - 1} \qquad 2$$

where $r_{p'q'} =$ the mean correlation between the various gradings for p and those for q,

$r_{p'1p'2} =$ the average correlation between one and another of these several independently obtained series of values for p,

$r_{q'1q'2} =$ the same as regards q,

$r_{p''q''} =$ the correlation of an amalgamated series of measurements for p with an amalgamated series for q,

m and n = the number of independent gradings for p and q respectively,

and $r_{pq} =$ the required real correlation between the true objective values of p and q.

It will be found exceedingly important to employ both formulae simultaneously, for they are independent of one another and each has different sources of fallacy, so that the most essential information is gained by a comparison between their respective results.

When we say that a series of objects correlates entirely with a second series, we do not assert that every set of measurements of the one will absolutely coincide with those of the other, seeing that discrepancies must inevitably arise from errors in measuring; we only mean that whatever all sets of measurements of the one series have in common with each other will also be found common to all measurements of the other series; then, either of the above formulae will exactly eliminate the observational discrepancies and thus present the correlation in its entirety.

But much more often the measurements for the same series are connected with one another by *more* than connects them with the measurements of the other series, and then the case is ambiguous. Either the surplus really lies in the series measured, which is equivalent to saying that this series contains elements not common to the other series, and that the correlation is to this extent incomplete; here, once more, both formulae will produce the properly corrected amount. Or, as is usual, the excess of agreement between the measurements for the same series may partly (or wholly) derive from their having the same constant fallacies; and now it will be found that both formulae give a correction still in the right direction but too small in quantity; further, this deficiency will be much greater for the theoretical formula than for the empirical one, so that *when both formulae give the same result, we can assume that the latter has not been appreciably falsified by any constant fallacy common to the several sets of measurements for the same series.*

Under special circumstances, the contrary case may occur of the sets of measurements for the one series being connected with each other by *less* than connects them with those of the other series. This will happen whenever several sets of measurements supposed to be taken from the same lot of objects are really procured from different ones and their several correspondences with the second series have arisen from independent causes. In physical matters, this danger is not serious; if two persons decide independently to measure a fossil cave-bear, they are unlikely to make the mistake of going to different animals. But in psychology it is otherwise: persons may honestly endeavor to appraise the same mental faculty, and yet, owing to diversity of procedure and ignorance of organic uniformities, they may really obtain measurements of quite independent functions. In such cases, the sets of measurements, however accurate they may be, will show no correspondence with one another; and if the functions are even only partially different, the measurements will correspond with one another to that extent less than they would by reason solely of errors of observation.

The effect will be to falsify any corrections by the theoretical formula, for the latter begins by assuming only one lot of objects to have been measured and therefore the correspondence between the sets of measurements to be at least as great as might be expected from their accuracy – an assumption generally fair enough, but under the special conditions delusively reducing the denominator and thus producing a final value proportionally too large. Now, this same fallacy affects corrections by the empirical formula in exactly the opposite direction; for the latter bases itself upon the fact that an amalgamation of several sets of measurements constantly emphasizes whatever elements are common to them all and simultaneously obliterates all that are not common; thus in the normal case of only one lot of objects underlying the sets and determining their correlations to the other series, amalgamation will continually raise the correlation towards its full amount; but if there be more than one underlying lot of objects, each correlating the other series independently, then amalgamation will not emphasize but obliterate these independent influences and consequently not raise but lower the correlation. Hence, when several functions really corresponding with the second series independently have been confounded together and taken for different measurements of a single correspondence, the results as corrected by the respective formulae will sharply diverge. Conversely, if, when a double set of measurements has been made, the empirical corrective formula produces an increase of correlation, then these sets of measurements may be regarded as certainly deriving from some single common faculty (any influences specific to each set of measurements being theoretically subtracted from the faculty and viewed as merely so many sources of observational error); and *if the two corrective formulae lead to the same final amount of correlation, then this latter concerns wholly and solely the common faculty*.

Further, it is of great importance to remark that the last fallacy, namely the case when measurements believed to be taken from the same function really derive from different ones correlating with the other series independently, may, by the first corrective formula, easily come to any values greater than 1 and therefore be impossible, seeing that 1 represents entirety. By the empirical formula, on the other hand, this can never occur; for whether the sets of measurements be connected with one another by either anything more or anything less than connects them with the measurements of any other compared series, then the correspondence between the two series will in both cases be reduced and therefore must necessarily be less than 1;[2] in other words, *the empirically corrected correlation can only amount to full unity when all the sets of measurements for both series have one common element and differ in every other systematic constituent.*

Fuller explanation and illustration are given in the article devoted to the topic of measuring correlation.

3. *Elimination of irrelevant factors.* This is the final operation necessary to obtain a true result. Unlike the preceding one, it may often be altogether escaped; for if the conditions are favorable and if the preliminary investigation has been sufficiently thorough the experiment need not be affected by any irrelevant factor of large enough magnitude sensibly to vitiate the result. Here, also, the necessary mathematical work has been reduced to brief and elementary arithmetic; for more explanation, the reader must again be referred to the special article.

If the irrelevant factor be connected with *only one* of the two compared series, the equation is:

$$r_{pq} = \frac{r'_{pq}}{\sqrt{1 - r^2_{pv}}}$$

where r'_{pq} = the apparent correlation of p and q, the two variants to be compared,

r_{pv} = the correlation of one of the above variants with a third and irrelevantly admitted variant v,

and r_{pq} = the required real correlation between p and q, after compensating for the illegitimate influence of v.

If the irrelevant factor be connected with *both* series compared, the equation becomes:

$$r_{pq} = \frac{r'_{pq} - r_{pv} \cdot r_{qv}}{\sqrt{(1 - r^2_{pv})(1 - r^2_{qv})}}$$

where all the terms have the same meaning as before.

2. Except for deviations due to mere chance, whose range will vary with the probable error.

The present results
Method and meaning of the demonstration

As the reader will have noticed, the formulae given at the end of the previous chapter are equations whereby from several observed correlations we are able to deduce a single true one. This latter alone is of real scientific significance, and under the ordinary unsystematic conditions – such as governed the great majority of work reviewed in the second chapter – the actually observed correlations will rarely be of much interest in their primitive raw state; for after passing through the proper corrections, they would come forth transfigured in every conceivable manner; some would increase in size, some diminish, some entirely disappear, and some even become inverted. Nevertheless, our true correlation in no way deserves the reproach of being a theoretical abstraction for it only represents the limit to which the observed correlation itself will continually approach as improvement is made in the experimental procedure; and not even the most perfect methodics can afford to dispense with the formulae, seeing that these are the sole means by which the perfection may be adequately ascertained.

Our method of demonstration implies four distinct steps, all of which are believed to be absolutely indispensable for work intending to be more than merely suggestive. First, we must exactly determine the quantity of correlation actually observable and we must compare it with the probable error; then, if the former be no more than about twice as large as the latter, the whole experiment may indeed have produced a substantial negative result, but cannot possibly warrant any positive conclusion other than to suggest the desirability of extending the investigation until it acquires more evidential value; but if, on the other hand, the observed correlation be four or five times greater than the probable error, we may then consider a *prima facie* case of correspondence to have been established and we may legitimately go on to the corrective processes so as to bring our raw figure to its most probable real amount. Accordingly, the second step will be to form an estimate of the errors in observing the two series compared; for this purpose we must have obtained two or more independent sets of measurements for each series, or at least must be acquainted with the relations found between other such sets under sufficiently similar circumstances. The third proceeding is to look for any factors irrelevantly admitted (or, more rarely, excluded); any suspicions must be carefully verified in succession. Finally, we have to critically review the whole argument, paying particular attention to such disturbing factors as have not been disposed of very satisfactorily; in this way we come to a final estimate, not only as to the most probable amount of real correspondence, but also as to the degree of confidence to which our evidence is entitled; for these two things are by no means always parallel, a high apparent correlation often having but small evidential value and *vice versa*.

A few words may now be said concerning the eventual *meaning* attachable to the result which we hope to obtain. To put it briefly, the usual direction of inquiry is in the present work reversed. The customary procedure consists in determining some matter of research subjectively, say, 'Perception', 'Attention,' 'Imagination', 'Fatigue', etc., and then ascertaining its relation to other similarly pre-determined psychoses or neuroses. Here, on the contrary, although every effort has been made to render the mental phenomena as unequivocal and significant as possible, yet in the beginning not the least note is taken of any psychological import beyond such as is barely necessary to define the subject of discussion in the most positive and objective manner; while the structure of language necessitates the continued use of such terms as 'Discrimination', 'Faculty', 'Intelligence', etc., these words must be understood as implying nothing more than a bare unequivocal indication of the factual conditions of experiment. For the moment we are only inquiring how closely the values gained in the several different series coincide with one another, and all our corrections are intended to introduce greater accuracy, not fuller connotation. The subjective problems are wholly reserved for later investigation. It is no new thing thus elaborately to deal with and precisely measure things whose real nature is concealed from view; of this nature, for instance, is obviously the study of electricity, of biology, and indeed of all physical science whatever.

Let us, then, consider the extent of connection between two series of things implied by this sole fact of their presenting a numerical correlation with one another; such a correspondence, when beyond the range of mere chance coincidence, may be forthwith assumed to indicate and measure *something common to* both series in question. Such a community may often consist of a definite so-called 'substance'; A's changes of wealth will show some correlation with those of B, if both possess some shares in the same stock. Or, on the other hand, the community may derive from a more complicated interaction of forces; thus, the weather is supposed to correlate with the state of the spots on the sun. But this distinction is superficial even in physical matters; thingness may well be an indispensable crutch for popular thought, and indeed in metaphysics becomes a serious enough topic, but it has no place in strict natural science and still less in psychology, where a fast limit has never been securely traceable between thing, qualities, and conditions.

But the same simple mathematical formulae which have brought us so far will take us yet farther. As from several sets of inaccurate measurements it has been found possible to arrive at the accurate correlation of the two real series, so now in a similar manner from any number of real series we can proceed on to dealing exclusively and precisely with any element that may be found common to these series; from ascertaining the intercorrelations of, say, auditory discrimination, visual discrimination, the capacity for learning Greek, and that for playing the piano, we can arrive at estimating the correspondence of whatever may be common to the first pair of faculties with whatever may be common to the second pair. By combining such correlations of higher order, it is feasible to execute any required amount of elimination and selection, so that eventually a dissociation and exactness may be introduced into psychology such as can only be compared with quantitative chemical analysis; even in the present work, it is hoped to obtain results of sufficient fineness to be independent of local conditions of experiment, and therefore to be precisely verifiable by any other workers. All the time, the relations discovered by us will wholly retain their impartial objective character; however accurately we may learn the distribution of the community, it will remain as a later and very different task to detect and analyse its psychical nature. But we shall find that the successful positive ascertainment of objective relations continually reduces and simplifies the thinkable explanatory hypotheses, so that practically our method of investigation is bringing us towards the introspective psychological solution also – and perhaps in the end by the shortest route.

Up to now we have only discussed the correspondence of the various Intelligences with the various sensory activities, Hearing, Sight, Touch, etc. Such isolated facts are interesting enough, but quite otherwise important is the relation of *any common and essential element in the Intelligences to any common and essential element in the Sensory Functions.* For brevity, we will term these common elements 'General Intelligence' and 'General Discrimination', but always with the reservations made in the first section of this chapter.

Curiously, this more general correspondence can in the present case be settled with much greater precision than was possible for the specific relations. This is due to our now having adequate data wherewith to measure the errors of observation, seeing that all the experimentally obtained gradings of specific Discrimination constitute so many one-sided independent attempts to grade the General Discrimination; the amount of observational error will be quantitatively revealed in the correlations between one grading and another.

(a) *The village school*. Here our calculation is as follows. The average of the nine correlations between the Intelligences and the Discriminations comes, as we have seen, to 0.38;[3] the two kinds of intellective gradings correlate with one another by an average of 0.55; and the three gradings in Discrimination do so by 0.25.[4] Therefore by the theoretical formula the true correlation between General Intelligence and General Discrimination comes to

$$\frac{0.38}{\sqrt{0.55 \times 0.25}} = 1.01.$$

Checking this by the second or empirical method, we find that on taking an amalgamation of the three intellective gradings with an amalgamation of the three gradings in Discrimination, the correlation rises to 0.66. Therefore the true correlation between General Intelligence and General Discrimination comes in this way to

$$\frac{\sqrt{3} \times 0.66 - 0.38}{\sqrt{3} - 1} = 1.04.$$

This again may be further checked by taking our amalgamation two instead of three lists at a time; in this way we get nine different correlations which present an average of 0.55, so that our required result now becomes 0.96.[5] Therefore an average again gives us as nearly as possible 1.00.

3. These correlations are here taken as actual measurements, and therefore are obviously required raw, not corrected; the correction then issues from their joint product according to the formula.

4. This value is precisely the same as that found for adults.

5. $\dfrac{\sqrt{2} \times 0.55 - 0.38}{\sqrt{2} - 1} = 0.96$

Thus we arrive at the remarkable result that the *common and essential element in the Intelligences wholly coincides with the common and essential element in the Sensory Functions.*

(*b*) *The high-class school.* Here also, the children were tested in the three senses, but unfortunately, as we have seen, the results for Light and Weight are not seriously usable,[6] so that we no longer have sufficient material for constructing a 'General' Discrimination.

This default, however, has been made good by what appears to be a very happy substitute. Our main correlations have dealt with reagents all undergoing musical instruction, and I have kindly been furnished with a complete order of their relative abilities in this department. Musical talent has always been recognized as being not so much an intellective as a sensory function; whole nations appear almost devoid of it, without therefore showing themselves any less intelligent; lunatic asylums, on the contrary, often contain a surprising share of the faculty. We will, then, take this as our second sensory function, will note whether it presents any community with Discrimination of Pitch, and if so will compare this common element with that obtaining between the intellective functions. As regards the first point, it may be noted that hitherto very conflicting opinions have been stoutly maintained; the great majority of writers have held Musical Talent and Pitch Discrimination to be very intimately connected and even go so far as to directly term the discriminative power 'musical sensitiveness'; while a few, but including perhaps the ablest judges, flatly deny any such correspondence whatever. The actual facts would at first sight seem to lie wholly on the side of the former tenet, seeing that the correlation works out to the substantial amount of 0·40 (or about 0·63, when corrected for errors). Next, these two auditory functions correlate with the Intelligences by 0·57 and 0·55 respectively, and the latter correlate with one another to the amount of 0·71. Thus the relation between the element common to the two former and that common to the four latter will be given by

$$\frac{0 \cdot 56}{\sqrt{0 \cdot 40 \times 0 \cdot 71}} = 1 \cdot 04.$$

We can now check the result by the empirical formula; for we find that the amalgamated order derived from the two sensory

6. As far as they go, they indicate results entirely similar to those above.

faculties correlates with the amalgamated order derived from the four Intelligences by 0·72; so that the required correlation comes to

$$\frac{\sqrt[4]{8} \times 0·72 - 0·56}{\sqrt[4]{8} - 1} = 0·96.$$

Taking as usual the mean,[7] we again reach a final correlation of precisely 1·00, and therefore once more must conclude that the element common to the sensory activities also wholly coincides with that common to the intelligences.

Before passing, it may be remarked that thus after all those were virtually in the right who maintained Musicality and Pitch Discrimination to have no correspondence with one another; for though a correspondence does really exist, yet it is not to the smallest degree of the specific character contemplated by those who talk of 'musical sensitivity'. It must here also be noted that this surprising intellectuality of musical talent by no means annihilates the many well-evidenced phenomena seeming to indicate to the contrary; one fact cannot destroy another, and any apparent conflict merely proves our imperfect acquaintance with their true nature.

(c) *Practical verification of the argument.* The conclusion above arrived at is so important and the method of argument is so new, that I have endeavored to reproduce analogous circumstances artificially, so that any one may easily test any portion of the reasoning.

The main argument was repeated as follows. A target was constructed of a great many horizontal bands, numbered from top to bottom. Then a man shot successively at a particular series of numbers in a particular order; clearly, the better the shot, the less numerical difference between any number hit and that aimed at; now, just as the measurement of any object is termed a 'shot' at its real value, so, conversely, we may perfectly well consider the series of numbers actually hit in the light of a series of measurements of the numbers aimed at. When the same man fired again at the same series, he thereby obtained a new and independent[8]

7. If this small difference of value between the theoretical and empirical results can be minutely investigated, it can be clearly seen to be solely attributable to mere chance, as indeed might well be expected from its small dimensions.

8. Provided, of course, that there be no appreciable constant error.

series of measurements of the same set of objects. Next, a woman had the same number of shots at some set numbers in a similar manner. If, then, our above reasoning and formulae are correct, it should be possible, by observing the numbers hit and working out their correlations, to ascertain the exact resemblance between the series aimed at by the man and woman respectively. In actual fact, the sets of numbers hit by the man turned out to correlate with those hit by the woman to the extent of 0·52; but it was noted that the man's sets correlated with one another to 0·74, and the woman's sets with one another to 0·36; thence the true correspondence between the set aimed at by the man and that aimed at by the woman was not the raw 0·52, but

$$\frac{0·52}{\sqrt{0·74 \times 0·36}} = 1·00,$$

that is to say, the two persons had fired at exactly the same series of bands, which was really the case. I repeated this experiment, testing three times by the first or theoretical formula and four times by the empirical one; by both methods the average came to just upon 1·00, with a mean variation above and below of precisely similar dimensions to those in our instances of Discrimination and Intelligence. Thus the experimental justification of our method of argumentation was as complete as could well be desired.

4. *Conclusion.* On the whole, then, we reach the profoundly important conclusion that *there really exists a something that we may provisionally term 'General Sensory Discrimination' and similarly a 'General Intelligence', and further that the functional correspondence between these two is not appreciably less than absolute.*

Besides its intrinsic value, such a general theorem has the enormous advantage over the specific results of the last section of being independent of any particular conditions; it has nothing to do with the procedure selected for testing Discrimination and Intelligence, nor even with the accuracy of its execution, nor indeed even with the homogeneousness of the experimental subjects; if correct, the proof should be reproducible in all times, places and manners – on the sole condition of adequate methodics.

In view of this community being discovered between such diverse functions as in-school Cleverness, out-of-school Common Sense, Sensory Discrimination, and Musical Talent, we need scarcely be astonished to continually come upon it no less paramount in other forms of intellectual activity. Always in the present experiments, approximately,

$$\frac{r_{pq}}{\sqrt{r_{pq} \cdot r_{pq}}} = 1.[9]$$

I have actually tested this relation in twelve pairs of such groups taken at random, and have found the average value to be precisely 1·00 for the first two decimal places with a mean deviation of only 0·05. All examination, therefore, in the different sensory, school, or other specific intellectual faculties, may be regarded as so many independently obtained estimates of the one great common Intellective Function.

Though the range of this central Function appears so universal and that of the specific functions so vanishingly minute, the latter must not be supposed to be altogether non-existent. We can always come upon them eventually, if we sufficiently narrow our field of view and consider branches of activity closely enough resembling one another. When, for instance, in this same preparatory school we take on the one side Latin translation with Latin grammar and on the other side French prose with French dictation, then our formula gives us a new result; for the two Latin studies correlate with the French ones by an average of 0·59, while the former correlate together by 0·66 and the latter by 0·71; so that the element common to the Latin correlates with the element common to the French by

$$\frac{0 \cdot 59}{\sqrt{0 \cdot 66 \times 0 \cdot 71}} = 0 \cdot 86 \text{ only.}$$

That is to say, the two common elements by no means coincide completely this time, but only to the extent of $0 \cdot 86^2$ or 74 per cent[10]; so that, in the remaining 26 per cent, each pair must possess a community purely specific and unshared by the other pair.[11]

9. Where r_{pq} = the mean of the correlations between the members of the one group p with the members of the other group q,

r_{pp} = the mean of the inter-correlations of the members of the group p among themselves,

and r_{qq} = the same as regards group q.

10. The influence of an element is measured by the *square* of its correlational value. *See* 'The association between two things'.

11. Of course this specific community is further resolvable into natural talent and favoring circumstances, of which factors the latter may often be paramount.

We therefore bring our general theorem to the following form. *Whenever branches of intellectual activity are at all dissimilar, then their correlations with one another appear wholly due to their being all variously saturated with some common fundamental Function (or group of Functions).* This law of the Universal Unity of the Intellective Function is both theoretically and practically so momentous, that it must acquire a much vaster corroborative basis before we can accept it even as a general principle and apart from its inevitable eventual corrections and limitations. Discussion of the *subjective* nature of this great central Function has been excluded from the scope of the present work. But clearly, if it be mental at all, it must inevitably become one of the foundation pillars of any psychological system claiming to accord with actual fact – and the majority of prevalent theories may have a difficulty in reckoning with it.

Of its objective relations, the principal is its unique universality, seeing that it reappears always the same in all the divers forms of intellectual activity tested; whereas the specific factor seems in every instance new and wholly different from that in all others. As regards amount, next, there seems to be an immense diversity; already in the present examples, the central factor varies from less than a fifth to over fifteen times the size of the accompanying specific one. But all cases appear equally susceptible of positive accurate measurement; thus we are becoming able to give a precise arithmetical limitation to the famous assertion that 'at bottom, the Great Man is ever the same kind of thing'.

Finally, there is the exceedingly significant fact that this central Function, whatever it may be, is hardly anywhere more prominent than in the simple act of discriminating two nearly identical tones; here we find a correlation exceeding 0·90, indicating the central Function to be more than four times larger than all the other influences upon individual differentiation. Not only the psychical content but also the external relations of Sensory Discrimination offer a most valuable simplicity; for it is a single monotonous act, almost independent of age, previous general education, memory, industry, and many other factors that inextricably complicate the other functions. Moreover, the specific element can to a great extent be readily eliminated by varying and combining the kind of test. For these reasons, Discrimination has unrivalled advantages for investigating and diagnosing the central Function.

The Theorem of Intellective Unity leads us to consider a corollary proceeding from it logically, testing it critically, and at once indicating some of its important practical uses. This corollary may be termed that of the Hierarchy of the Specific Intelligences.

For if we consider the correspondences between the four branches of school study, a very remarkable uniformity may be observed. English and French, for instance, agree with one another in having a higher correlation with Classics than with Mathematics. Quite similarly, French and Mathematics agree in both having a higher correlation with Classics than with English. And the same will be found to be the case when any other pair is compared with the remainder. The whole thus forms a *perfectly constant Hierarchy* in the following order: Classics, French, English, and Mathematics. This unbroken regularity becomes especially astonishing when we regard the minuteness of the variations involved, for the four branches have average correlations of 0·77, 0·72, 0·70, and 0·67 respectively.

When in the same experimental series we turn to the Discrimination of Pitch, we find its correlations to be of slightly less magnitude (raw) but in precisely the same relative rank, being: 0·66 with Classics, 0·65 with French, 0·54 with English, and 0·45 with Mathematics. Even in the crude correlations furnished by the whole school without excluding the non-musicians, exactly the same order is repeated, though with the general diminution caused by the impurity: Classics 0·60, French 0·56, English 0·45, and Mathematics 0·39.

Just the same principle governs even Musical Talent, a faculty that is usually set up on a pedestal entirely apart. For it is not only correlated with all the other functions, but once again in precisely the same order: with Classics 0·63, with French 0·57, with English 0·51, with Mathematics 0·51, and with Discrimination 0·40. Ability for music corresponds substantially with Discrimination of tones, but nevertheless not so much as it does with algebra, irregular verbs, etc.[12]

12. Of course, notable instances will easily be found where Musical Ability is apparently divorced from General Intelligence; in this very school, for example, the best musician is far from standing high intellectually. But not even the most extreme cases necessarily contravene the above rule. A correlation does not state any absolute coincidence between two faculties, but only a limited and precisely measured tendency in this direction; so far from excluding deviations, it proclaims them and even estimates their exact probability. If we may assume the normal law of frequency to approximately hold good and may abstract from further influences, then the proportion of persons with any given amount of musical talent who will attain to any given degree of stupidity (or vice versa)

The actual degree of uniformity in this Hierarchy can be most conveniently and summarily judged from the following table of correlation (*see* Table 1); the values given are those actually observed (theoretical correction would modify the relative order,

Table 1

	Classics	French	English	Maths	Discrim.	Music
Classics	*0·87*	0·83	0·78	0·70	0·66	0·63
French	0·83	*0·84*	0·67	0·67	0·65	0·57
English	0·78	0·67	*0·89*	0·64	0·54	0·51
Maths	0·70	0·67	0·64	*0·88*	0·45	0·51
Discrim.	0·66	0·65	0·54	0·45		0·40
Music	0·63	0·57	0·51	0·51	0·40	

but in no degree affect the amount of Hierarchy or otherwise). Each number shows the correlation between the faculty vertically above and that horizontally to the left; except in the oblique line italicized, the value always becomes smaller as the eye travels either to the right or downwards.

Altogether, we have a uniformity that is very nearly perfect and far surpasses the conceivable limits of chance coincidence. When we consider that the probable error varies between about 0·01 for the ordinary studies to about 0·03 for music, it is only surprising that the deviations are not greater. The general Hierarchy becomes even more striking when compared with the oblique line, which is no measure of the central Function and where consequently the gradation abruptly and entirely vanishes.[13]

$$= \frac{1}{2} \frac{1}{\sqrt{\pi}} \int e^{ah - t^2} \, dt,$$

where h is a measure of the correlation between Musicality and Intelligence and $a =$ the given inferiority in the latter faculty.

13. The only other data of this kind with which I am acquainted are some comparisons made between the different branches of study at the Columbia University. The correlations here obtained, which were throughout somewhat smaller than the above, manifest only a limited concordance with our above principle of Hierarchy. But a university is clearly not the place in which to look for natural correspondence between functions; at that time of life, strong ties of a wholly artificial sort have intervened; each student singles out for himself that particular group of studies tending to his main purpose and devotes to them the most judicious amounts of relative energy. To determine natural correlations, we must go to where the pupils meet each other in every department on relatively equal terms.

The above correlations are raw, and therefore do not tell us either the true rank of the respective activities or the full absolute saturation of each with General Intelligence. For the former purpose we must eliminate the observational errors, and for the latter our result must further be *squared*.[14] Thus we get:

Table 2

Activity	Correlation with Gen. Intelligence	Ratio of the common factor to the specific factor	
Classics	0·99	99 to	1
Common Sense	0·98	96	4
Pitch Dis.	0·94	89	11
French	0·92	84	16
Cleverness[15]	0·90	81	19
English	0·90	81	19
Mathematics[16]	0·86	74	26
Pitch Dis. among the uncultured[17]	0·72	52	48
Music	0·70	49	51
Light Dis.[17]	0·57	32	68
Weight Dis.[17]	0·44	19	81

It is clear how much the amount of any observable raw correlation depends upon the two very different influences: first, there is the above intellective saturation, or extent to which the considered faculty is functionally identical with General Intelligence; and secondly, there is the accuracy with which we have estimated the faculty. As regards the ordinary school studies, this accuracy is indicated by the oblique italicized line, and therefore appears about equal in all cases (not in the least following the direction of the Hierarchy); but in other cases there is a large divergence on this head, which leads to important practical consequences. Mathematics, for example, has a saturation of 74 and Common

14. See previous note.

15. Here so termed for brevity; really that quality is meant which causes a person to be regarded by his teachers as 'clever'.

16. The opposite and more usual view, namely, that mathematics form an entirely independent faculty, will be found expounded in 331 pages 'Über die Anlage zur Mathematik' by the well-known psychiatrist, Moebius. Similar evidence is brought by him to the effect that this talent is proportional to the development of the upper outer orbit of the eyes, especially the left.

17. As has been before mentioned, the rank of these three faculties remains ambiguous until their observational errors have been ascertained.

Sense has one of about 96; but in actual use the worth of these indications becomes reversed, so that a subjective impression as to a child's 'brightness' is a less reliable sign than the latter's rank in the arithmetic class; almost as good as either appears a few minutes' test with a monochord.

In the above Hierarchy one of the most noticeable features is the high position of languages; to myself, at any rate, it was no small surprise to find Classics and even French placed unequivocally above English (note that this term does not refer to any study of the native tongue, but merely to the aggregate of all the lessons conducted therein, such as History, Geography, Dictation, Scripture, and Repetition).

However it may be with these or any other special facts, here would seem to lie the long-wanted general rational basis for public examinations. Instead of continuing ineffectively to protest that high marks in Greek syntax are no test as to the capacity of men to command troops or to administer provinces, we shall at last actually determine the precise accuracy of the various means of measuring General Intelligence, and then we shall in an equally positive objective manner ascertain the exact relative importance of this General Intelligence as compared with other characteristics desirable for the particular post which the candidate is to assume (such as any required Specific Intelligences, also Instruction, Force of Will, Physical Constitution, Honesty, Zeal, etc.; though some of these factors cannot easily be estimated separately, there is no insuperable obstacle to weighing their *total influence* as compared with General Intelligence). Thus, it is to be hoped, we shall eventually reach our pedagogical conclusions, not by easy subjective theories, nor by the insignificant range of personal experiences, nor yet by some catchpenny exceptional cases, but rather by an adequately representative array of established facts. [. . .]

To conclude, the following is a brief summary of the principal conclusions indicated by the foregoing experiments:

1. The results hitherto obtained in respect of psychic correlation would, if true, be almost fatal to experimental psychology as a profitable branch of science. But none of these results, as at present standing, can be considered to possess any value other than suggestive only; this fact is not so much due to individual shortcomings of the investigators, as to the general non-existence of any adequate system of investigation.

2. On making good this methodological deficiency, there is found to actually occur a correspondence – continually varying in size according to the experimental conditions – between all the forms of Sensory Discrimination and the more complicated Intellectual Activities of practical life.

3. By this same new system of methodics, there is also shown to exist a correspondence between what may provisionally be called 'General Discrimination' and 'General Intelligence' which works out with great approximation[18] to *one or absoluteness*. Unlike the result quoted in the preceding paragraph, this phenomenon appears independent of the particular experimental circumstances; it has nothing to do with the procedure selected for testing either Discrimination or Intelligence, nor with the true representativeness of the values obtained by these tests, nor even with the homogeneousness of the experimental reagents; if the thesis be correct, its proof should be reproducible in all times, places, and manners – on the sole conditino of adequate methodics.

4. The above and other analogous observed facts indicate *that all branches of intellectual activity have in common one fundamental function (or group of functions), whereas the remaining or specific elements of the activity seem in every case to be wholly different from that in all the others.* The relative influence of the general to the specific function varies in the ten departments here investigated from 15:1 to 1:4.

5. As an important practical consequence of this universal Unity of the Intellectual Function, the various actual forms of mental activity constitute a stably interconnected Hierarchy according to their different degrees of intellective saturation. Hence, the value of any method of examination as to intellectual fitness for any given post is capable of being precisely ascertained, since it depends upon:

(a) the accuracy with which it can be conducted;
(b) the hierarchical intellective rank of the test;
(c) the hierarchical intellective rank of the duties involved in the post.

Methods have been given whereby all these three points can be sufficiently ascertained.

6. Discussion as to the psychical nature of this fundamental Function has been reserved until a more complete acquaintance

18. In the present experiments, as far as the second decimal place.

has been gained concerning its objective relations. Among the latter, the principal and determining one is its unique position as indicated in 4. The chief further evidence is to the following effect:

The Function appears to become fully developed in children by about their ninth year, and possibly even much earlier. From this moment, there normally occurs no further change even into extreme old age.

In adult life, there would seem no appreciable difference between the two sexes.

The Function almost entirely controls the relative position of children at school (after making due allowance for difference of age), and is nine parts out of ten responsible for success in such a simple act as Discrimination of Pitch.

Its relation to the intellectual activity does not appear to be of any loosely connected or auxiliary character (such as willingness to make an effort, readiness in adaptation to unfamiliar tests, or dexterity in the fashion of executing them), but rather to be intimately bound up in the very essence of the process.

3 T. L. Kelley

The Boundaries of Mental Life

Excerpts from T. L. Kelley, *Crossroads in the Mind of Man*, Stanford University Press, 1928, chapter 1, pp. 1–23.

The study of the nature and scope of mental traits is as broad as the entire field of psychology, and just about as evasive as the all-pervasive ether. He who dedicates his services to 'human welfare' is rather less likely to ease the progress of mankind than, say, an ear doctor who limits his attention to a narrower field. Nevertheless it is necessary to envisage an entire realm in order to maintain a proper perspective, to keep poised in the turmoil of separate schools, neo-schools and counter-schools. Each separate school is generally willing to ignore the others with the fine tolerance of the wise toward the harmlessly demented. If perchance a behaviorist takes issue with a psychoanalyst, the latter blandly informs him that he does not know the facts and the principles of the latter's study, and in this he is probably right. How, then, as each school becomes more specialized in technique, more confined within its self-made walls, and more dependent upon the rapidly increasing fruits of its own garden, is there any chance for helpful criticism of school by school, or any prospect of coordination of their several doctrines? Not only is there prospect, but sooner or later coordination is inevitable, for the doctrines meet at the crossroads of life. Professor Blank found bluejays breaking the eggs in a quail's nest, and killed seven in as many shots. He was 'so mad that he couldn't miss'. What a fine interplay of traits! Usually emotions and motor coordinations run separate courses, but here they met at the quail's nest.

It would seem that just two things are necessary to a comparative and coordinative study: First, a technique that is universal in its applicability in the sense that it serves not only at the cross-roads, but along the remote stretches where no other highway is near. And, second, the will and the opportunity on the part of someone to apply this technique to the divergent and convergent paths of modern psychology. The technique that is necessary is to be merely deductive, for its object is to test the validity of claims made and supported by sundry schools, and it is not primarily interested in the way these various claims happen to have been conceived in the first instance.

This single method of valuation applies to all schools of psychology, because in one important regard they all do the same thing, in that each advances certain psychological elements as underlying its particular system – the behaviorist has his original tendencies and 'given' nervous structure, the gestalt psychologist his configurations and *e pluribus unum* doctrine, the Freudian his underlying sexual urges, and so on. Without expressly so stating, the very postulation of these different elements constitutes a claim that each is an entity in itself and is entitled to an independent status in the field of mental life. Thus all that is needed in the way of technique by him who would investigate the entire field is a device for testing the independence of any given element from all others or at least from such as may be thought to be somewhat similar to it.

Before such testing there must be a definition of the element, and the school of psychology in question is obligated to supply this. This definition must be invariable, and expressible in terms of conduct. Certainly it would be in reason to demand as much in any other field. If a certain doctor maintains that hives are caused in one person by tomatoes, in some other individual by any sort of protein and in a third person by some particular protein, unless caused by the lack of some protein, his very comprehensive formulation is not subject to experimental test. About all that can be done with such a formulation, whether in psychology, medicine, astrology, economics or any other department of human activity, is to let it alone and see that it does not intrude upon more promising hypotheses.

The multiplicity of causes put forward by certain psychoanalysts for a single outcome nearly precludes the subjection of their claims to scientific inquiry. If it is claimed that one performance is consequent to one certain capacity, the matter may be readily tested. Even if the performance is a compound of two capacities check-up is possible. As the number of possible causes increases to three, four, or more, the possibility of check-up rapidly vanishes, and science goes through pseudo-science to speculation or to charlatanry. The trouble is not primarily in postulating several contributing causes but in doing this antecedent to the development of a method of proof. In any true science the formulation and the means of at least partial verification, generally by noting necessary objective consequences, run hand in hand.

Thus, in the field of psychology, if a designation of some trait or capacity, as a category of mental life, is to be given serious consideration, it must be such as to reveal itself as a measurable difference in conduct, that is, as a measurable difference in the same individual at different times, or in different individuals at the same time. Does a trait like introversion meet these conditions? The number of different verbal statements of the meaning to be attached to this term falls but a little short of the number of people using it in writing. Many of these meanings are so subjective as to lead one to doubt whether differences of conduct can be related to them. No method of verification can be hoped for or in fact desired that will investigate the reality of so indefinite a concept. If one or more of the users of the term state that they mean thereby high scoring on a designated test which is definite, administered in a standardized manner, and which yields an objective score, then, and practically only then, can the matter be subjected to test.

This demand that a concept be subjected to objective measurement before it is worthy of serious consideration as an independent category of mental life, though sweeping, is not too sweeping, if we limit objective measurements to such as are definable and verifiable. How about the large class of concepts which are definable only in a rough way and verifiable only in part? Suppose we define 'honesty' in the following manner: 'It is a trait possessed in varying amounts by school children and recognized by teachers, with the result that when teachers rank their pupils on the basis of honesty, a measure of the trait is obtained.' Let us first note that in this statement no precise distinction has been made between honesty itself and the measure of it. To determine whether such a lack of distinction is justified we should attempt to verify the measure. If a second equally trustworthy teacher having equal familiarity with certain pupils gives a rank order which is the same as a first teacher's, and if a third teacher, a fourth teacher, etc., all do the same, then the measure is verified and there is no need of distinction between the trait and the measure of it. Such a situation would arise in practice if height instead of honesty were the trait in question. We say 'John is four feet eight inches tall' and do not quibble over the fact that 'four feet eight inches' is merely some person's measurement of John. If there is complete agreement the measurement is the trait for all practical purposes.

In the case of honesty there would be no complete agreement but partial agreement only. Does such a measure provide a basis for scientific investigation? It seems to the writer that it does, provided firstly the degree of agreement of a measure in hand with a second equally trustworthy measure is known, secondly, the technique adopted takes the unreliability of the measure into account and allows for it so that no systematic error is introduced, and thirdly the technique adopted guards, by drawing tentative conclusions where necessary, against any chance error which may be introduced due to this unreliability of the measure.

These are necessary qualifications, but when these precautions are taken it would seem that objective measures in the sense earlier insisted upon may be derived from sources no more specific than the judgements of acquaintances. Though this is true, it is surely the part of wisdom to utilize performance records which are independent, or nearly independent, of human judgements whenever possible and when dealing with the more far-reaching issues.

Some very suggestive studies of mental capacity based upon judgements have been made [. . .]

After exercising all possible care there remain ambiguities in the interpretation of judgement measures. Should ten, twenty, or even one hundred acquaintances give judgements, which, pooled, characterize a person as one standard deviation above the average for his age in honesty, still no one knows just what is meant by them, and probably never can know, for he has no way of discovering how his independent concept agrees or disagrees with the average concept of these judges. On the other hand, if honesty is defined as a trait tending toward higher scores on a designated test, when administered and scored as directed, then any particular student can study the relationships of this 'honesty', even though he might individually misinterpret the purport of the test questions.

A few years ago Garnett made an analysis of Webb's study based upon judgements, and concluded that there is a mental factor 'cleverness'. Certainly to understand this, 'cleverness' is to be interpreted as by Garnett, but this we can only approximate. And, further, Garnett deduced his 'cleverness' from 'quickness', 'profoundness', 'common sense', 'originality', etc. (of forty-eight mental traits investigated, forty-three came from judgements), which were traits appraised by Webb's judges. The meaning of these traits is certainly to be interpreted as by the average of Webb's judges, but as to these meanings both we and Garnett can secure only rough approximations, so that our final belief in 'cleverness' as a factor must be most uncertain. Still more serious is the fact that it is incapable of verification, for we cannot duplicate by reproduction of the investigation, step by step, our own intepretation of Garnett's interpretation of Webb's judges' interpretation of the traits of the unknown subjects. All these difficulties except the last – differences in supposedly similar populations – are avoided when a trait is defined in terms of an objective measure which is capable of being duplicated and thus verified.

Because of the uncertainty of outcome when dealing with judgements in a study, the purpose of which is to determine disparate mental rubrics, this type of psychological investigation is only incidentally investigated in connection with the delightful study by Shen. It is probably an important and legitimate field in the matter of discovery and preliminary survey, but it is truly of doubtful value in the subsequent steps of proof,

Definition and reproducibility are essential characteristics of the psychological data to be dealt with. Having data with these characteristics, and having purposes as unified as is the case with investigators, there is provided a situation which is amenable to a single type of analysis. The avowed purposes of psychologists sound quite different, but this need not deter us from approaching all investigations with a single comparative technique, because there is a fundamental underlying unity in these purposes. The determination of some difference is the object of every psychological formulation. For convenience, these differences may be characterized as of three types, or of some composite of the three. Thus the difference may be chiefly affected by a change in time, as in the case of growth and fatigue, chiefly affected by spatial consideration, as are all of our sensory and motor functions, or chiefly related to differences in type of central nervous activity, as are the emotions and the several intellectual modes of thought, reasoning, memorizing, etc.

The technique of Spearman, based upon tetrad differences for determining the discreteness of mental phenomena, and that used by the writer, involving much of Spearman's technique but also a considerable extension of it, is entirely adequate to determine whether two things, say a set of visual and a set of auditory measures, are basically the same or different. The case cited is so simple that its solution seems obvious. Much simpler devices than tetrad differences are available here, as perhaps in the case of all differences affected by spatial considerations, which enable one to establish that the auditory and visual phenomena are disparate. It would be ridiculous to measure both the visual and the auditory acuity of a large number of people, measure still other traits, and then calculate a lot of tetrad differences to see if they would warrant the conclusion that visual and auditory acuities are different things. Also, dealing with a single individual, it would be absurd to measure the sensitivity to light, to sound, to heat, etc., of different areas of the body surface, calculate tetrad differences and conclude that visual and the other sensitivities are not the same. However, this could be done, and by this technique each measurable sensory and motor trait of mankind that does stand alone could be so proved. We thus see that the technique in question is much broader in its applicability than one might judge from the field to which it has been applied. However ponderous the tetrad-difference method is in the case of these sensory and motor traits, it seems to be the only way, other than that of intro-spection, available in connection with purely mental phenomena. Apparently the reason is that the usual concomitants of sensory and motor traits, namely, space and time, are not conditions of mental life. One's reasoning power has not been localized in any particular end organ, and it is approximately timeless, operating with equal facility yesterday, today, and tomorrow. Mental phenomena are not entirely devoid of temporal characteristics, as will be discussed at greater length in connection with growth, but in so far as they are independent of it they are not amenable to study by the simple procedures which suffice with sensory and motor traits.

We may characterize the entire realm of psychological thought by saying that it is concerned with:

1. Differentiating between traits, or more broadly, though without a change in meaning, with studying the relationship between traits.
2. Determining changes in single traits (growth, fatigue) as time changes.
3. Modification as locus (end-organ) changes.

From a different point of view, the first of these is to be recognized as a study of individual differences. Of these three problems of difference, we are here concerned only with the first, for a trait must be determined as independent before it is very useful to attempt to determine its growth, if it does grow, or its locale, if it has one. Further, as to differentiating between traits, we are here concerned only with those the independent status of which is open to question – memory, analysis, persistence, etc., but not visual acuity, right-hand grip, etc.

Though our field is thus limited, it may not be amiss to attempt to picture the structure of a human organism which is possessed of traits as wide apart as those of mankind. Walker found that there are many independent motor and sensory capacities in children, thus suggesting specific independently conditioned origins. Spearman (1927) reports much the same thing. Accordingly, so far as these things are concerned we may look to a rich and varied original genetic structure. The writer has argued elsewhere that this many-particled original nature is limited in its development by environmental pressure. If there are forty chromosomes, each with 1000 genetic elements, and if there are five allelomorphic alternates for each element, then the number of permutations conceivable is $5^{40 \times 100}$. The earth could thus be populated millions of times without duplicating in genetic structure any individual. However, probably many of these permutations are lethal, for the embryo in the main develops in one certain milieu only. Certainly medical science indicates a wonderful similarity in metabolism and tolerance, both in infants and in older people. If we carry this thought a step farther we can well believe that in the case of traits concerned with social contacts (love, hate, mental agility at argument, intellectual keenness in finding one's way, subtlety in conflict, tolerance toward the views of associates, etc.), certain permutations only are favorable to survival. Perhaps through generations the allelomorphic elements in these surviving combinations have become linked through mechanisms not unlike those of symbiosis. Thus genetic origins almost infinitely extensive, interacting with physiological and social environment, find their fruition in beings running more or less true to survival types in essential mental and physical make-up, but of great variability in non-essential physiological detail. To illustrate, we might readily conceive of almost an infinite number of intergrades in the matter of sex; but conditions of survival have determined that most of these must vanish, so that as a final result male and female children are born and few hermaphrodites. This picture[1] of

1. The conclusions of Stewart in his ' Mendelism in bacteriology' of 1926, as reported by Symmes (1927), are very pertinent in this connection: 'The variations exhibited occur only in adaptation to the stimulus presented, this

genetic structure, though merely a picture, seems adequate to a portrayal of all the conditions of inter-relationship found, while it is at the same time not sufficiently specific to prejudice any of the experimental treatment. It has two important features in addition to those mentioned, in that it suggests in what evolution consists and it gives a definite place to both heredity and environment in this process.

We have noted that mental traits which we wish to study with a view to differentiating between them are of the class not readily localized in space and time. Even so the field is very extensive and includes what are commonly called the higher mental processes. Our problem is difficult because of the complexity of these processes and because of their number, for they cannot be studied singly. A single mental trait can be studied with reference to growth without any attention to other traits, but obviously when the issue is the difference between traits, it must be studied in conjunction with other traits.

It is here argued that such an approach should logically precede all detailed studies of a trait. Spearman argues that 'perseveration', as measured by Muller, is the same as 'introversion', as proposed by Jung. Surely so vital an issue as this could well be made a matter of first importance, even if the investigator is studying merely the one or the other trait, and not primarily trying to see things in proper perspective. If this latter is the object, then not only should introversion and perseveration be studied together, but also along with many other traits, of which some will probably be related to these two and some will be entirely independent. A comprehensive study of this last sort has never been made. The experimental work of the present volume has dealt jointly with general ability (probably, in the main, maturity),

fact establishing an important hypothesis for evolutionary theory – that a race can adapt itself by variation directly to its environment and that such an adaptation is rigorously inherited. Such an acquired character, however, is inherited only by unicellular organisms; in higher forms it doubtless would affect the soma only, and not the germ-plasm, and therefore not be inherited.' This is quoted because so far as unicellular organisms are concerned it very fully supports the hypothesis here mentioned. So far as higher forms of life are involved it need not be considered a reversal of Mendelian doctrine to postulate some functional relationship between environmental influences and linkage of the genetic elements possessed by surviving individuals, thus in fact giving hereditary conditions operating, though much more slowly, as in the case of the bacteria studied by Stewart.

manipulation of spatial relationships, facility with verbal material, memory, mental speed, and certain other less clearly defined traits. Spearman and his students have studied these same abilities, except facility with verbal material as here defined, and other traits, but his studies have not been of all the traits at once. Generally speaking they have been investigations of the independence of each of the traits singly, from Spearman's general factor g. These studies have been most fruitful in indicating real differences between certain traits and certain gs (the writer does not quite subscribe to the view that the thing called g in all of these investigations is the same throughout), and in suggesting differences between these; but the much-needed comprehensive examination of relationships between many differently labeled, derived, measured, and variously sponsored mental traits is still to be made. Certainly such an investigation should take into consideration the following factors: (1) maturity; (2) sex; (3) race; (4) manipulation of spatial relationships in so far as independent of differences in visual acuity, etc.; (5) manipulation of auditory relationships in so far as independent of auditory acuity, etc.; (6) verbal facility; (7) number facility; (8) memory – one or more kinds; (9) mental speed; (10) one or more traits involving general motor organization and skill; (11) purpose or purposes; (12) ebullience or cleverness; (13) perseveration or intro-extraversion; (14) oscillation or variability in performance; (15) one or more traits connected with social interest and activities; (16) any remaining general factors not included in the preceding. The only adequate attack is to study all of these at once upon the same population, as otherwise certain relationships, perhaps of great importance, will be missed. Owing to previous work, mainly that of Spearman, the list as drawn up is very select and very promising for future study. The writer believes that the techniques herein employed are adequate for such a study and rather more comprehensive than those of Spearman, in spite of the fact that Spearman's have already yielded rich return.

In the study of independent mental capacities, Spearman has in the past utilized quite a number of different criteria. Though he claims that these early criteria are sound, because in harmony with results based upon what he now considers his final technique, there is considerable room for argument. If Technique B is sound and leads to a certain conclusion, then it does not follow that Technique A is sound because in some given instance it leads to the same conclusion. We are, however, not concerned at this time with Spearman's earlier techniques. His last one, for which he claims finality and universality, must be carefully scrutinized.

It is readily shown that if four variables have one, and only one, common factor running through them (in, the writer would add, a linear manner) then every tetrad difference involving the correlation coefficients of these four variables will be equal to zero. In the notation of this text, tetrad differences are denoted by the letter t with appropriate subscripts, and are defined as follows:

$$\left. \begin{array}{l} t_{1\,2\,3\,4} = r_{12}r_{34} - r_{13}r_{24} \\ t_{1\,2\,4\,3} = r_{12}r_{34} - r_{14}r_{23} \\ t_{1\,3\,4\,2} = r_{13}r_{24} - r_{14}r_{23} \end{array} \right\} \qquad \mathbf{1}$$

The equality of these tetrads to zero in the case when one general factor is sufficient was first pointed out by Spearman. It is very easily proved in a number of ways, one of which is given in chapter 3 [not reproduced here].

If there are more than four variables, if one general factor only runs through the variables, and if they contain no group factor, i.e., a factor found in a number of the variables but not all of them, then every tetrad will equal zero. The converse of this is also readily proved, namely, if every tetrad does equal zero, then the variables may be thought of as having one general factor and no group factors. With this as a starting-point Spearman argues that if the distribution of obtained tetrad differences shows a variability no greater than would be expected as a matter of chance, then one and only one factor, other than factors specific to the separate variables, may be looked for in the several measures. To carry this argument into effect the distribution of tetrads must be made (based on all the possible tetrads resulting from the variables employed), and its standard deviation must be calculated and compared with the theoretical standard deviation in case all tetrads deviate from zero merely as a matter of chance. This line of reasoning and the execution of it must be examined very critically, for it constitutes Spearman's major technique and, according to him, the only technique which is adequate. First, as to the execution of it: The formula (Spearman, 1927, Formula 16a) which Spearman and Holzinger have derived for the standard deviation of the distribution of a population of tetrad differences is

$$\sigma = 2 \left(\frac{r^2(1-r)^2 + (1-R)s^2}{N} \right)^{\frac{1}{2}} \qquad \mathbf{2}$$

wherein r is the mean of all the rs and s^2 is their variance, and

$$R = 3r\frac{n-4}{n-2}\ 2r^2\frac{n-6}{n-2}.$$

In these equations n is the number of variables and N is the size of the population.

The writer has criticized the earlier formula, now replaced by this one, and of the use of this later formula Spearman (1927) writes: 'although on some theoretical points still awaiting further elucidation in practice at any rate [it] appears to be far more convenient, and even more reliable than [Spearman and Holzinger's formulas giving the probable errors of single tetrads].' The proof of this very critical Formula 2 has not as yet appeared in print.

Formula 2 may be called not merely a critical formula, but *the* critical formula. Spearman states (1927): 'whenever the tetrad equation holds throughout any table of correlations, and *only* when it does so, then every individual measurement of every ability can be divided into two independent parts . . . [a general and a specific factor].' Formula 2 is the final criterion that Spearman uses to determine if the tetrads throughout the entire table are merely chance deviations from zero. He writes (1927):

To begin with, a note of warning must be sounded against all attempts to replace the rigorously demonstrated criterion by anything else. Many writers have tried to invent a new one for themselves; others have declared that so many are in the field as to produce a difficulty in choosing between them. Against this, we must formally declare that no other rigorous criterion than that demonstrated here (including mere equivalent conversions of it) has ever been proved *or ever can be.*

Spearman is presumably referring to the tetrad-difference formula $r_{12}r_{34} - r_{13}r_{24} = 0$, but we must note that the crux of the matter is not in the proposition that all tetrad differences equal zero, but in the standard errors of their actual values, which deviate by chance or otherwise from zero. According to Spearman's method this leads back to Formula 2. Clearly it is the basic formula in the entire treatment. If we grant that Formula 2 is correct, we may still question the use made of it, for Spearman assumes that chance would yield a normal distribution of tetrad differences with this standard deviation. This assumption of a normal distribution, even in situations where one general factor only is present, does not seem reasonable, for the chance errors in the correlation coefficients are known to be correlated, so that we may expect the chance errors in the tetrads also to be correlated, and to an appreciable extent, for they are only functions of four correlation coefficients and the products of correlation coefficients in pairs are repeated many times in the total population of tetrad differences. This would yield a non-normal distribution, of just what form the writer does not know. The obvious way of using the chance standard deviation of a population of tetrad differences would be to compare it with the obtained standard deviation, find the difference between the two, and the standard error of this difference. This standard error, which will certainly be very small, is not known, and it probably cannot be determined by any means sufficiently simple to be serviceable. Should one object to this proposed method of interpretation on grounds similar to those just raised, namely, that the distribution of differences between these two standard deviations will not be normal and thus not readily interpretable, it can be shown that the point, though not without foundation, is much less material here than in the former case.

How material this particular criticism of Spearman's use of Formula 2 is, is not known. It may be quite trivial. A more important criticism from the writer's point of view is the fact that the situations in which one is really interested are not those to which it can usefully be applied. According to Spearman's latest conclusions there are no less than three general cognitive factors – g, oscillation, and perseveration – and a much larger number of group factors, including memory, a spatial factor, a conjunction factor (probably identical with what the present writer calls a number factor), a music factor, etc., as well as 'conative' factors. All that Spearman's criterion could tell us would be that one factor was or was not sufficient to explain a given situation. All of the writer's data do show, and he ventures to prophesy that all of the forthcoming as well as much of the earlier data from Spearman's laboratory will show, the need for more than a single factor; thus Spearman's tool proves inadequate. We are no longer concerned with the first step, 'Does one factor suffice?' but with the later steps, 'How many and what factors suffice?', The writer presents herein the complete solution of the adequacy of two factors in the case of variables up to the number five, but he has found even this to be inadequate, for there are found in his data more than two general or group factors. Finally, the writer presents an iteration method for handling the problem when more factors and more variables are present. This method seems to be a powerful analytical device. It calls, however, for a wider use and more detailed mathematical scrutiny than it has as yet received. As to the needed mathematical scrutiny, it can, in brief, be said that the writer has been using an iteration method and obtaining a convergency in a series without having first proved that convergency is a mathematical necessity.

The fundamental technique of Spearman has been supplemented by him by a partial correlation procedure. When he has found that one independent factor was insufficient, he has partialed out g and by a study of the residual correlations has found additional factors. This procedure depends upon the ability to obtain a measure of g uncontaminated by other factors. The difficulty of doing this is great, because of the special hazards involved in partialing out just what is needed and no more when dealing with measures having large chance elements in them, and perhaps also having disconcerting specific and group factors in them. The writer has not attempted to follow carefully all of this partial correlation treatment, because Spearman's populations have been very small, the partial correlations very small, and the resulting probable errors very large and, most unfortunately, unknown. He would, however, express the belief that in spite of these special hazards the method has much to commend it.

Though certain shortcomings in the tools used by Spearman have been pointed out, nevertheless the writer believes that on the whole he has used them with rare judgement and has determined the existence of many important mental factors. In short, as Spearman's technique and point of view with reference to the significance of differences seems too rigorous, or, in other words, unfavorable to the discovery of factors in addition to g, we may place rather special confidence in the reality of such special factors as he does report. The very thorough review of these to be found in his *Abilities of Man* (1927) makes it unnecessary to give more than a brief discussion of them here. Spearman clearly distinguishes cognitive, conative, and affective traits, as well as various other traits, for example, retentivity and fatigue. It does not seem to the writer that he has established by his own method of tetrad differences the independence of these things. We will therefore, even at the risk of not doing full justice to his view, make no attempt to preserve this classification of traits and capacities. We will list those that he has found disparate, but we should bear in mind that in the main, by his technique, differences of each from g are established rather than complete difference of each from each other.

First in this list is Spearman's g. As measures of it, which involve nothing else except specific factors, are the 'usual sets of mental tests'. The number of specific tests which could here be mentioned is very great, including, in addition to many others, opposites, synonyms, classification, completion, questions, analogies, paragraphs, meanings, memory, abstract thought, accuracy, inferences and likelihood. Owing to the universality of g, Spearman states that 'any test will do just as well as any other, provided only that its correlation with g is equally high'. The saturation of measures with g is not markedly affected by any differences in the fields of cognition. Again, 'g proved to be a factor which enters into the measurements of ability of all kinds, and which is throughout constant for any individual, although varying greatly for different individuals. It showed itself to be involved invariably and exclusively in all operations of deductive nature, whatever might be the class of relation or the sort of fundamentals at issue. It was found to be equally concerned with each of two general dimensions of ability, Clearness and Speed. It also applied in similar manner to both the dimensions of span, which are Intensity and Extensity. But it revealed a surprisingly complete independence of all manifestations of Retentivity. Whether there is any advantage in attaching to this g the old mishandled label of "intelligence" seems at least dubious'. In brief, Spearman's concept is that g is the ability to deduce relations and correlates, and is dependent upon a central fund of energy.

The experimental results reported in later chapters hardly support this concept, because there seem to be two, and perhaps three, traits combined in this one concept. First, there is a factor making for correlation between variables due to maturity, race, sex differences, and differences of antecedent nurture. That these things would strongly tend to introduce a general factor is shown in chapter 2 of this book [not reproduced here], and that Spearman pays far too little attention to them is very obvious to one going over the various experimental investigations that have been made in his laboratory and under his direction. In fact, he writes, 'Also worthy of mention, though hardly of prolonged examination, is the taking of g to have reference only to children, being in fact no more than a measurement of their maturity. One child does better at the tests than another of the same age, it is said, only because of being more precocious' (1927, p. 90). Though this statement implies the comparison of children of the same age, Spearman's groups typically have not been children of the same age, and he has not resorted to a partial correlation technique to reduce his data to a constant age basis. Certainly race and nurture have not been partialed out, and only very occasionally has sex been experimentally treated as a separate factor. It is regrettable that this very fundamental matter[1] of maturity has not been thought worthy of prolonged examination. On *a priori* grounds why should one consider it of less significance in connection with intellect than with bodily structure?

The second factor which the writer finds clearly indicated in his own data, and which is undoubtedly present in the tests measuring g, is a verbal factor, for the tests that Spearman regularly uses as the better measures of g are very similar to those in which the writer has found a large verbal factor. One might say that this is merely quibbling over terms, and that what the present writer means by a verbal factor is what Spearman means by g. This does describe the situation in part, though the writer finds that the verbal factor is more limited in its scope than the statements of Spearman would indicate his g to be. It is, nevertheless, probably true that fully one-half of Spearman's g is represented by what is here called a verbal factor.

A very recent study by one of Spearman's students (Davey, 1926) gives data from which the author concludes that there is no general verbal factor. Davey reports the distribution of tetrads of the form $t_{1\ 2\ 3\ 4}$, in which x_1 equals the score on an oral test, x_3, that on a second oral test, x_2, that on a pictorial test, and x_4, that on a second pictorial test. The median of such tetrads is 0·021, and the probable error (of the distribution, not of the median) by Spearman's Formula 2 is 0·019. This clearly shows a verbal factor, but Davey, picking out four of the eight verbal tests which have contributed the greatest to the creation of this median difference

1. It may be that neglect of nurture as a factor has been caused by a belief that its influence is specific. We find one of Spearman's students (Slocombe, 1926) stating: 'How is it then, that practice, though present and producing an increase in score, does not influence g as measured? It is inferred that the influence of practice is specific to the form of test. Thus when a number of test forms are combined, practice enters as an uncorrelated specific factor.'

The data of Slocombe, based upon a growth or nurture period of three months only, are most inadequate for so important a conclusion. The contradictory view is indicated upon many counts in Kelley (1926), which includes data extending over a considerable range of years.

finds that the median of the distribution of the remaining tetrads is approximately zero. This process of selection is unwarranted, for the very act of *a posteriori* selecting the four tests has capitalized chance in one direction, that of not yielding a verbal factor. We are surely warranted in disagreeing with Davey and in fact in citing his data as indicating a verbal factor of fairly wide extent.

Finally, there may be a third factor – not variability, in maturity in sex, in race, in nurture; and not verbal – present in Spearman's g. The writer believes that if such a residual factor remains, after an allowance for the things mentioned, it is very small. A general factor, not verbal, is found by the writer throughout his work, but as he has not allowed for sex, race, or nurture, and probably not adequately for maturity, it is truly an open question whether any g factor at all would exist if these things had been properly taken into account.

The data which most adequately takes into account maturity and sex is the Army Alpha data quoted very disparagingly by Spearman. As to the facts we can all agree that a single general factor is not indicated. As to the cause, Spearman writes that by the procedure followed, 'the subjects, and still more so the testing must have become heterogeneous to the last degree'. Knowing something of the care with which this testing work was done, the writer does not believe the second of these charges is justified. As to the first charge, it is true that the group was rather heterogeneous, but this fact would introduce a g factor, not take out one already there. In brief, these data, almost unique in that they allow for maturity and sex, for the group consisted of adult men, do not yield a comprehensive g factor. A further study of the Army Alpha data is made in chapter 9 below [not reproduced here].

The relationship pictured by Spearman between education and g is stated in the following words: 'On the whole, the most reasonable conclusion for the present appears to be that education has a dominant influence upon individual differences in respect of s (specific factors), but normally it has little if any in respect of g' (1927). The writer has shown in an earlier study that there is a great community of function between general intelligence and general scholastic achievement. If Spearman is correct in his statement, then general scholastic achievement is of necessity little affected by education. Though this may be so to an extent not ordinarily suspected, at least in certain respects it has been found by the writer not to be the case. Further data and comment upon this important point are given below in chapter 6 [not reproduced here].

From Spearman's great dependence upon a central fund of intellective energy as a highly important category of mental life to a view wherein no general factor exists is indeed a far step, but one quite within the realm of possibility, judging by all the data at hand.

The nurture element earlier mentioned as a source of a general factor would be a general nurture, i.e. a tendency of the environment to stimulate or repress all intellectual development. Over and above this there may be a nurture operating on particular phases only of intellectual life, for example, an environment tending to stimulate or repress number ability. In either case there is no way, except by studying different age groups, to differentiate between native and acquired traits. Accordingly, with reference to the group traits found, we must, while noting Spearman's findings, be content to be concerned with the question of their existence rather than of the original or acquired nature of their origins.

A trait designated 'perseveration' is considered by Spearman to be a universal factor. It is an expression of his fundamental 'law of inertia'. The sensory tests (speed of rotation of a color disk to cause fusion; seconds needed for adaptation to darkness) employed by Wiersma showed rather systematic differences in the case of eleven maniacs, nine normals, and eighteen melancholics. Heymans and Brugmans with these same tests and with others obtained, in the case of fifteen normal subjects, such low correlations that no very likely conclusion is indicated from their data. Next, Wynn Jones (*see* Spearman, 1927) gave 'seventy-seven children about twelve years of age' tests, all of which involve motor activity and habits. The attempt was made to eliminate the motor factor by employing other motor tests not involving 'perseveration', but this should surely be called unsuccessful, because the inter-correlations were very low, averaging 0·09, which we may expect to have been due largely to the unreliability of the tests. Spearman writes, 'nothing of this diminutive size could possibly account for – or even by being eliminated sensibly diminish – the correlations shown in the foregoing table'. This is true but altogether insufficient, as the author of the correction for attenuation should know, for one cannot partial out a motor factor by partialing out the scores on motor tests of very low reliability. Finally, there is the study of Lankes involving forty-seven students in the Islington Day Training College (ages and sex not indicated). His array of tests is quite extensive, but his inter-correlations are so low, running from -0.05 to 0.51, and averaging 0.22, and his population so small, that probable errors are very large. The data are hardly serviceable in proving the existence of a 'perseveration' factor. From the Wiersma, Heymans and Brugmans, Wyn Jones, and Lankes data, Spearman not only deduces a 'perseveration' factor, but he defines many of its characteristics. These data are surely a feeble foundation for so imposing a superstructure. The writer believes that factors other than g are indicated by these data, but that it is hazardous to say more than this.

A trait called 'oscillation' is presented as a third universal cognitive factor. Its experimental foundation is perhaps a trifle more adequate than in the case of 'perseveration', for the largest population studied was of 'about eighty children aged about twelve years'. Here the inter-correlations ranged from 0.00 to 0.44, with an average of 0.21. Somewhat more adequate intelligence measures were available for this group.

One further general factor, this time connected with the field of conation, is considered to be present. This is Webb's 'persistence of motives', and Garnett's 'purpose' factor. The difficulty of establishing this is greatly increased by the fact that it is deduced from personal judgements and not from objective test scores. However, the population was large, '200 students with an average age of twenty-one years', and the evidence quite clear-cut that there is more than one factor present – the factors being g and 'persistence of motives' according to Webb, and g, 'purpose', and 'cleverness' according to Garnett. A thing much to be hoped for is the measurement of these factors in a more objective manner, and a more exact establishment of their place in mental life.

Let us now note briefly other factors which Spearman calls group factors, because he considers them of less universality than the general factors. There has been no criterion established justifying, say 'perseveration' as a general factor, and 'memory' as a group factor. In either instance, and also in the case of g, the evidence of the generality of the factor depends upon the measures employed in the investigation. With reference to a designated set of measurements through all of which runs a certain factor A, through several of which runs a factor B, and in one of which is a factor C, the writer sees a value in the terms general, group, and specific; but this value is only in the descriptive power of these terms for the particular situation which is being investigated.

Given other tests, the *A* factor might become specific, the *B* factor become general, and the *C* factor become a group factor. To determine factors which are not thus dependent upon a particular set of tests, it is necessary to utilize many measures at once, thus making a very exhaustive survey of the mental ability of the subjects tested. In noting factors reported by Spearman additional to those already mentioned we will not draw a distinction between general and group factors.

There is a memory factor certainly extending to different sensory fields and to verbal material.

One of Spearman's 'ideal' relations is 'conjunction', and he finds a factor of this nature. The writer prefers to call it a 'numbers' or 'arithmetical' factor as being more descriptive of the content and nature of the tests revealing it.

There is a constructive mechanical ability factor which may be related to that characterized by the writer as 'manipulation of spatial relationships'.

Dealing with this trait, McFarlane (1925) reports that the factor is found in the case of boys and not in that of girls. Certain other evidence of sex differences is cited, but no extensive treatment of sex as a factor in mental life is undertaken by Spearman. There is a great deal of literature bearing upon this matter. Noteworthy in this is the study already made by Terman, as well as a further investigation by him now under way. They suggest rather far-reaching mental differences which are correlated with sex.

The reader must not conclude because of the criticisms that have been made of Spearman's technique and interpretation that there is wide disagreement between his findings and those of the present writer. On the whole the two sets of findings are quite remarkably in harmony, the agreements being in the matter of a spatial, a numerical, a memory, and even a general factor, though this last is differently interpreted, and also in the conclusion that a large number of specific motor (probably also sensory) factors exist. There is scarcely a disagreement in the matters of music, purpose, cleverness, and sex, though here the data are inadequate. There does seem to be a real disagreement in the importance and extent of a verbal factor and in that of a mental speed factor [. . .]

It is admitted that the treatment of the present chapter and related treatments by the writer are an inadequate discussion of psychological points of view, varied both as to phenomena dealt with and methods employed. They may, however, suffice to emphasize the variety of mental activity of which man is master and to outline a picture of mental life which future study will fill in. In brief, the boundaries of mental traits are ruts, not far-flung indefinite fringes of consciousness. Mental life does not operate in a plain but in a network of canals. Though each canal may have indefinite limits in length and depth, it does not in width; though each mental trait may grow and become more and more subtle, it does not lose its character and discreteness from other traits.

References

DAVEY, C. M. (1926), 'Group verbal and pictorial tests of intelligence, *Brit J. Psychol.*, vol. 17.

KELLEY, T. L. (1926), *The Influence of Nurture Upon Native Differences*, Stanford University Press.

McFARLANE, M. (1925), 'Study of practical ability', *Brit. J. Psychol. Monogr. Supp.* no. 8.

SLOCOMBE, C. S. (1926), 'The constancy of intelligence', *Brit. J. Psychol.*, no. 17.

SPEARMAN, C. (1904), 'General intelligence objectively determined and measured', *Amer. J. Psychol.*, vol. 15, pp. 201–293.

SPEARMAN, C. (1927), *The Abilities of Man*, Macmillan.

SYMMES, E. H. (1927), 'Aesthetic preferences by comparison with standards', *Psychol. Abstracts*, vol. 1, no. 5.

WEBB, E. (1915), 'Character and intelligence', *Brit. J. Psychol.*, *Monogr.*, no. 3.

4 G. Thomson

Intelligence and Civilization

G. Thomson, *Intelligence and Civilisation*, the Ludwig Mond lecture
delivered at the University of Manchester, 23 October 1936, Edinburgh,
Constable at the University Press.

Introduction

When I was asked to name a subject for this lecture, my first
thought was to use the occasion to tell my audience in entirely
non-technical terms something of the work which has been done
during the past three decades in the endeavour to measure intelligence, to define what it is, and to analyse it into its constituents
if that be possible. Something of this I still intend to do, for one
cannot well discuss Intelligence and Civilization without asking
oneself what each of them is. But as I thought further over the
subject of my lecture I remembered the motives which had first
led me to take an interest in the measurement of intelligence and
which have continued to keep me at work on it. Those motives
arose out of the observation that our educational system, through
its secondary school scholarships, often favoured the well taught
or at least well-crammed mediocrity of one school at the expense
of the clever boy of another school: for example, favoured the
boy from a large and well-staffed suburban elementary school at
the expense of a boy from a small and remote country school,
where the only teacher had too much on his hands to have time
for specializing in scholarship-winning, and where, since there
was but one teacher, it was to a great extent a matter of chance
whether the child enjoyed good teaching or suffered under bad.
It was because in a heterogeneous county like Northumberland,
including suburban residential districts, large mining areas, and
sparsely populated dales, it had been found that many schools in
the latter two types of district simply made no attempt to enter
children for secondary school scholarships, well knowing that
they had no chance. We introduced intelligence tests in the hope
of righting this injustice to the individual, and to an increasing
extent by this and by other means it has been in some measure
righted, and the intelligent children have more and more

efficiently been selected and assisted to obtain secondary education. The motive was individual.

But as the years have gone on, the other side of the old problem of the individual and the community has also never been far from my mind, and I have asked myself, as I have also often enough been asked by others, whether we are doing the right thing both for the individual and the community when we thus take pains, through the medium of our educational system, to direct children of different degrees of intelligence into different types of school.

Tonight I want to discuss this. It is my faith that we must do individual justice. But it is our duty to do so without wrecking civilization or hindering its progress, if we can choose between methods. For anyone who hopes, as I do, that furthering the education of intelligent children also furthers civilization, it is necessary to ask about the dependence of civilization on intelligence and about the relative importance, to civilization, of intelligence and other qualities. We have seen in the years since the Great War a remarkable movement away from a belief in intelligence, in more than one European nation; a movement which can find nothing worse to say about a man than that he is a latecomer of the century of the Illumination;[1] a movement which preaches Irrationalism and decries Reason; and those of us who feel opposed to that retrograde movement have a duty laid upon us to show how much civilization has owed to intelligence.

Intelligence

I turn first, however, to the definition and measurement of intelligence, a province where also there have been controversies, though not such soul-shaking controversies likely to split the world to its foundations. It is one of the peculiarities of the idea of intelligence, and has often been made a reproach to those of us engaged in endeavouring to measure and analyse it, that it is difficult to define. Some of the difficulties are, I think, due to trying to define 'intelligence', and diminish when we confine ourselves to defining 'intelligent' behaviour or thought. The noun intelligence tends to invoke the idea of some entity called intelligence, whereas the adjective intelligent, more correctly, merely calls attention to an attribute of behaviour – for sooner or later thought finds issue in behaviour, especially if we include speaking

1. Krieck calls Herbart 'der Spätling der Aufklärung', a remark which I confess appears to me an undeserved compliment to Herbart, but was not so intended.

and writing under behaviour – and although we cannot define intelligent behaviour briefly, we can enumerate some of its symptoms.

Before there can be intelligent behaviour there must be some purpose to be achieved (though it may be a very general and vague purpose and only become clearer as the events succeed one another), and the behaviour has to have the appearance of being directed towards that end in such a way as to achieve it as quickly, as economically, as cleanly as possible. By cleanly I mean that the behaviour, in solving the given problem, must not unnecessarily create others, though it will lead on, through this problem, to others, beyond. By economically I mean not merely of time or of energy, but in the sense of solving simultaneously many similar problems and not leaving the work to be done afresh on each occasion.

We do not call behaviour intelligent if it has been learned by training – in the sense of rewarding certain overt actions and punishing others until the desired set of actions comes to be exclusively performed – as by a performing seal, or an indoctrinated partisan. Here I come upon a distinction which is very important for me, for in a certain sense I think that almost all our behaviour is due to training by reward and punishment, and yet I do not think that almost all our behaviour is unintelligent – though it would not, alas, be altogether hopeless to defend that thesis in the world of today. The difference is that I do not call a piece of behaviour intelligent until some at least of the trial and error involved is done inside us, by means of images or words or some kind of proxy for the actual behaviour. When a chicken is shut up in a simple maze and supplied with a motive for escape (loneliness will do) it does ultimately escape, by the process of running hither and thither until it chances to escape. If it is repeatedly shut in the maze under the same circumstances as regards motivation, it will in time come to take the correct path, without any digressions into blind alleys. But its action is not then to be called intelligent. On the other hand, when the unpractised townsman is faced with the unfamiliar task of driving a flock of sheep along a road, we call his action intelligent if on seeing an opening in the hedge some little distance ahead he sends a boy to guard it until the sheep are past. It would have been unintelligent to let the sheep first go in and then drive them out. It is intelligent to see them first go in in the mind's eye, and take steps to prevent it. Actual behaviour has been short-circuited by internal thinking. On a higher level the problem confronting the man may be more and more difficult, but the principle is the same – imaginary or symbolic behaviour replaces actual, and to the extent that he is capable of this, the man is potentially intelligent.

I may satisfy myself by actual individual trials in repeated instances that the sum of the series of consecutive odd numbers beginning with unity is always a perfect square; thus 1, 3, 5, 7 give 16, the square of 4. I shall probably do the earlier examples in my head, but the later ones on paper. Human curiosity will make me want to see this remarkable fact more as a whole, want to prove it as we say. In endeavouring to do so I shall again carry out plenty of trial and error, both in my head and on paper, the latter mainly to complete trials suggested and begun mentally. The algebraist, from his training, will at an early stage be led to reverse the series and add it to itself, and thus see that every pair of terms gives the same result, whence he will soon arrive at a proof. The Greek mathematicians saw the same truth in a more direct fashion by thinking of each square number as a square of dots, each of which squares is made into the next larger by adding an L-shaped row of dots along the west and along the south side of the preceding square, which new set of dots will clearly be the next odd number. Thus the square 2×2 is enlarged to 3×3 by adding an L of 5 dots (2 on the west, 2 on the south, and one in the corner – it is the one in the corner which makes it odd); this 3×3 square is increased to 4×4 by adding an L of 7 dots, and so on. The modern accountant would probably see, in his special way, that the average of consecutive odd numbers is equal to the number of them.

This is of course very incomplete, but time forbids me to illustrate and to delimit further. I will only add that if to the power of making internal trials we add a trained habit of making many, and accepting or rejecting according to the imagined consequences, we have, I think, got the major parts of the definition of intelligence in action; and I will add also that I think this power and habit mainly dependent, on its physiological side, on the actual number of elementary connections which the nervous system can make, and has practised making.

Whatever this intelligence is, there have been those during the present century who have ventured to endeavour to 'measure' it. When philosophically examined the measurement turns out to be no more than an ordering of magnitudes, even if it is that; but then still deeper philosophical examination might, and I think would, show that the same can be said of physical measurement (*see* Brown and Thomson, 1921). The 'unit' used has been either the amount by which an average child grows in intelligence in one year, or the statistical unit of the standard deviation of the intelligences of a number of children all of the same age. In the first case, it is a mere assumption that the mental growth from five to six, say, is equal to the mental growth from six to seven. Indeed everything points to this not being so. In the second case there is similarly no guarantee that the standard deviation remains constant from year to year, in real mental units. In late years there have been some heroic attempts, notably that of Thurstone, to arrive at an absolute zero and true mental unit of intelligence, attempts which depend in the main on the assumption that intelligence, if measured in real mental units, should be Gaussian in distribution; but they are not very convincing.

Yet in spite of the absence of a universally recognized definition of intelligence, and in spite of the very unsatisfactory foundations of its system of units, the measurement of intelligence has become more and more practicable and practised. Perhaps an analogy with the measurement of temperature will show how this can be. In the ordinary thermometer we have an instrument with a quite arbitrary zero, and which shows in actual fact the expansion of mercury in units marked on a glass tube. There is grave difficulty in believing that the change in our feelings of warmth is the same when the thermometer rises from 6° to 7° as when it rises from 66° to 67°. We have no guarantee that the mental units bear any fixed ratio to the mercury units. And I defy anyone to define what temperature is, in the mental sense, any more easily than he can define intelligence. Yet we find thermometers in practice very useful.

Finally, before turning away from this very sketchy account of the measurement of intelligence, I may be permitted to note the pioneering work of Spearman in trying to base the whole study on the one hand on experimental researches followed by mathematical deductions, and on explicitly stated 'neogenetic' principles on the other. As it is well known that I have opposed some of the views of Spearman, perhaps too I may be allowed to delimit the extent of my disagreement. Spearman, having noted empirically a certain relationship between the correlation coefficients of scores in mental tests, based upon this a theory of Two Factors – to which later a number of auxiliary Group Factors were added – the principal factor being g, usually identified with intelligence, though Spearman himself is careful to avoid naming it except by a letter. The analysis of human ability into these factors can be carried out by methods devised by Spearman and his school, or by other methods, mathematically but not philosophically different, devised by Kelley, Thurstone and others. My opposition is based on the fact that the analysis is not unique, but that innumerable alternative analyses are possible, all fulfilling the experimental conditions; and further, that among these alternatives is one which is intrinsically more probable than the others, not an analysis into large discrete factors but into innumerable bonds grouped in intermingled ramifications, the mind in my view being an integrated whole, though with aspects, not a bundle of factors. But it is impossible to do more than mention this controversy here. I must turn to the intelligence as we roughly estimate it by our actual examinations and tests, and to the way in which our educational system in England acts as a selective agency in furthering the higher education of the more intelligent.

The educational sieve

England has always had a scholarship system designed to assist clever poor boys to obtain a higher education culminating in a university degree. The system has been recently described, in its historical aspect, by Sadler in a scholarly and well-documented essay (1936). Since the Balfour Education Act of 1902 this system has been enormously broadened, in its lower reaches, by the institution of Free or Special Places in Secondary Schools for both boys and girls, awarded on an examination held usually within six months of the child's eleventh birthday. About 40 per cent of the children in our English Secondary Schools thus pay no fee, or only a very small fee. (The others, called fee-payers, pay usually about £9 per annum, which is about one-third of the running costs.) The object of thus assisting clever children to a secondary education, leading perhaps to still higher education, is not often explicitly stated. The actual motive of many who share in furthering the movement, whether by their votes as constituents, their actions as Town or County Councillors, their contributions to the force of public opinion, or in any other way direct or indirect, is mainly, I think, a desire to give the individual poor boy a chance of getting on in the world. The equally laudable desire of keeping up the supply of educated persons needed by the community in its administrative services, in its professional classes, and in the ranks of technical workers, is in the background. It is a motive often stated by pious benefactors, but not, I think, very prominent in the minds of administrators or of those who take an active part in the public life of our cities and counties. They tend to view the matter as giving the individual his chance, not as assisting the community by providing it with trained intelligences. Indeed there are not wanting those who openly state that the community is getting more trained intelligences than it can deal with. These are undoubtedly taking a communal view, and presumably would wish to reduce the provision of higher education, at least of higher academic education, to conform with their notion of the community need. They might, however, desire on the other hand to increase the provision of technical schools and to facilitate the vocational education of clever boys who could be directed into engineering or textiles or shipbuilding or what not. The main motive of such views is the communal one. True, those who hold them might and probably would claim that John Doe and Richard Roe would be far happier as mechanics in overalls than as clerks in white collars or teachers in black gowns, but their main motive is communal.

The first problem on which we have stumbled is then the question whether every sufficiently intelligent child is entitled to a higher education, or whether the State has a right to set a limit, if it can only use a certain number of such educated intelligences. Three subsidiary questions bound up with the main problem are:

1. How many educated intelligences does the modern community need, and in particular how many university graduates can it absorb?

2. To what extent does each sufficiently intelligent child at present actually have the opportunity to proceed to higher education, or to speak definitely, to attend a secondary school?

3. What is the distribution of intelligence among mankind, and is intelligence an inborn or an acquired quality?

Obviously we cannot debate at length all the questions which arise, and the third of these I shall dismiss arbitrarily by giving the view of most psychologists that individuals, at birth, do differ considerably in potential intelligence, and that the actual differences of intelligence observable in adults are, to at least one half of their extent and frequency and perhaps more than one half, due to these inborn differences. The scatter of intelligence among children of ten years of chronological age is such that about one-quarter of them are mentally eleven years of age and more, and

10 per cent of them are mentally twelve years of age and more. Something like 3 per cent of them are thirteen years and more old mentally, and a few of these 3 per cent will even exceed fourteen, fifteen, sixteen or seventeen years of mental age, although their chronological age is only ten. In short, the scatter is very great, and is certainly in part innate.

Do those children who are sufficiently intelligent all have the opportunity of secondary education? The answer to this is certainly no, whatever boundary we assign to the intelligence necessary to profit by a secondary education. Fifteen years ago, in the course of some extensive experiments in Northumberland, I took occasion to remark that were the secondary school population to be suddenly annihilated it could at once be replaced, intelligence quotient for intelligence quotient, from the children who had remained in elementary schools or had gone to work in the mines or elsewhere. But it could not be replaced twice. In other words, in Northumberland in 1921 only about half the children with the requisite intelligence actually entered secondary schools. There has been a very considerable advance since that date in Northumberland. But in the main the statement is still approximately true for the country as a whole, and it has been in particular verified for London by recent research by Gray and Moshinsky (1935). Something like one-half of even the most intelligent children – indeed more than half if Gray and Moshinsky are right – are denied the opportunity of secondary school education. It must not be too hastily assumed that they are denied it by hard-hearted Local Education Authorities who do not supply a sufficiency of free secondary school places. There are certainly other reasons: for the category of children who do not enter secondary schools includes substantial numbers of the very highest ranks of intelligence, who undoubtedly could win free places if they tried, and many of whom indeed have won free places but have not accepted them. Denial of opportunity arises from other factors of our social system; from the desire of parents that the children should go to work at once; from the fact – an unfortunate fact I think – that a secondary school boy cannot usually be apprenticed to a trade, since that in many trades must be done before the age of sixteen; from the need for a boy to enter his father's shop or business as soon as possible; from the boy's own distaste for further bookish study and his natural desire to get to 'a man's work'; and so on.

The situation in Scotland is different. Proportionately to population, more than twice as many children enter secondary schools in Scotland as in England. The wastage however is very great, and by sixteen years of age the numerical difference has almost disappeared. The Scottish children who leave a secondary school early have obviously had the opportunity of a higher education, in the sense that a place in school was open to them. It should be added that after sixteen years of age the Scottish superiority in numbers reappears, owing to the exit from English schools after the First School Certificate examination, not held in Scotland. There is only one examination in Scotland, taken on an average at seventeen and a half. Exactly twice as many Scots as English (proportionately to population) proceed to a university.

In England, then, only about one-half of those children who are intelligent enough to profit by it go to a secondary school, but the factors which deny this opportunity to the others are at least as much sociological as educational. The best way in which our educational administrators could help to prevent this denial would be by offering more alternative courses in the secondary schools, and by endeavouring to arrange with trades that years in a secondary school (including years in academic courses) should count as part apprenticeship, or at least that apprenticeship should not be denied to a secondary school boy because he has passed the usual age.

But we have still to face the chief of our three subsidiary questions, *viz.* how many educated intelligences does a modern community need? Now for my own part I reply to this without hesitation with the answer, as many as it can possibly get. It all depends on what is meant by the word 'need'. A modern nation can in a certain sense get along with fewer university graduates than England turns out today, and might be embarrassed by an oversupply, as is said to be the case in some countries, and even in our own country by some. But there seems to me to be a far greater danger in turning out too few than too many. Not only would those services which require university graduates be starved (among which services we in Scotland count the elementary branch of the teaching profession). There would also be the split in the nation between the educated and the uneducated, which means, if not civil war, then a state of disguised warfare. We are about to raise the school-leaving age to fifteen in three years' time. It is my own opinion that, if we are to survive, we shall have to raise it a great deal further than that during the coming few decades, or at least raise, if not the compulsory school age, then at least the age up to which free education can be claimed if it is desired. It is not generally realized in this country that in most American States of the Union, in addition to the compulsory school age, there is such a permissive school age, usually twenty-one, embodied either in the State's constitution or in its laws. One of the results of the Depression of four years ago was that the 'children' of eighteen and nineteen years of age who had finished High School in America simply declined to leave, and the headmasters were embarrassed by large classes of ex-pupils; the schools in fact began to grow unofficial Junior Colleges on top of their orthodox structure.

I have just said that I fear a split in the nation between the more educated and the less educated. This does seem to me to be a very real danger. It is the danger of Plato's 'two nations' in another form. 'Such a state is not one, but two states, the one of poor, the other of rich men; and they are living in the same spot and always conspiring against one another' (Jowett, 1908). Substitute 'elementary scholars' for poor, and 'secondary scholars' for rich men, and you have a dichotomy every whit as dangerous.

That is why I regret the forking of the ways in England, at the early age of eleven years, into elementary and secondary education, and why I prefer the American system of one High School for all. I know that a common reply to this is to point to the lower standards prevalent in American High School and College education, and to attribute these to the dilution of talent which occurs when the less intelligent are mixed with the more intelligent in one school. But while admitting the lower American standards I do not attribute them to this cause. For in Scotland, where I think no one can complain of lower standards, there is also a very considerable approach to the common secondary school. I have already said that more than twice as many enter, one reason being that entry is by qualification not by competition. In theory at least, and in most parts of the country in practice as well, every child who passes the qualifying examination, at whatever age, is entitled to free secondary education; and more than three quarters of the child population do qualify. If only one quarter enter secondary schools, that is caused by other reasons, regrettable but not so likely to engender bitterness as the long distances which necessarily separate secondary schools in the sparsely populated Highlands and Islands, or family reasons, or the provision of 'Advanced Divisions' which (at least in the cities) give as good an education as the secondary school though with a different bias – in some places, and this is in my eyes best, they are in the same block of buildings and under the same headmaster as the academic secondary school.

But although I think of the common High School as the ideal, I am practical-minded enough to know that England will not open her present secondary schools to make them common High Schools, and I look therefore to the generous development of the free Central or Senior Schools to perform this function. But this will only be if these schools are made more equal to secondary schools in the amount of money spent on their buildings, playing fields, equipment, and teachers, and if it becomes somehow possible, without chaining them to examinations, to reach a university through them, which will probably come through admission to faculties of commerce and of applied science, as the German *Realschule* got its first footing in the university, and as the product of the French *Ecole primaire supérieure* can get in by the doorway called 'PCN'.

In answering the subsidiary questions I have, I imagine, betrayed my opinion on the problem itself. I not only think that every sufficiently intelligent child is entitled to a higher education, but I think it would be in its own interest for the State to strain every nerve to see that he got it, and got it if possible in a way which would not create social differences, based on intelligence, in the same school as his less intelligent comrade.

Intelligence and truth

For the history of the advance of civilization has been the history of the conquest of the world by intelligence. The most astonishing example is, of course, the rapid advance during the sixth, fifth and fourth centuries B.C. in Greece, when not only the beginnings of our modern science were made, but the beginnings of our ideas of government, of economics and of philosophy. Many factors no doubt contributed. The city-states of Greece were in sheltered valleys separated by mountains, or on islands. But these valleys were not so sheltered as to be immune from trouble and war. The Greek civilization grew first and mainly in Ionia, where their new and vigorous race came up against earlier civilizations and learned from Persia and from Babylon; or in Argos, where their first-comers found a Minoan civilization. But history shows plainly enough that although there is something in this, yet it is not an infallible recipe for progress to bring vigorous primitive races up against an older civilization. No, clearly the main cause must lie in the intelligence of the Greeks. Terman of California has estimated the intelligence quotients of great men of a more recent past. I wonder at what level he would place Thales of Miletus, Herakleitos of Ephesus, Pythagoras of Samos and Kroton, Socrates, Plato, Aristotle.

Nor are the troubles of civilization today caused by over-much intelligence or over-much education, but by over-little. It is not because intelligence has made travel quicker, has made it possible for one man to speak to millions scattered over the whole globe, has made production easily catch up to and far surpass the geometrical increase of population which scared Malthus. It is not because we have too many scientists and too few poets. Poets are far more dangerous than scientists. I heard and admired and was much moved by Mr Baldwin's Cambridge address to the Congress of Universities of the Empire, but on reflection I did not agree with it. Rather do I think with M. Julien Benda (1927) when he says:

Ce qui étonnera surtout l'histoire dans ce mouvement des clercs, c'est avec quelle perfection ils l'ont exécuté. Ils ont exhorté les peuples à se sentir dans ce qui les fait le plus distincts, *dans leurs poètes plutôt que dans leurs savants, la poésie étant infiniment plus nationale, plus séparante, comme ils l'ont bien su voir, que les produits de la pure intelligence.*

Scientists have unwillingly and sometimes unwittingly supplied warring mankind with means of destruction, but they have not preached the doctrine. Civilization has advanced just as much as it has worshipped truth, and has been rewarded by finding that beauty and the graces follow in its train; and the worship of truth is the function of intelligence. You may expostulate that the science of the nineteenth century brought ugliness and destroyed beauty. But that we may surely hope was only a passing phase due to the velocity of change, and the very fact emphasizes still more urgently the need of trained intelligences to understand this changing world and to guide it aright. Take for example finance, capitalism, money. Men of affairs have to grapple with their mysteries as well as they can, like the doctors of the Dark Ages fighting disease, heroically but blindly. What is wanted is knowledge, classified, generalized, tested; and with understanding will come the cure. Intelligence has in the past made striking steps forward in this matter of finance; the invention of metal money, of drafts on distant treasuries, of joint stock companies, limited liability, cheques, and so on. We ourselves have lived through a period of experimenting with money, with commodity dollars and registered marks and what not. Intelligence, which *is* experiment, but experiment done as much as possible inside the mind, will find the solution, and *only* intelligence: and unless it does so, the Graces will have to beg their bread or earn it in misery and in sin. And it will only find the solution if it works for the sake of the truth only, not for any party or country or cause. Despite M. Charles Maurras, '*l'avenir de l'intelligence*' is not to be the servitor of nationalism, and scientists and philosophers must not commit that '*trahison des clercs*' which M. Julien Benda so bitterly and brilliantly bewails.

In passing, I may note a contradiction between pragmatism, for which in many respects I have a regard, and this belief that intelligence must serve truth only; for to the pragmatist truth does not exist waiting to be found, but is in the making. Pragmatism judges entirely by consequences, and would therefore judge intellectual work by its practical results, judging the eminence of a physicist by the application of his studies. Most men of science however chafe at the public demand for results, and believe that intelligence, in the persons of its most exclusive devotees, must serve no lower master than truth. Plato's philosopher came back into the Cave. In actual practice there are those who see the true Forms, and make no attempt to return to the Cave, and those middlemen who cannot themselves explore outside the Cave, but can go to the boundary Wall and learn at second hand from the pioneers outside, returning then to apply their knowledge within the Cave itself. This is physical science. In ethics and morality, which Plato had most in mind, I doubt if anyone has ever been over the Wall.

Intelligence and character

And this remark brings me to the objection perhaps most commonly and immediately voiced in opposition to the doctrine I am preaching, the objection that in world progress character has counted for more than intelligence. But here I have another heresy to confess to. I think that intelligence and character are positively correlated. Although a keen and well-trained intellect does not necessarily mean a good character; although there have been criminals of genius and many good men of only moderate intelligence; yet the tendency is for a correlation of intellect with good character. It is in intellect that man differs most from the beasts of the field. It is in the use of intellect that civilized man differs from savage and barbarian. And just as bestiality and savagery are bad traits in character, so are the self-control and tolerance which, in the main, go with intellect, good points of character. If we think there has been progress in the evolutionary scale at all, then that progress has, up to the present, culminated in man: and man is essentially more *rational* than any other animal, as he is more praiseworthy in character. Men have bad characters. But it is also in man that the highest traits of good character are found, and they are associated, broadly and secularly, though not individually and definitely, with intellectual advance. Intellect is, in the main, necessary to character, or at least is its accompaniment. And although in my haste I called this belief a heresy, was I not mistaken in thus naming it? Is it not 'more universally admitted than any other fact about him' that Socrates held the doctrine that 'badness is, in the last resort, a form of ignorance' and that the reason, not the feelings, must govern. The intelligence must of course be fed with a good education. I do not mean an education of the character, which invariably means indoctrination with some code or other, but a good intellectual education (Jowett). The Soul is to be *turned* from the world of becoming to that of being by a true art of education.

And whereas the other so-called virtues of the soul seem to be akin to bodily qualities, for even when they are not originally innate they can be implanted later by habit and exercise, the virtue of wisdom more than anything else contains a divine element which always remains, and by this conversion is rendered useful and profitable; or, on the other hand, hurtful and useless.

And the way to turn such misused intelligence from ethically bad to ethically good paths is to introduce it, through a suitable and graduated education, to things which the intellect recognizes as worthy of its steel, to difficult and abstract things; though what is difficult and abstract will of course depend upon the individual mind, and vary with it.

Luckily it is possible to refer those who demand experimental evidence to what is almost an objective proof of the positive correlation of character with either intelligence or education or both, in Bagley's book *Determinism in Education* (1925). This work was not written with that object; it had a polemical aim, directed against the doctrine that intelligence is entirely a matter of heredity and is measurable with fatal exactness at an early age, after which the child's intellectual rank among mankind is fixed by an

immutable doom, an extreme doctrine which Bagley had no difficulty in confuting, and which is probably held by no psychologist,
though Bagley was no doubt justified in saying that the public
misunderstood psychologists to say this. In the course of his inquiries, however, Bagley in effect proved my heretical assertion
that intelligence and character go together. He first showed that
intelligence and education go together, using as data the same
array of facts as his opponents, namely the scores of nearly two
million soldiers of the American army of 1917 and 1918 in an
intelligence test, the Army Alpha Test. For the most intelligent
soldiers came from those States in the Union, and in the case of
immigrants from those foreign countries, which had in their boy-
hood the best educational systems. His opponents said that was
because intelligent populations insist on good schools; Bagley,
that good schools make intelligent populations. For our purpose
the difference is immaterial. For he next went on to show that
those States with the best showing in the intelligence tests (and
also the best schools) were best in any of the ways in which one
can objectively measure goodness of character in a community,
for example had less crime of this or that sort. As I say, it is immaterial to me whether this is due to education or to intelligence,
since Bagley shows that they go together; the only point of
importance is that intelligence, education, and law-abiding go
together, all three.

Irrationalism today

It is true that Plato anticipated a scanty supply of persons endowed with the highest intelligence and also with exceptional
reliability and steadiness of character. That is only natural. We
must recognize with him further that reliability is often found
apart from the highest intelligence, and that the latter is tempted
to be impatient and unsteady. Discrepancies there will be, and
yet these are not incompatible with a general tendency. I cannot
really think that, – in such a state as his, and with such a first
education, music and gymnastics learned in play and without com-
pulsion, amidst scenes and objects of good taste, and with literature purged of its baser elements – he could seriously anticipate
the occurrence of men, intelligent enough to have become true
guardians, among his third class, kept there by lack of character,
men who would have been a serious source of trouble and revolution. Nor I think need we, if we are at equal pains to give an
equally good education to all. The way in which revolution *will*

come to his city is, he thinks, through a neglect of the laws of eugenics, which will cause a scarcity of the highly gifted: and the less gifted then necessarily coming to power will esteem education too lightly. The things really essential to the state are, a good first education to everyone, and a sufficient supply of the highly gifted, intellectually.

It seems then to be an extremely short-sighted policy of certain communities today to decry intelligence to such an extent as they do, to expel from their posts of office in the community and even drive away from the country intelligent men, not only because they hold opposed political views (that is perhaps understandable though I think wrong) but because they are neutral, because they are not active partisans of the governing political party. This seems incredibly stupid whether it is done by American party machines after a new election, or by dictatorship in Europe, and will surely revenge itself. The only province in which it can be confidently asserted that competent men who understand the problems will agree with one another is in matters of the intellect, where though there are different hypotheses in conflict at the boundary of knowledge, there is an ever-growing settled country of full agreement, and an undisputed referee, agreement with facts and with the laws of thought. In all other matters men disagree, or are brought to an agreement only by training, propaganda, sentimental appeal, factors which separate masses of mankind as much as they weld together partisans.

The only hope for unity, permanent unity, among mankind is through the rule of intelligence, through the cultivation, by an education proper to each, of the intelligence of all. The school-master is right who considers that his sole business is to lead his pupils to see truth clearly, and who holds that that is in itself character-training, and the only character-training the school may lend itself to, if it is to refrain from serving party or class, colour or race, or prejudice of whatever kind, but is to serve civilization and all mankind.

References

BAGLEY, W. C. (1925), *Determinism in Education*, Baltimore, Warwick & York, Inc.
BENDA, J. (1927), *La Trahison des Clercs*, Editions Grasset.
BROWN, W. and THOMSON, G. H. (1921), *The Essentials of Mental Measurement*, Cambridge University Press.
GRAY, J. L. and MOSHINSKY, P. (1935), *Sociolog. Rev*, April.
JOWETT, B. (1908), (trans.) Plato's *Republic*, Oxford University Press.
SADLER, M. (1936), *Essays on Examinations*, Macmillan.

Part Two
Structure of the Mind

It is time to look at a wider range of man's abilities and aptitudes. General intelligence has been the main topic so far; but what of memory, imagination, manual dexterity and all the abilities associated with schooling: verbal, numerical, scientific, aesthetic? How far are these separate and distinct entities? Are they truly specific in operation, or are they related? Questions such as these tend to be answered differently by British and by American psychologists. The British tend to see the structure of the mind as an hierarchy: general ability, g, subsumed by many group factors, each of which may be broken down into smaller elements. Thurstone and other American writers, on the other hand, conceive of the mind as consisting of a miscellaneous assortment of 'primary abilities'. These, however, are themselves related to each other, and by the technique of 'second-order factors' more pervasive and wide-ranging abilities may be postulated. Both views, in the end, reach the concept of hierarchical structure, and the end products of the two opposing schools bear strong resemblances. No doubt it will not be long before further research will bring the emergence of a *rapprochement*.

Vernon's contribution comes from his important book *The Structure of Human Abilities*, and gives an account of the hierarchical structure which is quite brilliant in its clarity and economy of words. Burt's paper – specially revised by him for this book – offers a masterly review of research in many fields, together with an integration and overview having such qualities of breadth and grasp that only someone of his experience and stature could encompass.

The final extract is a reprint of a now famous paper by

Guilford, and one which emphasizes the contrast between the approaches on either side of the Atlantic. The student will find a comparison between Guilford and Vernon a rewarding task: the search for an underlying unity will be of great help in leading him to a firmer grasp of 'the structure of the mind'.

5 P. E. Vernon

The Hierarchy of Ability

Excerpts from P. E. Vernon, *The Structure of Human Abilities*, Methuen, 1950, chapters 2 and 3, pp. 11–36.

Hierarchical group factor theory

In Britain where most work was done on less selected samples of the population such as Navy and Army conscript recruits, the importance of *g* was amply confirmed. In eight analyses *g* was found to cover more than twice as much variance as all group factors combined. Table 1 shows an analysis of thirteen tests given to 1000 Army recruits, and brings out a feature which appears to be highly characteristic of mental structure, namely hierarchy. After the removal of *g*, tests tend to fall into two main groups: the verbal–numerical–educational on the one hand (referred to as *v:ed* factor), and the practical–mechanical–spatial–physical on the other hand (referred to as *k:m* factor). If the analysis is sufficiently detailed, i.e. if sufficient tests are included, these types themselves subdivide. The *v:ed* factor in Table 1 gives minor *v* and *n* (number) group factors. In other analyses *k:m* splits similarly into mechanical information, spatial and manual sub-factors. Thus a first approximation to mental structure is provided by the hierarchical diagram of Figure 1, resembling a genealogical tree.

The relations between group-factor and multiple-factor analyses

Table 1 also serves to illustrate some of the resemblances and differences of centroid and group-factor analyses. In a centroid analysis the first factor represents the highest common element in all the tests. It is not usually the same as *g*, but is a kind of average of the particular tests applied in the investigation. Subsequent factors, 2, 3 and 4, are known as *bipolar*, since roughly half the tests receive positive, half negative, signs. These successively divide the tests into contrasted groups, and although they may have no psychological meaning as they stand, yet they do usually reveal what group factors are present. Often this classification by bipolar factors tells us all we need to know, and in several ex-

Table 1 Simple Summation and Group Factor Analyses of Tests given to 1000 Army Recruits

Tests	Unrotated centroid factors				Group factors						
	1	2	3	4	h^2	g	$k:m$	$v:ed$	v	n	h^2
0 Progressive Matrices	0·77	+0·23	+0·10	−0·16	0·68	0·79	0·17				0·65
Dominoes (non-verbal)	0·80	+0·09	+0·19	−0·12	0·70	0·87					0·75
Group Test 70, Pt 1	0·74	+0·16	+0·03	−0·08	0·58	0·78	0·13				0·62
4 Squares	0·63	+0·35	−0·00	+0·01	0·52	0·59	0·44				0·54
8 Assembly	0·37	+0·54	−0·15	+0·28	0·52	0·24	0·89				0·85
2 Bennett Mechanical	0·69	+0·35	−0·17	+0·07	0·62	0·66	0·31				0·54
25 Verbal	0·88	−0·24	−0·26	−0·14	0·92	0·79		0·29	0·45		0·90
Dictation	0·79	−0·42	−0·25	−0·11	0·88	0·62		0·54	0·48		0·90
14 ATS Spelling	0·81	−0·32	−0·20	−0·11	0·80	0·68		0·41	0·43		
21 Instructions	0·89	−0·06	+0·11	−0·15	0·82	0·87		0·23	0·09		0·82
3A Arithmetic, Pt 1	0·84	−0·29	+0·22	+0·23	0·89	0·72		0·49		0·39	0·91
Arithmetic, Pt 2	0·86	−0·16	+0·12	+0·13	0·80	0·80		0·38		0·16	0·82
23 ATS Arithmetic	0·84	−0·21	+0·26	+0·14	0·84	0·77		0·36		0·32	0·82
Variance per cent	59·8	8·5	3·1	2·2	73·5	52·5	− 8·7	8·4		6·9	76·5

amples in subsequent chapters the original, or *unrotated*, centroid factors alone are quoted. But it is preferable to transform the first and the bipolar factors into a series of factors where all the tests have either positive loadings, or zero or insignificant negative loadings, by means of what is called *rotation of axes*. This of course redistributes much of the variance of the first factor among the remaining ones. Actually the aim of rotation is to maximize the number of zero or insignificant loadings on each factor, so that as much as possible of the variance of each test is confined to a single factor. Thurstone (1931) calls this *Simple Structure*. Often such rotation does yield a general factor running through most or all of the tests, and smaller factors each confined to a few tests, in other words a group-factor pattern. But true group-factor analysis is carried out by assessing *g*-loadings first, and then analysing the residual correlations in each group of tests [. . .] A clear and much fuller account of these different types of analysis, and their inter-convertibility, is given by Burt (1944).

Other methods of analysis

This historical résumé must not omit to mention, however briefly, certain other approaches to factor analysis which have been less widely applied than general or group factor, and simple summation or centroid methods. Broadly speaking they are more accurate mathematically, but do not provide appreciably more psychological information about the make-up of the analysed tests, which would compensate for their much greater complexity and tediousness of calculation. They include Burt's Weighted Summation, Lawley's Maximum Likelihood, Hotelling's Principal Components, and Kelley's Principal Axes, methods. Explanations may be found in Thomson's (1939) and Burt's (1944) textbooks.

The hierarchical diagram should be regarded only as an approximation

The hierarchical theory was first put forward by Burt, under the influence of McDougall. In a recent article Burt describes how it originated, and shows that it applies in the fields of temperament and of anthropometric measurements, as well as to abilities. Though it is certainly an improvement both on the original two-factor theory and on the 'neo-faculty' theory of American writers, it has numerous limitations and implications which we must now discuss.

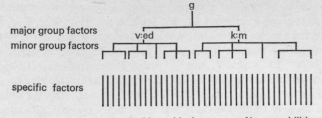

Figure 1 Diagram illustrating the hierarchical structure of human abilities

A diagram such as Figure 1 would be obtained only if an extensive battery of tests, covering – or at least sampling – most of the varieties of human abilities, could be applied to a very large and representative sample of the population. With one or two hundred testees the correlations are usually too unreliable for more than two to four group factors to be established at a time. In general a minimum of three tests is needed to define a factor, hence only a few factors can be resolved in any one investigation with a limited battery of tests. Further, if such a battery consists only, or predominantly, of a specialized type of test (e.g. all tests of sensory-motor abilities), the g and major group factors may fail to reveal themselves. The diagram is, in other words, a hypothetical integration of all the factorial investigations that have been carried out, rather than an established fact.

Broad and narrow group factors

Nevertheless there is ample evidence to support the view that group factors are almost infinitely subdivisible, depending only on the degree of detail to which the analysis is carried. Indeed, by including sufficiently similar tests, any specific factor (in Spearman's sense) can become a group factor. The only truly specific element is the unreliability or error variance of the test. Thus in a complete factorial investigation the communality of each test should approximate to its reliability coefficient. It is even possible, when analysing specialized tests, for a specific factor to become a general one. For example, a reaction time test analysed in a battery of paper-and-pencil mental tests might obtain a g and major group-factor variance of about 10 per cent, specificity 90 per cent. On including two other kinds of reaction time, a small group factor would appear, while in a battery consisting only of such tests, a general reaction time factor with 30 per cent or higher variance might be found; and we should be unaware that this was composed partly of 'higher' factors such as g and $k:m$. Thus there is no absolute distinction between general and specific factors as Spearman believed.

An important problem, as yet unsolved, is how broad a group factor should be before it is accepted as a useful element in our picture of mental structure. Some of the primary factors of Thurstone, Guilford and others – rote memory, for example – are so narrow in content that it may be more harmful than helpful to name them. It is unlikely that the rote memory tests which make up Thurstone's M factor have any predictive value of the rote memory in which teachers are interested. Only if it were possible to establish a common factor (over and above g and $v:ed$) in rote memory tests and in the learning of spellings, multiplication tables and poetry, would the notion of a rote memory group factor be acceptable. The same stricture holds for most of the manual dexterity, sensory-motor, and coordination factors that have so far been proposed. At the present moment the writer cannot think of any objective basis for distinguishing between acceptable group factors, and narrow factors confined to the highly specialized types of test which psychologists delight in constructing. But he would suggest that factors which fail to contribute at least 5 per cent to the variance of some measure of educational or occupational proficiency or other capacity in daily life should be relegated to the latter category. If, for example, g and v tests alone predict the ability to learn and retain poetry to the extent of a correlation of 0·60 (i.e. a variance of 36 per cent), then the addition of tests of rote memory to the predictive battery should raise the correlation to at least 0·64 (variance 41 per cent) if the factor measured by these tests is to be acceptable.[1] Such a criterion

1. This suggestion recalls Thomson's (1939) argument that factor analysis is of little use in vocational or educational psychology, because the predictive value of tests can be established much more efficiently by multiple correlation technique. The writer would agree that the content of a test as determined by factor analysis at the present time often fails to reveal its true predictive value, because the test's specificity may embody other group factors which are particularly relevant or irrelevant to some job. For example a test of graph-reading is very useful in selecting radar operators, but when analysed it usually appears to consist purely of $g + n +$ specificity. More detailed analysis would however break down part of the specificity into a minor group factor for graph-reading, i.e. a sub-division of n. This is the line that Guilford and Lacey (1947) followed in the USAAF. After considerable experience of multiple correlation, the writer has come to the conclusion that it is much too efficient. It does not, like the factorial approach suggested in this note, sufficiently allow for the chance errors in the

involves subjective judgement as to what constitutes a 'capacity in daily life', and is beset with many difficulties. But it appears preferable to a judgement of the broadness *versus* narrowness of the tests which yield a distinctive factor.

Relative importance of factors at different levels

The hierarchical group-factor viewpoint implies that most of the variance of human abilities in daily life is attributable to g and to highly specific (or very small group) factors, and that the role of the broader group factors is rather meagre. If our diagram could be worked out completely to cover all human abilities, the g-variance might amount to about 40 per cent, the major and minor group factors to some 10 per cent each, and the remaining 40 per cent would consist of very narrow group factors and unreliability. This means that fairly good predictions of ability in education, industry, or everyday life, can be achieved by g tests alone, and that somewhat more ground can be covered by tests of the main group factors. But only by much more detailed experimentation on tests relevant to particular jobs, or by work-sample methods (i.e. trying candidates out on the actual work), can much more than 50 per cent accuracy be obtained. This explains why Stanford–Binet or Terman–Merrill IQ tests, or all-round intelligence as measured by reliable group tests, have considerable practical value both among children and adults, whereas more specialized tests add something but not very much in educational and vocational guidance.

Effects of range of ability and selection on factor patterns

However, these quantitative estimates of the importance of different 'levels' of factors are dangerous, since so much depends on the degree of heterogeneity of the people concerned. When the same tests which, among unselected recruits, gave g and group-factor variances of 50 per cent and 20–25 per cent, respectively, were analysed among high-grade mechanics or officer candidates, g often fell to 15 per cent and group factors rose to 35 per cent. Similarly it has often been observed that the g and $k:m$ content of manual dexterity tests sinks almost to zero among such selected groups as technical school pupils or college students; such tests no longer correlate at all with paper-and-pencil tests of mental

---

validity coefficients of selection tests, and prohibits the inclusion of two or more rather similar tests in order to improve the reliability of prediction.

abilities. Since the people receiving any special type of education (e.g. grammar school or university), and those engaged in any one job, almost always constitute a strongly selected group, there is usually more scope for tests of major and minor group factors and less for g tests, than the preceding paragraph suggests. (The relatively unpredictable portion is however generally larger among such groups.) It also follows from Thomson's (1939) demonstration of the effects of selection on factors that not only the general degree but also the type of selection is important. For example, if a battery of mechanical and other tests is applied to a group of men with an engineering background, and to another group with the same range of g but without experience, the factor patterns are liable to differ. This accounts for many of the discrepancies between the results of different investigators, and makes it extremely difficult to fill out the details of our diagram accurately. We cannot expect to reach a final and complete map of the structure of abilities, since it necessarily varies with the kind of population studied.

Differentiation of specialized abilities with age

The relative prominence of g has often been thought to depend considerably on age. The writer at one time accepted the view that g tends to differentiate into more specialized abilities during adolescence and early adulthood. This view is advocated by Garrett (1946), who summarizes several confirmatory investigations. But most of these compare college with high school, or high school with elementary school, populations, hence the smaller g-variance in the older groups may be due merely to their greater selectivity.

Clark (1944) did choose groups of 11-, 13- and 15-year-old pupils with the same distribution of group test IQs, and found a decline in the average inter-correlation of the Primary Mental Abilities tests from 0·488 to 0·393. Other studies such as those of Swineford, Reichard and Doppelt fail to support the theory. Anastasi summarizes a large number of investigations and shows that, though there are strong indications of alterations in factor patterns with age and training, the evidence for differentiation is far from unanimous. McNemar carried out fourteen factorizations of Terman–Merrill scale items at mental age levels ranging from two years to eighteen years. His results are irregular and show no sign of any consistent trend towards greater differentiation at later ages. This might be criticized on the grounds that the later items are less diverse in content than those for young children. However Balinsky factorized an identical battery of tests, namely the Wechsler–Bellevue scale, among groups aged 9, 12, 15, 25–9, 35–44 and 50–9, all with average IQ 100. He obtained the following first factor variances: 38, 36, 24, 20, 33 and 45. These suggest differentiation from 9 to 30 and then greater integration. But he neglected to ensure the same degree of heterogeneity among the testees at all ages, and when correction is made for this, his first factor variances show much the same irregularity and lack of any clear trend as McNemar's.[2]

Particularly striking are Williams's results from the application of the same battery of ten intelligence, spatial and mechanical tests to samples of 250 boys, carefully chosen to be representative, at the ages of twelve, thirteen and fourteen. Here the first factor variances were 51, 56 and 62 per cent, respectively, indicating that secondary education tends to produce greater integration, not specialization, of verbal and practical abilities. In a research by the writer the standard British naval battery of five tests was given to 1171 boys leaving school at fourteen, and the results were compared with those of 265 seamen recruits who had also left at fourteen in the same district some four years previously. Scores tended to rise with age on the spatial and mechanical tests, and to drop on the arithmetical ones, but the average inter-correlation and g-saturations were almost identical. The only significant change was a drop in the correlation of mechanical arithmetic with mathematics (from 0·642 to 0·379). The correlations of $k:m$ tests with these educational tests were slightly lower, but with a verbal reasoning test (mainly a measure of g) they were slightly higher. Similarly two parallel groups of about 240 naval artificer apprentices aged 15+ and 18+ took nine varied tests and most of the correlations were slightly higher in the older group, although the nature of the group factors altered considerably.

Another approach to this problem was to calculate tetrachoric inter-correlations among ten tests, first by contrasting the top 25 per cent of a group of 993 Army recruits with the bottom 75 per cent, secondly contrasting the top 75 per cent with the bottom 25 per cent. If abilities are more differentiated among the more able

2. It is difficult to see how a crucial investigation of this problem could be planned even if strictly random samples could be tested at several age levels. For as Emmett (1949) points out, the content of the tests should be equally appropriate at all ages, otherwise reliability is affected, and with it the first factor variance. This condition may have disturbed both Williams's and the writer's results reported in the next paragraph.

and intellectually mature, the former correlations should be lower than the latter, but actually the reverse occurred. Many more men were very high on all tests than were very low on all tests, and the first factor variances were 75·6 and 66·3 per cent, respectively.

From these and other bits of evidence the writer would conclude that there is no general tendency towards differentiation, except perhaps in early infancy, and that everything depends on the type of educational and vocational training. Usually when abilities are practised at school or in jobs they tend to become more specialized, though sometimes the teaching is of such a nature as to increase integration. Again regression or de-differentiation may often occur as the effects of past training wear off. It is conceivable that secondary schooling is more fragmentary in America than in Britain, and so apt to produce more differentiation between twelve and eighteen than is usual here. But undoubtedly the main reason for the apparent reduction in the importance of g in adults is that the testees are more homogeneous in ability.

It is because the majority of American investigations are conducted with college students, aircraft pilots, high-school pupils and other selected groups, that their results so readily fall into independent primary factors instead of g and group factors. But when more heterogeneous adult groups have been studied, a g has usually appeared. Thus Anastasi quotes American Army studies which showed almost as high correlations between verbal, numerical, spatial and mechanical tests as between different numerical, or different mechanical tests. An analysis of the US Navy battery gave a g with variance of over 30 per cent, together with smaller mechanical, spatial and educational group factors. The emergence of a g in the Division of Occupational Analysis's investigations has already been mentioned.

Psychological nature of factors

We must next consider the nature of g and the group factors a little more closely. Thomson has shown that the statistical fact that test inter-correlations can be largely accounted for by a single factor does not prove that such a factor represents any unitary power, or organ of the mind. It might also arise if the mind is thought to consist of an immense number of 'bonds', including inherited reflexes, acquired habits and associations, etc. A person's performance at any one test would involve the activation of a large number of such bonds, and if a miscellaneous set of tests is given, the extensive sampling of bonds would result in the positive correlations that actually tend to occur. But he agrees that factors are useful concepts for describing the content of the various kinds of examples that may be taken, provided that they are not reified into organs or faculties. In this book we accept Thomson's view, and hold that factors over and above g arise, partly perhaps from hereditary influences, but mainly because an individual's upbringing and education imposes a certain grouping on his bonds. The $v:ed$ factor is, as we shall see, a rather strongly unified group because our society gives a fairly uniform education to all its members. It does not readily break down into separate verbal, number, speed, reasoning, attention, memory or other factors because the abilities covered by these names tend to be developed differently in different schools and homes, though partially distinct minor group factors can often be established, especially in fairly homogeneous groups such as university arts students. On the practical or $k:m$ side there is, as Anastasi points out, less cultural standardization, hence the $k:m$ pole is more heterogeneous and amorphous than $v:ed$. It would appear to be not so much a positive practical ability as an aggregate of all non-symbolic capacities, or of bonds that are not usually affected by primary schooling. Nevertheless, evidence is given below that not only mechanical and spatial, but physical and manual, and some non-verbal g, perceptual and performance tests all have something in common over and above g. The kind of test which is most strongly saturated with this factor is the mechanical assembly test, presumably because this epitomizes, as it were, non-scholastic activities. A rather significant point is that boys and men (at least in Western European civilization) tend to surpass girls and women on most aspects of $k:m$ whereas females tend to be superior in the linguistic aspects of $v:ed$. Though this might be attributable to cultural norms, it suggests the operation of hereditary influences. Thus it cannot be due to upbringing that girl babies usually start to talk earlier, or that boys and men have on the average greater physical size and strength.

Modifications of the hierarchical picture

It follows that there is no need to regard the hierarchical or genealogical principle as pre-eminent. Minor group factors are not always 'descendants' of *either* v:ed *or* k:m. And we shall see later that several factors cut across this dichotomous grouping, scientific ability, for example. Probably also there are other group factors which split off from g but are not subdivisions of either type. Auditory and musical abilities seem to constitute one such cluster, and others are mentioned in chapter 8 [not reproduced here]. It is merely because $v:ed$ and $k:m$ have the widest practical importance, and have received most investigation, that they alone are listed in Figure 1 (page 104).

Temperamental and other influences

In yet another respect the diagram over simplifies matters. It does not allow for personality, physique and other factors which have complex interactions with ability factors. Physique and physical health constitute an important dimension (or set of dimensions) which certainly affects practical abilities; and physical defects of the senses in particular react on educational attainments. Sex influences not only $v:ed–k:m$, but also most of the lower-order group factors, such as manual, imagery, etc. Age is important in spite of the conclusions reached above. Thus among adults the spatial, manual and physical aspects of $k:m$ tend to decline, whereas specialized mechanical skills and information probably go on increasing almost to senility. Cattell has pointed out that g is somehow associated with such personality traits as conscientiousness and with cultured interests. Terman's work on gifted children, and studies of mental defectives, confirm this. Apparently therefore the bonds established by character training, and by the development of sentiments and attitudes, are linked with the bonds responsible for our cognitive or intellectual activities. Doubtless interests greatly affect our more specialized abilities. It is known also that the fluency factor, measured by tests of richness of association with words or pictures, is connected with extraverted or cycloid trends, and that such physical or manual capacities as visual acuity, dark adaptation, agility, and finger dexterities are impaired among neurotics. Again Eysenck (1947) finds speed *versus* accuracy in mental and manual operations to differ among hysteric and dysthymic (anxiety or obsessional) neurotics.

Clearly then we are very far from a complete theory of the structure and nature of human abilities, and though it is useful to analyse them in isolation as though they were purely cognitive or motor, we should not forget that they are abstractions from the total personality structure.

Conclusions regarding g

Finally it may be seen from Thomson's theory that g is not a fixed, purely inherited, quantity. Thomson interprets it as the total number of bonds. Presumably that is largely dependent on some psycho-physiological and innate property of the higher nervous system, but there is no reason why its number should not be affected by the use made of the mind, and by organic conditions such as brain injury and ageing. This fits in with modern research on the highly individual nature of mental growth, on the effects of schooling and the intellectual stimulus provided by people's jobs and on deterioration of mental efficiency in pathological conditions.

Compensation theories

We have considered the relation of the hierarchical theory to Spearman's and Thurstone's views. How does it stand *vis-à-vis* the popular notion of compensation, and of opposed *types* of people? Actually it admits a large measure of truth in the contrast between the theoretical or academic and the practical, since they roughly describe our two major group factors. But these abilities are not inversely correlated, i.e. opposed, and they are independent only when the influence of g is ignored. Thus in fact the majority of children who are superior educationally are also above average in mechanical ability, in doing things with their hands, and even in physique, because of the common influence of g. The Norwood Report's separation of academic and practical-technical types of children is unsound for several reasons, but chiefly because the child with high g who is likely to do well at a grammar school would also do well at a technical school. So far, however, we have been talking about average tendencies; and as correlations between intelligence, educational, practical and physical tests are far from perfect, they admit of many exceptional individual cases. Thus there is a proportion of children who are suited to grammar school education not because their g is very high, but because of strong $v:ed$ factor, and such cases may well be poor in $k:m$ factor, and therefore unsuited to technical education. There are many cases too who are exceptionally well-developed physically, or good at athletics or at certain manual skills, whose $g+v:ed$ are low, who therefore conform to the layman's stereotype. But it is none the less true that such cases are much rarer than those who are above average, or below average, all round.

There are several reasons why the compensation theory gains such wide credence. First, whenever g-saturations or correlations with educational attainment are low, bright or dull children will tend to be nearer the average, in non-educational activities. The child who is very high in intelligence and school work will usually be less high in manual, practical or artistic work, and the scholastically dull pupil will on the average be less retarded in non-scholastic fields. This can readily be deduced by studying the scatter for a low correlation.

Secondly, the groups with which we are most familiar above the age of $11+$ are selected ones, and as already pointed out this reduces the g-loadings and exaggerates the group factors. Hence it is quite conceivable that in a grammar school there may be an inverse, or at least a negligible, correlation between, say, mathematical attainment and football. But if we could study the whole range of 15-year pupils we should find that grammar school pupils are usually superior to secondary modern pupils not only in mathematics, but also at football.

Thirdly, we are concerned here only with abilities, not with interests. The latter probably show much stronger contrasts than the former. Thus the adolescent with keen interests in reading or other $v{:}ed$ activities is frequently (perhaps more often than not) weakly interested in mechanical or athletic activities, and it may be that he devotes so little time to them that his potentially superior ability at such activities deteriorates. Nevertheless, the university professor with his high g can usually, if put to it, do better at things in which he is not much interested such as cooking a dinner and washing up without breaking the crockery, than can a low-g domestic servant. And it is by no means fanciful to suggest that the victories of the Jews in Palestine in 1948 over the Arabs (who tend to be more bellicose in interests) was largely due to their superior g and $v{:}ed$.

'Slow but sure' is another popular compensation theory, which likewise ignores the influences of g and other factors that tend to make the quick worker more rather than less accurate. However, it is considered in more detail in chapter 7 [not reproduced here], and is shown there to possess a modicum of truth.

The notion of types of people, as distinct from types of ability, should also be discouraged. As Burt (1944) points out, there is no more justification for talking of an academic or practical type of child than for a tall or a short type. Just as the majority are intermediate in height, so there are many more who are about equally able in educational and practical activities than there are extreme cases. Ability types themselves are abstractions, since many abilities when factorized will be found to be loaded on two or more group factors, i.e. to be intermediate. But the grouping is more clear-cut than in the case of individuals, because it is often imposed by school syllabuses and other cultural institutions or norms.

Note that our insistence on g does not involve any denial of special talents in individual cases. Apart from such rarities as *idiots savants*, there certainly exist children and adults of mediocre g and educational attainment who develop outstanding talents in the fields of art or scientific invention, or become leaders in business, politics, warfare, etc. Such talents can to some extent be attributed to the possession of strong group factors, but personality influences, drives and interests are probably still more important. The analysis and measurement of such influences by psychologists is far less advanced than that of abilities. Thus the warning given against regarding factors as covering the whole psychology of human achievements should be reiterated.

References

BURT, C. (1944), 'Mental abilities and mental factors', *Brit. J. educ. Psychol.*, vol. 14, pp. 35–94.

CLARK, M. P. (1944), 'Changes in primary mental abilities with age', *Arch. Psychol.*, vol. 291, p. 30.

EMMETT, W. G. (1949), 'Evidence of a spare factor at 11 + and earlier', *Brit. J. psychol. Stats.*, vol. 2, pp. 3–16.

EYSENCK, H. J. (1947), *Dimensions of Personality*, Kegan Paul, Trench & Trubner.

GARRETT, H. E. (1946), 'A developmental theory of intelligence', *Amer. Psychologist*, vol. 1, pp. 372–8.

GUILFORD, J. P. and LACEY, J. I. (1947), *Printed Classification Tests*, Army, Air Forces Aviation Psychol. Progress Research Report, no. 5, Washington DC, US Government Printing.

THOMSON, G. H. (1939), *The Factorial Analysis of Human Ability*, University of London Press.

THURSTONE, L. L. (1931), 'Multiple factor analysis', *Psychol. Rev.*, vol. 38, pp. 406–27.

6 C. Burt

The Structure of the Mind

Abridged and revised by the author from 'The structure of the mind: a review of the results of factor analysis', *British Journal of Educational Psychology*, vol. 19, 1949, pp. 100–111, and 176–99. (Full references are there given but, have been limited in the present résumé.)

The hierarchical structure of the mind
Factors and faculties

Practically all the books dealing with the subject of factor analysis consist of descriptions or discussions of the methods employed. None attempts a systematic survey of the results already achieved. Today, with the rare exception of one or two of Spearman's followers, few factorists still believe in the simplified hypothesis of a single general factor; practically all of them, whether in this country or in America, assume the existence of a number of so-called 'group factors', i.e. 'elementary' or 'primary abilities' not unlike the faculties of the old-fashioned 'faculty school'. But how many factors are there? How far do they correspond with the traditional lists? How cogent is the experimental and statistical evidence in favour of each one? These are questions which no one hitherto has systematically discussed. Accordingly, in the following paper I propose to collate and compare the more reliable conclusions reached in the numerous articles and theses which report results of factorial research, and then to inquire what light they throw on the general structure of the human mind.

The idea of studying individual characteristics by strict scientific techniques – by standardized measurement, experimental tests, and mathematical analyses of the data obtained – is due primarily to Galton (1869, 1883).[1] Galton, it may be remembered, departed

1. In an address (1905), Galton describes his aim as that of 'measuring physical and mental faculties', so as to secure 'a shorthand description of any individual pupil by assessing a small sample of his dimensions or qualities'. As early as 1881 a London schoolmaster, C. H. Lake, had applied tests of intelligence, discrimination, and retentiveness to 120 boys in his school at Chelsea, and described a 'schedule for child study'. A few years later another of Galton's keen disciples, Miss Sophie Bryant, Head Mistress of the Camden High School, applied other tests to her own pupils (1886). If their contributions are now forgotten, they paved the way for more extensive investigations when the London County Council introduced an official psychologist into its inspectorate.

from the traditional theory of 'faculties' as set forth by the Scottish philosophers of the preceding century and popularized by nineteenth-century phrenologists, in two important ways: first, he introduced various novel procedures for assessing the mental capacities of individuals; and secondly, as a result of the facts he thus collected, he contended that it was necessary to distinguish a new kind of super-faculty, which he called 'general ability' or 'intelligence', in addition to the various specialized aptitudes or faculties of the more familiar kind. Most of the psychologists who followed in his steps readily accepted his demand for more rigorous procedures, but were inclined to reject or at any rate to simplify his twofold hypothesis. In America, for example, Thorndike and later on Thurstone and their disciples have striven to dispense with the novel concept of 'general intelligence', and retain only a miscellaneous set of 'primary abilities'. In this country, on the other hand, Spearman and his research students have sought to discard the notion of special abilities, and have maintained that all intellectual differences between one individual and another are due either to differences in general intelligence or else to incidental circumstances – education, occupation, and personal interest.

My own view, based largely on Sherrington's anatomical and physiological studies of the brain and nervous system, was that the structure of the mind is essentially hierarchical. Mental processes and mental capacities appear to consist of systems within systems. According to their relative complexity, the various components seem assignable to one or other of four or five distinguishable levels. In the nervous system the simplest types of process are the innate reflexes, some of which enter into almost every form of mental activity: these, however, are essentially unconscious, and therefore do not concern us here. If we confine ourselves solely to so-called 'cognitive' (or as I should prefer to say 'directive') processes, the simplest forms of all consist either of elementary sensory impressions or of elementary motor reactions. These constitute the lowest mental level. The next includes the more complex processes of perception with equally complex reactions on the motor side. The third is the level of mechanical association – of memory and of habit. The fourth and highest level of all involves the apprehension and application of relations. 'Intelligence', as the 'integrative function of the mind', is involved at every level; and its manifestations therefore differ not only in degree, but also in their qualitative nature.

Now, however plausible it may sound, unless we can also find some kind of empirical confirmation, any such scheme must necessarily remain a mere speculative hypothesis. By its very nature it postulates a multiplicity of mental factors, of varying grades of generality, and distinguishable in theory though not actually separable in practice. To verify it therefore we need some method of multifactorial analysis. And, as I pointed out in my earliest paper on the subject, such a method was already to hand in Pearson's statistical technique of 'principal components'. This, with certain minor simplifications, was the procedure I used. The formulae thus derived were identical with those subsequently adopted by Thurstone and his followers, and now commonly known as the 'centroid method'.

Most of our early work, from 1903 onwards, was carried out on boys and girls of school age. With younger children relatively few special or 'group' factors could be demonstrated; and, even when present, their influence was usually swamped by the all-pervasive general factor. But, as the children grew older, the general factor appeared, as it were, to generate a series of broad group factors, and these in turn to generate still more specialized sub-factors, as different capacities progressively matured. This factorial scheme, therefore, though primarily a scheme for classifying intellectual characteristics into genera, species, subspecies, and so on, seemed to provide a rough indication of the way in which cognitive capacities had evolved in the race and developed in the individual. At the same time it furnished a means of reconciling the pluralistic assumptions of the faculty school (including Thorndike and his co-workers) with the monistic assumptions of the newer academic school (including Ward, Spearman, and their various disciples).[2]

It will be convenient to begin our general review with the most elementary types of process, and work upwards to the more complex, since the latter almost inevitably incorporate two or more of the simpler processes.

2. *See* McDougall (1912), Burt (1927), and various earlier and later papers. The general notion of a 'hierarchical structure' has since been accepted by Vernon (1950), and by Eysenck (1953). Let me emphasize that the scheme is itself highly schematic, and only represents what appears to be the most important trend; mental development proceeds by integration as well as by differentiation. But into these minor qualifications there is no space to enter here.

Group-factors involved in cognitive processes

1 Lowest levels: simple sensory processes

Although methods for investigating sensory capacities were among the earliest quantitative procedures to be used in the psychological laboratory, nevertheless comparatively little factorial work has been carried out upon the results obtained by such means.

(*a*) *Sight*. In the field of vision there are grounds for supposing that the sensory processes involved in the 'apprehension of form'[3] are relatively independent of those involved in the 'apprehension of colour'. But intensive research has been chiefly concentrated on the problems of colour vision. Here the correlations between efficiency in discriminating colours can be expressed in terms of three main group factors, which correspond approximately to the three primary colours. At first sight this would seem to corroborate the Young–Helmholtz theory. Yet, in point of fact, the data can be fitted just as well by a set of bipolar factors: and these correspond almost exactly with the pairs of mutually antagonistic processes postulated by the Hering theory. In passing it may be noted that, long before factorial analysis had been elaborated into a special technique, experimental psychologists, like Wundt, had claimed that the primary colours should be regarded as *Faktoren oder Komponenten*, obeying the laws of vector-addition, just like the factors of the modern statistical psychologist, and had illustrated them by 'configuration-diagrams' similar to those printed by present-day factorists (*see* Burt, 1946 and Wundt, 1902).

(*b*) *Hearing*. With laboratory tests of auditory discrimination we usually find a small general factor and four or five slightly overlapping group factors, namely, factors for the discrimination of (i) pitch, (ii) chords (harmony), (iii) tonal pattern (melody), (iv) loudness, and (v) rhythm (*see* Wing, 1941 and Karlin, 1942). In several of these factors, however, the more complex perceptual

3. The reader should be warned that, when physicians and oculists speak of testing 'form-vision' (as distinct from 'colour-vision'), they are as a rule referring to tests of sensory acuity or discrimination. The recognition of 'form' in the sense of 'shape' is a more complex process belonging to the perceptual level. The distinction proves to be of great practical importance in dealing with cases of reading disability, and is often overlooked both by teachers and by school doctors with no psychological training: the difficulties of the backward reader are more often due to difficulties of perception than to mere difficulties of sight which can readily be corrected by spectacles.

components may not have been completely eliminated. Experiments on children of various ages indicate that the different factors mature at different rates.

(c) *Smell.* Experimental studies with olfactory stimuli suggest a complicated system of factors and sub-factors. Collating results of various investigators (Eysenck, 1944, Henning, 1924, Hsu, 1946) they may be tentatively arranged as follows:

(A) Salubrious (and more or less pleasant): (i) Vegetable: (a) flowery; (b) fruity; (ii) Animal: (a) fleshy; (b) cutaneous; (B) Insalubrious (and more or less unpleasant): (i) Vegetable: (a) resinous; (b) burnt; (ii) Animal: (a) fishy; (b) excremental – eight sub-factors in all.

(d) *Touch and kinaesthesis.* On touch and cutaneous sensation only one or two minor researches seem to have been carried out; these indicate a small general factor and a bipolar factor contrasting epicritic with protopathic sensations. In the activities both of the school and of ordinary life, kinaesthetic discrimination (in popular discussion often described as a form of 'touch') plays a far greater part than is commonly realized; but, strange to say, hardly any factorial studies have been attempted on this process at the simple sensory level.

In the main therefore it would seem that, at this lowest level of all, we have to deal with a large number of highly specialized factors. Apparently there are no formal factors, only factors for content; and these, like most other content factors, appear to be highly differentiated.

2 Perceptual level: perceptual and motor processes

(a) *General sense perception.* Both popular psychology and books on phrenology assume the existence of a 'perceptual' or observant type, which is generally contrasted with the 'practical' type on the one hand and with the 'reflective' type on the other. In the early days of individual psychology, methods of measuring perceptual discrimination and the like were among the commonest tests suggested for studying mental differences between individuals. Spearman indeed maintained that all such tests really measured a *general* function of discrimination; and this function (as we have already seen) he regarded as the essential element in general intelligence. In later investigations, however, it appeared that, when more numerous and more adequate tests were used to eliminate the influence of general intelligence, a special group-factor covering various forms of perceptual discrimination seemed clearly discernible. This further factor, entering into all the perceptual tests and into these alone, seemed to be a factor for the formal activity of discrimination, regardless of sensory content. This however is by no means the only characteristic of the so-called 'perceptual person'. He commonly belongs to what Binet called the 'objective type' and Jung the 'extravert'; and thus shows distinctive temperamental characteristics. Moreover, within this broader 'objective' type, 'analytic' and 'synthetic' sub-types (Burt and Moore, 1911)[4] may often be distinguished, analogous to Binet's contrast between *simplistes* and *interprétateurs*.

Sub-factors. When both auditory and visual tests are included in the same battery, minor perceptual factors emerge corresponding to differences in sensory 'mode'. The differences thus indicated have a direct bearing on the teaching of various school subjects, particularly reading and spelling. Children who are defective in the visual perception of form or the auditory perception of sound-patterns are apt to be backward in reading and spelling; but their difficulties and their errors are not the same, and they require different remedial treatment.

(b) *Motor capacity.* In the field of individual differences one of the earliest distinctions to be suggested by experimental work was the antithesis between the 'sensory' and 'motor' types. The contrast was originally suggested in speed of reaction. But it was extended to include differences in every form of active behaviour. Recent work has demonstrated a small, specialized factor, common to practically all tests of a muscular or motor type. The highest saturations are shown by tests requiring delicate neuro-muscular coordination, such as the tests of manual skill.

The hypothesis of a general motor factor is corroborated by evidence from other fields. The practical psychologist continually comes across pupils of average or even high intelligence who are slow and clumsy in all forms of manual coordination – whose fingers, as the teacher puts it, 'are all thumbs', and who are often just as awkward and ungainly with their arms and legs. Emotional and unstable children, and those who are suffering from mild ataxic conditions such as may be observed in choreic and post-

4. The 'synthetic' type appeared to be strongly influenced by an intuitive apprehension of complex forms or *Gestalten*; the 'analytic' type had more difficulty in effecting their 'closures' (to borrow a convenient term from Gestalt psychology). *See* Vernon (1947).

encephalitic states, also seem to manifest a generalized disturbance of muscular coordination and control. This 'motor factor', however, includes a number of subordinate factors. Both in tests of athletic performance and in experiments of a laboratory type my colleagues and I have found factors for (i) strength, (ii) steadiness, (iii) quickness, and (iv) skill or dexterity of muscular actions. Of these, 'steadiness' apparently includes postural control and coordination of the larger muscles; 'dexterity' relates chiefly to the control of the finer muscles (including those of the eyes and the vocal organs, as well as the fingers and hands). There seems also to be a cross-division depending on a factor entering into skilled activities or games where muscular action is guided chiefly by eye, as distinct from those in which it is guided solely by kinaesthetic impressions.

3 Intermediate (associative) level

Form and content. We now come to the third mental level, that of association. Here the distinction between factors depending on the formal similarity of the activities and those depending on the material nature of the mental content becomes more marked. It is factors of the former type that have provoked the most vigorous criticisms. 'There are,' wrote Thorndike, 'no elemental "faculties", or forms of mental activity, which work alike with any and every content.' Spearman's objections are couched in much the same terms. Certainly content factors are far more readily demonstrated. But Wolfle, as well as several later writers, has noted that many of the factors established in recent American research 'cut across subject-matter lines, and so suggest the action of mental processes more general than any subject-matter classification' (*Factor Analysis to 1940*, p. 34).

(a) Formal factors

(i) *Memory.* The assumption that memory constitutes a single self-contained faculty was a feature in the traditional faculty doctrine that was most persistently attacked by the early associationists. 'We possess,' so they argued, 'not a memory in the abstract, but only memories in the concrete; and each of these is essentially a separate association of ideas.' James, however, while accepting the associationist criticisms so far as the memory-training is concerned, held that there was an innate quality of 'general retentiveness' which he interpreted as a kind of 'physiological plasticity of the brain'. Accordingly, in the hope of checking these alternative views, Flugel and I included in our first experiments a number of memory tests, chiefly modelled on those of Meumann. We found that all of them correlated closely with teachers' estimates of intelligence (by about 0·6) and with the results of school examinations (by about 0·7), but much less closely with the other tests of cognitive processes (only about 0·3) or with estimates of intelligence as exhibited outside the classroom (about 0·2). 'School teachers, and still more school examinations,' so we inferred, 'tend too often to rate the quick and retentive learner brighter or more intelligent than the pupil who shows superior powers of thinking or superior common sense.' It was largely as a result of these observations that we concluded that, in researches on intelligence tests, the simple correlational technique used by previous investigators – based on comparisons with an *external* criterion (such as the teachers' judgement) required to be supplemented by some form of *internal* criterion.

Later investigations fully confirmed the hypothesis of a general factor of memory entering into all kinds of activities, visual and auditory, verbal and numerical, tests and school work, that depend essentially on retentiveness; and Wolfle in his recent survey describes 'memory' as 'the fourth most frequently reported factor'. This is in keeping with everyday experience. When a child of normal intelligence and character proves to be seriously backward in his elementary school work one of the commonest causes is a weakness in mechanical memory. On the other hand, the cases of *idiots savants* demonstrate clearly that a person may possess an exceptional retentiveness for figures or words, and yet be highly deficient in general intelligence; and every University examiner can cite cases of dull students who nevertheless scrape through all their written examinations by dint of a good memory.

Within the broader field covered by 'general factor' for memory a number of more specialized sub-factors can be discerned. Thus, according to its formal nature, what we loosely call memory appears to be divisible into two main types – short distance (or immediate) memory and long distance (or deferred) memory. The former depends largely on the 'primary memory image' of the item learnt; the latter on the formation of 'associations' between the items. The former thus seems to be an effect of what is sometimes called 'perseveration', the latter of 'retentivity' in the more usual sense. As J. Z. Young and others have recently shown the difference is also found in animals, and appears to have a discernible physiological basis.

McDougall and May Smith (1920) believed that, as a result of an analysis of the inter- and cross-correlations between various tests, they could offer clear empirical evidence to support Bergson's distinction between two further types of memory – recognition-memory and habit-memory – the former they considered to be much the same as memory for meaningful material.

(ii) *Productive association.* In the old lists of faculties, Imagination usually follows Memory; and together the pair constitute the two main faculties on the intermediate level between the lower plane of 'Sense-Perception' and the higher plane of 'Rational Thought'. Later textbooks, written under the influence of the associationist school, commonly contrast 'productive (or divergent) association' with 'reproductive (or convergent) association'. Binet, in his studies of the feeble-minded, distinguished between what he called 'intellectual *level*' and 'intellectual *activity*'. 'Intellectual activity,' he maintained, is revealed most clearly by an abundant 'flow of ideas'; and he sought to show how such exhibitions of creative fancy could be elicited by means of appropriate tests. In a number of minor experiments R. C. Moore and I endeavoured to follow up Binet's ingenious investigations by applying procedures that permitted more rigorous standardization and measurement. The correlations obtained clearly indicated a common factor of 'productive imagination' or 'inventiveness', after general intelligence had been partialed out. Later still, in experiments with children in London schools, Hargreaves found a similar factor which he designated 'fluency'. (The term was suggested by Galton's use of 'fluency' (1883) to describe 'the vivid and rapid flow of imagination' exhibited by those with creative gifts.) Spearman, on the other hand, held that 'no such special creative power exists: that which is usually attributed to such a special imaginative operation can be simply resolved into correlate-eduction combined with mere reproduction'. In his view, therefore, so-called 'imagination' – in the sense of 'creativeness or originality' – depends solely on the general factor of intelligence.

Most experienced teachers seem strongly of the opinion that fertility of imagination is by no means an automatic result of high intelligence: it is, they point out, often exhibited by pupils with comparatively low IQs, and may be absent in many whose intelligence is exceptionally good. Mere abundance in the 'flow of ideas', however, is not of itself sufficient to form a creative mind. The ideas must be relevant; and they must be selected and combined so as to form a new and satisfying answer to some unsolved problem. This implies not merely intellectual activity, but intellectual construction. The factor for 'productive imagination' therefore must itself be complex, and plainly there is here yet another field of cognitive activity calling for far closer analytic study than it has hitherto received.[5]

(b) Content factors

(i) *Imagery (reproductive imagination).* Of all the individual differences observed by earlier investigators, the most striking are those relating to mental imagery. To investigate them Galton introduced a device which was at that time entirely new in psychological research – the questionnaire; and so was able to demonstrate that different persons varied surprisingly in the ease and clearness with which they could reproduce 'inner or mental images' from different sensory spheres. The issue thus raised is manifestly a problem for factor-analysis, and was one of the earliest which my research students and I attacked (Burt and Moore, 1912).[6] Strange to say, comparatively few factorial studies have been made by later investigators.

So far as the available evidence goes, there would seem to be, first, a general factor for vividness of imagery of every kind, secondly, particularly with older children and adults, a bipolar factor indicating a clear contrast between those whose thinking is mainly verbal and those whose thinking is mainly concrete and therefore, non-verbal, and thirdly, a set of still more specialized group factors superposed upon the others – the best-established being factors for visual, auditory, kinaesthetic, and olfactory imagery. Thus, here as elsewhere, the so-called mental types are not clear-cut classes; they are extreme instances of mental tendencies which may vary in almost every degree.

(ii) *Verbal ability.* The ability to speak is a mental function possessed by man and by no other animal. It has therefore long been

5. For a review of recent American work on 'creativity' and earlier British work on the components involved, see Burt (1962).
6. The results were fully confirmed by a later study carried out by Moore and Davies in Liverpool, and Carey and myself in London (1915). The neglect of mental imagery by American factorists is attributed by McKenna to 'the influence of Watson and the behaviourist school, who excluded all reference to inner, private, or conscious experiences from psychology as a natural science'. The excessive enthusiasm of some of the earlier educationists for classifying pupils according to supposed 'imaginal types' also helped to bring the subjects into disrepute.

regarded as a distinct and self-contained faculty. Its phrenological location seemed confirmed by early pathological research. In 1825, J. B. Bouillaud, a disciple of Gall and professor of clinical medicine at Paris, succeeded in connecting loss of speech with a lesion in the frontal lobes of the brain; and some years later Broca published his famous monograph giving evidence for the existence of a 'speech centre' in the third left frontal convolution. Thus both the phrenologists and the faculty psychologists claimed that their views had been vindicated. The earliest statistical evidence for a verbal or linguistic factor (or rather for a group of such factors) was that obtained in a series of LCC researches (Burt, 1915a; Burt and Bickersteth, 1916, LCC, 1917). To the educational psychologists its existence seemed of interest on various grounds. First, its absence, or rather its deficiency, accounted for the frequent occurrence of pupils suffering from specific verbal disabilities (e.g. the so-called word-blind child). Secondly, its presence, or rather its development to a high degree, appeared essential for those pupils whose later education took a verbal or bookish direction, e.g. pupils suited for what are now called 'secondary schools of a grammar school type'. Thirdly, its influence implied that intelligence tests with a verbal bias, like the Binet scale and many of the ordinary written group tests, could not safely be relied on for detecting high intelligence among pupils of a non-verbal type. The superior verbal fluency of the feminine sex, marked verbal deficiencies of certain families and stocks, the appearance of both verbal abilities and verbal disabilities at an early age, the fact that in orphanages and similar institutions children showing exceptional verbal ability often prove to have had at least one parent who was verbally gifted, and finally the positive correlation between factor-measurements for members (often remote members) of the same family – all these facts taken together lend strong support to the hypothesis that verbal aptitude is to a large extent inborn.

In our first account of the verbal factor my co-workers and I observed that it seemed to manifest itself in two different forms – as a vocabulary factor (in reading and spelling, for example) and as a literary factor (in English composition and the like). Later work indicated that within each of these forms there is a further sub-division according as the processes involved are mainly afferent (or receptive) or mainly efferent (or executive). And there were even indications of various minor sub-factors still more specialized.

The scheme so reached may be set out as follows. The results are, on the whole, in agreement with the views on speech-mechanisms put forward by head teachers on the basis of tests and clinical observations.

I Word factor (dealing with words in isolation)

(A) *Receptive* (factor for recognizing words and understanding the ideas expressed by them): (i) *Visual* (understanding printed or written words); (ii) *Audio-motor* (understanding words heard or uttered).

(B) *Executive* (factor for finding or selecting the right word to express a given idea; cf. Head's (1926) 'nominal' defects): (i) *Articulatory* (in speech); (ii) *Graphic* (in writing).

II Language factor (dealing with words in their context)

(A) *Receptive* (factor for understanding statements; cf. Head's 'semantic' defects).

(B) *Executive* (factor for literary expression: 'verbal fluency'; cf. Head's syntactical defects).

(iii) *Arithmetical ability*. Of all special capacities perhaps the best established is that underlying efficiency in numerical computation. Mathematical ability has almost always been regarded as a distinct ability or gift. A group factor entering into arithmetic tests was observed in the early LCC investigations already cited; and its existence was further confirmed by a specific investigation undertaken by Collar in LCC schools. The inheritance[7] of special ability and special disability in arithmetic was studied by Hewlett, who found correlations of 0·37 between siblings and 0·28 between parents and children.

Like the verbal factor, it is undoubtedly composite. The essential constituent would seem to be an ability to form, retain, and use associations between numerical, or at least non-verbal, symbols. But with younger children more especially, there is ample

7. Galton, strange to say, doubted the inheritance of specific mathematical ability (1869). But the family histories of the Bernouilli brothers, of Gauss, Bidder, Diamondi, and many Cambridge wranglers (and, I may add, cases of special arithmetic ability and disability in my own surveys) all strongly suggest the inheritability of some underlying peculiarity (*see also* Bramwell, 1948). This is further borne out by the well-known sex-difference. The inherited conditions, however, would seem to be in part temperamental; pupils of an emotionally unstable disposition seem, as a rule, to be badly handicapped; introverts on the other hand, usually do better in arithmetic than extraverts of equal intelligence.

evidence for distinguishing speed of computation and accuracy, mechanical arithmetic and problem arithmetic, mental arithmetic and written arithmetic, and between sums involving addition and multiplication and those involving subtraction and division. With older children of secondary school level, earlier investigations suggested a broad distinction between an 'arithmetical' or computational factor (depending mainly on the routine use of memorized *associations*) and a 'mathematical' factor (involving the ability to perceive, attend to, and combine numerical *relations*). Some investigators claim also to have found three more specialized group factors for : (i) Arithmetic; (ii) Algebra; and (iii) Geometry (including Trigonometry). But it is difficult to decide how far these narrower factors may be the effect of teaching methods and of class organization.

(iv) *Practical ability.* In my work as psychologist in the London schools one of the chief tasks was to investigate the methods of awarding scholarships, not only to secondary schools of the 'grammar' type, but also to trade schools and technical institutes. Children so selected were 'required to possess, in addition to a satisfactory degree of general intelligence, a marked or definite aptitude for practical or technical work'. In our endeavour to assess their intelligence, we found that, although verbal tests (such as those in the Binet scale or those given in group form) might be admirable for selecting scholars for the grammar school, they often failed to do full justice to clever children of a non-verbal type. Accordingly, non-verbal tests of a more practical kind – so-called performance tests – were tentatively introduced into some of the examinations. Their introduction at once raises an important question. Do these 'practical tests' involve a new group-factor, much as the older 'verbal' tests involved a verbal or linguistic factor, and if so what is its relation to the supposed aptitude for technical work?

The results of further research left little doubt that some such factor was involved. It appeared to be closely related to efficiency in tests designed specifically to measure 'mechanical' ability, and to have the highest saturation in tests of 'mechanical constructiveness'. This type of ability was sharply distinguished from manual (or motor) ability and seemed to depend largely on the power to appreciate *relations in space*. The fact that this practical factor has proved much harder to establish than the last two factors is due chiefly to the fact that it matures much later. The main conclusion of recent studies on the problem may provisionally be summed up as follows: (1) what may reasonably be termed a 'practical factor' is undoubtedly discernible by the age of eleven, but at that age still contributes very little to the individual variance; (2) its contribution increases steadily up to the age of about fifteen; (3) after adolescence the factor becomes more and more specialized, partly as a result of occupational interests and habits; (4) at almost every age it is much more prominent among boys than among girls.

As numerous investigations show, the factor is decidedly complex. Visual perception and visual imagery play a part, but by no means the most important. Kinaesthetic imagery, or rather cognitive schemata apprehended in kinaesthetic terms, seem to be more essential, and for this reason the factor has sometimes been designated k. Such imagery and schemata appear to be of two or three kinds: (1) that concerned in the appreciation of *position and movement*, or possibilities of movement (*a*) of the observer's own limits or organs (especially hands and eyes), (*b*) of the objects observed, and (2) that concerned in the appreciation of *force* exerted or resisted. The factor thus divided into two distinguishable components – a 'spatial' factor and a 'mechanical' factor. The one is predominantly, but not exclusively, a perceptual or receptive factor; the other, a constructive or executive factor.

(*a*) *Spatial factor.* The first component appears to be primarily concerned with the ability to perceive, interpret, or mentally rearrange objects as spatially related. Some of our test-results, obtained with boys at trade schools and with older engineering apprentices, suggested the need for distinguishing at least two sub-factors under this head – a factor for *static* spatial relations and a factor for *kinetic* spatial relations. Kinetic relations, involved in the actual movements of external objects, are apprehended mainly by the movements of the observer's own organs, especially his eyes. Yet even when space relations are apprehended statically, as with objects seen by the eye, their correct perception rests on schemes built up as a result of the movements of the observer's own body and limbs. As regards static relations there seems a further distinction between the ability to perceive and visualize relations (i) in two dimensions only and (ii) in three dimensions. This perhaps may in part explain the wide differences in the ease with which different pupils can master the rudiments of plane and solid geometry respectively – differences so often noticed by mathematical teachers. The spatial factor was later subjected to an intensive study in our laboratory by El Koussy (1935)[8] whose results are summarized in a monograph which has formed the starting point for most of the later researches on the subject – e.g. those of Thurstone, Garrett, Holzinger, and other investigators.

(b) *Mechanical factor.* In theoretical studies it is important to distinguish between the abstract 'mechanical factor' as it appears in experimental and statistical researches and the rather vague and complex characteristic that is commonly denoted by the phrase 'mechanical ability' in non-psychological discussions: the latter must involve general intelligence, the spatial factor and to a smaller extent manual and numerical factors, possibly some such factor as speed (both perceptual and motor), and above all such further qualities as mechanical interest, mechanical experience, and technical knowledge.[9] For purposes of educational and vocational guidance, especially in the engineering trades, a number of studies of mechanical ability have been carried out at the National Institute of Industrial Psychology. One factor repeatedly emerged which usually accounted for more of the variance than any other single factor except general intelligence. It seemed clearly distinguishable both from the manual and the spatial factor, and appeared to be chiefly concerned with ability to appreciate processes of mechanical causation. It thus involved an understanding of dynamic rather than merely static relations, and manifested itself in tests not only of apprehension and comprehension, but also of construction and performance. Like the arithmetical factor, its development depends largely on experience and training. But there are also indications of an innate, underlying aptitude leading its possessor to learn more speedily and more efficiently when the appropriate training or experience is supplied.

4. *Higher relational level*

Thought processes
We now come to cognitive processes on the highest plane of all, those which scholastic psychology summed up under the generic

8. For a recent study of the subject, *see* MacFarlane Smith (1964).

9. With older children we found a test of elementary technical knowledge (e.g. acquaintance with the use of certain tools) far more effective than any single test of a more practical kind – largely because of the very low reliability-coefficients of most practical tests. Much the same result was noted by those who attempted to develop tests for 'mechanical ability' in the Army and Navy during the war.

names of 'Thought' or 'Understanding'. On this level there appear to be two main groups of factors. They are manifested most typically (i) in scientific or logical thinking and (ii) in artistic or aesthetic appreciation. Both depend on the apprehension, explicit or implicit, of abstract relations.

In traditional psychology under the general head of Intellect or Thought, three species of activities were commonly recognized: (1) Generalization or Abstraction, the results of which are expressed by general terms or abstract nouns; (2) Judgement, the results of which are expressed by single sentences or propositions; and (3) Reasoning, the results of which are expressed by arguments, made up of a series of propositions or sentences, logically connected. To measure the capacity for each of the three processes tests can readily be devised. Charles Dodgson (Lewis Carroll) was fertile in devising neat and amusing logical problems, which required no special knowledge or information, and were set as exercises by logic tutors in the Oxford of my day; and the earlier tests of 'Reasoning Ability' that I employed were largely suggested by problems such as these, and were selected so as to represent all the commoner logical processes as currently classified.

In the joint investigations carried out by Moore, Corkhill and myself with tests of these various processes, we found, after differences of intelligence had been ruled out, the following subsidiary factors: (a) a verbal factor; (b) a factor of productive association; (c) a factor for the apprehension of relations; and (d) a factor for the combination of relations. The first two are by no means confined to tests of higher cognitive levels; but the last two appear only in tests that turn essentially on processes of thought and understanding. The factor for the *apprehension of relations* emerges most conspicuously in tests of judgement and of deductive reasoning, as well as in problems requiring an appreciation of functional dependence; the factor for the *combination of relations* yields fairly high saturations in tests of concept-formation and of inductive reasoning (two processes that seem more closely allied psychologically than the traditional classification of the logicians might suggest), somewhat higher saturations for tests turning on the conception of 'class' and of 'order', and the highest saturations of all for tests involving syllogistic reasoning. Moreover, these two factors appear, not only when the problems are expressed in verbal, spatial or pictorial form, but also when they are embodied in mathematical exercises. Here, therefore, we have psychological evidence for the view which Bertrand Russell has so plausibly argued, namely, that mathematics is essentially a branch of logic. A word or two seems desirable about each factor.

(i) *Explicit and implicit apprehension of relations.* Tests involving relational processes furnish high saturations with the general cognitive factor of intelligence. For that reason it is always difficult to secure clear evidence for or against the presence of more specialized factors in tests of this type. Nevertheless, the following conclusions appear to be well established. First, nearly all the relational tests, and nearly all the methods of attacking relational problems, fall into two contrasted groups. These correspond with two different ways of comprehending a relational complex – either explicit or analytic, or implicit or synthetic.

Many of the persons we tested, particularly children and students with a 'fixating' type of attention, usually began by dissecting or analysing the complex whole that is presented by the test problem, and expressly noted the way the items are connected or related; they then applied these relations in a conscious and more or less systematic fashion to elicit a suitable solution. Others, particularly those of a 'fluctuating' type, seemed to depend more on 'a complex synthetic activity comparable to the activity often popularly described as intuition – the activity whereby we implicitly comprehend the essential character of a whole, without analysing it into its component parts, or distinctly formulating their relations.' (Burt and Moore, 1911.) In other words, the characteristic method of the former group was some form of analytic reasoning, proceeding by a succession of logical steps, and of the latter, a synthetic apperception of what later psychologists have called *Gestalten* or configurations, depending chiefly on an intuitive insight which embraces the component aspects almost simultaneously. The former type includes most of those who possess a marked scientific bias; the latter, most of those who possess a marked gift for aesthetic appreciation

Secondly, there is some evidence suggesting the existence of separate group factors for the apprehension of different kinds of relations, i.e. of content factors as well as formal factors. Tiny children can usually grasp relations of difference long before they grasp those of similarity; both can be explicitly apprehended before the age of six; at a later stage comes synthesis by attribution (age seven); and this in turn seems easier than synthesis by degree (age eight); the explicit use of space-relations appears somewhat later, and that of time-relations later still. In every case, of course much depends on the context within which the relations are set. (Burt, 1919.)

(ii) *The combination of relations.* To test the intelligence of any given individual – whether child, adult, or a sub-human animal – we must test his power of combining the highest and most difficult type of information that he is capable of apprehending; and on the relational level, as elsewhere, it is the 'integrative' (i.e. the combining) processes that show the closest correlation with the general factor. At older ages the distinctive characteristic of the intelligent child is his ability to rearrange a set of related data and combine them into a coherent rational whole. And of all the tests devised to measure cognitive or intellectual capacities, those that require an explicit synthesis of explicitly perceived relations provide the best indicators of general intelligence. Nevertheless, in most of the researches carried out on these higher levels, a small but statistically significant group factor for 'combining relations' (as distinct from other forms of combination) is also demonstrable; and this conclusion is further confirmed by the facts that the ability to reason is to a large extent a trainable technique, and that pupils or students of approximately equal intelligence may display marked differences in their aptitude for this type of training.

Here again a bipolar factor divides the broader factor into sections or sub-factors. The ground of division seems much the same as before; and suggests a distinction between the inductive or constructive type of thinker and the deductive or critical. The intuitive type of mind seems to succeed better with test-problems involving generalization – the formation of general concepts and the perception of general laws or rules; the analytic type of mind with problems requiring formal inference – deductive and particularly syllogistic reasoning.

Aesthetic processes

The aesthetic processes that concern us here are those of aesthetic cognition rather than of aesthetic feeling or expression, though the latter are scarcely possible without the former. It has often been observed that 'there are two higher modes of understanding – logical and aesthetic'. If so, we may plausibly include aesthetic appreciation as a process belonging to the highest cognitive level; and this is on the whole borne out by our experimental results.

The initial reasons for attempting a factor analysis of aesthetic activities were practical rather than theoretical. The education authority for London used to award 'special talent scholarships' in art and allied subjects; and with a view to improving the methods of selection, Pelling and I, with the assistance of the staff and pupils at the various schools of art maintained by the London County Council, undertook a series of factorial studies. The tests employed were mainly pictorial, but tests of poetical and musical appreciation, and of skill in imaginative sketching and painting were also included. As usual, we found that differences in intelligence played an appreciable part; but, when these had been ruled out, there still remained a large and well-defined factor common to all the tests involving aesthetic appreciation or execution – in short, what I termed 'a general factor for artistic ability' (Burt, 1924, 1933).[10] It is to be noted that this factor is not limited to 'art' in the narrower sense, but enters into every manifestation of aesthetic taste – auditory or visual, verbal or concrete. Much the same view has since been expressed by Fry (1926). 'If,' he writes, 'we compare responses experienced in face of works of art of the most diverse kinds – architectural, pictorial, musical, or literary – we see in all these different expressions a general similarity in our mental attitude; and further the attitude common to all these activities is also peculiar to them, and clearly distinguishable from our attitude in other experiences.'

These early experiments were followed by a succession of more intensive investigations in our laboratory in which research-students with a specialized knowledge have taken part – e.g. Dewar, Wing, Stephenson, Eysenck, Crane, and Cancardas (*see* Dewar, 1938; Eysenck, 1940; Williams *et al.*, 1938. A number of more specialized factors were found for the appreciation of (1) literature (prose as well as poetry), (2) painting, architecture, and sculpture, (3) music, (4) humour, and (5) dancing and the ballet – in short, for the aesthetic appreciation of different kinds of content. Cutting across these subdivisions, we also find two marked bipolar factors indicating a preference for (1) *classical* styles as contrasted with *romantic*, and (2) *realistic* styles as contrasted with *impressionistic*. These preferences are, in part at least, dependent upon temperamental factors, more especially on the bipolar factor which (as we shall see in a moment) may be roughly identified with extraversion versus introversion.

10. A brief but accessible indication of the material used, together with references to other suitable tests will be found in Cattell (1936 and 1938). Conclusions reached in these earlier studies were later confirmed by Bulley (1933).

General processes

Certain factors of a highly general type appear at every level. Intelligence, as we have seen, is merely another name for 'general mental efficiency' in so far as it results from cognitive (or directive) rather than from dynamic (or motivational) characteristics. Since its variations depend on the general structural characteristics of each individual's brain or nervous tissue, it is manifested in every kind of cognitive process; but the same appears to be true of several other factor qualities or factors, which are not so readily established.

(i) *Receptive and executive functions*. The brain, as the 'integrative mechanism of the body' (a built-in apparatus for processing information) has both input and output systems, namely, the sensory or 'afferent' nerves and the motor or 'efferent' nerves with their respective peripheral and central organs. Hence, after differences in the general factor of intelligence have been eliminated, the next most conspicuous factor is usually a bipolar factor contrasting receptive capacities with executive. On the lower levels it contrasts sensory types with motor, perceptual types with manipulative, and on the higher levels intellectual types with practical.[11]

(ii) *Speed*. With most cognitive capacities as commonly tested a high degree of efficiency seems usually to imply speed as well as accuracy. This raises several important questions. How far is speed specific to the process concerned? If it is in some sense a general characteristic, how closely does it vary with general intelligence? Or is there yet another general factor making for high or low speed in all mental capacities?

This was in fact one of the first issues to be studied by correlational techniques based on mental tests. 'People usually assume,' wrote Wissler in 1901, 'that quickness is a fundamental quality, characterizing the individual in *every* direction' (Wissler, 1901). His own results failed to yield any evidence for such an all-pervasive characteristic. He adds, however, that since 'this

11. This bipolar factor (or the corresponding group factors) emerged in the earliest of the investigations quoted above. It presumably underlies the two 'major group factors' later obtained by Vernon (1950) and renamed '*v:ed*' and '*k:m*' respectively. *Cf. also* MacFarlane Smith (1964) and the 'hierarchical structure' there shown (a simplified version of my own 'hierarchical diagram').

negative conclusion is out of harmony with all general belief', a final verdict should be deferred until more comprehensive data are available. Wissler worked mainly with adults whose abilities are always more or less specialized. My colleagues and I, working with school children, found clear evidence for a general speed-factor at the younger ages, although, as the children grew older, they too seemed progressively to specialize. Later work is fully in agreement with this result. Wolfle cites no less than a dozen American investigators who have reported such a factor. But there are undoubtedly more specific group factors for speed in different fields and under different conditions – e.g. for motor or bodily speed as contrasted with verbal speed, perceptual speed as contrasted with associative speed, speed in short-reaction tests as contrasted with sustained speed in prolonged activities, and finally preferred or voluntary speed as contrasted with maximal speed.

(iii) *Attention*. Reference to 'attention' – a word with many different meanings – cropped up constantly in early factorial discussions. Ward, who was among the first to advance the theory that there is but one essential cognitive function, used 'attention' to designate it; and several later writers identified attention with the general factor of intelligence. Wundt (1911), for example, held that 'die *Energie der Aufmerksamkeit* den Centralfaktor abgibt, der die einzelnen Tätigkeiten bestimmt'.[12] The traditional conception, however, has been to regard attention as a separate capacity or faculty. In this sense it is commonly said to cover both the capacity for cognizing a large number of items *simultaneously* as parts of an organized whole, and the capacity for *sustaining* the cognition of an organized whole while examining its several aspects or items in an orderly *succession*, and so resisting distraction by irrelevant items. In our own researches tests involving the first type of process usually showed a high correlation with

12. In a note, added in small print, he discusses Spearman's preference for explaining the general or central factor in terms of 'nervous plasticity', and concludes that Spearman's arguments are 'scarcely sufficient to reject the theory of attention'. For Wundt, it may be noted, the word 'attention' denotes much the same as what he elsewhere terms 'Apperception', regarded as a 'teils *verbindende*, teils *zerlegende* Funktion', and this identification brings Wundt's theory closely into line with McDougall's. In his later writings, Spearman, influenced apparently by these criticisms of his former teacher, dropped the theory of 'nervous plasticity', and proposed to treat the central function (*g*) as 'equivalent to Mental Energy'.

intelligence; tests involving the latter correlated more closely with conative or temperamental stability. But we found no evidence for any separate factor.

When we consider more precisely *how* different persons cognize an organized whole, i.e. the particular *way* in which they attend, a suggestive difference is discernible. Faced with some unfamiliar patterns – say a sentence to be read aloud, like 'Fair waved the golden corn' – one child will focus its glance fixedly on one group of letters after another, uttering the whole in detached instalments: 'Fair, wave-ed, the, gold-en, corn.' Another, whose eye roves rapidly up and down the line, will produce some impressionistic version superficially corresponding to the general visible scheme: 'A fairy waved her golden crown.' The difference between these two modes of attack has been noted again and again. Meumann, whose description is perhaps the most complete, speaks of 'attention-types', and calls them the 'concentrating' or 'fixating' type and the 'diffusive' or 'fluctuating' type.[13]

To verify this classification, and determine its connection with other intellectual differences, Flugel, Moore, and I, in our earliest correlational studies, included a number of tests of attention and apperception. And with most of these tests, particularly the tachistoscopic 'spot-pattern test' devised by McDougall, we repeatedly noted opposite methods of attack and different modes of apperception. The same difference was noticed at every mental level. It emerged most clearly, however, in experiments on the teaching of reading. But the same bipolar factor seemed to underlie analogous contrasts in a number of different activities – e.g. the contrast first between the 'objective' (*observateur*) type of apprehension and the 'subjective' (*interprétateur*) type as revealed in perceptual tests; second between the 'perseverating' and 'non-perseverating' types as revealed in tests of memory and the like; third between the stable and unstable temperaments, and fourth (according to several investigators) between the introverted and the extraverted types (*cf.* pp. 120, 133).

Emotional factors

This survey is concerned primarily with what are commonly described as the 'cognitive' aspects of mental life. It is, however, impossible to draw a sharp and rigid distinction between 'cognitive' capacities which guide or direct the individual's behaviour and the various 'affective' and 'conative' tendencies which supply

13. *See* pp. 131–2.

the dynamic or motivational energy. Already we have had occasion to note how the two aspects continually overlap. In my early work as educational psychologist I found it essential to have some broad and workable conception of the various components of the individual's total personality,[13] which would include non-cognitive aspects as well as cognitive, dynamic aspects as well as directive.

In dealing with young children, it is always helpful to distinguish, whenever possible, between those tendencies that appear to be innate and those which are mainly acquired postnatally as a result of environmental influence and personal experiences. Unfortunately, in the case of dynamic or motivational characteristics this distinction is even harder to make than in the case of cognitive characteristics. The most we can say is that certain 'primary emotions' (i.e. those accompanying 'instinctive' tendencies, in McDougall's sense of the term) and certain general temperamental qualities seem to show signs of genetic differences. But here further research is badly needed.

In our earliest investigations my co-workers and I confined our attention chiefly to assessments for the strength of these primary emotional tendencies. Our main group consisted of 172 children of school age. The methods employed – tests, observations, behavioural reports, etc. – are fully described elsewhere. The main result was to demonstrate, on the non-cognitive side as well as on the cognitive side, a broad hierarchical structure. As in the case of cognitive qualities, there was first a general factor accounting for nearly half the total variance; this I termed 'general emotionality'. The next most important appeared to be two bipolar factors: of these the first which classified the various emotional characteristics into (1) the assertive or 'sthenic' (self-assertion, anger, sociability, curiosity, etc.) and (2) the inhibitive or 'asthenic' (fear, self-submission, tenderness, disgust, etc.): their effect was to divide the various individuals into two contrasted groups or 'types', roughly answering to what Jung subsequently called extraverts and introverts. The second bipolar factor cross-classified the emotions into (1) the pleasurable or 'euphoric' (joy, sociability, self-assertion, tenderness) and (2) the

13. I use the word 'personality' in the traditional sense – that, for example, which was adopted by writers like Galton, Ward and McDougall. Later American writers have tended to give it a much narrower connotation, roughly equivalent to what older writers would have called 'character' or 'temperament'. This is the usage adopted by psychologists like Cattell and Vernon and by others who have been influenced by German work, e.g. Eysenck.

unpleasurable or 'dysphoric' (sorrow, anger, disgust, etc.), and thus divided the persons assessed into those of a cheerful or optimistic type and those of a morose or pessimistic type. The resulting fourfold scheme was not unlike the traditional classification of temperaments based on the so-called 'humours' – the choleric, the phlegmatic, the sanguine and the melancholic. Finally, there were a number of narrower group-factors, largely corresponding to the several 'instincts' or 'primary emotions'. As with cognitive characteristics the frequency distributions for the factor measurements were all approximately normal; thus the so-called 'types' are really the more extreme examples of the various distinguishable tendencies. (Burt, 1915b.)[15] Similar methods were used to factorize acquired emotional characteristics – interests, sentiments, complexes etc.; and once again a hierarchical structure of progressively complex levels was obtained.[16]

Summary and conclusions

Let me now briefly summarize the more general conclusions emerging from this condensed review.

1. Many British psychologists and educationists, influenced chiefly by Ward or Spearman, still cling[17] to the attractive and highly simplified theory that there is only one basic, all-pervasive cognitive factor, and that what are mistakenly regarded as special factors or 'faculties' are merely the effects of environmental opportunity, personal interest, education, occupation, and the like. The cumulative evidence set forth in the preceding pages should, I think, finally dispose of this unitarian doctrine. At least eighteen of the special or 'group' factors mentioned in the previous sections have been established by at least three independent investigators; many of them by more than half a dozen. And of these the vast majority would seem to be partly, if not mainly, determined by genetic variations, though here the evidence is by no means conclusive.

2. The opposite theory put forward by Thurstone and still favoured by most American writers – that the mind consists of a

15. For a fuller discussion of these acquired factors *see* Reymert (1950).

16. This early research was fully confirmed by later and more extensive investigations (Burt, 1947) and other papers there cited. The first two factors have since been obtained both by Eysenck and by Cattell, though their terminology differs from that here adopted.

17. This refers to the period when this article was originally written. Even today, however, many writers on educational topics still apparently regard Spearman's doctrine as orthodox.

miscellaneous assortment of 'primary abilities', showing little or no system or order, and no definite or intelligible relations with each other appears to be equally inadequate. The mind, like the central nervous system, exhibits a systematic type of organization – a hierarchical scheme, arranged in four or five levels of increasing complexity and generality. The more general factors can be sub-divided into less general, the broader factors into narrower, and each narrow factor into sub-factors, and so on.

3. All the main cognitive factors of importance to the educationist would now seem to have been determined; but there is still an obvious and urgent need for further research. We need to know far more about the precise nature of the several factors, about their relations to the neural mechanisms and processes of the brain, and above all about the influence of genetic tendencies; and this holds both of cognitive and of temperamental factors. The scheme I have outlined is no more than a scheme. It is not put forward as a fixed and final conception, but simply as a working basis for current practice and for future investigation.

References

BRAMWELL, B. S. (1948), *Eug. Rev.* vol. 39, pp. 150.

BRYANT, S. (1886), Experiments in testing school children', *Anthrop., Inst.,* vol. 15, pp. 338–49.

BULLEY, M. (1933), *Have You Good Taste?*

BURT, C. (1909), *Brit. J. Psychol.,* vol. 3, pp. 94–178.

BURT, C. (1915), *Annual Report of the LCC Psychologist.*

BURT, C. (1915), 'The general and specific factors underlying the primary emotions', *Brit. Assoc. Ann. Rep.,* p. 694.

BURT, C. (1919), 'The development of reasoning in school children', *J. Exp. Pedag.,* p. 36–50.

BURT, C. (1924), *Report on Psychological Tests of Educable Ability,* Board of Education, HMSO.

BURT, C. (1927), The Measurement of Mental Capacities, Oliver & Boyd.

BURT, C. (1933), 'The psychology of art', *How the Mind Works,* University of London Press.

BURT, C. (1938), 'The analysis of temperament', *Brit. J. Psychol.,* vol. 12, p. 184.

BURT, C. (1938), *Brit. J. Educ. Psychol.* vol. 8, pp. 29–49 and 265–85.

BURT, C. (1946), *Eugenics Rev.,* vol. 38, p. 155.

BURT, C. (1947), 'The factorial study of temperamental traits', *Brit. J. Statist. Psychol.*

BURT, C. (1962), 'Creativity and intelligence', *Brit. J. Educ. Psychol.,* vol. 32, pp. 292–8.

BURT, C. and BISKERSTETH, M. (1916), 'Some results of mental and scholastic tests', *Rep. Conf. of Educ. Assoc.,* p. 34.

BURT, C. and MOORE, R. C. (1911), 'Experimental tests of higher mental processes', *J. Exp. Pedag.,* vol. 1, pp. 93–112, and 251–9.

CATTELL, R. (1936), 'Burt's test in aesthetics', *Guide to Mental Testing.*
CATTELL, R. (1938), *Brit. J. Educ. Psychol.*, vol. 8.
CATTELL, R. (1949), Burt's test in aesthetics', *Guide to Mental Testing.*
CAREY, N. and BURT, C. (1915), *Brit. J. Psychol.*, vol. 8, p. 38.
CHRISTAL, R. E. (1958), 'Factor analytic study of visual memory',
   Psychol. Monograph, vol. 72, no. 13, (whole no. 466).
DEWAR, H. (1938), *Brit. J. Educ. Psychol.*, vol. 8, pp. 29–49.
EYSENCK, H. J. (1940), Ph. D. thesis, London.
EYSENCK, H. J. (1940), 'The general factor in aesthetic judgement', *Brit. J.
   Psychol.*, vol. 30, pp. 94–102 and 262–70.
EYSENCK, H. J. (1953), *The Structure of Human Personality*, Methuen.
EYSENCK, M. D. (1944), 'An experimental and statistical study of small
   preferences', *J. exp. Psychol.*, vol. 39, pp. 246–52.
FRY, R. (1926), Transformations.
GALTON, F. (1869), *Hereditary Genius*, Macmillan,
GALTON, F. (1883), *Inquiries into Human Faculty*, Macmillan.
GALTON, F. (1905), 'Anthropometry in schools', *Congress of Public Health.*
GUILFORD, J. P. (1956), 'The structure of intellect', *Psychol. Bull.*, vol. 53,
   pp. 267–93.
GUILFORD, J. P. (1959), *Personality*, McGraw-Hill.
HEAD, H. (1926), *Aphasia and Kindred Disorders of Speech*, Cambridge
   University Press.
HENNING, H. (1924), *Der Geruch*, Leipzig.
HSU, E. H. (1946), 'A factor analysis of olfaction', *Psychometrika*, vol. 11
   pp. 31–42.
KARLIN, J. E. (1942), 'A factorial study of auditory appreciation',
   Psychometrika, vol. 7, p. 251.
EL KOUSSY, A. A. H. (1935), 'The visual perception of space', *Brit. J. Mon.
   Sup.*, no. 20.
LCC (1917), *Distribution and Relations of Educational Abilities.*
MCDOUGALL, W. (1912), '*Psychology the Study of Behaviour*', Hutchinson.
MCDOUGALL, W. and SMITH, M. (1920), *Brit. J. Psychol.*, vol. 10,
   pp. 198–209.
MCFARLANE SMITH, I. (1964), *Spacial Ability*, University of London
   Press.
REYMART, M. L. (1950), 'The factorial study of emotions', *Feelings and
   Emotions*, Hafner.
VERNON, M. D. (1947), 'Different types of perceptual ability', *Brit. J.
   Psychol.*, vol. 37, pp. 79–89.
VERNON, P. E. (1961), *The Structure of Human Abilities*, Methuen, 2nd edn.
WILLIAMS, E. D. *et al* (1938), 'Tests of literary appreciation', *Brit. J. Educ.
   Psychol.*, vol. 8, pp. 265–86.
WING, H. D. (1941), *Musical Appreciation*, Ph.D. thesis, University College,
   London.
WISSLER, C. (1901), 'The correlation of mental and physical tests', *Psychol.
   Mon. Sup.*, vol. 3, p. 29.
WUNDT, W. (1902), *Grundzüge der Physiologischen Psychologie*, vol. 2,
   p. 243.
WUNDT, W. (1911), *Grundzüge der Psysiologischen Psychologie*, vol. 3.
   p. 598.

7 J. P. Guilford

Three Faces of Intellect

J. P. Guilford, 'Three faces of intellect', *American, Psychologist* (1959),
vol. 14, 1959 pp. 469–79.

My subject is in the area of human intelligence, in connection
with which the names of Terman and Stanford have become
known the world over. The Stanford Revision of the Binet intelligence scale has been the standard against which all other instruments for the measurement of intelligence have been compared.
The term IQ or intelligence quotient has become a household
word in this country. This is illustrated by two brief stories.

A few years ago, one of my neighbors came home from the PTA meeting, remarking: 'That Mrs So-And-So thinks she knows so much. She
kept talking about the "intelligence *quota*" of the children; "intelligence *quota*"; imagine. Why, everybody knows that IQ stands for
"intelligence *quiz*".'

The other story comes from a little comic strip in a Los Angeles
morning newspaper, called *Junior Grade*. In the first picture a little
boy meets a little girl, both apparently about the first-grade level. The
little girl remarks, 'I have a high IQ.' The little boy, puzzled, said, 'You
have a what?' The little girl repeated, 'I have a high IQ,' then went on
her way. The little boy, looking thoughtful, said, 'And she looks like
such a nice little girl, too.'

It is my purpose to speak about the analysis of this thing called
human intelligence into its components. I do not believe that
either Binet or Terman, if they were still with us, would object to
the idea of a searching and detailed study of intelligence, aimed
toward a better understanding of its nature. Preceding the development of his intelligence scale, Binet had done much research
on different kinds of thinking activities and apparently recognized
that intelligence has a number of aspects. It is to the lasting credit
of both Binet and Terman that they introduced such a great
variety of tasks into their intelligence scales.

Two related events of very recent history make it imperative
that we learn all we can regarding the nature of intelligence. I am
referring to the advent of the artificial satellites and planets and

to the crisis in education that has arisen in part as a consequence. The preservation of our way of life and our future security depend upon our most important national resources: our intellectual abilities and, more particularly, our creative abilities. It is time, then, that we learn all we can about those resources.

Our knowledge of the components of human intelligence has come about mostly within the last twenty-five years. The major sources of this information in this country have been Thurstone and his associates, the wartime research of psychologists in the United States Air Force, and more recently the Aptitudes Project[1] at the University of Southern California, now in its tenth year of research on cognitive and thinking abilities. The results from the Aptitudes Project that have gained perhaps the most attention have pertained to creative-thinking abilities. These are mostly novel findings. But to me, the most significant outcome has been the development of a unified theory of human intellect, which organizes the known, unique or primary intellectual abilities into a single system called the 'structure of intellect'. It is to this system that I shall devote the major part of my remarks, with very brief mentions of some of the implications for the psychology of thinking and problem solving, for vocational testing and for education.

The discovery of the components of intelligence has been by means of the experimental application of the method of factor analysis. It is not necessary for you to know anything about the theory or method of factor analysis in order to follow the discussion of the components. I should like to say, however, that factor analysis has no connection with or resemblance to psychoanalysis. A positive statement would be more helpful, so I will say that each intellectual component or factor is a unique ability that is needed to do well in a certain class of tasks or tests. As a general principle we find that certain individuals do well in the tests of a certain class, but they may do poorly in the tests of another class. We conclude that a factor has certain properties from the features that the tests of a class have in common. I shall give you very soon a number of examples of tests, each representing a factor.

The structure of intellect

Although each factor is sufficiently distinct to be detected by factor analysis, in very recent years it has become apparent that the

1. Under Contract N6 ONR–23810 with the Office of Naval Research (Personnel and Training Branch).

factors themselves can be classified because they resemble one another in certain ways. One basis of classification is according to the basic kind of process or operation performed. This kind of classification gives us five major groups of intellectual abilities: factors of cognition, memory, convergent thinking, divergent thinking, and evaluation.

Cognition means discovery or rediscovery or recognition. Memory means retention of what is cognized. Two kinds of productive-thinking operations generate new information from known information and remembered information. In divergent-thinking operations we think in different directions, sometimes searching, sometimes seeking variety. In convergent thinking the information leads to one right answer or to a recognized best or conventional answer. In evaluation we reach decisions as to goodness, correctness, suitability, or adequacy of what we know, what we remember, and what we produce in productive thinking.

A second way of classifying the intellectual factors is according to the kind of material or content involved. The factors known thus far involve three kinds of material or content: the content may be figural, symbolic, or semantic. Figural content is concrete material such as is perceived through the senses. It does not represent anything except itself. Visual material has properties such as size, form, color, location, or texture. Things we hear or feel provide other examples of figural material. Symbolic content is composed of letters, digits, and other conventional signs, usually organized in general systems, such as the alphabet or the number system. Semantic content is in the form of verbal meanings or ideas, for which no examples are necessary.

When a certain operation is applied to a certain kind of content, as many as six general kinds of products may be involved. There is enough evidence available to suggest that, regardless of the combinations of operations and content, the same six kinds of products may be found associated. The six kinds of products are: units, classes, relations, systems, transformations, and implications. So far as we have determined from factor analysis, these are the only fundamental kinds of products that we can know. As such, they may serve as basic classes into which one might fit all kinds of information psychologically.

The three kinds of classifications of the factors of intellect can be represented by means of a single solid model, shown in Figure 1. In this model, which we call the 'structure of intellect', each dimension represents one of the modes of variation of the factors.[2] Along one dimension are found the various kinds of operations, along a second one are the various kinds of products, and along the third are various kinds of content. Along the dimension of content a fourth category has been added, its kind of content being designated as 'behavioral'. This category has been added on a purely theoretical basis to represent the general area sometimes called 'social intelligence'. More will be said about this section of the model later.

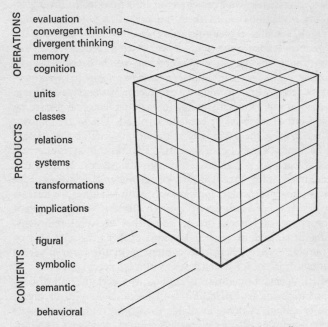

Figure 1 A cubical model representing the structure of the intellect

In order to provide a better basis for understanding the model and a better basis for accepting it as a picture of human intellect, I shall do some exploring of it with you systematically, giving some examples of tests. Each cell in the model calls for a certain kind of ability that can be described in terms of operation, content, and product, for each cell is at the intersection of a unique combination of kinds of operation, content, and product. A test

2. For an earlier presentation of the concept, *see* Guilford (1956).

for that ability would have the same three properties. In our exploration of the model, we shall take one vertical layer at a time, beginning with the front face. The first layer provides us with a matrix of eighteen cells (if we ignore the behavioral column for which there are as yet no known factors) each of which should contain a cognitive ability.

The cognitive abilities

We know at present the unique abilities that fit logically into fifteen of the eighteen cells for cognitive abilities. Each row presents a triad of similar abilities, having a single kind of product in common. The factors of the first row are concerned with the knowing of units. A good test of the ability to cognize figural units is the Street Gestalt Completion Test. In this test, the recognition of familiar pictured objects in silhouette form is made difficult for testing purposes by blocking out parts of those objects. There is another factor that is known to involve the perception of auditory figures – in the form of melodies, rhythms, and speech sounds – and still another factor involving kinaesthetic forms. The presence of three factors in one cell (they are conceivably distinct abilities, although this has not been tested) suggests that more generally, in the figural column, at least, we should expect to find more than one ability. A fourth dimension pertaining to variations in sense modality may thus apply in connection with figural content. The model could be extended in this manner, if the facts call for such an extension.

The ability to cognize symbolic units is measured by tests like the following:

Put vowels in the following blanks to make real words:
P—W—R
M—R V—L
C—R T—N

Rearrange the letters to make real words:
R A C I H
T V O E S
K L C C O

The first of these two tests is called Disemboweled Words, and the second Scrambled Words.

The ability to cognize semantic units is the well-known factor of verbal comprehension, which is best measured by means of a vocabulary test, with items such as:

GRAVITY means ———
CIRCUS means ———
VIRTUE means ———

From the comparison of these two factors it is obvious that recognizing familiar words as letter structures and knowing what words mean depend upon quite different abilities.

For testing the abilities to know classes of units, we may present the following kinds of items, one with symbolic content and one with semantic content:

Which letter group does not belong?
XECM PVAA QXIN VTRO

Which object does not belong?
clam tree oven rose

A figural test is constructed in a completely parallel form, presenting in each item four figures, three of which have a property in common and the fourth lacking that property.

The three abilities to see relationships are also readily measured by a common kind of test, differing only in terms of content. The well-known analogies test is applicable, two items in symbolic and semantic form being:

JIRE   : KIRE : : FORA : KORE KORA LIRE GORA GIRE
poetry : prose : : dance : music walk sing talk jump

Such tests usually involve more than the ability to cognize relations, but we are not concerned with this problem at this point.

The three factors for cognizing systems do not at present appear in tests so closely resembling one another as in the case of the examples just given. There is nevertheless an underlying common core of logical similarity. Ordinary space tests, such as Thurstone's Flags, Figures, and Cards or Part 5 (Spatial Orientation) of the Guilford–Zimmerman Aptitude Survey (GZAS), serve in the figural column. The system involved is an order or arrangement of objects in space. A system that uses symbolic elements is illustrated by the Letter Triangle Test, a sample item of which is:

What letter belongs at the place of the question mark?

The ability to understand a semantic system has been known for some time as the factor called general reasoning. One of its most faithful indicators is a test composed of arithmetic-reasoning items. That the phase of understanding only is important for measuring this ability is shown by the fact that such a test works even if the examinee is not asked to give a complete solution; he need only show that he structures the problem properly. For example, an item from the test Necessary Arithmetical Operations simply asks what operations are needed to solve the problem:

A city lot 48 feet wide and 149 feet deep costs $79.432. What is the cost per square foot?

A add and multiply
B multiply and divide
C subtract and divide
D add and subtract
E divide and add

Placing the factor of general reasoning in this cell of the structure of intellect gives us some new conceptions of its nature. It should be a broad ability to grasp all kinds of systems that are conceived in terms of verbal concepts, not restricted to the understanding of problems of an arithmetical type.

Transformations are changes of various kinds, including modifications in arrangement, organization, or meaning. In the figural column for the transformations row, we find the factor known as visualization. Common measuring instruments for this factor are the surface-development tests, and an example of a different kind is Part 6 (Spatial Visualization) of the GZAS. A test of the ability to make transformations of meaning, for the factor in the semantic column, is called Similarities. The examinee is asked to state several ways in which two objects, such as an apple and an orange, are alike. Only by shifting the meanings of both is the examinee able to give many responses to such an item.

In the set of abilities having to do with the cognition of implications, we find that the individual goes beyond the information given, but not to the extent of what might be called drawing conclusions. We may say that he extrapolates. From the given information he expects or foresees certain consequences, for example. The two factors found in this row of the cognition matrix were first called 'foresight' factors. Foresight in connection with figural material can be tested by means of paper-and-pencil mazes. Foresight in connection with ideas, those pertaining to events, for example, is indicated by a test such as Pertinent Questions:

In planning to open a new hamburger stand in a certain community, what four questions should be considered in deciding upon its location?

The more questions the examinee asks in response to a list of such problems, the more he evidently foresees contingencies.

The memory abilities

The area of memory abilities has been explored less than some of the other areas of operation, and only seven of the potential cells of the memory matrix have known factors in them. These cells are restricted to three rows: for units, relations, and systems. The first cell in the memory matrix is now occupied by two factors, parallel to two in the corresponding cognition matrix: visual memory and auditory memory. Memory for series of letters or numbers, as in memory span tests, conforms to the conception of memory for symbolic units. Memory for the ideas in a paragraph conforms to the conception of memory for semantic units.

The formation of associations between units, such as visual forms, syllables, and meaningful words, as in the method of paired associates, would seem to represent three abilities to remember relationships involving three kinds of content. We know of two such abilities, for the symbolic and semantic columns. The memory for known systems is represented by two abilities very recently discovered (Christal, 1958). Remembering the arrangement of objects in space is the nature of an ability in the figural column, and remembering a sequence of events is the nature of a corresponding ability in the semantic column. The differentiation between these two abilities implies that a person may be able to say where he saw an object on a page, but he might not be able to say on which of several pages he saw it after leafing through several pages that included the right one. Considering the blank rows in the memory matrix, we should expect to find abilities also to remember classes, transformations, and implications, as well as units, relations, and systems.

The divergent-thinking abilities

The unique feature of divergent production is that a *variety* of responses is produced. The product is not completely determined by the given information. This is not to say that divergent thinking does not come into play in the total process of reaching a unique conclusion, for it comes into play wherever there is trial-and-error thinking.

The well-known ability of word fluency is tested by asking the examinee to list words satisfying a specified letter requirement, such as words beginning with the letter 's' or words ending in

'-tion'. This ability is now regarded as a facility in divergent production of symbolic units. The parallel semantic ability has been known as ideational fluency. A typical test item calls for listing objects that are round and edible. Winston Churchill must have possessed this ability to a high degree. Clement Attlee is reported to have said about him recently that, no matter what problem came up, Churchill always seemed to have about ten ideas. The trouble was, Attlee continued, he did not know which was the good one. The last comment implies some weakness in one or more of the evaluative abilities.

The divergent production of class ideas is believed to be the unique feature of a factor called 'spontaneous flexibility'. A typical test instructs the examinee to list all the uses he can think of for a common brick, and he is given eight minutes. If his responses are: build a house, build a barn, build a garage, build a school, build a church, build a chimney, build a walk, and build a barbecue, he would earn a fairly high score for ideational fluency but a very low score for spontaneous flexibility, because all these uses fall into the same class. If another person said: make a door stop, make a paper weight, throw it at a dog, make a bookcase, drown a cat, drive a nail, make a red powder, and use for baseball bases, he would also receive a high score for flexibility. He has gone frequently from one class to another.

A current study of unknown but predicted divergent-production abilities includes testing whether there are also figural and symbolic abilities to produce multiple classes. An experimental figural test presents a number of figures that can be classified in groups of three in various ways, each figure being usable in more than one class. An experimental symbolic test presents a few numbers that are also to be classified in multiple ways.

A unique ability involving relations is called 'associational fluency'. It calls for the production of a variety of things related in a specified way to a given thing. For example, the examinee is asked to list words meaning about the same as 'good' or to list words meaning about the opposite of 'hard'. In these instances the response produced is to complete a relationship, and semantic content is involved. Some of our present experimental tests call for the production of varieties of relations, as such, and involve figural and symbolic content also. For example, given four small digits, in how many ways can they be related in order to produce a sum of eight?

One factor pertaining to the production of systems is known as expressional fluency. The rapid formation of phrases or sentences is the essence of certain tests of this factor. For example, given the initial letters:

W——— c——— e——— n———

with different sentences to be produced, the examinee might write 'We can eat nuts' or 'Whence came Eve Newton?' In interpreting the factor, we regard the sentence as a symbolic system. By analogy, a figural system would be some kind of organization of lines and other elements, and a semantic system would be in the form of a verbally stated problem or perhaps something as complex as a theory.

In the row of the divergent-production matrix devoted to transformations, we find some very interesting factors. The one called 'adaptive flexibility' is now recognized as belonging in the figural column. A faithful test of it has been Match Problems. This is based upon the common game that uses squares, the sides of which are formed by match sticks. The examinee is told to take away a given number of matches to leave a stated number of squares with nothing left over. Nothing is said about the sizes of the squares to be left. If the examinee imposes upon himself the restriction that the squares that he leaves must be of the same size, he will fail in his attempts to do items like that in Figure 2. Other odd kinds of solutions are introduced in other items, such as overlapping squares and squares within squares, and so on. In another variation of Match Problems the examinee is told to produce two or more solutions for each problem.

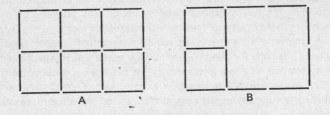

take away four matches in A leaving
three squares and nothing more   Answer B

Figure 2   A sample item from the test Match Problems. The problem in this item is to take away four matches and leave three squares
The solution is given

A factor that has been called 'originality' is now recognized as adaptive flexibility with semantic material, where there must be a shifting of meanings. The examinee must produce the shifts or changes in meaning and so come up with novel, unusual, clever, or farfetched ideas. The Plot Titles Test present a short story, the examinee being told to list as many appropriate titles as he can to head the story. One story is about a missionary who has been captured by cannibals in Africa. He is in the pot and about to be boiled when a princess of the tribe obtains a promise for his release if he will become her mate. He refuses and is boiled to death.

In scoring the test, we separate the responses into two categories, clever and nonclever. Examples of nonclever responses are: African Death, Defeat of a Princess, Eaten by Savages, The Princess, The African Missionary, In Darkest Africa, and Boiled by Savages. These titles are appropriate but commonplace. The number of such responses serves as a score for ideational fluency. Examples of clever responses are: Pot's Plot, Potluck Dinner, Stewed Parson, Goil or Boil, A Mate Worse Than Death, He Left a Dish for a Pot, Chaste in Haste, and A Hot Price for Freedom. The number of clever responses given by an examinee is his score for originality, or the divergent production of semantic transformations.

Another test of originality presents a very novel task so that any acceptable response is unusual for the individual. In the Symbol Production Test the examinee is to produce a simple symbol to stand for a noun or a verb in each short sentence, in other words to invent something like pictographic symbols. Still another test of originality asks for writing the 'punch lines' for cartoons, a task that almost automatically challenges the examinee to be clever. Thus, quite a variety of tests offer approaches to the measurement of originality, including one or two others that I have not mentioned.

Abilities to produce a variety of implications are assessed by tests calling for elaboration of given information. A figural test of this type provides the examinee with a line or two, to which he is to add other lines to produce an object. The more lines he adds, the greater his score. A semantic test gives the examinee the outlines of a plan to which he is to respond by stating all the details he can think of to make the plan work. A new test we are trying out in the symbolic area presents two simple equations such as $B - C = D$ and $z = A + D$. The examinee is to make as many other equations as he can from this information.

The convergent-production abilities

Of the eighteen convergent-production abilities expected in the three content columns, twelve are now recognized. In the first row, pertaining to units, we have an ability to name figural properties (forms or colors) and an ability to name abstractions (classes, relations, and so on). It may be that the ability in common to the speed of naming forms and the speed of naming colors is not appropriately placed in the convergent-thinking matrix. One might expect that the thing to be produced in a test of the convergent production of figural units would be in the form of figures rather than words. A better test of such an ability might somehow specify the need for one particular object, the examinee to furnish the object.

A test for the convergent production of classes (Word Grouping) presents a list of twelve words that are to be classified in four, and only four, meaningful groups, no word to appear in more than one group. A parallel test (Figure Concepts Test) presents twenty pictured real objects that are to be grouped in meaningful classes of two or more each.

Convergent production having to do with relationships is represented by three known factors, all involving the 'eduction of correlates', as Spearman called it. The given information includes one unit and a stated relation, the examinee to supply the other unit. Analogies tests that call for completion rather than a choice between alternative answers emphasize this kind of ability. With symbolic content such an item might read:

pots   stop   bard   drab   rats   ?

A semantic item that measures eduction of correlates is:

The absence of sound is ———

Incidentally, the latter item is from a vocabulary-completion test, and its relation to the factor of ability to produce correlates indicates how, by change of form, a vocabulary test may indicate an ability other than that for which vocabulary tests are usually intended, namely, the factor of verbal comprehension.

Only one factor for convergent production of systems is known, and it is in the semantic column. It is measured by a class of tests that may be called ordering tests. The examinee may be presented with a number of events that ordinarily have a best or most logical order, the events being presented in scrambled order. The presentation may be pictorial, as in the Picture Arrangement Test, or verbal. The pictures may be taken from a cartoon strip. The verbally presented events may be in the form of the various steps needed to plant a new lawn. There are undoubtedly other kinds of systems than temporal order that could be utilized for testing abilities in this row of the convergent-production matrix.

In the way of producing transformations of a unique variety, we have three recognized factors, known as redefinition abilities. In each case, redefinition involves the changing of functions or uses of parts of one unit and giving them new functions or uses in some new unit. For testing the ability of figural redefinition, a task based upon the Gottschaldt figures is suitable. Figure 3 shows the kind of item for such a test. In recognizing the simpler figure within the structure of a more complex figure, certain lines must take on new roles.

In terms of symbolic material, the following sample items will illustrate how groups of letters in given words must be readapted to use in other words. In the test Camouflaged Words, each sentence contains the name of a sport or game:

I did not know that he was ailing.
To beat the Hun, tin goes a long way.

For the factor of semantic redefinition, the Gestalt Transformation Test may be used. A sample item reads:

From which object could you most likely make a needle?
A a cabbage
B a splice
C a steak
D a paper box
E a fish

The convergent production of implications means the drawing of fully determined conclusions from given information. The well-known factor of numerical facility belongs in the symbolic column. For the parallel ability in the figural column, we have a test known as Form Reasoning, in which rigorously defined operations with figures are used. For the parallel ability in the semantic column, the factor sometimes called 'deduction' probably qualifies. Items of the following type are sometimes used.

Charles is younger than Robert
Charles is older than Frank
Who is older: Robert or Frank?

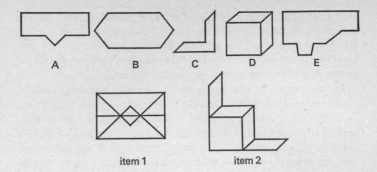

Figure 3 Sample items from a test, Hidden Figures, based upon Gottschaldt figures. Which of the simpler figures is concealed with each two more complex figures?

Evaluative abilities

The evaluative area has had the least investigation of all the operational categories. In fact, only one systematic analytical study has been devoted to this area. Only eight evaluative abilities are recognized as fitting into the evaluation matrix. But at least five rows have one or more factors each, and also three of the usual columns or content categories. In each case, evaluation involves reaching decisions as to the accuracy, goodness, suitability, or workability of information. In each row, for the particular kind of product of that row, some kind of criterion or standard of judgement is involved.

In the first row, for the evaluation of units, the important decision to be made pertains to the identity of a unit. Is this unit identical with that one? In the figural column we find the factor long known as 'perceptual speed'. Tests of this factor invariably call for decisions of identity, for example, Part 4 (Perceptual Speed) of the GZAS or Thurstone's Identical Forms. I think it has been generally wrongly thought that the ability involved is that of cognition of visual forms. But we have seen that another factor is a more suitable candidate for this definition and for being in the very first cell of the cognitive matrix. It is parallel to this evaluative ability but does not require the judgement of identity as one of its properties.

In the symbolic column is an ability to judge identity of symbolic units, in the form of series of letters or numbers or of names of individuals.

Are members of the following pairs identical or not:

    825170493———825176493
    dkcltvmpa———dkcltvmpa
C. S. Meyerson———C. E. Meyerson

Such items are common in tests of clerical aptitude.

There should be a parallel ability to decide whether two ideas are identical or different. Is the idea expressed in this sentence the same as the idea expressed in that one? Do these two proverbs express essentially the same idea? Such tests exist and will be used to test the hypothesis that such an ability can be demonstrated.

No evaluative abilities pertaining to classes have as yet been recognized. The abilities having to do with evaluation where relations are concerned must meet the criterion of logical consistency. Syllogistic-type tests involving letter symbols indicate a different ability than the same type of test involving verbal statements. In the figural column we might expect that tests incorporating geometric reasoning or proof would indicate a parallel ability to sense the soundness of conclusions regarding figural relationships.

The evaluation of systems seems to be concerned with the internal consistency of those systems, so far as we can tell from the knowledge of one such factor. The factor has been called 'experiential evaluation', and its representative test presents items like that in Figure 4 asking 'What is wrong with this picture?' The things wrong are often internal inconsistencies.

A semantic ability for evaluating transformations is thought to be that known for some time as 'judgement'. In typical judgement tests, the examinee is asked to tell which of five solutions to

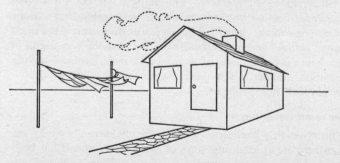

Figure 4 A sample item from the test Unusual Details. What two things are wrong in this picture?

a practical problem is most adequate or wise. The solutions frequently involve improvisations, in other words, adaptations of familiar objects to unusual uses. In this way the items present redefinitions to be evaluated.

A factor known first as 'sensitivity to problems' has become recognized as an evaluative ability having to do with implications. One test of the factor, the Apparatus Test, asks for two needed improvements with respect to each of several common devices, such as the telephone or the toaster. The Social Institutions Test, a measure of the same factor, asks what things are wrong with each of several institutions, such as tipping or national elections. We may say that defects or deficiencies are implications of an evaluative kind. Another interpretation would be that seeing defects and deficiencies are evaluations of implications to the effect that the various aspects of something are all right.[3]

Some implications of the structure of intellect
For psychological theory

Although factor analysis as generally employed is best designed to investigate ways in which individuals differ from one another, in other words, to discover traits, the results also tell us much about how individuals are alike. Consequently, information regarding the factors and their interrelationships gives us understanding of functioning individuals. The five kinds of intellectual abilities in terms of operations may be said to represent five ways of functioning. The kinds of intellectual abilities distinguished according to varieties of test content and the kinds of abilities distinguished according to varieties of products suggest a classification of basic forms of information or knowledge. The kind of organism suggested by this way of looking at intellect is that of an agency for dealing with information of various kinds in various ways. The concepts provided by the distinctions among the intellectual abilities and by their classifications may be very useful in our future investigations of learning, memory, problem-solving invention, and decision making, by whatever method we choose to approach those problems.

For vocational testing

With about fifty intellectual factors already known, we may say that there are at least fifty ways of being intelligent. It has been

3. For further details concerning the intellectual factors, illustrative tests, and the place of the factors in the structure of intellect, *see* Guilford (1959).

facetiously suggested that there seem to be a great many more ways of being stupid, unfortunately. The structure of intellect is a theoretical model that predicts as many as 120 distinct abilities, if every cell of the model contains a factor. Already we know that two cells contain two or more factors each, and there probably are actually other cells of this type. Since the model was first conceived, twelve factors predicted by it have found places in it. There is consequently hope of filling many of the other vacancies, and we may eventually end up with more than 120 abilities.

The major implication for the assessment of intelligence is that to know an individual's intellectual resources thoroughly we shall need a surprisingly large number of scores. It is expected that many of the factors are inter-correlated, so there is some possibility that by appropriate sampling we shall be able to cover the important abilities with a more limited number of tests. At any rate, a multiple-score approach to the assessment of intelligence is definitely indicated in connection with future vocational operations.

Considering the kinds of abilities classified as to content, we may speak roughly of four kinds of intelligence. The abilities involving the use of figural information may be regarded as 'concrete' intelligence. The people who depend most upon these abilities deal with concrete things and their properties. Among these people are mechanics, operators of machines, engineers (in some aspects of their work), artists, and musicians.

In the abilities pertaining to symbolic and semantic content, we have two kinds of 'abstract' intelligence. Symbolic abilities should be important in learning to recognize words, to spell, and to operate with numbers. Language and mathematics should depend very much upon them, except that in mathematics some aspects, such as geometry, have strong figural involvement. Semantic intelligence is important for understanding things in terms of verbal concepts and hence is important in all courses where the learning of facts and ideas is essential.

In the hypothesized behavioral column of the structure of intellect, which may be roughly described as 'social' intelligence, we have some of the most interesting possibilities. Understanding the behavior of others and of ourselves is largely nonverbal in character. The theory suggests as many as 30 abilities in this area, some having to do with understanding, some with productive thinking about behavior, and some with the evaluation of behavior. The theory also suggests that information regarding behavior is also in the form of the six kinds of products that apply elsewhere in the structure of intellect, including units, relations, systems, and so on. The abilities in the area of social intelligence, whatever they prove to be, will possess considerable importance in connection with all those individuals who deal most with other people: teachers, law officials, social workers, therapists, politicians, statesmen, and leaders of other kinds.

For education

The implications for education are numerous, and I have time just to mention a very few. The most fundamental implication is that we might well undergo transformations with respect to our conception of the learner and of the process of learning. Under the prevailing conception, the learner is a kind of stimulus-response device, much on the order of a vending machine. You put in a coin, and something comes out. The machine learns what reaction to put out when a certain coin is put in. If, instead, we think of the learner as an agent for dealing with information, where information is defined very broadly, we have something more analogous to an electronic computer. We feed a computer information; it stores that information; it uses that information for generating new information, either by way of divergent or convergent thinking; and it evaluates its own results. Advantages that a human learner has over a computer include the step of seeking and discovering new information from sources outside itself and the step of programing itself. Perhaps even these steps will be added to computers, if this has not already been done in some cases.

At any rate, this conception of the learner leads us to the idea that learning is discovery of information, not merely the formation of associations, particularly associations in the form of stimulus-response connections. I am aware of the fact that my proposal is rank heresy. But if we are to make significant progress in our understanding of human learning and particularly our understanding of the so-called higher mental processes of thinking, problem solving, and creative thinking, some drastic modifications are due in our theory.

The idea that education is a matter of training the mind or of training the intellect has been rather unpopular, wherever the prevailing psychological doctrines have been followed. In theory, at least, the emphasis has been upon the learning of rather specific habits or skills. If we take our cue from factor theory, however, we recognize that most learning probably has both specific and general aspects or components. The general aspects may be along the lines of the factors of intellect. This is not to say that the individual's status in each factor is entirely determined by learning. We do not know to what extent each factor is determined by heredity and to what extent by learning. The best position for educators to take is that possibly every intellectual factor can be developed in individuals at least to some extent by learning.

If education has the general objective of developing the intellects of students, it can be suggested that each intellectual factor provides a particular goal at which to aim. Defined by a certain combination of content, operation, and product, each goal ability then calls for certain kinds of practice in order to achieve improvement in it. This implies choice of curriculum and the choice or invention of teaching methods that will most likely accomplish the desired results.

Considering the very great variety of abilities revealed by the factorial exploration of intellect, we are in a better position to ask whether any general intellectual skills are now being neglected in education and whether appropriate balances are being observed. It is often observed these days that we have fallen down in the way of producing resourceful, creative graduates. How true this is, in comparison with other times, I do not know. Perhaps the deficit is noticed because the demands for inventiveness are so much greater at this time. At any rate, realizing that the more conspicuously creative abilities appear to be concentrated in the divergent-thinking category, and also to some extent in the transformation category, we now ask whether we have been giving these skills appropriate exercise. It is probable that we need a better balance of training in the divergent-thinking area as compared with training in convergent thinking and in critical thinking or evaluation.

The structure of intellect as I have presented it to you may or may not stand the test of time. Even if the general form persists, there are likely to be some modifications. Possibly some different kind of model will be invented. Be that as it may, the fact of a multiplicity of intellectual abilities seems well established.

There are many individuals who long for the good old days of simplicity, when we got along with one unanalysed intelligence. Simplicity certainly has its appeal. But human nature is exceedingly complex, and we may as well face that fact. The rapidly moving events of the world in which we live have forced upon us the need for knowing human intelligence thoroughly. Humanity's peaceful pursuit of happiness depends upon our control of nature and of our own behavior; and this, in turn, depends upon understanding ourselves, including our intellectual resources.

References

CHRISTAL, R. E. (1958), 'Factor analytic study of visual memory', *Psychol. Monograph*, vol. 72, no. 13.

GUILFORD, J. P. (1956), 'Structure of intellect', *Psychol. Bulletin*, vol. 53, pp. 267–93.

GUILFORD, J. P. (1959), *Personality*, McGraw-Hill.

Part Three
Nature *v.* Nurture

This section deals with the major problem, mentioned in the Introduction: the age-old controversy of heredity and environment. Galton, himself a notable example of hereditary influences, had few doubts about this. In his *Enquiries into Human Faculty* (1883) he states:

There is no escape from the conclusion that Nature prevails enormously over Nurture when the differences of Nurture do not exceed what is commonly to be found among persons of the same rank of society and in the same country. My theory is that my evidence may seem to prove too much and be discredited on that account as it appears contrary to all experience that Nurture should go for so little. But experience is often fallacious in ascribing great effects to trifling circumstances.

If we take note of the reservation in Galton's first sentence this perhaps does little violence to the present state of informed opinion. Radical differences in environment can produce large effects on measured intelligence: differences 'commonly found among persons of the same rank of society' have, however, less dramatic effects, as has been repeatedly demonstrated in research. Research work in this field has tended to concentrate on studies of foster-children and studies of twins. Identical twins are, of course, obvious subjects for investigation, since they possess identical genetic factors and if a sufficient number of such monozygotic twins can be found who have been separated at birth, and brought up in very different kinds of homes, the influence of nurture can be estimated with a considerable degree of accuracy. Many researches of this type have been mounted, and Erlenmeyer-Kimling and Jarvik have provided an informative survey of the results of fifty-two studies, yielding over 30,000 correlation coefficients. The summary of these in graphical form is a most telling confirmation of genetic theory

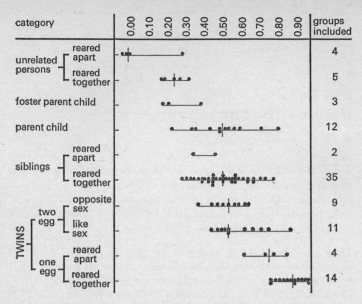

category		0.00	0.10	0.20	0.30	0.40	0.50	0.60	0.70	0.80	0.90	groups included

Figure 1 Correlation coefficients for 'intelligence' test scores from fifty-two studies. Some studies reported data for more than one relationship category; some included more than one sample per category, giving a total of ninety-nine groups. Over two-thirds of the correlation coefficients were derived from IQs the remainder from special tests (e.g., Primary Mental Abilities). Midparent-child correlation was used when available, otherwise mother-child correlation

(*see* Figure 1). As the authors put it, 'the median of the empirical correlations closely approaches the theoretical value predicted on the basis of genetic relationship alone'.

The first of our Readings is taken from Hebb's classic book *The Organization of Behavior*, in which he uses results from experiments in animal psychology and neuro-physiology, data from the hospital clinic as well as the psychological laboratory. This book made an immediate impact, and all students of psychology and education are now familiar with 'Intelligence A' and 'Intelligence B', the labels invented by Hebb to distinguish between 'the *innate potential*, the capacity for development', and 'the functioning of a brain in which development has gone on, determining an *average level of performance or comprehension* by the partly grown or mature person'. He agrees that 'the effects of early experience are more or less generalized and permanent', so that we 'can concede a major effect of experience on the IQ and still leave the IQ its constancy and validity as an index of future performance'.

The other contribution in this section is a revised version (revised by the author himself) of Burt's important paper 'The evidence for the concept of intelligence'. This is much more than a contribution to the nature–nurture controversy, and many students will find its historical survey of interest and value. Although Burt emphasizes the great importance of genetic factors, he is far from occupying the reactionary role sometimes attributed to him by the less discerning social scientists. He insists, for example, on the importance of the fact that differences within each social class are much greater than differences between the classes, and finishes his paper with a comment that what we already know 'presents an extremely complicated set of problems for the educationist, the politician, the social reformer, and the policy-makers of every truly democratic state', and he goes on to urge the need 'not only for further research but also for a more general understanding of the results of such research'.

8 D. O. Hebb

The Growth and Decline of Intelligence

Excerpts from D. O. Hebb, *The Organization of Behavior*, John Wiley, 1949, chapter 11, pp. 275–303.

Identifying intellectual deterioration

We feel, most of us, that we can make a reasonably good estimate of another's intellectual ability by conversation with him; and we are apt to feel, too, that we have in general a fairly good idea of what sort of problems can be solved by the healthy, 'average', 'normal' people in our own communities. Both convictions are frequently misleading. The first point on method is that the detection of intellectual defect, following brain injury, requires the test procedure and (in some form or other) the use of a control group.

Ordinarily, the person who is clear in conversation, quick to understand what is said to him, and coherent in his reply, is 'intelligent': that is, conversational ability is correlated with other abilities, and is not a bad basis of prediction. But these correlations sometimes break down with pathological changes in the brain, and then the prediction may be false. Also, one is apt to judge capacity by the patient's alertness and manner, apart from what he says. The physician is familiar with deterioration in the form of unresponsiveness, apathy, slowness, or inconstancy of purpose. Accordingly, when such signs are absent the physician may feel certain that intelligence is not impaired.

It is reasonably sure that this has been a major source of the disagreement about intellectual impairment in aphasia. Because the aphasic always tries to respond, is fully attentive, and gives the *impression* of being quite clear mentally, it is easy to conclude that he has lost nothing but the power of verbal recognition and expression. There are cases on record in which it has been 'proved' that aphasia does not affect intelligence, on the ground that the patient nodded and smiled when the physician greeted him, that he knew whether it was morning or afternoon, or that he was able to let an attendant know when he needed the bedpan.

Tests, on the other hand, show that the aphasic usually cannot fit blocks together to make a simple pattern, that he does not

recognize absurdities in pictures, cannot make a simple drawing –
even though he clearly knows what he is to do. In such performances the aphasic is almost certain to be at a much lower level
than a normal individual of the same background and original
ability. The aphasic patient is apt to have trouble in finding his
way about, even in a familiar region, and to have trouble in manipulating simple mechanical contrivances. There is no sense in
arguing over terminology, and each writer can define that equi-
vocal term 'intelligence' to suit himself (though one might expect
some consistency in its subsequent use); but because the aphasic
is alert, and persistent in trying to discover what 2 and 2 add up
to, or to discover what is missing in a picture of a dog with three
legs, it does not follow that he has lost only the capacity for communication. There is also a change in what would usually be
called intelligence.

To detect deterioration, one cannot depend on impression
alone but must also use test methods; and this requires a normal
control group. It is most dangerous to assume knowledge of what
the 'average' person knows and can do. Let me give some examples, based on data obtained in the standardization of some
adult tests. Somewhere in the neighborhood of half the adult
English-speaking population cannot complete the analogy *foot* is
to *ankle* as *hand* is to *what?* or *under*: *over* – *down*:*?* (though almost everyone can do *dog*: *bark* – *cat*:?). About half the adult
population think that *priceless* means 'of no value'; nearly the
same number are unaware that *brunette* refers to a dark com-
plexion, and many think it a synonym for 'blonde' – meaning
any lively young woman. Figure 1 shows some simple problems –
apparently simple – that cannot be solved by some fraction,
between 10 and 25 per cent, of the adult population.

The subjects in these tests were able to earn a living and conduct their own affairs with ordinary prudence, and would not be
classed as anything but normal in the clinic. If such a person
happened to have a brain injury, and the examiner did not know
what other persons of the same class would do with such tests, he
would be bound to conclude that the brain injury was the reason
for the subject's incompetence. No matter how simple one's tests
may seem to be, the brain-injured patient's performance must be
interpreted in the light of the scores of a normal control group.
The professional man's idea of the average intelligence is colored
by his preoccupation with the abstract and academic, and by the
fact that his intimacy is mainly with others in the professional

community whose preoccupations, interests, and abilities are of the same kind as his own.

How is a normal control group to be chosen? Despite some recent discussion making this an esoteric question, almost impossible to understand, the desiderata are comparatively simple. There might be no need of a control group if one could compare the patient's scores after brain operation with his scores before anything was wrong with his brain; all one can get, however, is a

Figure 1 Problems from a performance test (upper line) and attempted solutions (lower line) by a person not in any way classified as feeble-minded. A pattern in cardboard was placed before the subject, and left there while he tried to duplicate it, using two or more identical wooden triangles. Each of the shaded diagrams shows a subject's placing of the blocks in an attempt to duplicate the pattern immediately above (by BG, female thirty years of age, a 'normal control subject' convalescent after appendicitis). A fairly large proportion of the adult population will make such errors and have difficulty in seeing how to change the placing of the blocks when told that the solution is not correct

pre- and post-operative comparison, which must be a different matter. The condition for which he is being operated on must itself affect his scores, and in fact the operation quite often causes a *rise* in score. The purpose of the control group, then, is to let us know as far as possible what the brain-operated patient would have done if his brain had remained healthy and undamaged. This tells us what to look for in a control group. The object is to find persons who are like the patients being studied in every way that, as far as one knows, affects intelligence-test scores, except in the one respect, that the normal control subjects have undamaged brains.

Now test scores are related to education, social background, and occupation – a concatenation that can be summarized as the factor of sophistication. Scores are also affected by age, rising to a peak in the teens and declining (for almost all tests) after the twenties. These are the correlates of intelligence in normal persons, as far as they are known at present; if they are controlled, one can estimate, by comparing clinical and control groups, the degree and kind of impairment that results from brain damage; but if they are not controlled this is not possible. It is not possible to show that brain damage affects intelligence, by the use of a control group that is made up of hospital employees, or college students, or clerical workers, when the clinical group includes truck drivers, farmers, and unskilled laborers – persons who are apt to have been long away from clerical work, with a lower average level of education. It is not possible to compare a man who went to high school ten years ago with a student now in high school. If the clinical subjects are older adults, or less sophisticated, they are bound to have lower scores than the normal subjects.

These considerations are what should determine the nature of the *normal* control group. One must then go farther, and use *clinical* controls, if one wishes to know not only that a certain kind of injury produces intellectual defects but also whether it produces more defect than some other kind of injury. If one wanted to show that frontal-lobe damage is more serious than damage elsewhere in the brain, one would use two groups, a frontal-lobe group and a parietal, temporal, occipital group. But note this: everything that was said above about making the normal group equivalent to the clinical group is equally necessary in the comparison of two clinical groups. They must be the same in age, in sophistication, and, in addition, in the size and type of lesion.

Differences between early and late brain injury

The study of brain operations in human patients has not so far provided the data that would allow one to be very definite about the way in which higher functions are related to special parts of the cerebral cortex; but it has raised one problem that gives us a valuable lead concerning the nature of intelligence. The problem has been referred to already – it arises from the discovery that an IQ of 160 or higher is possible after the removal of one prefrontal lobe or an IQ of 115 after hemidecortication, and from the frequency with which above-average scores are reported after cortical injury in any except the speech area. It appears possible, however, that similar damage to the infant brain has a much greater effect on the subsequent IQ. This possibility suggests a clue to the nature of adult intelligence and suggests a distinction between two quite different meanings of the term 'intelligence' – a distinction that may help to resolve current theoretical disagreements.

The average IQ after brain operation, in all cases in which an IQ was reported up to the end of 1941, was 108 – at least 8 points above the normal adult average, which is probably well below 100 according to the US Army data of 1917 and Weisenburg, Roe, and McBride's (1936) data. When brain damage is traumatic or pathological, instead of surgical, there are also frequent indications that on certain kinds of test (on which the Stanford-Binet IQ is mainly based) the patient's score is not much lower than it would have been had the brain damage not occurred. These data are given in more detail elsewhere (Hebb, 1942). But in practically all such cases the use of other tests shows that there is a definite intellectual loss. That is, some tests such as the Stanford-Binet show little sign of a loss of intelligence, others show much greater loss. There are then two kinds of test material, or two extremes in test content that shade into one another. The same picture appears when older adult subjects are examined: some (Binet-type) tests show no deterioration due to advancing age; others show a marked deterioration; and most tests fall somewhere between the two extremes.

The Binet IQ is determined by the use of a composite test, and it amounts to an average level of performance in a miscellany of tasks. It is mainly verbal, however, and mainly involves a kind of problem to which the answer is rather obvious, to the subject who can solve it at all. Tests of intelligence may also consist of non-verbal tasks, and puzzle-like tasks – ones that require an effort and have to be worked out logically. Analysis of the test scores made after brain operation, when aphasia is not present, indicates that it is the first of these two kinds of task that is little affected by brain damage, the second that is much affected. The IQ shows little effect of brain damage outside the speech areas because it is mainly based on 'Binet-type' tasks. These consist particularly of tests of vocabulary, information, digit repetition, digits backward, understanding of the meaning of fables or proverbs, and certain problems of a familiar kind, dependent usually on common sense (in the form of a cultural sophistication).

Now, for normal persons, vocabulary and information tests are among the most valid tests of intelligence, and the Binet-type test in general is what best predicts the subject's level of problem-solving outside the laboratory or clinic, in a wide range of situations. This is what presents us with our problem: how can they also be the ones that show the least effect of brain operation, and the degenerative changes of senescence?

But we must consider at once a further fact: that *in certain essential respects, 'intelligence' does not decrease after the age of twenty or thirty, and the brain-operated patient very frequently demonstrates an unimpaired level of functioning in his daily occupations.* The patient with an IQ of 160 after prefrontal lobectomy graduated with honors in his arts course and went on to do well in medical school; the patients with half the cortex removed *clearly did not act in any respect like the feeble-minded,* in their daily affairs. Certain intellectual capacities *are* well retained by the patient; in some respects, the prediction made by the Binet-type test *is* valid. The puzzle is not why the Binet suddenly loses its diagnostic value after brain injury; but why an important part of intelligence is little affected by the injury. The fact that it is not, at once suggests that this part of intelligence is not directly correlated with the integrity of the brain; and, since the problems in which 'intelligence' is unimpaired are in general those with which the patient is familiar, a further suggestion is that part of intelligence is a product of experience.

An idea of this sort led to the examination of the effects of early brain injury (with the help of Doctor Heinz Werner); the results, in short, indicated that any damage to the infant brain would affect later performance on vocabulary tests, information, and the like at least as much as performance on other tests. The situation apparently is this. Unless every known case of large damage to the infant cortex is a case of speech-area damage (a most improbable situation), destruction of tissue outside the speech areas will prevent the development of verbal abilities, but the same destruction may not greatly affect these abilities once development has occurred.

The evidence for this interpretation is not perfect, but it is rather strong. The one flaw appears to be the possibility that the known cortical-type birth-injury population is made up predominantly or entirely of patients with speech-area lesions. It is conceivable that when palsy is not present only speech-area cases are detected – that all the 'exogenous' cases of mental deficiency are discovered because of damage to this particular cortical area alone. But against this possibility is the fact that cases of palsy, presumably detected because of it, also have the low verbal test scores characteristic of other birth-injury cases. The twelve cases reported by Doll, Phelps and Melcher (1932) showed marked vocabulary retardation. The low vocabulary score of the birth-injured is not due to deficient opportunity to learn the meaning of words – a conclusion supported by the almost identical retardations of vocabulary and digit-repetition scores reported by Doll, Phelps and Melcher. Further, Doll (1933) reported that there is no correlation of speech defect and IQ in the birth-injured.

It appears, therefore, that an early injury may prevent the development of some intellectual capacities that an equally extensive injury, at maturity, would not have destroyed. To complete the picture, it should be said again that this relationship does not hold – at least not to the same degree – for all intellectual capacities; and sensory and motor capacities after damage to the infant brain tend to reach a higher level than that attained after destruction of the same regions at maturity.

How are we to understand the first type of capacity in the adult, the one that is not greatly affected by brain damage at maturity? Psychologically, the matter might be put this way. The actual modifications of behavior that occur in intellectual development are from one point of view qualitative; faced with a complex situation, the more intelligent subject sees it in a different way, and makes a different response – not more responses, or responses that take more effort. The chief intellectual effort, in such behavior, is demanded on the *first* occasion on which the new way of seeing the situation occurs. Learning to solve a problem usually demands more effort than solving other problems of the same kind on later occasions when one has discovered the principle involved. The same is often true of perception, whether one is solving a formal problem or not; once one has seen a certain relationship in a picture, or heard it in music, it may take no effort to find it again in similar pictures or music. This perception of relationships is essential in problem-solving, and one would steadily accumulate an increasing stock of such ways of seeing and attacking problem situations, as age advances; so, in a familiar field, the fifty-year-old may be definitely more 'intelligent' (as defined by the problems he can solve) than a twenty-year-old. At the same time, the problem that requires a radically new approach, or new ways of perceiving, is not likely to be solved by the older man with his shrunken brain. The difference in the demands that are made by different professions, or different fields of investigation, would account for the fact that some fields are characteristically the domain of young men, others of the middle-aged. We cannot simply generalize, and say that intellectual capacity, objectively defined, decreases from the age of twenty-five onward. Some capacities do; others do not.

Physiologically, the matter may be put as follows: some types of behavior that require a large amount of brain tissue for their first establishment can then persist when the amount of available tissue has been decreased. This of course is consistent with the theory of cell-assemblies that has been presented in this monograph. It has been postulated that, with the enlargement of synaptic knobs, the number of fibers necessary for transmission at the synapse decreases. In the first establishment of an assembly, then, more fibers are necessary than for its later functioning.

Also, it has been said that there is a possibility of 'short-circuiting' in the phase sequence so that, after a phase sequence has been well established, some assemblies may no longer be necessary to it. If brain injury occurs in a limited region of the brain, it would presumably remove a small number of transmission paths from each of a very large number of assemblies. These assemblies might still function, though they would have smaller safety margins and therefore would function less reliably. In other assemblies, the loss might be great enough to prevent any functioning; but a phase sequence in which some of these assemblies were originally essential might later short-circuit them, and produce the same ultimate insight or understanding of the situation, though some of the steps of inference would have been omitted.

Visual stimulation may have been involved in the formation of some concept, and yet not be necessary to its later arousal. Thus the congenitally blind would be incapable of insights and understanding possessed by those who have become blind after having had vision. In the same way, an area-18 lesion might prevent certain 'visual' assemblies from functioning. These may have been originally necessary, as a connecting link, in the establishment of connections between other assemblies, constituting a particular conceptual activity; but once the connections are established, the connecting link may not be needed any longer. The same area-18 lesion in infancy thus might prevent a conceptual development but not destroy it at maturity.

The two meanings of 'intelligence'

The clinical evidence has indicated, in effect, that there are two components in intelligence-test performance and in any intelligent behavior. One is diminished immediately by damage to the brain, and amounts to a factor of heredity; one is related more to experience, consisting of permanent changes in the organization of pathways in the cerebrum (in the present theory, these changes are the establishment first of assemblies of cells, and secondly of interfacilitation between assemblies). The hereditary factor is essentially the capacity for elaborating perceptions and conceptual activities; the experiential factor is the degree to which such elaboration has occurred (and particularly, when we speak of intelligence, the conceptual elaboration that is not specific to one occupation or situation, but that enters into many human activities; concepts of number, of causal relations, of common human behavior, and so on).

From this point of view it appears that the word 'intelligence' has *two* valuable meanings. One is (*A*) an *innate potential*, the capacity for development, a fully innate property that amounts to the possession of a good brain and a good neural metabolism. The second is (*B*) the functioning of a brain in which development has gone on, determining an *average level of performance or comprehension* by the partly grown or mature person. Neither, of course, is observed directly; but *intelligence B*, a hypothetical level of development in brain function, is a much more direct inference from behavior than *intelligence A*, the original potential. (I emphasize that these are not two parallel kinds of intelligence, coexistent, but two different meanings of 'intelligence'.) It is true that estimating intelligence *B* requires a summation of observations of behavior in many different situations, at different times; however, if we assume that such an estimate is possible, what we actually know about an intelligence-test score is that it is primarily related to intelligence *B* rather than intelligence *A*. The relationship to *A* is less direct.

Most of the disagreement in recent years over the nature of 'intelligence' concerns the relation of *A*, innate potential, to *B*, the estimated level of functioning at maturity. If *A* determines *B* fully, 'intelligence' is a matter of heredity and maturation only; the IQ is not dependent on experience. But if intelligence *A* is only one of the conditions of intelligence *B*, not the sole determinant, what then? Intelligence *A* is still hereditary, and it would not be true to say that 'intelligence' (without qualification) is influenced by experience: only intelligence B is so affected.

The dispute in the current literature has arisen, I believe, partly because of the double reference of the term 'intelligence' and partly because it has not been realized that if the effects of early experience are more or less generalized and permanent one can concede a major effect of experience on the IQ, and still leave the IQ its constancy and validity as an index of future performance.

An innate potential for development is not logically a guarantee that the development will occur. There is in fact an overwhelming body of evidence to show that experience is essential to the development (the original potentiality is of course equally essential). Binet himself assumed the necessity of adequate experience in the subject to be examined by his method; the content of intelligence tests still makes this a necessary precondition; and all psychologists recognize that one cannot compare the innate intelligence of subjects from two different cultures: experience affects their IQs to an unknown degree. Why then should we object to the idea that enriching an inadequate environment will raise the IQ, as Stoddard and Wellman (1940) and others have urged?

Some of the objection, certainly, may be occasioned by a faulty use of evidence and be due to the impression that the case for an environmental influence on the IQ has been overstated. But the roots of the objection, I believe, are to be found in certain ideas about the nature of learning. It is apt to be assumed that learning is more or less specific to particular situations; that what is learned can always be forgotten; or that if something can be learned in infancy it can also be learned at maturity. Assuming the truth of such propositions, one might then think as follows: 'If the IQ has any great dependence on learning it must fluctuate easily; it might be raised from 100 to 150 in the adult, or might fall from 100 to 70 if a child is removed from school and other stimulating influences. But the IQ does not in fact behave so – therefore learning does not contribute to it. It must be hereditary, because it is so stable.'

However, there are definite limits to the 'constancy' of the IQ; and most of the facts that seem to show that it is hereditarily determined would be accounted for if we assume that heredity only sets a *limit* to the IQ, and assume also that early learning tends to be permanent, that it has generalized transfer effects, and that it is not specific to particular situations. That early learning has such properties has already been suggested, in the first part of

Chapter 6 [not reproduced here]. I wish now to report some preliminary experiments with the rat, which seem to show that some aspects of this animal's intelligence at maturity are a function of his early experience. If this principle can be established by means of animal experiment, we can then see how it could be applied to the known facts of human intelligence and intelligence-test performance.

Experiment: infant experience and adult problem-solving

When we test human intelligence, we always assume that the subject has had a certain body of experience common to all 'normal' children in the community, the experience whose *lack* may invalidate comparison of the innate potential of subjects from different communities. Apart entirely from controversy about the effect of special experiences on the IQ, we are all agreed, in this sense, on the effect of a certain kind of experience (which is not, however, well defined).

One purpose of the experimental work briefly described here was to find out more about how the ordinary experience of infancy affects mature behavior. It was not certain that such effects could be found in rat behavior, even if they exist for man; but if one could find some trace of them in rat behavior their nature could be investigated much more easily in a species that reaches maturity in three months than in one that takes fifteen years. Also, the clinical evidence reviewed in this chapter has indicated that the effect of early experience is not found equally in all forms of behavior. Accordingly, these were exploratory experiments, with the main object of establishing the existence of some lasting effect of early experience on the later problem-solving of the rat. The first explorations gave wholly negative results, but they have the value of showing that some behavior is *not* affected by early experience; that is, they serve to delimit the effect.

In the first part of the study, one group of seven animals were blinded in infancy, and a group of seven litter-mates were blinded at maturity. Both groups were handled frequently, and were allowed daily to run outside their cages in a large space in which there were a number of objects. The question asked was this. Would the group with vision during growth learn something about finding their way around that they would retain after being blinded at maturity? Would this affect their behavior permanently, in other situations than those in which their visual experience occurred?

At the age of five months – two months after the second group were blinded – the rats were trained to find food in one of four containers in an open field. Two hundred trials were given, and the learning was not complete for most of the animals in this time – so this presumably is to be classed as rote learning rather than insightful. A second period of training in a similar task also appeared to give rote learning, and in neither could any significant difference be found between the two groups, early- and late-blinded.

At this point, however, a chance observation suggested the possibility that an 'intelligence test' for the rat might reveal differences between the groups. Although the test had been meant for normal animals, it might work with the blind as well.

The test showed a clear difference between the groups. By this time the experiment was being done with only three late-blinded animals and four early-blinded, a small number for statistical significance. However, there was no overlap of scores in the two groups – all three late-blinded were better than all four early-blinded, which is certainly significant.[1]

Before repeating and confirming this result, it appeared profitable to explore further. The effect of vision during development, on the behavior of rats after being blinded at maturity, was great; would other variations of experience also have effects that could be detected by this – apparently sensitive – method of testing? The obvious experiment was to compare rats reared in ordinary small cages with others that had the run of a wider environment. Two litters were taken home to be reared as pets,[2] a first group of three after one mortality at home, and a second group of four. They were out of their cages a good deal of the time and running about the house. While this was being done, twenty-five cage-reared rats from the same colony were tested.

When the pet group were tested, all seven scored in the top

1. The experiments described in this section are now being repeated and carried further by Hymovitch and Lansdell, and will be reported in detail later. The method has been considerably improved since the first report of Hebb and Williams; it will be described in detail in a separate publication. The essential features of the method are: (1) 10 to 14 days' preliminary training gets the animal used to handling, to the test situation, and to daily changes in the route he must take to food, and teaches him where the food is to be found (its position is constant throughout); (2) the test itself is a series of 20 to 24 separate problems, each relatively easy for the seeing rat; he is given between 6 and 10 trials with each, and his score is the total number of entries into error zones.

2. Grateful acknowledgements are due to the Misses Jane and Ellen Hebb, aged seven and five, for their enthusiastic assistance in the investigation.

third of the total distribution for cage-reared and pets. More important still, the pets improved their relative standing in the last ten days of testing, following ten days of preliminary training, and eleven days of testing (a total of twenty-one tests was used). One explanation of the better scores of the pets is just that they were tamer, more used to handling, and less disturbed by testing. But, if this were so, the longer the cage-reared animals were worked with the closer they would come to the pet group, as the cage-reared became tamer with prolonged handling. On the contrary, the pets improved more than the cage-reared. This means that *the richer experience of the pet group during development made them better able to profit by new experiences at maturity* – one of the characteristics of the 'intelligent' human being. Furthermore, a measure of motivation and tameness in the cage-reared was available, and the correlation of this with the test score was negligible ($0.130 \pm .19$).

These results show a permanent effect of early experience on problem-solving at maturity: 'permanent' because, in the first experiment with early- and late-blinded, visual experience that ended at three months of age had marked effects at eight months of age (a long period in the life of a rat); and because, in the second experiment, the pet group improved its standing compared to the others as experience increased. Differences of early experience can produce differences in adult problem-solving that further experience does not erase.

These preliminary results are already being confirmed by more elaborate experiments now going on, and a principle is established that, first, is fully in accord with other evidence showing lasting and generalized effects of early experience and, secondly, clarifies the interpretation of existing data concerning human intelligence-test performance.

The nature and nurture of intelligence

Actually, some of the data on normal human intelligence (as well as the clinical data) allow only one interpretation, namely, that there is a major effect of experience on the IQ. One difficulty in accepting this interpretation is that it may seem to deny the validity of the intelligence-test method. But, if the principle of a lasting and generalized effect of early learning is accepted, not only on the IQ but also on the every-day problem-solving of the adult, the validity of the intelligence-test method may be extended, not reduced. It is common to say that an intelligence test is not valid when given to a foreigner or a Negro. Not valid in what sense? As an estimate of innate potentiality, of intelligence A. It may be quite valid, on a purely empirical footing, for estimating intelligence B – the actual level of comprehension, learning, and problem-solving *in this culture*. Separating these two meanings of 'intelligence' allows one to show where the test is valid, as well as where it is invalid.

Look closer at this question of the relationship between test score and culture. It is agreed by psychologists that the IQs of different peoples should not be compared, since intelligence tests are culture-loaded and not equally fair to subjects from different cultures. Now it is quite clear from the context of such discussion that the 'unfairness' lies in estimating a subject's hereditary endowment. Negroes living in the United States make lower average scores on intelligence tests than whites do, but we cannot conclude that the Negro has a poorer brain than the white. Why? Negro and white speak the same language, are taught in the same curriculum and sometimes in the same schools, work at the same plants, and on the whole intermingle very freely. Why then does the Negro's IQ not have the same meaning as a white man's? Because Negro and white do not have the opportunity to learn to speak the language with equal range and accuracy, are not usually taught in equally good schools, and do not have equally good jobs or equal exposure to cultural influences that usually require a fairly good income.

All this we can accept; but when we do so we must recognize that we have completely undermined the argument that differences of IQ among white, native Americans are determined by heredity.

In what respect does the argument, concerning the Negro's IQ and his innate endowment, differ for the poor white in the South and the white tenement dweller in the North? *They* do not have opportunity to acquire the same vocabulary, are often taught in poor schools, do not get good jobs or have good salaries. The extent of this influence of experience is quite unknown; conceivably, it is small; but one cannot argue that Negro and white IQs cannot be compared, and at the same time that those of white and white can be, when the white subjects have different social backgrounds. The IQ can be trusted as an index of intelligence A only when the social backgrounds of the subjects compared are identical; and this adds up to the proposition that we cannot in any rigorous sense measure a subject's innate endowment, for no two social backgrounds are identical and we do not know what the important environmental variables are in the development of intellectual functions. Intelligence *A* may sometimes be estimated, but it cannot be measured.

Intelligence in sense *B* is a different matter. We know, beyond dispute, that the adolescent with generally low intelligence-test scores, whether Negro, poor white American, or foreigner, is a poor prospect for college training, or training as a mechanic, or Army officer, or dress designer. The inability to determine intelligence *A* from a test score should not blind us to the fact that a foreigner's intelligence *B* can be estimated, as far as its operation in this culture is concerned.

To be a bank manager, an airplane pilot, a mathematician, a secretary, or a surgeon requires a certain common conceptual development that must occur in this or a closely related culture, and in childhood mainly; and intelligence tests on the whole can provide a rather good index of the extent to which that development has occurred. No other interpretation seems possible of the differences, *both in educability and in intelligence-test scores*, of first- and second-generation immigrants. Supposing that both have an adequate nutrition, father and son must have on the average the same intelligence *A*; the son very often has a much higher intelligence *B*.

The nature of the cultural environment that is necessary to this conceptual development cannot be described accurately. It does not necessarily consist of a formal schooling, and it may be present in spite of poverty. In general, one might guess, it consists of an exposure to ideas, to books, and to intelligent conversation; the opportunity to acquire common technical knowledge and skills; and exposure to persons with social skills, who are good at getting along with other persons. Besides being a guess, of course, such a statement is pretty vague and shows rather clearly how much we cannot say about the matter. Also, we have no way of knowing what ceiling there is on this environmental influence, at what age it is greatest, and so on. Such questions can be answered only by further research.

Our information at present is scanty, almost entirely naturalistic rather than experimental in origin. Neff's (1938) review will show the interested reader how definite the evidence is that environment has a major effect on the IQ. Identical-twin data, for example, are commonly supposed to have shown that heredity is the only major determinant of 'intelligence'. In none of the studied pairs, however, was one twin brought up in an entirely favorable environment, one in an entirely unfavorable environment; usually they were brought up in about the same stratum of society, so that similar IQs may be the result of similar environment, a similar heredity, or both.

What we really want, as evidence on this point, is one twin brought up in a good home, with books, toys, kindergarten training, and plenty of exposure to intelligent adults; the other brought up by illiterate, poverty-stricken, anti-social mountaineers with low IQs: *then* test their intelligences at maturity, and try making doctors, or politicians, of both twins. When this is done, and when it has been shown that the twin with a poor environment (for the first fifteen years of life) can with time become as good a diagnostician or committeeman as his genetically identical brother, it will then be in order to say that the factual evidence shows that 'intelligence' and the IQ are without any major effect from experience; not before.

If the Iowa studies (Stoddard and Wellman, 1940) are distrusted, the studies of Gordon, Asher, and Jordan, among others reviewed by Neff, all tell the same story. The constancy of the IQ is the main argument for its being determined by heredity; but the fact is that the IQ is not constant – it is stable, and changes slowly, and more and more slowly as maturity is approached, so that the IQ *of the adult* may be constant (though there are few data on long-term comparisons even here). But prediction of the adult IQ, in infancy, is more accurate on the basis of the parents' IQs than on that of the infant himself; from an IQ at the age of five, prediction of the IQ at twelve is about 20 per cent better than chance prediction, very little better than can be done from knowing what kind of home the child is growing up in.

There are then two determinants of intellectual growth: a *completely necessary* innate potential (intelligence *A*), and a *completely necessary* stimulating environment. It is not to the point to ask which is more important; hypothetically, we might suppose that intelligence will rise to the limit set by heredity *or* environment, whichever is lower. Given a perfect environment, the inherited constitution will set the pace; given the heredity of a genius, the environment will do so.

The essentials of this environmental influence cannot be specified. Though we know that wealth, prolonged schooling, or 'intelligent' parents (that is, with intelligence *B*) are not essential, these things all may contribute. Since the guess has been made that the essential is exposure to intelligence *B*, it is presumably true that the child must either have intelligent parents or intelligent acquaintances and teachers. Schooling also is becoming more and more necessary to an understanding of adult problems in this society; and a certain amount of wealth, of freedom from economic pressure, may be quite necessary to full intellectual development. The fact is, however, that we know almost nothing specific about the matter. The country may be full of potential geniuses, for all we know, and it should be a pressing concern for psychology to discover the conditions that will develop whatever potentialities a child may have.

References

DOLL, E. A. (1933), 'Psychological significance of cerebral birth lesions', *Amer. J. Psychol.*, vol. 45, pp. 444–52.

DOLL, E. A., PHELPS, W. M. and MELCHER, R. T. (1932), *Mental Deficiency Due to Birth Injuries*, Macmillan Co.

HEBB, D. O. (1942), 'The effect of early and late brain injury upon test scores, and the nature of normal adult intelligence', *Proc. Amer. Phil. Soc.*, vol. 85, pp. 275–92.

NEFF, W. S. (1938), 'Socioeconomic status and intelligence: a critical survey', *Psych. Bull.*, vol. 35, pp. 727–57.

STODDARD, G. D. and WELLMAN, B. L. (1940), 'Environment and the IQ', *Yearl. Nat. Soc. Stud. Educ.*, vol. 39, no. 1, pp. 405–42

WEISENBURG, T., ROE, A. and MCBRIDE, K. E. (1936), *Adult Intelligence: A Psychological Study of Test Performance*, Commonwealth Fund, New York.

9 C. Burt

The Evidence for the Concept of Intelligence

Abridged and revised by the author from 'The evidence for the concept of intelligence', *British Journal of Educational Psychology*, vol. 25, 1955, pp. 158–77.

The non-statistical evidence
Current criticisms

The concept of 'intelligence', and the attempt to measure intelligence by standardized tests, have of late become the subject of attack from several different quarters. The objections urged are partly practical and partly theoretical. Yet few of the critics show a clear or correct understanding of what the term really designates or of the reasons that led to its introduction. Two misconceptions are widely current. Writers who are chiefly interested in the more practical issues declare that intelligence 'is a popular and relatively unambiguous word', and denotes a quality that 'all can recognize, though few can define': as such it is 'too elusive to measure'. Hence, instead of pinning IQs on to the coat of each child, we ought, so they tell us, to leave all such decisions to the intuitive insight of the teacher. Writers who discuss the more technical aspects of the subject seem for the most part to suppose that the concept, if not the name, was invented by a small band of statistical enthusiasts – one critic mentions Spearman, Pearson, and myself – who deduced their theories by primitive factorial procedures that have since been 'publicly discredited': the more accurate methods of Thurstone and his American followers, they say, have since clearly shown that the intellectual achievements of different individuals are the product, not of a single general factor, but of a number of more specialized 'primary abilities'. And this at once accounts for the difficulty that besets all attempts to produce an agreed definition. As Captain Kettle observed, when asked why the pictures of the Saghalien sea-serpent showed such incredible differences: '"Spects it's because there's no such crittur"; so each just draws his fancy.'

The definition of intelligence

Most of the critics who protest about 'the spate of incongruous definitions' rest their complaint on the results of the famous Symposium organized some twenty years ago (Thurstone, 1921). The editor of an American journal submitted two searching questions about the nature of intelligence to a dozen differing psychologists, and received a dozen different replies. But the varying descriptions suggested were not (as is commonly supposed by those who still quote them) intended to be 'definitions' in the strict logical sense; they were, in the language of J. S. Mill, merely 'attempts to explain the thing', not 'attempts to interpret the word'. As the editorial letter shows, the purpose of the discussion was primarily a practical one – to determine how intelligence appears to operate, with a view to ascertaining 'what material may most profitably be used in constructing tests'. But that is a separate question, and, except incidentally, will not concern us here. The questions I now want to settle are prior to all these: namely, (1) how precisely is the word to be defined, and (2) what evidence is there for believing that something really exists corresponding to the definition proposed? Instead of taking the term for granted and hunting round for a plausible formula, as is most frequently done, a sound scientific procedure requires us to start with the relevant facts: so let us take the second of our two questions first.

History of the concept

Many of the current criticisms spring largely from a manifest ignorance as to how the concept originated. A glance at the earlier literature is, therefore, necessary first of all.[1] As a brief historical review will show, long before the advent of statistical analysis several converging lines of evidence had already drawn attention to an important property of the mind, for which some special name seemed desirable.

1. *Observational*. The earliest attempts to analyse and classify mental activities were based partly on the observation of various types of person in everyday life and partly on introspection. Plato, to whom we owe the basic distinctions, drew a clear contrast between 'nature' and 'nurture', and then distinguished three 'parts' or aspects of the soul (*Republic*, 435A f.). The modern terms – intellectual, emotional, and moral – cognition, affection,

1. A more detailed account will be found in Burt (1924).

and conation – suggest rough but somewhat inexact equivalents for his untranslatable expressions. In a celebrated passage (*Phaedrus*, 253D) he sketches a picturesque analogy which conveys a better notion of the fundamental difference: the first component he compares to a charioteer who holds the reins, and the other to a pair of horses who draw the vehicle; the former guides, the latter supply the power; the former is the *cybernetic*[2] or directive element, the latter the *dynamic*. 'Intelligence,' said Sully, 'steers like a rudder; emotion and interest supply the steam.'

Aristotle makes a further contribution. He contrasts the actual or concrete activity with the hypothetical capacity[3] on which it depends, and thus introduces the idea of an 'ability'. Plato's threefold classification he reduces to a twofold. For him the main distinction is between what he calls the 'dianoetic' (cognitive or intellectual) capacities of the mind and the 'orectic' (emotional and moral). Finally, Cicero, in an endeavour to supply a Latin terminology for Greek philosophy, translated Aristotle's term for 'capacity' by *facultas*, and 'orexis' by *appetitio* (or sometimes *conatus*) respectively, while to designate *dianoia* he coined a new word, rendering the Greek work almost literally by the compound '*intelligentia*' (inter-legentia).

Here then we have the origin of both the concept and the name. So far from being a 'word of popular speech', whose meaning has been restricted and distorted by the modern psychologist, intelligence is a highly technical expression invented to denote a highly technical abstraction. From Aristotle and Cicero it descended to the mediaeval schoolmen, and the scholastic theories in turn became elaborated into the cut-and-dried schemes of the faculty psychologists and their phrenological followers.

2. *Biological.* As Guilford has remarked, the modern notion of 'intelligence as a unitary entity' was 'a gift to psychology from biology through the instrumentality of Herbert Spencer'. Following Aristotle and the later Scottish school, Spencer recognized two main aspects of mental life – the cognitive and the affective. All cognition (he explains) involves both an analytic or discriminative and a synthetic or integrative process; and its essential

2. As those who are familiar with the recent development of 'cybernetics' will be aware, the Greek noun (from which our own word 'governor' is derived) means 'a steersman, or director'.

3. *De Anima*, II, 3, 414a, 31. *Eth. Nic.*, I, 13, 18, 1102b, 30. The usual rendering 'power' must not be taken to imply causal agency: Aristotle is simply describing what Professor Broad has called a 'dispositional property'.

function is to enable the organism to adjust itself more effectively to a complex and ever-changing environment. During the evolution of the animal kingdom, and during the growth of the individual child, the fundamental capacity of cognition 'progressively differentiates into a hierarchy of more specialized abilities' – sensory, perceptual, associative, and relational, much as the trunk of a tree sprouts into boughs, branches, and twigs. To designate the basic characteristic he revived the term 'intelligence' (Spencer, 1870). Evidence favouring Spencer's somewhat speculative theories was adduced by Lloyd Morgan and other pioneers of comparative psychology; and his views on intelligence were accepted, not only by British biologists like Darwin, but also by continental writers like Binet and Claparède, and more recently by Piaget (1950). Mendel's earliest disciples maintained that his whole doctrine of unit-characters was utterly irreconcilable with the inheritability of a *graded* trait, such as intelligence; but as we shall see in a moment, the later developments of the Mendelian hypothesis not only permit it, but actually suggest it.

3. *Physiological.* The clinical work of Hughlings Jackson, the experimental investigations of Sherrington, and the microscopical studies of the brain carried out by Campbell, Brodmann, and others, have done much to confirm Spencer's theory of a 'hierarchy of neural functions', with a basic type of activity developing by fairly definite stages into higher and more specialized forms. In particular, the examination of the cortex, both in mental defectives and in normal persons, suggests that the quality of the nervous tissue in any given individual tends to be predominantly the same throughout. Defectives, for instance, exhibit a 'general cerebral immaturity'; their nerve cells tend to be 'visibly deficient in number, branching, and regularity of arrangement in every part of the cortex'. After all, as Sherrington himself observes, much the same is true of almost every tissue of which the human frame is composed – of a man's skin, bones, hair, or muscles; each is of the same general character all over the body, although minor local variations are usually discernible. In the adult human brain marked differences in the architecture of different areas and of different cell-layers are perceptible under the microscope; and these specializations emerge and develop progressively during the early months of infant life. And, of course, such differentiation is precisely what the Spencerian theory would entail. The earlier histologists, whose maps of the brain still figure in elementary textbooks of physiology as Sholl and others have recently pointed

out, 'greatly exaggerated the definiteness in the localization of different functions in the brain, and overlooked the enormous amount of difference between different human brains'. (Sholl, 1956.)

The experimental study of the brain leads to the same conclusion. The intact brain always acts as a whole (*see* Lashley, 1929). No part of the brain functions in total isolation from the rest, as the older champions of cortical localization originally assumed. The activity, in Sherrington's phrase, is 'patterned, not indifferently diffuse'; but the patterning itself 'involves and implies integration'. The evidence of neurology, therefore, suggests something very like a theory of general ability, which gradually differentiates into more specific functions, though we must beware of picturing such functions as separate 'faculties' located in certain centres or compartments of the brain, after the fashion of the older phrenologists.

4. *Individual psychology.* All these earlier writers were interested primarily in the working of the mind as such, that is to say, in problems of *general* psychology. The first to apply scientific methods for the problems of *individual* psychology was Galton, Charles Darwin's half-cousin. Darwin and Spencer had maintained that the basic capacities of the human mind were hereditary, transmitted as part of our common racial endowment. Galton went farther and maintained that individual differences in these capacities were also innate. As a result of his investigations into 'hereditary genius', he was led to discard the traditional explanation in terms of faculties and types, and to substitute a classification in terms of 'general ability' and 'special aptitudes'. Of the two he considered general ability to be 'by far the most powerful'. 'Numerous instances,' he says,

recorded in this book, show in how small a degree eminence is due to purely special faculties: people lay too much stress on specialties, thinking that because a man shines in some particular pursuit, he could not have succeeded in anything else. They might just as well say that because a youth has fallen in love with a brunette, he could not have fallen in love with a blonde. It is as probable as not that the whole affair was due to a *general* amorousness. It is the same with mental pursuits. . . . Without a special gift for mathematics, a man cannot be a mathematician; but without a high degree of general ability he will never make a *great* mathematician. (Galton, 1869.)

Much the same view was maintained by Dr Johnson. Robertson, the historian, had argued that it was by virtue of very different gifts that Newton had become a great scientist, Caesar a great commander, Shakespeare a great poet. 'No,' replied Johnson, 'it is only that one man has more mind than another, though he may prefer this matter to that. Sir, the man who has vigour may walk to the North as well as to the South, to the East as well as to the West.' (Boswell, 1791.)[4]

The definition implied

These converging lines of inquiry, therefore, furnished strong presumptive evidence for a mental trait of fundamental import-ance defined by three verifiable attributes: first, it is a *general* quality; it enters into every form of mental activity; secondly, it is (in a broad sense of the word) an *intellectual* quality – that is, it characterizes the cognitive rather than the affective or conative aspects of conscious behaviour; thirdly, it is inherited or at least *innate*; differences in its strength or amount are due to differences in the individual's genetic constitution. We thus arrive at the concept of an *innate, general, cognitive ability*. We cannot, how-ever, keep repeating a cumbersome phrase of twelve syllables every time we wish to mention it. And, since a name that suggests its own meaning seems preferable to a brand-new esoteric symbol, what better label can be found than the traditional term 'intelli-gence'?

Here then is a clearly formulated hypothesis, the outcome of centuries of shrewd observation and plausible conjecture – a psychological hypothesis fully in accord with the findings of the biologist and neurologist. Nevertheless, each of the three pro-positions that I have just laid down has been vigorously chal-lenged; and at this point, therefore, the need for *ad hoc* inquiries based on more rigorous experimental and statistical techniques becomes plain.

The statistical evidence

1. *The general factor*. At the beginning of the century the problem which chiefly exercised students of individual psychology was, in

4. Carlyle defends much the same conclusion: 'I have no notion of a truly great man who couldn't be all sorts of men – poet, prophet, priest, king, or what you will' (*On Heroes*, Lect. III). Galton's usual term was 'general ability'. In French, however, the corresponding word (*habileté*) has a differ-ent meaning. Hence Binet (1905), in adopting Galton's view, substituted the term 'intelligence'; and, largely as a result of the wide popularity of his 'intelligence tests' in this country, 'intelligence' became the more usual name.

Bain's phrase, 'the classification of intellectual abilities or *powers*'.

(a) Were there, as the faculty psychologists maintained, a number of specialized abilities, each independent of the rest – observation, practical ability, memory, language, reasoning, and the like? (b) Or was there, as Ward maintained, 'not a congeries of faculties, but only a single subjective activity' – a general capacity for cognition as such? (c) Were there, as Galton[5] believed, both a general ability and a number of more or less specialized capacities? (d) Or, finally, might there be, as the earlier associationists and most of the later behaviourists alleged, no discernible structure in the mind at all?

Each hypothesis entailed its own distinctive corollaries; and Galton's technique of correlation offered a ready-made method of checking them. Thus, the obvious plan for attacking such a many-sided issue was to devise and apply experimental tests to measure the main forms of mental activity, and then calculate the correlations between each test and the rest. If, for example, the behaviourist view is right, and there is 'no organized structure in the mind, no ground for classifying mental performances under one or more broad headings, no basis for inferring efficiency in one type of activity from efficiency in another', then we should expect *all the inter-correlations to be zero* or at least non-significant.[6] If, on the other hand, the mind consists of a number of specialized faculties or abilities, such as 'observation' (assessed

5. Many contemporary writers, particularly in the field of education, attribute the antithesis between 'general' and 'special' abilities to Spearman. Spearman himself, however, frankly admitted his own theories were prompted by those of Galton and Spencer. However, in his earlier writings he definitely rejected the notion of 'special aptitudes', as merely a relic of 'the discredited faculties of the older school' (1904).

6. Thomson's sampling theory, though expressed in language similar to that of the 'anti-structural psychologists', leads to very different corollaries. 'The Mind,' he says (1948), 'has little structure: unlike the body, it is not subdivided into distinct organs, but forms a comparatively undifferentiated complex of innumerable elements.' These he pictures as 'bonds', i.e. interconnecting neural paths: they have the same character or quality throughout the brain. But, so far from the effects of specific stimuli being limited to specific neural paths (as the earlier opponents of structure assumed), '*any* sample whatever of these elements can be assembled in the activity called for by a "test"'.

by tests of sensory capacity), and 'practical ability' (assessed by tests of motor capacity), and so on, then we should expect that all the inter-correlations between the sensory tests would be positive and similarly that all the inter-correlations between the motor tests would be positive; on the other hand, we should expect that *all the cross-correlations between the one group and the other would be approximately zero*. Lastly, if there were no specific faculties at all, but only 'a single cognitive activity' – 'attention', as Ward believed, 'sensory discriminations', as Sully, and later Spearman, maintained – then we should expect the entire table of correlations to exhibit what Spearman called 'a perfect hierarchical order', or (in the more precise language of the mathematical textbook) to form 'a matrix of rank one' – apart, of course, from minor aberrations due to sampling errors.

The results of the earlier inquiries revealed, almost without exception, *positive and significant correlations between every form of cognitive activity*. This disproves hypotheses (a) and (d). Further, except when the sample was small and the sampling errors large, there were nearly always *well-marked clusters of augmented correlations confined to similar forms of cognitive activity*, and leaving significant residuals after the general factor was removed. This rules out hypothesis (b). We are thus left with hypothesis (c) as the only alternative consistent with the facts. And, accordingly, the unavoidable inference is that *both* a 'general factor' *and* a number of 'group factors' must be at work. (Burt, 1909.)[7]

But we are not yet justified in identifying this abstract 'general factor' with anything so concrete as 'general intelligence'. In Spearman's investigations 'general intelligence' was always represented by an *external* criterion, i.e. by teachers' assessments for intelligence as popularly understood, or (in later researches) by standard tests, selected as furnishing accredited 'reference values'. In my own investigations, the 'general cognitive factor' formed an *internal* criterion, namely, what I called the 'highest common factor' in the battery of tests. And to determine the concrete nature of such a factor, or rather of the processes that give rise to it, a supplementary investigation was used, based on

7. Since Spearman did not believe in the existence of multiple factors, he never used 'factor analysis' as the term is commonly understood. This method was in fact devised by Pearson to analyse bodily measurements: *see* Burt (1949).

observations and introspections, and on the correlation of the factor measurements with independent gradings.[8]

Later investigators, notably Brown, Thomson, and more recently Thurstone, have argued that, if we accept the existence of group factors or 'primary abilities', we can dispense with the hypothesis of a general factor by assuming that the group factors overlap. Thurstone in his earlier researches used the same simplified formula which I had proposed (Burt, 1917)[9] – the so-called 'centroid formula' – but rotated the factors thus obtained so as to secure a 'simple structure' of 'primary abilities'. But, to get a satisfactory fit, it was nearly always necessary to allow these 'primary abilities' (the 'first-order factors') to be correlated with each other. Later, however, he put forward a method for deriving uncorrelated 'second-order factors' which should include a 'general factor' accounting for the correlations between the 'primary abilities'. Thus his final scheme was practically identical with that which my co-workers and I had produced. In their more recent writings both Brown and Thomson eventually acknowledged that 'the evidence for a general factor now seems conclusive'. Thomson indeed constructed numerous booklets for testing intelligence, notably the 'Moray House Tests' which have been so widely used in the eleven-plus examinations. (Brown and Stephenson 1933; Thomson, 1948; Thurstone, 1947.)

Granted the existence of a general factor, what is its relative importance? In nearly every study of cognitive abilities among children of school age, it appears that the general factor accounts

8. Actually teachers' gradings for 'intelligence' (as I showed in my 1909 research) are markedly biased in favour of memory or capacity to learn; Spearman, following Sully and the sensationist school, originally equated intelligence with 'sensory discrimination' as the basic form of mental *analysis*. Ward, Stout and others inclined to identify it with 'attention' or 'apperception', i.e. mental or 'noetic' *synthesis*. This early disagreement about the 'nature of intelligence' is no reason for repudiating the concept: after all, there is little agreement about the 'nature' of gravity: but that is no reason for discarding the principle. And, in point of fact, the conflict can easily be reconciled if we borrow the suggestion of the neurologists and supposes its function to be that of 'integration', i.e. organization, which involves both analysis and synthesis.

9. Much of the work of Thurstone and his followers was carried out with students and older persons, who show far more specialization than school children; moreover the older groups available for testing are nearly always partly selected for intelligence, and consequently exhibit a narrower range of variation. Thurstone and most American investigators ignore all the concurrent biological and physiological evidence, and rely almost exclusively on statistical analysis.

for about 50 per cent of the individual variability – rather more in the case of the younger age-groups, rather less as their age increases and special abilities begin to mature. Hence, for purposes of prediction – forecasting what this or that particular child is likely to achieve in school or in after-life the general factor is by far the most useful, though by no means the only, guide.

2. *The factor as cognitive.* Merely to demonstrate the presence of a general factor common to all cognitive activities does not of itself suffice to prove that this factor is specifically cognitive. Impressed by this obvious ambiguity, several writers went on to argue that in all probability the factor common to all mental and scholastic activities was not cognitive but conative. Such an interpretation had a warm appeal for those who cherished the doctrine of intellectual equality. When a pupil lagged behindhand in nearly every subject, many teachers laid the blame on what Ballard dubbed the 'general factor of laziness'. Conversely, when a bright child forged ahead in all he undertook, he found himself applauded as a paragon of industry and held up to his fellows as a model of zeal; 'genius,' said the apostles of the gospel of work, 'is just an infinite capacity for taking pains'. It was partly as a result of this alternative interpretation that Spearman dropped his earlier identifications ('sensory discrimination' in his first paper, 'neural plasticity' in the second) and proposed instead a hypothesis of 'mental energy'.

Accordingly, in our later experiments, my co-workers and I correlated assessments for intellectual performances with assessments for physical, temperamental, and moral qualities. This time most of the cross-correlations were still positive, but extremely low: it seemed as if there was a small but far more comprehensive general factor – a super-factor, as it were – making for excellence in every direction, while the older and more conspicuous factor for cognitive efficiency now appeared simply as a broad group factor, confined to cognitive activities alone: in short, the so-called 'general cognitive factor' turned out to be merely one of the largest of a number of 'group factors' varying in extent and size. At the same time, another broad group factor emerged underlying the temperamental and moral assessments: this was obviously identifiable with what we had previously called 'the general factor for emotionality'. No sharp division, however, was found which would separate affective (or emotional) characteristics from conative (or moral). And the so-called cognitive factor was found to be quite as prominent in tests of practical efficiency as in tests of intellectual activity in the narrower sense. In the light of this further evidence, there was no need to surrender the idea of a cognitive factor. But it certainly appeared necessary to revise the implications conveyed by the word cognition. The basic contrast seems to lie, not so much between cognitive processes and non-cognitive (i.e. affective or conative) in the old introspective sense of those terms, but rather between the capacity for adapting, guiding, or directing mental activities by means of discriminative and integrative processes, and the capacity for responding promptly, actively, and energetically.

3. *The factor as innate.* The evidence we have so far reviewed seems fully to vindicate the notion of a 'general cognitive factor'; and during recent years the most frequent target for attack has been, not so much the existence of such a factor, but rather the assumption that differences in this factor are to a large extent hereditary or at least inborn. The first to collect factual evidence in support of such a conclusion was, once again, Galton. In his earliest inquiries he relied mainly on an analysis of pedigrees (1869). His aim was to show that, if a child had a genius among his various relatives, the likelihood that he himself would be a genius was enormously increased. He collected family histories for nearly a thousand 'eminent men' in various walks of life. An 'eminent' person was defined as the ablest in 4000: from the definition, therefore, it follows that the chance that a boy picked at random would achieve 'eminence' was 1 in 4000. Galton found that, if the boy was the son of a genius, his chance would be increased to about 1 in 4; if the grandson, it would be 1 in 29; if the nephew, 1 in 40; if a first cousin, 1 in 100. He readily recognized that a gifted father would be likely to provide his son with a better education and perhaps use his influence in the boy's favour. This objection he met in various ways: first, by trying to find 'two classes of men with equal advantages, in one of which they have high hereditary gifts, while in the other they have not'; secondly, by noting cases in which the eminent relatives did not in fact influence the child; and thirdly, by noting cases in which the unmistakable genius appeared by a kind of 'spontaneous variation'. Sir Isaac Newton's father, for example, was a simple yeoman–farmer who died before the boy was born; his mother took him from school at the age of fourteen to help run the farm; instead, he devoted himself to mathematics and scientific experiments, showing (according to numerous anecdotes) an amazing precocity. He was accepted at Trinity College, Cambridge, as a

subsizar, which meant that he paid his way by menial work. He became Lucasian Professor at the early age of twenty-seven. As Galton records, later investigations have discovered two exceptionally able scientists among his mother's relatives, one of whom later became secretary to the Royal Society; but the connection seems to have been unrecognized at the time. And Galton goes on to emphasize that 'abundant instances of this emergence from obscurity' are to be found in the pages of his book. D'Alembert was a foundling, afterwards shown to be well-bred in respect of ability, put out to nurse as a pauper baby; largely self-educated, he 'attained first rank as a celebrity by the time he was twenty-four'. Galton's list of 'inborn geniuses who owed little or nothing to their social circumstances' could easily be extended. Gauss, still acclaimed as the greatest mathematician of all time, was the son of a bricklayer; Laplace, almost as brilliant, the son of a farm labourer; James Watt, Whewell, Opie, Lincoln, and Carlyle were sons of carpenters; Marlowe, Winckelmann, and James Mill, sons of cobblers; Thomas Cromwell, David Cox, and Michael Faraday, sons of blacksmiths; Defoe and Wolsey, sons of butchers; Luther, Zwingli, and John Knox, sons of peasants; Kant's father was a strap-maker, Tieck's a rope-maker, Bunyan's a tinker, Franklin's a soap-boiler, Kepler's a drunken inn-keeper; and so one might go on. Still more significant is the amazing precocity of most of those I have named. Many eventually entered a university; but it was generally by their intelligence and hard work that they gained their education, not their education that produced their high intelligence.[10]

Galton fully recognized that these family histories could furnish no more than strong *prima facie* evidence; and for this reason he suggested various new and fruitful methods of investigation – the calculation of correlations, the application of standardized tests, the study of foster-children, and of identical and non-identical twins – many of which he later took up himself. As he pointed out, three distinct questions are really involved: (a) what evidence is there for the *fact* of inheritance, (b) what precisely is the *mode*

10. For my data I have relied chiefly on Havelock Ellis, Terman and Cox, as well as the *Dictionary of National Biography*, and various foreign biographies. The descriptions do not always agree, usually perhaps because the fathers changed their occupations. Many of the fathers, e.g. those of Watt and Gauss, became more or less well-to-do; but they commonly wanted their sons to follow in their footsteps, and 'learn a trade'. Indeed most of the sons might well have adopted Jacques Bernoulli's motto: *Invito patre sidera verso*.

in which intelligence is inherited, and (c) what is the *relative importance* of the genetic factor as compared with the environmental?

(a) *The fact.* In controversies about the fact of mental inheritance most critics have tended to assume that the two causal agencies commonly invoked – heredity and environment – are not merely antithetical, but mutually exclusive. The environmentalists suppose that, once they have shown that intelligence tests are affected by environment, it follows that all differences in intelligence are due to nothing but environment. Similarly the thoroughgoing hereditarians are apt to talk as though they believed that differences in intelligence were due to nothing but genetic constitution. This is the familiar fallacy which I am tempted to label 'nothing-buttery'. With a few rare exceptions, like eye colour or serological differences in the blood, every observable characteristic that geneticists have so far studied has proved to be the product of the joint action of both heredity and environment. There are no such things as hereditary characters; there are only hereditary tendencies.

Now, where two inexplicable factors, such as heredity and environment, are likely to be involved, the obvious procedure will be to keep first one and then the other as constant as possible, and observe the results in either case.

(i) *Uniform environment.* As psychological consultant to the London County Council, I had free access to its orphanages and other residential institutions, and to the private files of case records giving the history of each inmate. My co-workers and I were thus able to study large numbers of children who had been transferred thither during the earliest weeks of infancy and had thus been brought up in an environment that was much the same for all. We found that individual differences in intelligence, so far from being diminished, varied over an unusually wide range. In the majority of instances, they seemed to be correlated with differences in the intelligence of one or both of the parents. Some of the most striking cases were those of illegitimate children of high ability: often the father (as the case records showed) had been a casual acquaintance, of a social and intellectual status well above that of the mother, and had taken no further interest in the child. In instances like these it is out of the question to attribute the high intelligence of the child to the special cultural opportunities furnished by the home environment, since his only home has been the institution.

(ii) *Uniform heredity*. To secure cases in which the children's genetic endowment is the same, we may turn to the assessments obtained for monozygotic or 'identical' twins. Not infrequently the mother is unable or unwilling to bring up two children at the same time, and one is consequently sent to a relative or to a foster home. Owing to the popular prejudice against separating twins, she not unnaturally tries to keep these arrangements secret. But patient and tactful inquiries show that cases of twins brought up in different environments almost from birth are in fact much commoner than is usually believed. We have now collected as many as fifty-three such cases. (Burt, 1958.) I reproduce the more important correlations in Table 1 and for comparison have added corresponding coefficients obtained from other pairs, both related and unrelated. As regards intelligence the outstanding feature is the high correlation between the final assessments for the identical twins, even when reared apart: it is almost as high as the correlation between two successive testings for the same individuals. On the other hand, with school attainments the correlations are much lower for twins reared separately than for twins reared together in the same home.

Several of our critics – Maddox and Liam Hudson, for example – have cited the American study of twins, reported by Newman and his collaborators, as proving that intelligence is dependent on environment. Thus, to take an oft-quoted pair, 'Helen', who had been trained as a teacher, scored with the Stanford-Binet tests an IQ of 116; whereas her twin sister, 'Gladys', brought up for much of her childhood in an isolated district of the Canadian Rockies, scored only 92. But, says Newman, her score

was higher than we might expect considering her scant education; and ... it seems certain that the great deficiency in education had inhibitted the development of the rather higher grade of mental ability with which she was *endowed by heredity* (*see* Scheinfeld, 1942.)[11]

Thus Newman's interpretation in no way conflicts with ours, as will be obvious on comparing his figures with ours (*see* last three columns of Table 1).

It is sometimes alleged that, since twins are born at the same time, the intrauterine environment must have been the same for both before birth, even if later on their environments differ widely, and that it is the former that is crucial. As it happens, however, this gratuitous assumption reverses the actual facts. Embryological and obstetric records show that, particularly with twins

11. Newman's tests, it should be noted, were mainly verbal.

C. Burt 195

Table 1 Correlations for Mental and Educational Characteristics

	English children (Burt)					American adults (Newman)			
	Identical twins reared together	Identical twins reared apart	Non-identical twins reared together	Siblings reared together	Siblings reared apart	Unrelated children reared together	Identical twins reared together	Identical twins reared apart	Non-identical twins reared together
Number of pairs	95	53	127	124	151	130	50	19	51
Intelligence									
Group test	0·94	0·77	0·55	0·56	0·41	0·28	0·92	0·73	0·62
Individual test	0·92	0·86	0·53	0·50	0·42	0·29	0·88	0·77	0·63
Final assessment	0·93	0·87	0·54	0·53	0·44	0·27	—	—	—
Educational									
Reading	0·95	0·60	0·92	0·84	0·49	0·55	—	—	—
Arithmetic	0·86	0·71	0·75	0·75	0·56	0·48	—	—	—
General attainments	0·89	0·62	0·83	0·80	0·53	0·54	0·89	0·58	0·70

developed from split ova, the position of each in the uterus, and the subsequent development, is liable to differ widely. As a result twins usually display poorer health and energy than normal children; and often one twin suffers more than the other.

I think, therefore, it may be safely said that, apart from the influence of some preconceived theory, few psychologists nowadays would be inclined to deny the mere fact of mental inheritance: the most that can be plausibly alleged is that its influence is comparatively slight and distinctly elusive.

(b) *The mode of inheritance.* The majority of those who still question the importance of mental inheritance, and many of those who support it, seem to cherish rather antiquated notions of the way in which inheritable characteristics are transmitted. If, as is generally believed, mental capacities are dependent on the physical characteristics of the brain (or, to speak a little more precisely, on the structural and biochemical qualities of the nervous system), then we should expect those capacities to be inherited in accordance with the same principles that govern the inheritance of other physical characteristics; and these principles (except for obscure and apparently exceptional instances of extranuclear heredity) are essentially those commonly associated with the name of Mendel. Many British psychologists, however, feel a strong and not unreasonable prejudice against applying 'atomistic theories like Mendel's' to explain the facts of mental life, and consequently, so far as they admit the possibility of mental inheritance at all, still cling to the old Darwinian principle of blended inheritance. On this view heredity means 'the tendency of like to beget like' (the definition quoted by one of them from the *Oxford English Dictionary*). As a result, they commonly assume that the arguments for inheritance must consist in demonstrating resemblances between the parent and his children by means of correlations. When the two parents differ, then the child is expected to consist in an intermediate blend of both, much as Aristotle maintained that the 'offspring of a leopard and a camel would be a "cameleopard" or giraffe'.

The approach of the modern geneticist is the reverse of all this. As he views it, the real problem is rather to explain why in so many instances 'like begets unlike'. Both for the environmentalist and for the believer in blended inheritance, one of the most puzzling phenomena is the appearance, not only of extremely dull children in the families of the well-to-do professional classes, but also of extremely bright youngsters in families where both the cultural and the economic conditions of the parents would, one might imagine, doom every child to hopeless failure. With the Mendelian hypothesis these anomalies are just what we should anticipate. However, the few critics who are familiar with the Mendelian explanation seem, as a rule, to suppose that it can apply only to discontinuous variations, and point out that intelligence, like stature, exhibits not discontinuous but continuous or graded variation. Hence, so they contend (sometimes citing the experiments of De Vries on 'pure lines'), the apparent differences in intelligence between one individual and another must be due almost entirely to differences in environmental conditions.

Mendel himself was the first to indicate how his theory could be extended to account for the problem of graded characteristics. When supplementing his experiments on the hybridization of peas by hybridizing beans, and (as before) crossing white-flowered plants with purple, he found that, whereas with peas the two types sorted out with no hint of any intermediate colour, with beans the offspring displayed 'a whole range of hues from white to deep purple'. This, he suggested, might be explained by postulating that with beans the colour was determined, not by a single pair of alternative factors, but by a *number* of such pairs, each positive factor, when present, contributing a small additional amount of colour. And if, as before, the recombinations are the effects of chance unions, then the resulting frequencies would inevitably approximate to those of the normal curve.

However, in our early surveys of London children, we found that, when complete age groups were tested, the distribution of intelligence departed significantly from that of a perfect normal curve: there was a swollen tail at the lower end, due to an excess of mental defectives, and a smaller enlargement at the upper end. This and other considerations led me to put forward the tentative hypothesis that innate variations in intelligence are due partly to unifactorial and partly to multifactorial inheritance: i.e. they result from Mendelian factors of two main kinds (no doubt overlapping), (i) major genes responsible for comparatively *large* deviations, usually of an abnormal type, and (ii) multiple genes whose effects are *small*, *similar*, and *cumulative*.

Pearson (1904) endeavoured to test the Mendelian theory in its multifactorial form by comparing its implications with actual figures obtained for height, arm length, and similar physical measurements, collected from over 2000 students and their relatives. The expected correlations which he deduced for various degrees of kinship were in every case far smaller than those act-ually observed. He therefore rejected the hypothesis of Mendelian inheritance, and fell back on the older theory of blending. How-ever, in deriving his formulae and his expected values, Pearson relied on an oversimplified model. Contrary to what we now know to be the case, he assumed that the effect of assortative mating – the tendency of like to marry like – could be ignored as negligible, and that dominance would in every case be perfect. Fisher (1918) has since deduced more appropriate formulae, which allow for these and other complicating factors: when the necessary adjust-ments have thus been made the theoretical values fit Pearson's own figures as closely as could be wished.

My colleagues and I have applied Fisher's methods (suitably modified) to assessments for intelligence (Burt and Howard, 1956). The data were secured in the course of surveys of the entire school population in a representative London borough, and covered nearly 1000 pairs of siblings, together with the ratings for parents, and (so far as they were accessible) grandparents, uncles and aunts, and first cousins. The final assessments for the children were obtained by submitting the marks from the group tests to the judgement of the teachers who knew the children best; where the teacher disagreed, the child was interviewed personally, and sub-jected to further tests, often on several successive occasions. The assessments for the adults were naturally far less accurate. Never-theless, the correlations computed from the actual data agreed with the theoretical values deduced from the multifactorial hypo-thesis far better than the values deduced from any other hypo-thesis hitherto put forward. The only appreciable discrepancy occurred in the case of first cousins. Here, as for stature, the observed correlation for intelligence was larger than the theoreti-cal; but the difference could readily be explained if (as suggested above) variations in intelligence are affected by a few major genes as well as by numerous minor genes. The figures for cousins of maternal, paternal, and mixed kinship also show some slight evidence suggestive of sex linkage.

(c) *The relative influence of heredity and environment*. In practical work, however, the question most frequently raised is, not whether differences in intelligence are inherited, nor even how they are inherited, but rather what is the relative influence of heredity as compared with environment. To such a question there can be no single answer. We can only try to determine, for this or that type of environment, for this or that population, and for this or that type of assessment, how far the observable results appear to be influenced by each of the two main groups of factors.

Formulae analogous to those used to deduce the expected correlations from the theoretical variances can also be devised for comparing the amount of the constituent variances from the observed correlations. I have ventured to modify Fisher's methods so as to allow for unreliability and for the systematic effects of environment, i.e. for those environmental influences which are correlated with those of heredity, as well as for random effects. The genetic contribution may be regarded as comprising two distinguishable portions: that due to the 'fixable' component (or, as Fisher expresses it, to the 'essential genotypes') and that due to the 'nonfixable' part (i.e. deviations resulting from dominance and similar influences). The data analysed consist of (i) marks obtained from the intelligence tests of the ordinary type taken just as they stand and (ii) adjusted assessments obtained by the supplementary methods already described.

From Table 2 it will be seen that, with the crude test-results taken as they stand, nearly 23 per cent of the total variance appears due to nongenetic influences, i.e. to environment or to unreliability, and about 77 per cent to genetic factors; with the adjusted assessments only about 12 per cent (or slightly more) is apparently due to nongenetic influences and 88 per cent to genetic factors. The improvement implies that the practice of relying on tests alone – usually a group test applied once only – is by no means the best method of estimating a child's innate ability. More accurate assessments can almost always be secured by submitting the test scores to the teachers for criticism or correction, and where necessary adjusting them as described above.

Table 2 **Analysis of variance for assessments of intelligence**

Source	Unadjusted test scores	Adjusted assessments
Genetic component:		
fixable	40·5	47·9
nonfixable	16·7	21·7
Assortative mating	19·9	17·9
Environment:		
systematic	10·6	1·4
random	5·9	5·8
Unreliability	6·4	5·3
Total	100·0	100·0

Environment appears to influence the test results chiefly in three ways: (i) the cultural amenities of the home and the educational opportunities provided by the school can undoubtedly affect a child's performance in intelligence tests of the ordinary type, since so often they demand an acquired facility with abstract and verbal modes of expression; (ii) quite apart from what the child may learn, the constant presence of an intellectual background may stimulate (or seem to stimulate) his latent powers by inculcating a keener motivation, an interest in intellectual things, and a habit of accurate, speedy, and diligent work; (iii) in a few rare cases illness or malnutrition during the prenatal or early postnatal stages may, almost from the start, permanently impair the development of the child's central nervous system. The adjusted assessments may help to eliminate the irrelevant effects of the first two conditions; but it is doubtful whether they can adequately allow for the last.

Class differences. Since differences in 'intelligence' as we have defined it result from differences in genetic constitution, they are to a large and measurable extent transmitted from father to son. Moreover, as historical records amply testify, there has been, throughout the ages but more particularly during the last century, a natural tendency for individuals of high intelligence to rise in the social scale, and for those of low intelligence to drift downwards; and their children tend usually to inherit the high or low intelligence of their parents. The cumulative effect is a marked difference in the average intelligence of the different social classes. Thus the average IQ of children from the higher professional and administrative classes is 120; that of children from the ranks of unskilled labour only 92. But individual differences *within* each social class are far wider than the differences *between* the various classes; and since the numbers in the manual classes are vastly greater than the numbers in the non-manual classes, there are far more gifted children among the former than among the latter. Nevertheless a large proportion of the gifted children in the manual classes still fail to attain the type of advanced education that their high intelligence might seem to deserve. This, it would seem, is due partly to temperamental differences (which are themselves largely innate), and partly to social background, parental attitudes, and above all differences in interest, aims, and ideals.[12] Moreover, the birthrate is not only much bigger among the so-

12. For the data on which the conclusions are based see Burt 1943, 1962 and 1952, and the references there cited.

called 'lower' classes, but also among the less intelligent and more unstable families in every social class; and this has not unnaturally aroused considerable alarm lest, as a general result, the average level of intelligence among the nation as a whole might not be slowly but steadily deteriorating from one generation to another.

Summary and conclusion

The various lines of evidence we have now reviewed lead to the following conclusions.

1. The evidence from biology, from neurology, from introspection or self-observation, and from the impartial observation of the behaviour of other persons, suggests that there is a general mental factor which enters, with varying degrees, into all types of cognitive process (where the term 'cognitive' is to be interpreted as covering any and every kind of mental activity that guides or directs our actual behaviour as distinct from those processes that supply energy or motivation). This conclusion is fully confirmed by statistical data, particularly by the results of so-called factor-analysis.

2. Individual differences in this general factor are largely dependent on the individual's genetic constitution, and appear to be transmitted in accordance with the Mendelian theory of unifactorial and multifactorial inheritance. This implies that differences between members of the same family, as well as resemblances, are genetically determined.

3. These empirical findings suggest the concept of an innate, general, cognitive factor, which for convenience has been technically named 'intelligence' – a term which unfortunately is all too frequently misunderstood.

4. Differences in 'intelligence' as thus defined can be measured with a fair degree of accuracy by so-called 'intelligence tests', provided they are appropriately constructed and selected, and carefully checked.

5. The degree of intelligence with which any particular child is endowed is one of the most important factors determining his general efficiency all through life. In particular it sets an upper limit to what he can successfully perform, especially in the educational, vocational, and intellectual fields. Nevertheless, intelligence is by no means the only factor. His progress and achievement will also be affected by his special abilities and disabilities,

by his physical health and stamina, and above all by his emotional and conative qualities (i.e. by what is loosely termed his 'temperament', his 'character', or his 'personality'). At every stage heredity and environment, genetic constitution and postnatal influences are continually interacting. As a result the influence of the innate general factor is greatest during early childhood, but tends to be increasingly overlaid or masked during later years.

6. There is no discernible difference between the average intelligence of the two sexes; but there are well-marked differences between the average intelligence of the socio-economic classes — that of the manual classes being decidedly lower than that of the non-manual and professional classes. However, within each class individuals vary enormously, ranging in every case from the born imbecile to the born genius.

All this, it will be seen, presents an extremely complicated set of problems for the educationist, the politician, the social reformer, and the policy-makers of every truly democratic state. Too often both the facts and the origins of the various problems are ignored or misconceived. Here therefore is an urgent need not only for further research but also for a more general understanding of the results of such research.

References

BINET, A. (1905), *Année Psychologque*, vol. 11.

BOSWELL, J. (1791), *Life of Johnson*, vol. 2, Charles Dilly.

BROWN, W., and STEPHENSON, W. (1933), 'A test of the theory of two factors', *Brit. J. Psychol.*, vol. 23, p. 352.

BURT, C. (1909), 'Experimental tests of general intelligence' *Brit. J. Psychol.* vol. 3, pp. 94–177.

BURT, C. (1924), 'Historical sketch', in *Psychological Tests of Educable Capacity*, Board of Education, HMSO.

BURT, C. (1943), 'Ability and income', *Brit. J. Educ. Psychol.*, vol. 13, pp. 83–98.

BURT, C. (1949), 'Alternative methods of factor analysis', *Brit. J. Statist. Psychol.*, vol. 2, pp. 98–121.

BURT, C. (1955), 'The meaning and assessment of intelligence', Galton Lecture for 1955, *Eugenics Rev.*, vol. 47, pp. 81–91.

BURT, C. (1958), 'The inheritance of ability', *Amer. Psychologist*, vol. 13, p. 3.

BURT, C. (1962), 'Intelligence and social mobility', *Brit. J. Statist. Psychol.*, vol. 15, p. 3.

BURT, C., and HOWARD, M. (1956), 'The multifactoral theory of inheritance and its application to intelligence', *Brit. J. Statis. Psychol.*, vol. 9, pp. 93–131.

FISHER, R. A. (1918), 'Correlations between relatives of the suppositions of Mendelian inheritance', *Trans. Royal Soc. of Edinburgh*, vol. 52, pp. 399–433.

GALTON, F. (1869), *Hereditary Genius*, Macmillan.

LASHLEY, K. S. (1929), *Brain Mechanisms and Intelligence*, Chicago University Press.

PEARSON, K. (1904), 'On a generalized theory of alternative inheritance with special reference to Mendel's Laws', *Phil. Trans.*, vol. 203, pp. 53–87.

PIAGET, J. (1950), *The Psychology of Intelligence*, Routledge & Kegan Paul.

SCHEINFELD, A. (1942), *Twins and Supertwins*, Chatto & Windus.

SHOLL, D. A. (1956), *The Organization of the Cerebral Cortex*, Methuen.

SPEARMAN, C. (1904), 'A general intelligence objectively determined and measured', *American J. Psychol.*, vol. 15, pp. 202–92.

SPENCER, H. (1870), *Principles of Psychology*, Williams and Norgate.

THOMSON, G. (1948), *Factorial Analysis of Human Ability*, University of London Press.

THURSTONE, L. L. (1921), 'Symposium on intelligence and its measurement', *J. Educ. Psychol.*, vol. 12, pp. 123–47, 195–216.

THURSTONE, L. L. (1947), *Multiple Factor Analysis*, Chicago University Press.

Part Four
Theory *v.* Practice

The picture presented by Hebb and by Burt in the previous
section presents serious difficulties to the psychologist wishing
to make accurate measurements of intelligence and ability, since
his measurements are inevitably affected, to a greater or lesser
degree, by environmental factors. The more heterogeneous his
subjects in terms of socioeconomic level and cultural differences,
the greater the differences produced in this way. Intelligence A,
using Hebb's term, is inaccessible to measurement: we must be
content with Intelligence B, which in particular cases may differ
radically from A. And as Vernon points out, our measurement
(Intelligence C) is but a fallible estimate of B. For the
educational psychologist, concerned with child development in
general, and with cognitive growth in particular, this poses acute
problems. The slow learner offers a constant challenge to the
teacher: the educational psychologist is expected to provide
diagnosis and to recommend treatment. The first and most
obvious line of attack of the psychologist, faced with this problem,
was to seek to develop culture-free or culture-fair tests of
intelligence, and a great deal of time and energy has been spent
on this search during the past two or three decades – but with
little success. This is almost certainly the pursuit of a chimera,
particularly if the search is for a single overall measure of g.
Two other lines of attack exist, however: first, the relationship of
intelligence to *learning ability*, taking into account the hierarchical
nature of abilities covered in Part Two; and second, the
interaction of personality factors with intelligence and with
learning ability. The readings in this section exemplify these
approaches, and come from three of the outstanding researchers
and theoreticians in this field.

The first contribution comes from R. B. Cattell, a former pupil
of Burt. Although British by birth and by training, most of his
professional life has been spent in the United States, so that he

may be said to have a foot in both camps. The paper printed here presents further data in support of his theory of *fluid and crystallized general intelligence*. This denies the existence of one single factor of general ability, as propounded by Spearman, and substitutes two. Crystallized intelligence, says Cattell, is concerned mainly with 'culturally acquired judgemental skills' (and is thus strongly affected by environmental experience) while fluid intelligence is connected with 'insightful performances in which individual differences in learning experience play little part'. The results presented in this paper, from six-year-old pupils, show fluid intelligence revealing itself, in factor analysis, through typical subtests of intelligence scales, such as classification, directions, mazes and riddles; whilst crystallized intelligence had heaviest loadings on verbal-reading and number variables. Cattell also included measures of personality, some of which had obvious connections with the cognitive measures, and he suggests that 'the intelligence of the early years interacted with environment to develop certain personality factors'.

The second paper in this section comes from Jensen. He is one of the minority of American psychologists who lean towards Burt's viewpoint in ascribing the greater part of measured intelligence to genetic factors rather than environmental. This contribution examines the connection between socioeconomic status (SES) and measured intelligence. He starts from the observation 'that, in some ways, low SES children with low IQs appear brighter than middle-class children of the same IQ'. His method of attack was to study learning ability directly, by giving children something to learn and seeing how fast they succeeded. The learning tasks used included serial and paired-associated rote learning, trial-and-error learning, and digit span. He compared the learning ability of low SES and high SES groups *of the same measured IQ*. In the middle ranges of intelligence little difference was found, but children with IQs between sixty and eighty demonstrated large differences between the two groups, with the low SES children significantly *better* learners. The learning tasks chosen by Jensen are, of course, very simple ones, with short-term memory playing a decisive role. They fall, Jensen suggests, towards one end of a continuum stretching from the simplicity of associative learning to the complexity of abstract problem-solving and conceptual learning. Low SES children are not handicapped in comparison with high SES children in terms of *associative learning*. Tests can also be classified, Jensen goes on, in terms of culture-loading. While accepting the impossibility of a truly culture-free test, he argues that 'we cannot discard the concept of culture-free *v.* culture-loaded tests. This is a real and useful continuum, which should not be abandoned just because no existing tests of intelligence fall at either end of it.' And this continuum, he suggests, is one independent of (i.e. at right-angles to) the learning continuum associative *versus* abstract-conceptual. All tests can then be plotted on a diagram having two orthogonal axes. This goes a long way to explain some of the results of previous research: e.g. that disadvantaged children often perform better on verbal than on non-verbal intelligence tests; that Negro children do worse on Progressive Matrices than on the Stanford–Binet. Jensen's theory has obvious points of similarity to Cattell's: presumably tests of fluid intelligence fall predominantly within the south–west quadrant of Jensen's Figure 3, and measures of crystallized intelligence within the two northern quadrants.

The third contribution in this section comes from the pen of Eysenck, the well-known British psychologist. The scope of his paper is much wider than that of either Cattell or Jensen. He starts with a brief and highly-condensed history of intelligence testing, in which he recognizes four stages. The fourth stage is exemplified by Guilford's cube (*see* p. 144) with its dimensions of operations, contents and products. Eysenck notes that this model fails to reproduce the essentially hierarchical nature of the data, and

by omitting any mention of this central feature of the scene Guilford has truly cut out the Dane from his production of Hamlet. He suggests that the time has come to retrace our steps, and his paper is a plea for a fifth stage of development, so that 'notions such as intelligence, IQ, ability and factor will cease to be regarded as poor relations, and will return to the eminent and successful status they held before the war; it also furnishes the only means of making these concepts scientifically meaningful, academically respectable, and practically more useful.

Eysenck's suggestions for the strategy of research in the fifth stage are three in number.

1. Factor analysts and psychometricians correlate total test scores, thus assuming that equal scores are equivalent. This is patently untrue. The fundamental unit of analysis should be the

individual test item, categorizing responses as Right, Wrong, Abandoned or Not Attempted.

2. The mental speed factor should be reinstated to 'its theoretical pre-eminence as the main cognitive determinant of mental test solving ability'. He suggests that – for some test items at least – the only source of difference between individuals is the speed of solution. This accords with some interesting recent work on 'mastery' learning, which postulates that (to put it crudely and with some exaggeration) anyone can learn anything provided they are given enough time: the difference between the bright and the dull is really that between the quick-learners and the slow-learners.

3. This re-emphasis on speed makes it essential to consider personality and the way in which it affects response. Eysenck's own theories of personality postulate two orthogonal axes, extraversion/introversion and neuroticism/stability: these, he says, interact with learning in complex though meaningful ways.

This is a paper full of promising suggestions for further work. Eysenck himself disclaims any degree of finality for his hypotheses: they are, at the moment, merely 'guideposts pointing in the direction of interesting and important factors which will almost certainly have a bearing on the proper measure of intelligence.... What is required is clearly an integration of intelligence testing with the main stream of academic psychology.'

10 R. B. Cattell

The Theory of Fluid and Crystallized General Intelligence Checked at the Five- to Six-Year-Old Level

R. B. Cattell, 'The theory of fluid and crystallized general intelligence checked at the five- to six-year-old level', *British Journal of Educational Psychology*, vol. 37, 1967, part 2, pp. 209–224.

The hypothesis to be tested and its background in theory

According to the theory of fluid and crystallized general ability, there is not *one* general ability factor, as originally propounded by Spearman (1904) and supported by Thurstone (1938), but *two*. It states that these two broad[1] factors are distinguishable by one, called crystallized intelligence, g_c, loading most heavily the culturally acquired judgemental skills, while the other, called fluid ability, g_f, is found loading insightful performances in which individual differences in learning experience play little part.

That earlier researches did not discover this double structure seems partly due to the comparative crudity of early factor analytic techniques, e.g. in relation to estimation of communality and factor number, but especially to the highly prevalent defect of design which omitted the inclusion of *sufficient 'hyperplane stuff' to permit reliable rotation of any factor absolutely general to the whole ability domain*. When these circumstances were remedied, by providing a large enough 'ground' for factors spanning most cognitive performances to be rotated as discernible patterns, the resolution was plainly different. Now functionally independent, but appreciably correlated ($r = +0.47$), g_f and g_c factors appeared (Cattell, 1963), where only one g had been posited. This finding

1. As argued elsewhere (Cattell, 1966), 'broad' is a better antithesis to specific than is 'general'. In nature, no factor is general to all variables, nor does even the matrix in a well-designed single experiment permit a general factor – else it becomes rotationally indeterminate. The g_c and g_f factors, according to Horn's large experiment (1964), although not absolutely general even to the cognitive domain, are quite the broadest factors. However, two other factors approach them in breadth – visualization and speed. The former, by breadth of cognitive effect, has *some* claim to being called a third form of intelligence. If this were granted, however, there are probably other broad sensory structuring functions – auditory, kinesthetic, olfactory – which could claim the same. One may perhaps anticipate that these will form a collateral set of *relatively* broad, but not general, 'sensory and relational resolution powers' below general intelligence.

with twelve-to-thirteen-year-old children has been confirmed, on a larger scale, by Horn's study with adults (1964).

Demonstration of the *factorial separability* of the two concepts has been only a beginning, though a necessary one, for checking and extending the remaining parts of the theory which have to do with the differences of g_c and g_f in (1) age change plots, (2) population scatter of IQs, (3) relations to brain injury, (4) size of nature–nurture ratios, (5) expression in culture-fair as opposed to traditional intelligence tests, etc. (Cattell, 1963; Horn and Cattell, 1966; Hebb, 1942; Horn, 1966), and (6) a development theory of the generation of crystallized general ability by the joint action of fluid ability and experience-plus-motivation (whereby the fluid ability level over the preceding years would determine, in part, the crystallized ability this year). With these further implications, the present research is not directly concerned. It invokes them only insofar as they have implications for the hypothesis and design of experiments extending investigation of g_c and g_f factor structure to the early age of five to six years, with which this experiment is specifically concerned. However, Figure 1 is a brief schematic summary of what can be read in greater detail elsewhere (Cattell, 1963; Horn, 1964).

The theory of fluid ability is that it produces individual differences mostly in perceiving relations firstly in material equally new to all and secondly in material equally 'overlearnt' for all. Where the group has persons with widely varying degrees of familiarity with the material, less of the variance will be due to g_f and more to g_c. However, unless this length of experience and familiarity co-varies for a wide array of intellectual performances, this variance will show more in specifics than in g_c. Since more school-type performances are new to five year olds than say, fifteen year olds, we should expect that g_f would affect more types of performance, e.g. kinds of school, subject performances, in five than in fifteen year olds (Hypothesis 1). However, since the percentage of *variation* in 'time spent at school' is higher for five than fifteen year olds, we should expect experience to play a greater role than do the differences in g_f in building up g_c. The actual communality of those performances which *do* form a g_c could thus be very high. Consequently, g_c should be narrower than at later school ages and g_c and g_f should be less substantially positively correlated than in older persons, since differences of experience have had more to say than differences of fluid ability (Hypothesis 2). Since the uniformity of learning experience and

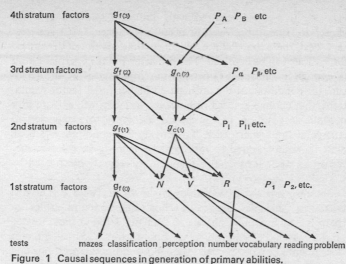

Figure 1 Causal sequences in generation of primary abilities.
Note Ps are personality factors described later

the power of 'aids' (Cattell, 1963) is likely to prevail in *special areas*, e.g. mastering numbers, learning to read, more than across the *whole* scholastic and cultural field, at this age (compared to later ages, when aids have sunk into the background), we might expect primary ability factors (or, at least, numerical ability and reading ability) to have greater absolute loading on performances of this kind at five than later, and to be more separate. For example, reading speed, vocabulary size, and precision of spelling would be larger and more inter-correlated than in adults (Hypothesis 3). The crystallized ability factor should show up as a second-order factor across these primaries (as it does at all ages) but because of the greater chances of uneven learning experiences in the different primary fields, it should not show as high a communality, i.e. should leave more specific variance *in the primaries*, than later (Hypothesis 4), i.e. the common variance in crystallized abilities should show up more in the primaries and less in g_c.

Design of the experiment

The choice of variables was carefully made to include firstly, ability measures – twenty in all – covering some which would definitely be considered fluid ability, some theoretically largely involved in crystallized ability, and some which would be expected to load both, and secondly, personality measures which could be expected to be uncorrelated with ability. These last are also chosen to 'spread out' well in personality space, i.e. it is necessary that there be definite evidence that several independent dimensions will be involved. The provision in the hyperplane stuff of enough independent dimensions is important if we are to insure the condition, at the anticipated higher order factor resolutions, that enough distinct non-ability variables will exist to give dependable rotation to the broad ability factors expected to emerge at the higher order. To provide this condition, we took material demonstrated to represent thirteen distinct personality factors in the questionnaire medium, as recently discovered by Cattell and Peterson (1958).

The resulting list of variables is shown in Table 1. The last twenty-six variables are quite short questionnaire scales or 'parcels', each containing one to four items found most loaded on the Cattell–Peterson nursery school factors. Each such factor is represented by *two* parcels, though we did not expect, nor is it necessary, that they be represented with high variance (for in at least four cases, the 'scale' was only a single item in length).

Table 1 **List of cognitive and personality measures applied in the experiment**

No. in matrix	Cognitive ability variables
1	Substitution. No. completed
2	Substitution. Inverse No. of errors
3	Classification (non-verbal)
4	Mazes
*⟨ 5	Selection of Named Objects
6	Following Directions
7	Detecting Wrong Pictures
8	Riddles
9	Similarities (non-verbal)
10	Cal. Ment. Mat. (Language)
11	Cal. Ment. Mat. (Non-lang.)
12	Reading Test. Word Mastery
13	Reading Test. Sentences
14	Reading Test. Information Gained
15	Reading Test. Following Maths
16	Handling numbers
17	Copying
18	(Ach.) Test of Readiness for Reading Work
19	(Ach.) Test of Readiness for Number Work
20	Drawing a Man (Scored for 'Intelligence')

Table 1 – *continued*

No. in matrix	Personality variables	PSPQ items (indexed as in Cattell and Dreger)
21	Cattell–Peterson No. 1 (a) (G(a))	(1)
22	C–P No. 1b (G(*b*))	(11, −42).
23	C–P No. 2a (Fa)	(−10, −31, 41, 57)
24	C–P No. 2b (Fb)	(109, 177, 179, −196)
25	C–P No. 3a (Aa)	(21, −33, 52)
26	C–P No. 3b (Ab)	(−40, 134)
27	C–P No. 4a (Da)	(4)
28	C–P No. 4b (Db)	(13, 17)
29	C–P No. 5a (Ia)	(8, −27, −39)
30	C–P No. 5b (Ib)	(−140, −165)
31	C–P No. 6a (Ea)	(−6, −15, 46, −156)
32	C–P No. 6b (Eb)	(69, 111, 184)
33	C–P No. 7a (Oa)	(9, 25)
34	C–P No. 7b (Ob)	(−28, 51)
35	C–P No. 8a (Ma)	(−7, −26, 38, −92)
36	C–P No. 8b (Mb)	(−47, −74, 101, −127)
37	C–P No. 9a (Ca)	(12, −23, 30, −45)
38	C–P No. 9b (Cb)	(67, 192)
39	C–P No. 10a (Ha)	(−16, −29, 55)
40	C–P No. 10b (Hb)	(−54, −178)
41	C–P No. 11a (Ma)	(−14)
42	C–P No. 11b (Mb)	(5, 44)
43	C–P No. 12a (Q$_2$a)	(3)
44	C–P No. 12b (Q$_2$b)	(36, −56)
45	C–P No. 13a (Q$_4$a)	(50)
46	C–P No. 13b (Q$_4$b)	(−18, −20)

*IPAT Culture Fair Scale 1 (1–9).

The ability tests consisted first of the eight subtests (one scored two ways) from the IPAT Culture Fair Intelligence Scale 1. As the Handbook (Cattell, 1950) explains, although the test is in the Culture Fair series, only a core of four subtests is considered substantially culture fair, i.e. of a type to measure fluid ability. (For in many practical situations, users wish to have a longer test where culture-fairness is no longer completely necessary.) To represent traditional tests, the California Mental Maturity (Intelligence) Test was included, but separating the score for the non-language part from the language score because, by content, the former could approach a culture fair subtest. After that, the ability measures are meant largely to represent reading and number performance, in various manifestations, as well as such skills as copying and drawing (the latter, however, scored for 'intelligence').

The choice of subjects necessarily had to be nursery school children, with a sprinkling of first-grade children. Some slight social selection is implied here, which should be kept in mind in later comparisons, in that it might produce a slightly early rise of crystallized ability structures. The age range was kept minimal to avoid spurious correlations of g_f and g_c (since both increase sharply with age). The characteristics of the subject sample are given in Table 2.

Table 2 **Properties of subjects**

Male=57	Female=57	Total=114
Mean Age=79·24 months (6 years 6 months)		
S.D. of Age=5.17	,,	,,

The testing was carried out by Killian and Nesselroade, to whose careful work we are much indebted. The intelligence test was given to groups of three and four children at a time and covered two sessions. The personality questionnaire items were administered similarly over three sessions. Voice-recorded instructions were used throughout the course of the test, and short rest periods were given about every ten minutes. The reading and number tests, the drawing of a man, and the California Test were given as a series of tests by the school to all children, and administered by the teachers of the different classrooms. Attention and interest by the children was maintained at a good level and we have no reason to believe that any major effects arose from motivation differences. The author is greatly indebted to the University of Illinois Nursery School and the Lottie Switzer and Garden Hills Schools, Champaign, for good advice and patient cooperation. The testing extended over the year 1963–64, and the sample in Table 2 represents those remaining when children with an incomplete test score were dropped.

Analysis of the data

The testing of hypotheses calls for a first-order factor analysis, which is then to be pursued into as many higher strata analyses as may be necessary to get complete resolution of the factors affecting the ability performance, just as has been attempted, up to a point, by three earlier studies (Cattell, 1963; Horn, 1964; Thurstone, 1938). For the main theory, as it affects cross-sectional studies, expresses itself as a model of higher-order relationships.

For the first order, the product-moment R matrix among the forty-six variables was subjected to a principal axis analysis, with unities in the diagonal carried to forty-six factors. Application of the Scree test (Figure 2) clearly indicated eighteen factors (the Kaiser–Guttmann criterion suggested seventeen). Six iterations yielded communality convergence at eighteen factors. The application of the Maxplane (Eber, 1966) automatic topological program for simple structure was followed by twenty-one blind rotations by Rotoplot (Cattell and Foster, 1963). The successive hyperplane counts (± 0.10) were plotted on a curve until an unimprovable plateau was reached at 50 per cent in the ± 0.05 and 73 per cent in the ± 0.10 hyperplane. (This is in the V_{rs}, i.e. reference vector structure: the corresponding and scarcely different values in the V_{fp}, i.e. factor pattern, can be seen in Table 3.)

The V_o (unrotated), L (transformation), and full V_{fp} (factor pattern) matrices may be obtained from ADI under no. A111. Since we are not concerned here with the personality factors *per se* (which exist only for hyperplane stuff) and only one of them, no. 3 (no. 7 in the V_{fp}) has noticeable loading on cognitive vari-

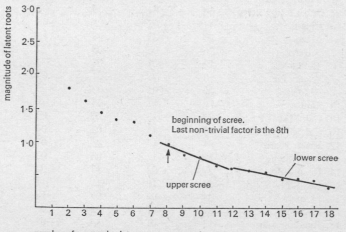

Figure 2 Decision on number of factors by scree test : first order

ables (namely, on the assiduous 'substitution coding' performances, nos. 1 and 2 in Table 1) nothing need be said about them,
except that they do confirm the markers for the Cattell–Peterson
personality factors listed on the left of Table 3. (Factor 18, though
wholly of a personality nature, is an extra and seems to represent
something at the personality second order.) The personality
factor structure as such is, in any case, set out fully elsewhere
(Cattell and Dreger, 1967) so that only the first four primaries –
the cognitive factors, arranged to come first – are shown in Table
3. (Drawing ability, as well as substitution skill, were exceptions
among abilities in having loading on personality factors, namely,
CP6; −0·35.)

Inspection of the full eighteen-factor V_{fp} matrix (ADI no. A111)
shows immediately that the design has fulfilled its expectations.
The thirteen Cattell–Peterson personality factors have replicated
themselves and are as fully determinate, by the two markers for
each, as one could expect from the short scales. They separate

Table 3 **Factor pattern matrix for the four of the eighteen factors
strongly involved in cognitive performances**

		Factors			
	Variables	1	2	3	4
Nos.	Names	$g_{f(0)}$	R or Vi	V	N
Cognitive:					
1.	Substit. (Spd)	−06	03	44	07
2.	Substit. (low error)	00	−04	−00	09
3.	Classif.	41	67	02	−06
4.	Maze	20	23	08	13
5.	Sel. Obj.	36	06	−05	22
6.	Directions	52	−01	08	21
7.	Wrong Pic.	50	72	−01	07
8.	Riddles	20	03	03	25
9.	Similar	−16	11	05	49
10.	Cal. MM (L)	45	−18	−06	00
11.	Cal. MM (NL)	62	15	−02	−06
12.	Read. Word	06	13	48	07
13.	Read. Sent.	19	−12	66	00
14.	Read. Info.	24	−03	17	−02
15.	Read. Fol. Math.	−02	16	59	11
16.	Number Skill	08	−04	09	94
17.	Copying	07	−01	62	27
18.	Reading Ach.	12	−01	86	−08
19.	Number Ach.	03	05	−07	83
20.	Draw (Intell.)	−07	19	−00	09

Table 3 – *continued*

Nos.	Variables Names	Factors 1 $g_{f(o)}$	2 R or Vi	3 V	4 N
Personality:					
21. CP*1a		−11	−10	06	−02
22. CP 1b		10	47	02	00
23. CP 2a		−14	−08	04	−06
24. CP 2b		14	12	07	−02
25. CP 3a		03	02	11	−09
26. CP 3b		00	−04	−07	16
27. CP 4a		−03	−17	54	02
28. CP 4b		02	10	03	02
29. CP 5a		−07	−11	−01	−15
30. CP 5b		00	17	−04	−09
31. CP 6a		07	−13	08	11
32. CP 6b		50	−12	−05	−15
33. CP 7a		10	−47	46	−02
34. CP 7b		−00	16	36	−10
35. CP 8a		−04	13	05	−34
36. CP 8b		−03	−01	−04	−06
37. CP 9a		06	−01	01	12
38. CP 9b		−03	−07	−03	13
39. CP 10a		−21	−06	01	01
49. CP 10b		−09	−24	−07	18
41. CP 11a		−02	−09	04	−11
42. CP 11b		−05	−09	01	05
43. CP 12a		01	25	−01	−07
44. CP 12b		−18	01	−09	19
45. CP 13a		−41	09	−08	10
46. CP 13b		10	−01	−01	05

* CP: Cattell–Peterson personality factor, from the questionnaire personality factor markers of their earlier study.

Note For economy of space only the four relevant factors, with cognitive ability loadings, are reproduced here. The remaining fourteen are clear doublets marking the thirteen known personality factors and an unknown fourteenth, also almost wholly in personality variance. Critical loadings for theory set in *boxes*.

clearly as a spectrum of primary personality factors approximately orthogonal, but actually precisely angularly oriented among themselves. They give the required distinct background to the four factors, set out in Table 3, which together handle all the cognitive performances. Among the latter, the presence of emphatic number facility (N) and verbal facility (V, though much concerned with reading) factors is at once evident. Interpretation of Factors 1 and 2, on the other hand, involves us in a thorough examination of our basic concepts. If we consider classification, mazes, directions, California Mental Maturity Non-language, and possibly riddles (for in the latter, the usual cultural skills might be an obstacle to solution, by negative transfer) as most embodying sheer non-cultural relation eduction with little benefit from culture, then we are faced by the problem that two of these are strongly and one weakly shared with the second factor, which is tentatively identified as Visualization.

Nevertheless, our identification of Factor 1 as the fluid general g_f, is aided firstly by its greater generality across other cognitive tests (loading, above $+0.15$, no fewer than nine variables, compared to five for Factor (2); and secondly by its substantial loading on intelligence performances that are not *only* perceptual in nature. At first glance, the interpretation of Factor 2 (Table 3) could be either that it is Reasoning, R, or Visualization, Vi (Thurstone, 1938; French, 1951; Horn, 1964).

The issue is not unimportant, for according to present views, R is taken as a regular primary ability (possibly covering deductive and inductive reasoning ability), whereas Vi, by Horn's analysis (1964) is almost as broad as g_f and g_c, and, along with other possible sense area structuring abilities, could be on the same stratum, or slightly below, the *general* ability level. If $F2$ is R, why does it not load more highly Following Directions, Riddles, and the traditional intelligence test items (Cal. MM)? If, on the other hand, it is Vi, why does it not load more highly Perceiving Similarities and why is it so high on Classifications? Only when the loading pattern of those factors has become more explored at four to five years can the decision be made. Because of the heavy involvement in Wrong Pictures, and some in Drawing, we lean a little to the Vi identification, but the arguments for R are probably equally good – and in the second order outcome better. Additionally, there is the possibility that through some insufficiency of items discriminating R and Vi (in hyperplane terms) at this age, F_2 is actually an unresolved *combination* of R and Vi.

Where then is the crystallized general ability factor? In this rich setting of varied abilities, it is perhaps not surprising that it does not appear immediately at the first order. Instead, we find two clear-cut primary abilities; first, in Factor 3, a very clear Verbal reading ability factor (variables twelve through fifteen and seventeen through eighteen, with slight overflow into substitution), and, second, in Factor 4, a very clear Number factor, with very high (0·83, 0·94) loadings on the two Number performances (but also slighter ones on the reasoning and exactitude types of performance, which might even suggest R).

The question now arises: 'Will the g_c pattern appear at the next order, i.e. as a second order factor, loading all three of these primaries (or possibly omitting Vi, if such it is), but preserving its distinction from the fluid ability of Factor 1?' Parenthetically, the g_f factor is labelled $g_{f(0)}$ in Table 3, because if g_f is truly cognate with g_c we should expect first to recognize it formally, as such, in an appearance at the *second* stratum level. That is to say, we are adhering for the present to the defining of g_f and g_c as they have appeared before, at the *second* stratum (Cattell, 1963). As we shall argue later that the g_f factor picked up at the 'primary' ability level is really a 'shorn' fluid ability, lacking the loadings which it may have on the primaries, we have indexed it as $g_{f(0)}$ – incomplete fluid ability pattern – making $g_{f(1)}$, later, the true span of fluid ability among all abilities. This stratum level issue is developed more fully in further discussing Figure 1 (p. 211) in the Summary on p. 233.

Accordingly, in pursuit of the second stratum patterns let us note that personality Factor 18 in Table 3 which, by content, is a neurotic or introversive factor, has the interesting property of being at this age positively related to fluid ability and negatively to crystallized. This may mean that high natural ability in the young child increases susceptibility to conflict but that the educational forces which develop crystallized ability simultaneously work to reduce conflict. (Negative loadings in Table 3.) A second-order analysis of the eighteen primary factors was begun with the factor correlations obtained from the very careful rotations made to simple structure at the first order. The Scree test, as Diagram 3 shows, indicated eight factors. Communalities were accordingly iterated to exactitude at three decimal places for eight factors and the resulting V_0 was rotated by Maxplane (Eber, 1966) to the first approach to simple structure. Thereafter, it was subjected to an extremely careful pursuit of blind simple structure by Rotoplot (Cattell and Foster, 1963) which eventually stabilized unimprovably after twenty rotations at ± 10 hyperplane count of 66 per cent. The R_f, V_0, and L (transformation) matrices are reserved at ADI under no. 222. The resulting factor pattern is shown in Table 4.

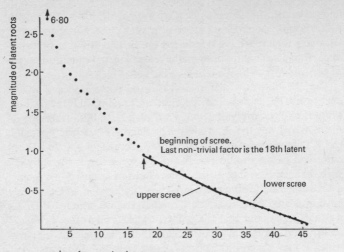

Figure 3 Decision on number of factors by scree test : second order

Now we see that the fluid general ability factor has retained its independence, though the loading (0·58) is not so high as to justify believing that $g_{f(0)}$ is the 'whole story' of the nature of $g_{f(1)}$. The second stratum $g_{f(1)}$ now appropriately loads N also (and, for some as yet unknown reason, a personality factor, possibly of anxiety engendered by the gift of high native ability). Meanwhile, the primaries V (verbal), N (numerical), and $R–Vi$ (visual or reasoning), have come together in a single second order which has the meaning commonly assigned to Crystallized General Ability, g_c. At least, it clearly does so as far as V and N are concerned, through if Primary no. 2 is Visualization, not Reasoning, we would have to adjust other aspects of ability theory to a new phenomenon, namely, the inclusion of Visualization in Crystallized General Ability. Personality factors D, E, A, and H load the latter as found elsewhere.

Beyond these two general ability factors lie six second-order personality factors which, unfortunately, cannot be identified until two researches now in press (Cattell and Dreger, in press; Cattell, Dreger, Coan and Baker, in preparation are) cross-checked. It is important to the present ability researches to have these identifications, because the fact that fluid ability positively affects personality factor CP3 and crystallized ability has a strong association with CP9, may or may not amplify and check our

Table 4 Second-order analysis: factor pattern

	$g_{f(1)}$	$g_{c(1)}$	CPI	CPII	CPIII	CPIV	CPV	CPVI
Fluid Ability $g_{(u)}$	58	−11	−03	−09	−09	14	01	−04
Vi or Reason	10	72	54	08	09	08	−05	02
Verbal (Read.)	−17	74	14	06	−05	−04	31	−53
Numerical	43	49	06	12	01	−06	05	04
CPF 1	14	−01	02	49	10	41	−08	09
CPF 2	04	−05	−08	−01	−10	−06	35	−01
CPF 3	07	−08	−05	03	10	14	−02	−65
CPF 4 (D)	−07	−33	−03	−02	−66	02	10	02
CPF 5 (I)	−13	−04	−10	06	−21	64	01	03
CPF 6 (E)	−12	−33	−05	01	−05	−07	−29	05
CPF 7 (O)	−00	−01	51	−01	05	01	−51	−07
CPF 8 (A)	08	50	−06	−02	−07	−08	−28	−31
CPF 9 (C)	−07	−09	−17	02	56	−15	18	−05
CPF 10 (H)	15	17	−06	−41	06	−04	−06	05
CPF 11 (M)	−03	−23	04	−33	41	05	−02	40
CPF 12 (Q_2)	01	02	11	−25	12	61	15	00
CPF 13 (Q_4)	−10	−02	−60	32	09	08	07	03
CPF (BI Dec.)	52	−53	09	−00	−01	−15	05	04

All decimal points have been omitted.
Note CPF now refers not to Cattell–Peterson *markers*, but to the Cattell–Peterson first-order personality factors *themselves*. The letters in parentheses after some of them indicate their very tentative 'content' identification (to be checked), with source traits in the 16 PF, HSPO, CPO, etc.

concepts of fluid and crystallized abilities. However, already we may note from Table 4 that whereas fluid general ability remains a relatively pure ability factor, crystallized intelligence begins to involve several personality factors (CPF 4, 6, 8 and 11, besides the last and unknown factor), such as one would expect if the realization of fluid ability in crystallized judgemental skills involved also temperament and interest influences. Parenthetically, the fact that $g_{(1)}$ now shows some loading on N but not V may imply that V abilities have been growing for some years (since birth), whereas N is more recent, and generally rests only on a year's schooling, so that advance in it is more dependent on recent leads in $g_{(1)}$.

Now, according to theory, and the previous findings with which it has been associated (Cattell, 1963; Horn, 1964, etc.), the next higher-order analysis should show $g_{c(1)}$ to be the offspring of $g_{f(2)}$ by time and interest, i.e. a $g_{f(2)}$ corresponding to the individual's g_f level over the immediately preceding years should appear, loading g_c, but not itself loaded *by* g_c. That is to say, $g_{f(1)}$ and $g_{c(1)}$ in Table 4 should be positively correlated and on factoring

R. B. Cattell 221

should yield a factor heavily loading $g_{f(1)}$ but also accounting for an appreciable part of the variance in g_c. Since most of the V and N learning in these children is very recent, and the $g_{c(1)}$ is the product of $g_{f(1)}$ acting in very recent times, the g should heavily load the g_f of today.

To test this, the next higher-order factoring was carried out. The Scree (not again reproduced) gave four factors and the rotation yielded the factor pattern shown in Table 5.

Table 5 **Third-order analysis: factor pattern**

	Third order factors			
2nd order variable	$g_{f(2)}$	$g_{c(2)}$	$CP\alpha$	$CP\beta$
$g_{f(1)}$	85	−01	04	−08
$g_{c(1)}$	05	73	−04	01
CPF I	00	−64	37	−66
CPF II	−33	−05	23	38
CPF III	03	−63	00	−41
CPF IV	−03	00	09	−54
CPF V	−01	−02	83	02
CPF VI	−80	68	00	−03

Note As in the usual convention, Roman numerals are introduced to indicate that these personality factors are at the second stratum level.

The unmistakable result is that the fluid and crystallized second orders still fall on two *different* factors at this third stratum. However, they are no longer on their own, for crystallized ability has quite substantial associations with three second order personality factors – CP I, III, and VI – while fluid general ability has substantial association only with one, namely, CPVI. Before discussing the meaning of this we sought the evidence of a fourth-order factor analysis. Here the Scree test gave definite indication of three factors in four variables, which renders simple iteration to stable and unique communalities impossible. Accordingly, we employed a community-estimating computer program by Nesselroade which employs a Jacobi Eigenvector routine and iterates to obtain communalities convergent for the number of positive roots demanded. It *may* not be able to reach the given required number of positive roots, but the fact that it succeeds, as in this case, is additional support for that number being acceptable. The V_0, L, etc., are available at ADI under no. 333.

Regarding the rotational resolution in Table 6, and to some extent in Table 5, the reader must be reminded of the methodological point that as the number of variables diminishes, sampling

Table 6 Fourth-order analysis: factor pattern and factor correlations

(a) Factor pattern.

	$g_{f(3)}$	$CP_{\alpha(2)}$	$CP_{\beta(2)}$
$g_{f(2)}$	94	−06	13
$g_{c(2)}$	41	38	−12
$CP_{\alpha(1)}$	10	89	03
$CP_{\beta(1)}$	01	−01	98

(b) Correlation among the fourth-order factors.

	$g_{f(3)}$	$CP_{\alpha(2)}$	$CP_{\beta(2)}$
$g_{f(3)}$	1·00	·38	·02
$CP_{\alpha(2)}$	·38	1·00	−·12
$CP_{\beta(2)}$	·02	−·12	1·00

problems become obtrusive. Roughly, one might say that when the number falls below, say, ten in a four-factor space, the sample becomes insufficient to permit a specific simple structure position to be accepted with a high level of confidence, from a single investigation. Thus, we know that alternative positions exist to those in Tables 5 and 6 which are almost as good in one or two cases and conceivably could be the 'true' positions. Only additional experiments and, hopefully, some additional variables can raise the confidence level of the conclusion we are drawing from rotation in this last stratum. However, certainly the $g_{f(2)}$ and $g_{c(2)}$ of Table 5 correlate positively so that a single higher order embracing both is likely. And, in fact, the simple structure, unusually good at so high an order, does end with a g_f embracing g_c as general theory would lead us to expect (Table 6). It shows three 'variables' from the lower order each loading a higher order factor so highly (possibly unity, allowing for error of rotation) that $CP\alpha$. $CP\beta$ and g_f substantially constitute the factors. Parenthetically, a two-factor analysis of the four variables, iterating for communalities, yielded only a poor simple structure, suggesting that the Scree test is correct in negating a two-factor resolution.

Summary and discussion

1. The theory of fluid and crystallized general ability factors has been briefly recapitulated as an introduction to this experiment, and some sub-hypotheses stated regarding differences of pattern to be expected at early and late ages, and with and without a large age span in the sample.

2. The experiment measures 114, five- to seven-year-old boys and girls on twenty cognitive ability variables and twenty-four questionnaire, brief, paired, personality scales. The variables were strategically chosen in the cognitive field to separate fluid and crystallized ability (mainly by the Cattell Culture Fair Scale 1; the California Mental Maturity Test and Verbal and Numerical performances). The second (personality domain) set employed the Cattell–Peterson finding of thirteen personality factors at this age to provide a contrasting 'ground' of hyperplane stuff by which factors general to abilities could be accurately rotated, if necessary as far as the third and fourth orders.

3. Using technical checks – notably (a) the Scree test for number of factors, (b) iteration of factoring to uniquely determined communalities, (c) unprejudiced (blind) rotation, initially by the Maxplane program, and (d) at least fifteen to twenty further visual shifts (without knowledge of individual variables) by the Rotoplot program, to an unimprovable total simple structure count – eighteen factors were located at the first order, eight at the second, four at the third, and three at the fourth.

4. Except for the clearly recognizable fluid ability factor, $g_{f(o)}$ (shorn of loadings on primaries, however) and the thirteen personality factors which appeared essentially as in the Cattell–Peterson study, the first order yielded no crystallized general ability, but only strong primary abilities – verbal, V, numerical, N, and a factor which could be either reasoning, R, or visualization, Vi, or a composite of both.

5. At the second order, the ability primaries became organized in what is a typical crystallized general ability factor $g_{c(1)}$, which remains separate from a typical, extensive fluid ability factor, $g_{f(1)}$, now loading also a little of the numerical primary, and a neuroticism-introversion-like personality factor.

So far, this structure matches very closely what has been found in the only previous analyses (Cattell, 1963; Horn, 1964) meeting the above technical conditions. But at this point, one must discuss the phenomenon here encountered, and to be encountered again in a moment, in which a higher stratum factor (Cattell, 1965) seems apparently to make its appearance also at a lower order ($g_{f(1)}$ as $g_{f(o)}$ here). This can happen if other primaries which it should load are not present in the first-order analysis except as single variables. One then has the alternative of 'stealing' some of the variance of these variables to appear as loadings on the second stratum factor, or of adding new variables to create the missing primaries and letting the second stratum factor properly show its loadings on these primaries at the next order. By this reasoning $g_{f(0)}$ has been described as a 'shorn' fluid ability factor, not having all its branches, and appearing at the same level as these branches.

The only circumstance here which does not fit this interpretation is the failure of $g_{f(0)}$ to have virtually a unit loading (actually it is $+0.58$) on $g_{f(1)}$. However, $g_{f(1)}$ as Table 4 shows, loads only two out of eighteen other variables (and it *could* with slight rotation load only one). Consequently, the communality of $g_{f(0)}$, by reason of $g_{f(0)}$ standing almost alone, could be seriously underestimated. Thus, 0.58 is a biased estimate of what might really reach unity. Parenthetically, one perceives in retrospect that a last small shift of $g_{f(0)}$ could have been made toward N which would have presented an alternative and perhaps equally good simple structure. The shorn $g_{f(0)}$ would then have been a little broader, but would have lost some loading on primary N at the next order. Fortunately, whichever way we choose to rotate it would not affect (except trivially) what we obtained at the next order.

6. At the third order the structure is reduced to two general-ability factors, indexed as $g_{f(2)}$, and $g_{c(2)}$ and two third-order personality factors, carrying the usual Greek letter indices, as CPα and CPβ, to indicate the third order. In the previous two studies, the two general ability factors have at this level come together as one 'historical' fluid-ability factor, the crystallized ability factor $g_{c(2)}$ being revealed at the same time as a product of the historical fluid ability interacting with certain historical personality factors. ('Historical' will be explained in a moment.) The same resolution comes here, *but only at the fourth order.*

Two possibilities have to be considered to explain this: one merely mechanical, one involving an amendment to theory. The mechanical possibility is that we made a wrong estimate, by taking four factors instead of three, at the third order. It can only be repeated that the evidence by the usual standards showed four. We are in process, however, of recalculating with three only to see whether, as one would expect, this would yield a result not unlike our fourth-order analysis here. It remains to be seen whether the general fit can be as good when one thus skips an order, and we doubt it.

To understand the alternative of fitting this best structural verdict by an amendment of theory, one needs to ask what meaning can be attached to the special mosaic (Cattell, 1965) we encounter in factor orders here. Stripped to its essentials it is shown in what we may call the hegemony mosaic or model in Figure 4.

Here, as instanced by the contrast of a 0·9 loading and loadings of 0·2 and 0·3 (a simpler picture of Tables 4, 5 and 6), a factor at each stratum accounts for virtually the whole of a factor at the next lower stratum. This degree of determination – i.e. of hegemony in determining a next lower stratum factor – justifies inferring some special conceptual continuity in the series of factors. In this case our first hypothesis is an historical continuity: $g_{f(3)}$ represents fluid ability as it operated and produced effects at some very early stage of the child's development; $g_{f(2)}$ represents it during the first year in nursery school; and $g_{f(1)}$ represents it as it stands functionally at the present moment. (An alternative for $g_{f(3)}$ is that it represents a single genetic influence which affects both fluid ability and certain temperament factors.)

At each upward step in stratum, in any case, additional affected traits come into the pattern of the factor. But $g_{f(1)}$, the factor defined as the presently operating fluid ability, will be almost, though not entirely, restricted to primary abilities. By contrast, $g_{f(2)}$ has substantial loadings on one or two broad personality factors, because the intelligence of the early years interacted with environment to develop certain personality factors too.

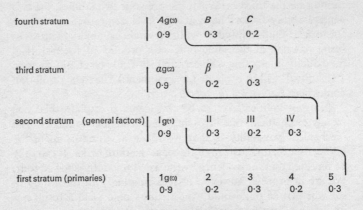

Figure 4 The hegemony mosaic in factor strata.
Note The individual *O C*s *B*s etc do not have same meaning as in tables, but the Greek letters still stand for third stratum and so on

7. The evidence of Table 6, at the fourth order, finally yields the same conclusion as from the pioneer researches: crystallized general ability is revealed as the product of investment of the earlier fluid ability, $g_{f(3)}$, of some personality traits, presumably of persistence and application, labelled CPA; and of time. But (unless the above mechanical, statistical estimate failure explains all) why has this relationship come at a stratum higher than usual?

Let it be noted that the same hegemony model and lineal descent (in $g_{c(1)}$ and $g_{c(2)}$) holds, in this experiment, for the g_cs as for the g_fs. The crystallized ability in the child today, at five or six years, $g_{c(1)}$ (which, incidentally, includes a pattern of personality and social skills – CP4, CP8 and 14 – as well as cognitive skills), is the product and descendant of the $g_{c(2)}$ pattern of the previous few years. This tendency of crystallized ability to beget crystallized ability through 'aids' has been expressly part of the fluid and crystallized general ability theory (Cattell, 1963, 1965). But why should the old g_{cs} influence on the new g_c be greater here than in more mature years? Presumably because the individual differences in opportunity to pick up aids are greater and more accidental over two or three extremely important early developmental years than when steadily accumulated over many years in a standardized school environment. However, even on this theory, of more active influence of $g_{c(2)}$ in generating individual differences in $g_{c(1)}$ in early childhood than later, we should expect $g_{f(2)}$ to have contributed something more than the 0·05 value in Table 5 to the $g_{c(1)}$ score during the immediately succeeding period.

Future experiment should aim at accurate determination of this value. It should obviously also check the general theory here by more than the cross sectional approach necessary in a first attack. A measuring and remeasuring of the same children over a one-year and two-year interval offers a means of checking the development sequences here inferred.

Recently, there has been some tendency to try to re-orient the concepts of some British psychologists (outstandingly of Vernon, 1950) – which contrast practical ability, k, with educational verbal ability, $v:ed$ – to fit the findings appearing around the fluid and crystallized ability concepts. But this attempt to creep from one conceptual position to the other, without clear rejection of false associations and different technical assumptions, is merely asking for confusion. The resemblance of the two dualities is only superficial and gross. Fluid and crystallized abilities are oblique factors: k and $v:ed$ are orthogonal. The g_f and g_c theory supersedes and abolishes the need for the Spearman g altogether, whereas the k and v:ed theory retains g. The crystallized ability factor, g_c, covers alike mechanical, practical, numerical and verbal skills, whereas the k and $v:ed$ divide them into two different categories. There are, besides, a whole set of connotations of the fluid and crystallized ability theory in physiological, cultural and developmental fields which do not belong to the theory of the k and $v:ed$ dichotomy.

Acknowledgements

The writer wishes to express his great indebtedness to research assistants John Nesselroade and Larry Killian who gathered the measurement data, to the principals of the schools which gave their facilities, and to Jack Ford who carefully performed the prolonged computer analyses. This investigation was supported in part by Public Health Service Research Grant No. 1733–10 from the National Institute of Mental Health.

References

BURT, C. (1941), *Factors of the Mind*, University of London Press.

CATTELL, R. B. (1941), 'Some theoretical issues in adult intelligence testing', *Psychol. Bull.*, vol. 38, p. 562.

CATTELL, R. B. (1950), *Culture Fair Intelligence Test Scale 1*, Instit. Pers. and Abil. Test., Champaign, Illinois.

CATTELL, R. B. (1963), 'Theory of fluid and crystallized intelligence: a critical experiment', *J. educ. Psychol.*, vol. 54, pp. 1–22.

CATTELL, R. B. (1965), *The Scientific Analysis of Personality*, Penguin.

CATTELL, R. B. (1965). 'Higher order factor structures and reticular-vs-hierarchical formulae for their interpretation', in C. Banks and P. L. Broadhurst (eds.), *Stephanos: Studies in Psychology Presented to Cyril Burt*, University of London Press.

CATTELL, R. B. (ed.) (1966), *Handbook of Multivariate Experimental Psychology*, Rand McNally.

CATTELL, R. B. and DREGER, R. M. (1967), *Personality Structure in 4–5 Year-Olds in the Q-data Medium* (in press).

CATTELL, R. B. DREGER, R. M., COAN, R. B., and BAKER, R. (1967), 'Identification, by ESPQ relations of checked personality source traits (Q-data) in 4–5 year-olds' (in preparation).

CATTELL, R. B. and FOSTER, M. J. (1963), 'The Rotoplot program for multiple, single plane, visually-guided rotation', *Behav. Sci.*, vol. 8, pp. 156–65.

CATTELL, R. B., and PETERSON, D. K. (1958), 'Personality source traits factored from the questionnaire responses of 4–5-year-olds', *Adv. Publ.* no. 15, Lab. of Pers. Anal. and Group Behav., University of Illinois.

EBER, H. W. (1966), 'Toward oblique simple structure: maxplane', *Multiv. Behav. Res.*, vol. 1, pp. 112–25.

FRENCH, J. W. (1951), 'The description of aptitude and achievement factors in terms of rotated factors', *Psychol. Monogr.*, no. 5.

HEBB, D. O. (1942), 'The effect of early and late brain injury upon test scores, and the nature of normal adult intelligence', *Proc. Amer. Phil. Soc.*, vol. 85, pp. 275–92.

HORN, L. J. (1964), *Fluid and Crystallized Intelligence: A Factor Analytic Study of the Structure Among Primary Mental Abilities*, unpublished doctoral thesis, Univ. of Illinois.

HORN, J. L., and CATTELL, R. B. (1966), 'Age differences in primary mental ability factors', *J. Gerontology*, vol. 21, no. 2, pp. 210–20.

SPEARMAN, C. (1904), 'General intelligence, objectively determined and measured', *Amer. J. Psychol.*, vol. 15, pp. 201–93.

THURSTONE, L. L. (1938), *Primary Mental Abilities*, University of Chicago Press.

VERNON, P. E. (1950), *The Structure of Human Abilities*, Methuen.

11 A. R. Jensen

Intelligence, Learning Ability and Socioeconomic Status[1]

From A. R. Jensen, *Journal of Special Education*, vol. 3, 1969, no. 1, pp. 23–35.

The research and theory presented here originated in the observation that low IQ children called 'culturally disadvantaged' appear in certain ways to be considerably brighter than their more advantaged middle-class counterparts of similar IQ.

We know that on standard intelligence tests, like the Stanford–Binet, the Wechsler scales, and group tests intended to measure the same abilities, children of low socioeconomic status (SES) perform almost one standard deviation below the general population mean, and upper-middle-class children about one standard deviation above it (Tyler, 1965).

Two theories have been formulated to account for these differences in the distribution of IQ as a function of SES.

The first theory holds that SES differences in IQ are due entirely to environmental or social-cultural influences (e.g. Eells *et al.*, 1951). According to this view, SES differences in measured intelligence do not have a biological basis, but reflect only the degree of cultural bias that exists in the tests, which are devised by middle-class persons, and standardized and validated on largely middle-class populations.

The second theory holds that SES differences in measured intelligence do reflect cultural differences to some degree; but they also reflect genetically-determined differences in potential for intellectual development (e.g. Burt, 1959, 1961).

Most of the evidence supports the conclusion that the first theory is inadequate, and that the second theory is essentially correct. The conclusion that SES intellectual differences have a major genetic component, and are not entirely attributable to environment, is now practically beyond dispute among scientists who have studied the relevant evidence, which comes from a

1. Based on a paper presented at a symposium on 'New Approaches to the Measurement of Intelligence', at the annual convention of the American Educational Research Association, Chicago, 8 February 1968.

variety of sources (Tyler, 1965; Burt, 1959 and 1961; Eckland, 1967; Jensen, 1968a and b). For example, identical twins separated in the first year of life, and reared in widely differing social classes, show greater resemblance in intelligence than unrelated children reared together; the IQs of children adopted in early infancy show a much lower correlation with the SES of the adopting parents than do the IQs of children reared by their own parents (Leahy, 1935); the IQs of children reared in orphanages from infacy, who have not known their parents, show approximately the same correlation with their true father's occupational status as do children reared by their own parents (0·23 v. 0·24) (Lawrence, 1931); the correlation between the IQs of children adopted in infancy and the education of their true mothers is close to that of children reared by their own mothers (0·44), while the correlation between children and their adopting parents is close to zero (Honzik, 1957); children of both low and high SES show, on the average, an amount of regression from the parental IQ toward the mean of the general population that is precisely predicted by a polygenic model (Burt, 1961); when full siblings (who have, on the average, at least 50 per cent of their genetic inheritance in common) differ significantly in intelligence, those who are above the family average tend to move up the SES scale, and those who are below it tend to move down (Young and Gibson, 1965).

Psychologists, educators, and sociologists have made intensive efforts to devise 'culture-free' or 'culture-fair' tests that would eliminate SES differences in measured intelligence; none of these efforts has succeeded (Lambert, 1964; Ludlow, 1956). There are no standard intelligence tests known which eliminate SES differences.

Then what about the common observation that, in some ways, low-SES children with low IQs appear brighter than middle-class children of the same IQ? Is this only because standard IQ tests are culturally biased so as not to give a true picture of the disadvantaged child's intellectual ability?

Direct learning tests

To study this phenomenon, we decided to measure children's learning abilities directly, by giving them something to learn and seeing how fast they succeeded. Many disadvantaged children with IQs of 60 to 80 showed a level of ability on these learning tests that would be entirely unexpected from their low IQs or their poor scholastic achievement. The children's learning performances, however, often correspond to the classroom teacher's judgement of the child's brightness as observed on the playground or in social situations. On the other hand, upper-middle-class children in the same IQ range (60 to 80) performed on the learning tasks in a way that was consistent with their low IQs and poor scholastic performances – they were consistently slow learners in a wide variety of situations.

The learning tasks were varied: serial and paired-associate rote learning (Jensen, 1961; Jensen and Rohwer, in press; Rapier, 1968), selective trial-and-error learning (Jensen, 1963), and free recall (Jensen, 1961), all using a variety of materials and methods of presentation. Our most recent work utilizes the digit span paradigm, which seems to be the purest measure of the learning ability factor measured by the other learning tests, and which shows the same interaction between IQ and SES as the other tests (*see* Jensen, 1968a).

Our subjects have been low-SES children (typically called culturally disadvantaged) and middle- and upper-middle-class children, as determined by the neighborhood of their home and their father's occupation. Their ages ranged in various studies from preschoolers to junior high school pupils, that is, from about ages four to fourteen. Mexican–American, Negro, and Caucasian populations have been sampled. Low-SES children in each of these groups were much alike, on the average, with respect to the phenomena here described.

Essentially the same results have been found so consistently with various learning tasks, different age groups, and different ethnic samples, that there can be little doubt that we are studying a substantial psychological phenomenon.

The essential results of these studies are summarized in Figure 1. Note the large average difference in learning ability between the high- and low-SES groups in the low IQ range. But also note that in the above-average range of IQ, the high- and low-SES groups do not differ appreciably in learning ability, as measured by our learning tests. (The slight difference between low- and high-SES groups of above-average IQ shown in Figure 1 is probably due to statistical regression, since the low-SES groups with IQs above 100 are above the general mean of all low-SES children.)

A related fact is that the learning tests show quite different correlations with IQ in the low-SES and middle-SES groups. In the low-SES groups, correlations between the learning tests and

IQ are in the range from 0·10 to 0·20. The correlations for middle-class children for various tests range between 0·60 and 0·80, which is about as high as the inter-correlations among various standard IQ tests. In other words, our learning tests could substitute for IQ tests in the middle-class segment of the population, but not in the lower-class segment.

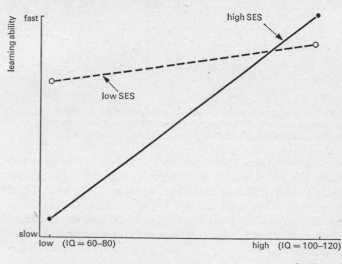

Figure 1 Summary graph of a number of studies, showing the relationship between learning ability (free recall, serial and paired-associate learning, and digit span) and I Q as a function of socioeconomic status (SES)

These SES differences in correlation are not attributable to SES differences in the variance on either the learning or the IQ tests; nor are they attributable to SES differences in test reliability. They are not due to any psychometric cause, as far as we can determine. This is a genuine phenomenon, calling for further analysis and theoretical explanation.

Examination of the correlation scatter diagrams for the two SES groups is revealing. The general finding is shown schematically in Figure 2, which illustrates the locus of the SES difference in the magnitudes of the correlation between associative learning ability and IQ.

Another interesting finding results when a number of learning

A. R. Jensen 233

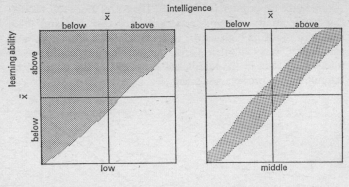

Figure 2 Contingency tables illustrating the essential form of the correlation scatter-diagram for the relationship between associative learning ability and I Q in low-SES and upper-middle-SES children

tests and intelligence tests are intercorrelated and subjected to factor analysis separately in low- and middle-SES groups. The general factor common to all tests accounts for a much larger proportion of the total variance in the middle-SES than in the low-SES groups. (This finding was markedly apparent in a comparison of low-SES Negro children with middle-SES Caucasian children.)

Two dimensions of SES differences

These results do not readily lend themselves to explanation in terms of greater cultural bias in the IQ tests than in the learning tests. A more complex formulation is needed to explain these results, as well as a number of other findings reported in the literature – findings which appear paradoxical if one thinks in terms of cultural bias in tests as the sole explanation of SES differences in test performance.

For example, culturally disadvantaged children often perform better on verbal than on non-verbal intelligence tests. By what rationale can one call the non-verbal tests more culturally biased than the verbal? Negro children perform much better on the digit span test than on the vocabulary test of the Stanford–Binet (*see* Jensen, 1968a; Kennedy, Van De Riet and White, 1963). Is this only because vocabulary is more culturally loaded than digit span? Then why do Negro children do worse on Raven's Progressive Matrices than on the Stanford–Binet (Higgins and Sivers,

1958; Sperrazzo and Wilkins, 1958, 1959)? Also, several studies have shown that Negro youths performed better, relative to whites, on intelligence test items judged to be cultural, than on items judged to be non-cultural (McGurk, 1951; Dreger and Miller, 1960, pp. 366–7).

Findings such as these lead to the conclusion that another dimension, in addition to the cultural loading of tests, must be hypothesized in order to comprehend all the relevant facts.

We cannot discard the concept of culture-free *v.* culture-loaded tests. This is a real and useful continuum, which should not be abandoned just because no existing tests of intelligence fall at either end of it. Various tests stand at different points on this continuum. Much of the discouragement of attempts to devise culture-free tests has resulted from the choice of the wrong criteria for determining the degree of 'culture-freeness' of a test. Those who chose as the criterion the degree to which the test minimized social class differences have utterly failed (e.g. Ludlow, 1956; Lambert, 1964). They have produced either tests having meager correlations with other measures of intelligence, even in culturally advantaged segments of the population, or tests which, on cross-validation, do not reduce SES differences in IQ.

The proper criterion for the 'culture-freeness' of a test is the magnitude of heritability estimates that can be obtained for the test in a specified population. The higher the heritability (h^2), the less culturally or environmentally biased is the test for the population in which the determination of h^2 is made. The magnitude of h^2 tells us the extent to which the test is measuring something that is genetically determined. (For a discussion of the meaning and computation of h^2, *see* Jensen, 1967 and 1968a.)

Intelligence test items can, of course, be classified, by factor analysis or related techniques, in many categories or dimensions (Guilford, 1967). The two dimensions we are hypothesizing as minimally necessary for comprehending the phenomena we have just described may be tentatively designated as *cultural loading* and *complexity of learning tasks*. Theoretically, these two dimensions are best thought of as completely orthogonal (uncorrelated), although their manifestations in actual test items may necessarily be correlated.

Little more need be said about the cultural-loading dimension at this point (*see* Figure 3). It is defined by the value of h^2 (heritability estimate) for the test in a given population. Research on social-class and race differences in abilities can be aided by taking

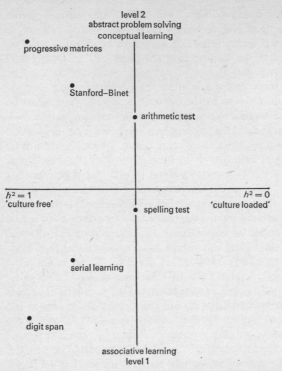

Figure 3 The two-dimensional space required for comprehending social-class differences in performance of tests of intelligence and learning ability. The locations of the various tests in this space are speculative

greater account of this dimension. Group comparisons should be made on two or more tests that stand at distinctly different points on this continuum for each of the groups being compared. Differences between the group means on the various tests should be plotted and studied as a function of h^2.

The second dimension, *complexity of learning tasks*, orthogonal to cultural loading, is more difficult to describe, partly because its nature is still being elucidated in our current research.

As depicted on the vertical axis in Figure 3, it represents a continuum of tests ranging from memory span and associative learning at the one extreme to conceptual learning, abstract reasoning and problem solving at the other. Near one end of this continuum are such tests as digit span, serial rote learning, paired-associate learning and free-recall. These tests stand at different points on the continuum, but they are all in the region below the horizontal axis in Figure 3. At the other extreme of the continuum are tests such as the Progressive Matrices, the Dominoes test, analogies tests, verbal similarities, and tests of the speed of concept attainment.

Another way of characterizing this test dimension would be in terms of the amount of self-initiated activity required of the testee. As we move up from the digit span test to the Progressive Matrices for example, the subject must spontaneously bring more and more covert 'mental' activity (discrimination, generalization, verbal mediation, deduction, induction, and hypothesis testing) to bear on the task in order to perform successfully.

The increasing complexity of the processes required for the noting of the tasks in the second dimension may be thought of as hierarchical – the more complex processes being functionally dependent upon the 'simpler' or more basic ones. Consequently, individual differences in test performance along this continuum should be asymmetrically correlated between tests of lower and higher levels. Poor performance at a lower level is sufficient cause for poor performance at a higher level, while good performance at a lower level is necessary but not sufficient for good performance at a higher level.

A minimum hypothesis

At the present stage of our research on this problem we are proposing the simplest possible model – a minimum hypothesis – to attempt to comprehend our findings and the related evidence in the literature already mentioned.

The hypothesis states that the continuum of tests going from associative to conceptual is the phenotypic expression of two functionally dependent but genotypically (or structurally) independent types of mental process, which we shall label Level 1 and Level 2. Level 1 processes are perhaps best measured by tests such as digit span and serial rote learning; Level 2 processes are represented in tests such as the Progressive Matrices.

1. The biological or structural bases of Levels 1 and 2 are thought of as independent (although they are functionally related, since the rate and asymptote of phenotypic development of Level 2 performance depends upon the individual's status on Level 1 processes). For example, short-term memory is necessary for solving Progressive Matrices, but the covert mediation and

abstraction needed for them are not necessary for digit span performance. The individual's performance on Level 2 tasks cannot rise much above the limitations set by his abilities on Level 1. Conversely, high status on Level 1 cannot express itself in Level 2 performance higher than the individual's ability on Level 2 functions.

2. Level 1 and Level 2 processes are distributed differently in the upper and lower social classes. Level 1 is distributed fairly evenly in all classes, while Level 2 is distributed about a higher mean in the upper classes than in the lower (*see* Figure 4). (The exact form of the distributions is not a crucial point in the present discussion.)

Our empirical findings can be explained by three hypotheses: (a) the genotypic independence of Level 1 and Level 2 processes, (b) the functional dependence of Level 2 upon Level 1, and (c) the differential distribution of individual differences in Level 1 and Level 2 genotypes in upper and lower social classes, as shown in Figure 4. (The terms *genotype* and *phenotype* are used very loosely, not in a strict genetic sense, in order to distinguish between test performance and the psychological or structural processes underlying performance.)

Type *A* children, who are above average on Level 1 but below average on Level 2 performance, usually appear to be bright and capable of normal learning and achievement in many life situations, although they have unusual difficulties in school work under the traditional methods of classroom instruction. Many of these children, who may be classed as mentally retarded in school, suddenly become socially adequate persons when they leave the academic situation. Type *B* children, who are far below average on both Level 1 and Level 2, seem to be much more handicapped. Not only is their scholastic performance poor, but their social and vocational potential also seems to be much less than those of children with normal Level 1 functions. Yet both type *A* and type *B* children look much alike in overall measures of IQ and scholastic achievement. This is a major shortcoming of our traditional testing procedures. Tests which clearly assess and distinguish between Level 1 and Level 2 abilities must be developed for general use in schools, clinics, personnel work, and the Armed Forces. Also, instructional methods which make better use of Level 1 abilities must be sought as a means of improving the educational outcome of children now called culturally disadvantaged.

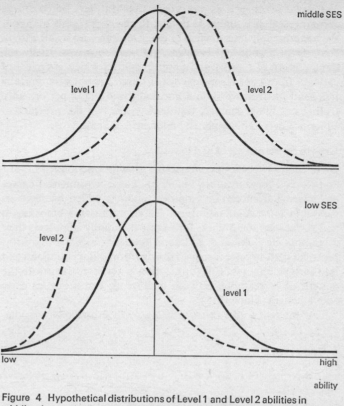

middle SES

level 1

level 2

low SES

level 2

level 1

low

high

ability

Figure 4 Hypothetical distributions of Level 1 and Level 2 abilities in middle-class and culturally disadvantaged populations

Determinants of Level 1 and Level 2

Level 1 abilities may be less affected by environmental deprivation than Level 2 abilities, since the distribution of Level 1 seems to be about the same across all SES and racial groups.

The extent to which Level 2 is dependent upon the quality of the environmental input is an open question. It could be composed of an acquired set of cognitive abilities. The rate and asymptote of their acquisition could be viewed as a joint function of inherited Level 1 ability and the quality of the environment. According to this view, individual differences in Level 2 could have no genetic component, other than that included in Level 1 abilities. This seems rather unlikely, however, considering the high heritability

A. R. Jensen 239

of Level 2 tasks such as the Progressive Matrices. Some of our current research is aimed at finding the answer to this question. We are especially interested in finding children who by all criteria come from a good environment, yet who show essentially the same pattern of Level 1 and Level 2 abilities which is typical of children from poor environments. If Level 2 is not genotypically independent, then we should not find low Level 2 performance (ruling out brain damage, test anxiety, etc.) in the presence of superior Level 1 ability plus superior environment.

Growth curves of Level 1 and Level 2

An ancillary hypothesis concerns the growth functions of Level 1 and Level 2 measures (*see* Figure 5). These hypothetical curves are inferred from certain empirical findings which we have reviewed in some detail elsewhere (Jensen in press). Memory span and serial learning ability, for example, rapidly approach their asymptote in childhood and soon level off, while Progressive Matrices performance increases slowly throughout childhood and into early adulthood. This formulation is also consistent with the pattern of correlations between intelligence test scores at early and later ages (Bloom 1964).

The different forms of these two growth functions in middle-

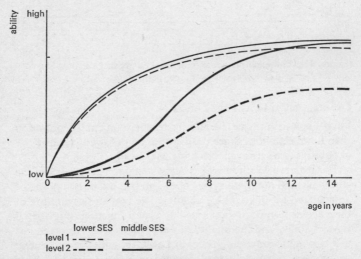

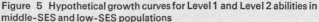

Figure 5 Hypothetical growth curves for Level 1 and Level 2 abilities in middle-SES and low-SES populations

and lower-class children would also account for the so-called 'cumulative deficit' phenomenon (the relative lowering of IQ and scholastic achievement) often found in culturally disadvantaged children as they progress from early childhood to maturity (Jensen, 1966).

Group v. individual testing

We have found that caution must be observed in obtaining and interpreting test results from low-SES children. It appears from recent findings in our laboratory that middle-class children perform about the same on Level 1 learning tasks whether they are tested individually or as a group in the classroom (the rest of the testing procedure being identical). Lower-class children, on the other hand, seem to perform considerably worse in the group situation than when tested individually. We have now begun to investigate this phenomenon in its own right. It may be crucial for the development of standard procedures for assessing the learning ability of disadvantaged children.

Summary and conclusions

Low-SES children with low measured IQs (60 to 80) are generally superior to their middle-class counterparts in IQ on tests of associative learning ability: free recall, serial learning, paired-associative learning, and digit span. Low-SES children of average IQ or above, on the other hand, do not differ from their middle-class counterparts on these associative learning tasks. This inter-action among IQ, associative learning ability, and socioeconomic status has been found in groups of children sampled from Caucasian, Mexican–American, and Negro populations.

The findings have been interpreted in terms of a hierarchic model of mental abilities, going from associative learning to conceptual thinking, in which the development of lower levels in the hierarchy is necessary but not sufficient for the developmental of higher levels.

The findings are important because they help to localize the nature of the intellectual deficit of many children called culturally disadvantaged; they bring a sharper focus to the nature–nurture problem as it relates to social class and racial differences in mental ability; they show that environmental deprivation does not have an equal effect on all mental abilities; and they emphasize the need for standard tests to assess a broader spectrum of mental abilities than is sampled by current tests of intelligence.

References

BLOOM, B. S. (1964), *Stability and Change in Human Characteristics*, Wiley.

BURT, C. (1959), 'Class differences in general intelligence: III', *Brit. J. statist. Psychol.*, vol. 12, pp. 15–33.

BURT, C. (1961), 'Intelligence and social mobility', *Brit. J. Stat. Psychol.*, vol. 14, pp. 3–24.

DREGER, R. M. and MILLER, K. S. (1960), 'Comparative psychological studies of Negroes and whites in the United States', *Psychol. Bull.*, vol. 57, pp. 361–402.

ECKLAND, B. K. (1967), 'Genetics and sociology: a reconsideration', *Amer. soc. Rev.*, vol. 32, pp. 173–94.

EELLS, K., DAVIS, A., HAVIGHURST, R. J., HERRICK, V. E., and TYLER, R. W. (1951), *Intelligence and Cultural Differences*, University of Chicago Press.

GUILFORD, J. P. (1967), *The Nature of Human Intelligence*, McGraw-Hill.

HIGGINS, C., and SIVERS, C. (1958), 'A comparison of Stanford-Binet and Raven Colored Progressive Matrices IQs for children with low socio-economic status', *J. consult. Psychol.*, vol. 22, pp. 465–68.

HONZIK, M. P. (1957), 'Developmental studies of parent–child resemblances in intelligence', *Child Development*, vol. 28, pp. 215–28.

JENSEN, A. R. (1961), 'Learning abilities in Mexican-American and Anglo-American children', *Calif. J. educ. Res.*, vol. 12, pp. 147–59.

JENSEN, A. R. (1963), 'Learning abilities in retarded, average, and gifted children', *Merill–Palmer Quart.*, vol. 9, pp. 123–40. Reprinted in J. P. DeCecco (ed.), *Educational Technology: Readings in Programmed Instruction*, Holt, Rinehart and Winston, 1964.

JENSEN, A. R. (1966), 'Cumulative deficit in compensatory education', *J. Sch. Psychol.*, vol. 4, pp. 37–47.

JENSEN, A. R. (1967), 'Estimation of the limits of heritability of traits by comparison of monozygotic and dizygotic twins', *Proc. Nat. Acad. Sci.*, vol. 58, pp. 149–57.

JENSEN, A. R. (1968a), 'Social class, race, and genetics: Implications for education', *Amer. Educ. Res. J.*, vol. 5, pp. 1–42.

JENSEN, A. R. (1968b), 'The culturally disadvantaged and the heredity-environment uncertainty', in J. Helmuth (ed.), *The Disadvantaged Child*, vol. 2. Special Child Pub., Seattle.

JENSEN, A. R., and ROHWER, W. D., Jr. (1968), 'Mental retardation, mental age, and learning rate', *J. educ. Psychol.*, vol. 59, pp. 402–3.

KENNEDY, W. A., VAN DE RIET, V. and WHITE, J. C., Jr. (1963), 'A normative sample of intelligence and achievement of Negro elementary school children in the Southeastern United States', *Monogr. Soc. Res. Child Development*, vol. 28, no. 6.

LAMBERT, N. M. (1964), 'The present status of the culture fair testing movement', *Psychol. Schools*, vol. 1, pp. 318–30.

LAWRENCE, E. M. (1931), 'An investigation into the relation between intelligence and inheritance', *Brit. J. Psychol. Monogr. Sup.*, vol. 16, no. 5.

LEAHY, A. M. (1935), 'Nature–nurture and intelligence', *Genet. Psychol. Monogr.*, vol. 17, pp. 241–305.

LUDLOW, H. G. (1956), 'Some recent research on the Davis–Eells Games', *Sch. and Soc.*, vol. 84, pp. 146–8.

McGurk, M. C. (1951), *Comparison of the Performance of Negro and White High School Seniors on Cultural and Non-Cultural Psychological Test Questions.* Catholic University Press, Washington.

Rapier, J. L. (1968), 'The learning abilities of normal and retarded children as a function of social class', *J. educ. Psychol.*, vol. 59, pp. 102 19.

Sperrazzo, G. and Wilkins, W. L. (1958), 'Further normative data on the Progressive Matrices', *J. consult. Psychol.*, vol. 22, pp. 35–7.

Sperrazzo, G. and Wilkins, W. L. (1959), 'Racial differences on Progressive Matrices', *J. consult., Psychol.*, vol. 23, pp. 273–4.

Tyler, L. A. (1965), *The Psychology of Human Differences*, 3rd edn. Appleton-Century-Crofts.

Young, M., and Gibson, J. B. (1965), 'Social mobility and fertility' in J. E. Meade and A. S. Parkes (eds.), *Biological Aspects of Social Problems*, Oliver & Boyd.

12 H. J. Eysenck

Intelligence Assessment:
A Theoretical and Experimental Approach[1]

H. J. Eysenck, 'Intelligence assessment: a theoretical and experimental approach', *British Journal of Educational Psychology*, vol. 37, 1967, pp. 81–98.

Development of a concept

Attempts to measure intelligence have passed through several stages since Galton tried to use the measurement of sensory processes to arrive at an estimate of the subject's intellectual level (1883), and McKeen Cattell (1890) employed tests of muscular strength, speed of movement, sensitivity to pain, reaction time and the like for a similar purpose. These largely abortive efforts were followed by the first stage of intelligence measurement properly so called; it may with truth be labelled the '*g*' phase because both Spearman (1904) and Binet and Simon (1905) stressed the importance of a *general factor of intellectual ability*, Binet contributing mainly by the construction of test items and the invention of the concept of mental age, Spearman contributing mainly by the application of correlational methods and the invention of factor analysis.

The second stage was concerned with the proper definition of intelligence, and theories regarding its nature. Several books concerned themselves with this problem (Thurstone, 1926; Spearman, 1923), and a number of symposia were held (*Brit. J. Psychol.*, 1910; *J. Educ. Psychol.*, 1921; *Internat. Congress of Psychol.*, 1923). Among the theories canvassed were 'mental speed' hypotheses which placed the burden of intellectual attainment on speed of mental functioning, and 'learning' hypotheses which protested that the ability to learn new material was fundamental. Both hypotheses faced difficulties; the fact that reaction times showed no relation to ability tended to discourage believers in the 'speed' hypothesis, and the negative results of the large-scale work of Woodrow (1946) on the relation between different learning tasks and intelligence discouraged believers in the 'learning'

1. This paper was originally delivered at a symposium on New Aspects of Intelligence Assessment at the Swansea Meeting of the BPS, on 3 April 1966. The preparation was assisted by a grant from the MRC.

hypothesis. Psychologists learned to agree to disagree, and to present their work with the dictum that 'intelligence is what intelligence tests measure' – a saying less circular than it sounds, but only acceptable if all intelligence tests did, in fact, measure the same thing, which they quite emphatically did not.

We thus reach the third stage, which is essentially a continuation of the early factor analytic approach, but now fortified by recourse to multiple factors and matrix algebra. This phase owes most to Thurstone, but Thomson, Burt, Holzinger, and many others made valiant contributions. In this factorial phase, investigators went back to Binet's idea of different mental faculties making up the complex concept of intelligence, and used factor analysis to sort out these alleged faculties; they merged with verbal, numerical, perceptual, memory, visuo-spatial and many other factors. At first, Thurstone and his followers believed that these 'primary factors' put paid altogether to the notion of intelligence, but when they found the primary factors to be themselves correlated they resurrected the concept of intelligence as a second-order factor, a solution already implicit in the earlier methods and theories of Burt (Eysenck, 1939).

The fourth stage constitutes essentially an extension of the third, and is associated specifically with Guilford (1966), whose publication of his '1965 model' of intelligence provided some of the motivation for this paper. This model, which shows some similarities to one I published in *Uses and Abuses of Psychology* (Eysenck, 1953), is illustrated in Figure 1 on p. 246. Guilford classifies the intellect into *operations* which it can perform, different *contents* of these operations, and different *products*; by taking all possible interactions we obtain 120 cells corresponding to different mental abilities. Of these Guilford claims to have evidence in actual factorial studies for eighty; he is optimistic about discovering the remainder. To some critics, this factorial extension of Thurstone's work has appeared almost as a *reductio ad absurdum* of the whole approach. There is a possibility of infinite sub-division inherent in the statistical method employed, and evidence is lacking that further and further sub-factors add anything either to the experimental analysis of intellectual functioning or the practical aim of forecasting success and failure in intellectual pursuits (Vernon, 1965). Worse, the model fails to reproduce the essentially hierarchical nature of the data; the one outstanding fact which recurs again and again in all analyses is the universality of positive correlations among all relevant tests, and the positive correlations between different factors (McNemar, 1964). By omitting any mention of this central feature of the scene Guilford has truly cut out the Dane from his production of Hamlet. If this is really the best model (1965 style) which psychology can offer of intelligence and intellect, then the time seems to have come to retrace our steps; something has gone very wrong indeed!

Limitation of the factor analysis approach

Zangwill has several times suggested that the whole intelligence testing movement is a technological rather than a scientific one, and in essence my own diagnosis is not too different from his. I would suggest that the psychometric approach has become almost completely divorced from both psychological theory and experiment, and that factor analysis, while an extremely useful tool, cannot by itself bear the whole burden which has been placed upon it. It is the purpose of this paper to raise certain questions in this connection rather than to give definitive answers: a few empirical results from some of our work will be presented more in order to illustrate an approach than because we believe that these results settle the questions the experiments were designed to investigate.

Table 1 **Five-item intelligence test, administered to five children all having a score of two**

	1	2	3	4	5	Total score
Jones	R	R	N	N	N	2
Charles	W	R	W	R	N	2
Smith	R	A	A	R	A	2
Lucy	R	A	N	N	N	2
Mary	R	W	R	W	W	2

R right answer; *W* wrong answer; *A* abandoned item; *N* item not attempted. (In most tests *A* and *N* cannot be distinguished.)

Our work started out with a fundamental criticism of the whole testing movement, directed at the unit of analysis chosen. Nearly all factor analysts and psychometrists correlate test scores and then proceed to work with these correlations; they thus assume that equal scores are equivalent. Such an assumption is unwarranted in the absence of proof, and consideration of typical intelligence-test papers shows that it is, in fact, mistaken. Consider Table 1, which shows the results of giving an imaginary five-item test to five candidates. Let R stand for an item correctly solved, W for an item incorrectly solved, A for an item abandoned and N for an item not attempted. Let us also assume that the items increase in difficulty. It will be seen that all five children obtain an identical mark of two; but it will also be seen that no two children obtain this mark in the same way. Jones gets the easiest two right, but uses up all his time and does not attempt any more; he works slowly and carefully. Charles gets some easy items wrong and some difficult ones right; he works quickly but carelessly. Smith gives up on three items; had he been more persistent, he might have solved some of them. Lucy is rather selective in the choice of item to be tackled; and Mary fails to check her answers, getting three of them wrong. Can it really be maintained that the mental processes and abilities of these five children are identical, merely because they all obtained the same final mark? This is the implicit assumption underlying the factor analysis of test scores, and it may be suggested that this assumption requires careful investigation before we can regard it as acceptable. Such investigations are notable by their absence, and factor analysts proceed throughout as if the problem did not exist. This, it may be suggested, is not a proper scientific procedure.

The Furneaux model

Our own approach has been to emphasize the point that the fundamental unit of analysis must be the individual test item, and that in addition to determining the category (R, W, A, N) into which it falls for each candidate, it is important to determine the *speed* with which each R item is solved, the length of time devoted to each A item (persistence or continuance), and the number of W items together with the time spent on each. Furneaux (1960) has given a detailed analysis of scores obtained in this fashion, and has suggested on the basis of this evidence that the solution of mental test problems has three main parameters:

1. Mental Speed, i.e. speed of solution of R items.

2. Continuance, or persistence in efforts to solve problems the solution to which is not immediately apparent.

3. Error Checking Mechanism, i.e. a mental set predisposing the individual to check his solution against the problem instead of writing it down immediately.

Two interesting and important consequences follow from this analysis. In the first instance, Furneaux reinstates the mental speed factor to its theoretical pre-eminence as the main cognitive determinant of mental test solving ability, and in the second instance he emphasizes the importance of non-cognitive (personality) factors in determining mental test performance – both persistence and carefulness in checking are personality attributes rather than cognitive abilities. I have attempted to incorporate some elements of this analysis into my own model of intellect (Eysenck, 1953), which is shown in Figure 1, and which may be compared with Guilford's. What I call 'mental processes' he calls 'operations'; what I call 'test material' he calls 'contents'; so far there is close agreement. But instead of having a third dimension concerned with 'products' (which seems to me a weak and not very important principle of division) I have suggested a dimension rather vaguely labelled 'quality' into which I wanted to incorporate concepts of mental speed and power, somewhat after the fashion of Thorndike's fundamental contribution (1926). The suggestion is that mental speed and power are fundamental aspects of all mental work, but that they are to some extent qualified by the mental processes involved and the materials used. This seems to me a more realistic concept than Guilford's, as well as having the advantage of retaining the central 'g' concept in hierarchical structure in which the major source of variation is mental speed, averaged over all processes and materials. 'Primary mental abilities', so called, would then emerge at a lower level of generality, and be related to different processes and different materials used.

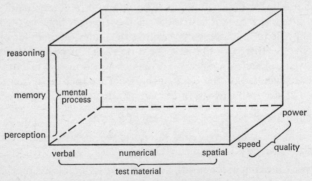

Figure 1 Model of the structure of the intellect
Source Eysenck, 1953

Furneaux has demonstrated the fundamental nature of the mental speed function by showing that when an individual's *R* latencies are plotted against the difficulty level of the items concerned, a negatively accelerated curve is obtained (Figure 2a); when the time units are then logarithmically transformed *all plots become linear and parallel* (Figure 2b). This may be interpreted to

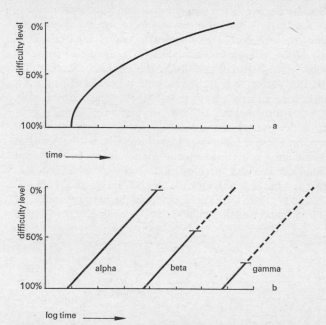

Figure 2 Relation between difficulty level of test items and time (a) and log time (b) needed for solution. Alpha, beta and gamma are three imaginary subjects of high, medium and low mental ability respectively. *Source* Eysenck, 1953

mean that the only source of difference in intellectual ability between individuals (in relation to the particular set of test items chosen at least) is the intercept on the abscissa. The increase in log latency with increase in item difficulty turns out to have the same slope for all individuals tested, and is thus a *constant*, one of the few which exist in psychology. It seems to me that the scientific study of intelligence would gain much by following up the important leads given by Furneaux in this extremely original and pathbreaking work.

Mental speed and intelligence

On the theoretical side Furneaux has suggested that what may be involved in problem-solving activity may be some kind of scanning mechanism the speed of which determines the probability of the right solution being brought into focus more or less quickly. If we join this notion with that of information processing, we may have here not only the suggestion of a useful theory of intellectual functioning, but also an argument against those who abandoned the whole theory of 'speed' as underlying intelligence because of the failure of reaction-time experiments to correlate with intelligence tests. Let us consider the amount of information conveyed by flashing a light and requiring the subject to press a button located underneath the light flashed. When there is only one light/button combination, no information is, in fact, conveyed. As the number of combinations increases, the amount of information conveyed increases logarithmically, so that one bit of information is conveyed with two combinations, two bits with four combinations and three bits with eight combinations. Response speed has been shown by Hick (1952), Hyman (1953) and Schmidtke (1961), to increase linearly with increasing number of bits of information, as shown in Figure 3 (Frank, 1963). We have

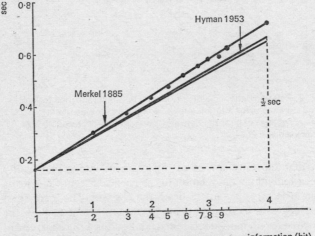

Figure 3 Relation between reaction time in seconds and complexity of task in bits. Data from Merkel (1885) and Hyman (1953). The latter shows results before and after practice.
Source Frank, 1963

two separate items of information for each subject: one is the raw reaction time, as shown by the intercept on the ordinate, the other is the slope of the regression line, i.e. the rate of increase in reaction time with increasing amount of information processed. If intelligence is conceived of as speed of information processing, then simple reaction time, involving 0 bits of information, should not correlate with intelligence, but the slope of the regression line, showing increase of reaction time with amount of information processed, should correlate (negatively) with intelligence; in other words, intelligent subjects would show less increase in reaction time with increase in number of light/button combinations than would dull ones. (This is a slightly more precise way of phrasing Spearman's first noegenetic law.) Experimentally, the prediction has been tested by Roth (1964) who demonstrated that while as expected simple reaction time was independent of IQ, speed of information processing (slope) correlated significantly with IQ, in the predicted direction. Reaction-time experiments, properly interpreted, do not appear to contradict a theory of intellectual functioning based on the motion of mental *speed*.

Learning and intelligence

The theory that *learning* is basic to intellectual functioning is not necessarily antagonistic to a theory stressing speed; within the more general speed theory we might expect that speedy learning would be characteristic of the bright, slow learning of the dull. In other words, learning would be one of the 'mental processes' sub-divisions in Figure 1. The early work of Woodrow (1946) was often considered to have disproved such an hypothesis, but his experiments were too simple altogether to throw much light on the problem; it is not adequate to take subjects who are at different stages of mastery and practice on various types of tasks, who are differentially motivated towards these tasks, and who vary considerably with respect to the abilities involved in these tasks, and then to correlate speed of learning on these tasks with each other and with IQ. Improved experimental and statistical methods have given more positive results regarding the relationship between IQ and learning (Stake, 1961; Duncanson, 1964).[2]

2. An early study showing the close relation obtaining between intelligence, on the one hand, and learning/memory, on the other, was an investigation by Eysenck and Halstead (1945) of fifteen learning/memory tests; these were found to be highly correlated with intelligence. A factorial analysis gave rise to a general factor of intelligence, leaving no residual evidence of any additional contribution by learning or memory.

Another argument has often been presented, e.g. by Wechsler; he has pointed out that a learning task such as 'memory span' correlates poorly with the other tests in the WAIS and does not predict final total score well. Jensen (1964) has argued that this view is based on a neglect of the low reliability of the test as described by Wechsler; this, in turn, can be raised to any height by simply lengthening the (very short) test, or by improving its design, or both. When correlations are corrected for attenuation, Jensen shows that digit span correlates 0·75 with total IQ, has a factor loading of 0·8 on a general factor extracted from the Wechsler tests, is more culture-free than other tests, and can be shown to obey the Spearman–Brown prophecy formula, thus making it possible to increase its reliability to any desired degree. The test can be made more predictive of IQ by measuring forward and backward span separately, rather than by throwing them together into one score; apparently these two measures are not, in fact, highly correlated and should not be averaged but combined in some multiple correlation formula, if at all.

Jensen has used digit span and serial learning experiments of the traditional laboratory kind in an extensive investigation into personality determinants of individual differences in these tests; we shall return to this study later. Here it is relevant to mention that he found a multiple correlation of +0·76 between learning ability as so measured and college Grade Point Average, a measure of academic standing. When it is considered that this value was obtained in a relatively homogeneous group of persons from the point of view of IQ, and that this correlation is considerably higher than those usually reported with highly regarded IQ tests, then it may become apparent why I am suggesting here that we should take seriously the theory relating the concept of 'intelligence' to learning efficiency and speed, and attempt, by means of laboratory studies such as those of Jensen and Roth, to investigate deductions from such an hypothesis. It seems reasonable to expect that such investigations are more likely to help in the elucidation of the nature of intellectual functioning than is the continued construction of IQ tests of a kind that has not materially altered in fifty years. And it is also possible that from the practical point of view, this method of procedure may result in tests and devices which enable us to give better predictions of school and university success than do existing tests.[3]

3. One interesting possibility which is suggested by Jensen's work relates to his finding that serial learning tasks and paired associate learning tasks

As an example of the much increased possibility of psychological analysis opened by the use of laboratory methods in this field, consider Schonfield's (1965) study of memory changes with age. The general loss of ability of the aged to do IQ tests well has been known for a long time, as has their failure to acquire new skills and information, or to retain acquired material. These defects may be due either to a loss of ability to retrieve memories from storage, or to a deficiency in the storage system itself. By comparing recall and recognition scores on a learning task, Schonfield showed that recall was impaired in aged subjects, but recognition was not; he concluded that it was retrieval from memory storage which was at fault, rather than storage itself, thus suggesting that learning itself might be unimpaired with age. This experiment is cited, not because the results are definitive in any way, but because they illustrate well the approach suggested here; simple IQ testing cannot in the nature of things do any more than reveal the existence of a deficit, but in order to reveal the precise psychological nature of the intellectual deficit in question more experimental methods are required.

Learning and personality

In our discussion of Furneaux's contribution, we found that of his three components of intellectual functioning, only one (speed) was cognitive, while two (persistence and the error-checking mechanism) seemed more orectic in origin, and likely to be related to personality. Most workers in the field of intelligence testing disregard personality factors altogether, but this is almost certainly a mistake. There are several experiments which bring out fairly clearly the importance of personality factors such as neuroticism and extraversion /introversion in the measurement of intelligence, and much of our work has centred on this aspect. Consider first of all the simple learning experiments which we have just discussed; here one can perhaps expect personality to play little if any role. This, however, is not so, and it may be interesting to speculate about the kind of relation which one

---

both correlate with IQ, but not with each other. In view of the dependence of paired-associate learning on verbal mediation, in contrast to the rote character of serial learning, it seems possible to regard serial learning as the prototype of Cattell's 'fluid' ability, and paired-associate learning as the prototype of his 'crystallized' ability (1964). If this suggestion has any value, it may show the way to the construction of a battery of tests less dependent on cultural factors and training than are most existing IQ tests.

might expect to find. We may with advantage begin by considering the well-known experiments of Kleinsmith and Kaplan (1963). These authors argued, briefly, that learning is mediated by a *consolidation process* which takes place after the learned material has been registered, but before it is transferred into permanent memory storage. Consolidation is a function of the state of arousal of the organism; the greater the arousal, the longer and more efficient the consolidation, so that higher arousal leads to better memory in the long run. However, while consolidation is proceeding, it interferes with recall, so that while the consolidation process is going on the highly aroused organism is at a disadvantage. Kleinsmith and Kaplan tested their theory by measuring the amount of arousal (GSR reaction) produced by different paired stimuli; for each subject they then picked the most arousing and the least arousing stimulus pairs and had the subject remember the paired stimulus after presentation of the original stimulus. Recall was arranged at different times after original learning for different groups of subjects, and Figure 4 shows the results; it will be seen that as expected high arousal words are poorly remembered immediately after learning, but show very marked reminiscence effects, while low arousal words are well remembered immediately after learning, but fade out quickly. There is little doubt of the reality of this phenomenon, which has since been demonstrated several times.

In this experiment stimuli were measured and grouped according to their arousing qualities. It is equally possible to group subjects according to their arousability, and I have argued that introverts are characterized by high arousal, extraverts by poor arousal (Eysenck, 1963, 1967). If this theory is along the right lines, we would expect extraverts to behave in the manner of the low arousal words in Figure 4, and introverts in the manner of the high arousal words. In other words, for short recall times, extraverts should be superior, while for long recall times introverts should be superior. There are about half-a-dozen experiments in the literature demonstrating the superiority of extraverts over short-term intervals, including the work of Jensen already mentioned; these have been summarized elsewhere (Eysenck, 1967), and all that need be said here is that results are in good agreement with prediction. Some unpublished work on pursuit rotor reminiscence also supports the prediction of better learning for introverts after long rest intervals.

A specially designed experiment by McLaughlin and Eysenck

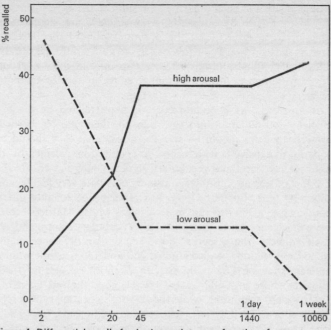

Figure 4 Differential recall of paired associates as a function of
arousal level.
Source Kleinsmith and Kaplan, 1963

was undertaken to test, in addition to the hypothesis stated above,
a further one relating to the personality dimension of neuroticism,
which we may regard as associated with drive (Spence, 1964).
Subjects were tested on either an easy list of seven pairs of nonsense syllables, or on a difficult list, difficulty being manipulated
through degree of response similarity. It was predicted that in
accordance with the Yerkes–Dodson law the optimum drive level
for the easy list would be higher than that for the difficult list, and
it was further assumed that N subjects (high scorers on the N
scale of the EPI) would be characterized by higher drive than S
subjects (stable, low scorers on the N scale of the EPI). Extraverts,
as already explained, were regarded as low in arousal, introverts
as high. There are thus four groups of subjects, which, in order of
drive, would be (from low to high): stable extraverts; neurotic
extraverts and stable introverts; neurotic introverts. (No prediction could be made about the position of the two intermediate

groups relative to each other.) The results of the experiment are shown in Figure 5; extraverts, as predicted, are significantly superior to introverts, and the optimum performance level of drive is shifted towards the low end as we go from the easy to the difficult list, thus shifting the SE group up and the NE group down. (The figures in the diagram refer to number of errors to criterion.)

If introverts, as hypothesized, are characterized by a more efficient consolidation process, due to their greater cortical arousal, then we should be able to predict that they should be superior to extraverts with respect to acquired knowledge. As an example, we may take vocabulary scores, which are clearly the product of learning, and which usually correlate very highly with other IQ tests. Eysenck (1947) has reported personality differences between 250 neurotic male soldiers whose Matrices scores were much superior to their Mill Hill Vocabulary scores, and 290 male soldiers whose scores showed a similar difference in the opposite direction; he also studied 200 and 140 neurotic women soldiers showing similar differences. In both sex groups those subjects whose vocabulary was relatively good showed dysthymic (introverted) symptoms, while those whose vocabulary was relatively poor showed hysteric (extraverted) symptoms. Farley (unpublished) has carried out a study of forty-seven normal subjects in which he found a substantial positive correlation ($r = +0.48$) between introversion and vocabulary. This is of course in line with the alleged 'bookish' character of the typical introvert. There was no such correlation between Introversion and Raven's Matrices.

It is possible to go further than this and argue that introverts should do rather better at school and university because of this superiority in consolidation of learned material; there is much evidence to indicate that such a prediction may be along the right lines (Furneaux, 1962; Lynn and Gordon, 1961; Savage, 1962; Bendig, 1958, 1960; Otto, 1965; Otto and Fredricks, 1963; Child, 1964; Ranking, 1963a, 1963b). Not all the results are favourable, but the overall impression is certainly in accordance with expectation. It might be suggested that some form of zone analysis (Eysenck, 1966) which included the N variable as well as the E variable would throw much-needed light on these relationships. It should be added that the results do not so much support the hypothesis, as rather fail to disprove it. There are so many alternative hypotheses to account for the finding that not too much should be read into the data.

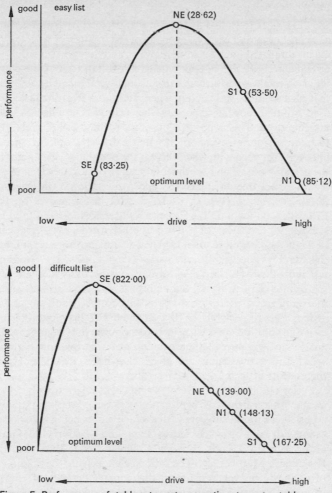

Figure 5 Performance of stable extroverts, neurotic extroverts, stable introverts and neurotic introverts on early and difficult paired associate learning tests.

Data from McLaughlin and Eysenck, unpublished

Intelligence and personality

It will be clear from this discussion that personality features such as neuroticism and extraversion–introversion interact with learning in complex though meaningful ways, and that great care has to be taken in the design of experiments not to fall foul of the complex laws relating performance to personality.[4] It might be objected that such relations only obtain when laboratory learning tasks are used, but that they fail to appear when orthodox intelligence tests are employed. This is not so. One of the earliest findings relating to extraversion/introversion was that extraverts opt for speed, introverts for accuracy, when there is the possibility of a choice in the carrying out of an experimental task (Eysenck, 1947), and we would expect this difference to appear in relation to intelligence tests also. Jensen (1964) correlated extraversion scores on the EPI with time spent on the Progressive Matrices test and found a significant correlation of -0.46; in other words, extraverts carried out the task more quickly. They also made more errors, but this trend was not significant. Farley (1966) applied the Nufferno test individually to thirty Ss, divided on the basis of their EPI scores into ten extraverts, ten ambiverts and ten introverts. The mean log speed scores on all problems correctly solved for the groups were respectively: 0·78, 0·88 and 0·93. This monotonic increase in solution time with introversion was fully significant by analysis of variance. Other examples of this relation between speed and extraversion are given elsewhere (Eysenck, 1967); there seems little doubt about its reality.

Farley (1966) also discovered a significant relation with neuroticism, but as might have been expected (Payne, 1960) this showed a non-linear trend, subjects with average scores being superior to those with high or low N scores. Lynn and Gordon (1961) have also published a study showing a similar trend; they used the Progressive Matrices test. The rationale underlying the prediction of a curvilinear relationship in this context derives, of course, from the Yerkes–Dodson law; it is believed that the optimum

4. The common belief that incentives and higher or depressed motivation generally do not affect intelligence test performance (Eysenck, 1944) may be mistaken; it is conceivable that here too we find the curvilinear Yerkes-Dodson relation, so that *overall* failure to find significant motivation and incentives may be due to compensating positive and negative effects of increased motivation on different types of subject. Some form of interaction terms should be included in analyses of this type, and by preference this should take the form of zone analysis. (Eysenck, 1966.)

drive level for complex and difficult tasks like those involved in an intelligence test lies below the high level reached by high N subjects, and above that reached by low N subjects. The general drive level of the group tested is, of course, quite critical in this connection, and it must be emphasized that unless this can be specified or measured, predictions will not always be fulfilled. Changes in difficulty level of the items, changes in the importance the result of the test assumes in the eyes of the subjects, and changes in the motivational value of the instructions may all lead to a general shift in the drive level of the subjects which may displace the optimum level in either direction. It would seem useful in tests of this prediction to have separate measures of drive, or of arousal, against which performance could be plotted (Eysenck, 1967): without such direct measures the subjects' N score may often be difficult to interpret, giving us essentially merely a measure of their *probability* of responding with autonomic activation to an anxiety-producing situation. If the situation is not perceived as anxiety-producing by the subjects, then differences in N cease to matter. This line of argument has led to a better understanding of the conditions under which N correlates with eyeblink conditioning (Eysenck, 1967), and it may be used to design experiments explicitly aimed at increasing the correlation posited.

This dependence of results on precise control of parameter values can also be illustrated by some recent unpublished experiments undertaken by Berger. We have noted that extraverts are faster and make more errors when conditions are such that the test is administered without stress on speed; in other words, when no explicit instructions are given emphasizing speed, extraverts opt for speed and neglect accuracy, while introverts opt for accuracy and go slow. These are response styles well familiar from other types of activity (Eysenck, 1960). What would we expect to happen when stress was placed, explicitly and implicitly, on speed of problem-solving activity? Let us return to Figure 5, in which we postulated that stable extraverts would have low drive level, neurotic introverts high drive level, with the other two groups (stable introverts and neurotic extraverts) intermediate. Given the specific stress on *speed* as the proper index of performance, we would expect the low-drive stable extraverts to have the slowest speed, and the neurotic introverts the highest, with the other two groups intermediate; we might also expect that the neurotic introverts would produce more errors in order to make up for the excessive speed shown.

Berger tested twenty-one thirteen-year-old school children in each of the four personality groups; the groups were equated for age, sex and intelligence, using their 11+records for this purpose. Fifty problems were presented for solution individually, followed by a rest, and finally by another set of thirty problems. Each problem was shown to the child on a screen, with numbered alternative solutions; having selected the correct solution, the child pressed a numbered button, which activated a time switch, thus recording solution latency, and also caused the projector to project the next problem on to the screen. Instructions emphasized speed of working, and the whole experimental set-up added to this impression; furthermore, the disappearance of the problem after the button had been pressed eliminated the possibility of checking the correctness of the answer. Figure 6 shows the results of the first fifty items; the next thirty showed similar results. The Figure is arranged in the form of a cumulative time record, with time arranged along the ordinate and the problems, one to fifty, along the abscissa. It will be clear that the stable extraverts are much the slowest, the neurotic introverts much the fastest, with the other two groups intermediate; these differences are highly significant. It was also found, at a high level of significance, that neurotic introverts compensated for their speed by making more errors than the other groups. Thus, the Yerkes–Dodson law appears to be working here very much as it did in the case of the McLaughlin–Eysenck experiment: the low-drive SE group does poorly because it is so slow, the high-drive NI group does poorly because it makes too many errors, and the intermediate NE and SI groups do best because they work at an optimum level of motivation.

Fluency and inhibition

This study illustrates the value of applying theories and laws from general and experimental psychology to intelligence testing. Another example may serve the same function. From the point of view of the experimental psychologist, a typical intelligence test is a good example of a task undertaken in the condition of massed practice; we would, therefore, expect it to generate reactive inhibition. Extraverts generate such inhibition more strongly and more quickly than do introverts (Eysenck, 1957, 1967), and consequently we would expect that when groups of extraverts and introverts are matched for performance during the earlier part of an intelligence test, then they will diverge towards the latter part,

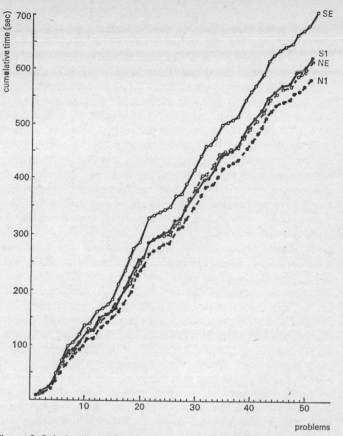

Figure 6 Solution times of stable extroverts, neurotic extroverts, stable introverts and neurotic introverts on fifty intelligence problems, timed separately and cumulated.
Data from Berger, unpublished

with the introverts superior in performance. Another way of saying the same thing would be to regard an intelligence test as a vigilance test, and use the well-known fact that introverts preserve vigilance better than extraverts to predict their better performance towards the end. Eysenck (1959) has reported such an experiment, in which he used sixty items from the Morrisby Compound Series test, individually but unobtrusively timed. Using speed of correct solutions, it was found that on the first forty-five problems introverts were slower than extraverts, but on the last fifteen items, the two groups reversed position and the extraverts were now the slower. On the last fifteen items, it was also found that the extraverts gave up more easily. It would thus seem true to say that extraverts do show the predicted decline in performance during the latter part of their performance on a typical test of intelligence, administered as far as the subjects were concerned in the usual manner, and without any special stress on speed. This experiment, taken in connection with the others already quoted, leaves little doubt that personality plays an important part in intelligence-test performance, and that its influence has hitherto been very much under-estimated.

Personality factors interact with intelligence-test performance in many ways, and neglect of these factors may easily lead to quite incorrect conclusions. As an example, we may, perhaps, take the large body of work recently done on convergent and divergent types of tests (Hudson, 1966). In studies of this kind, candidates good on divergent tests are often called 'creative', and the argument is sometimes extended to other desirable qualities of intellect, such as 'originality' (Barron, 1963; Taylor and Barron, 1963). In fact, divergent tests are by no means new; under the title of 'fluency' tests they were among the early discoveries of the London school, and a typical set of such tests is reprinted in Cattell's (1936) *Manual of Mental Tests*. Tests of this kind were found to be correlated with extraversion (Eysenck, 1960) and Spearman (1927) already pointed out that this particular factor 'has proved to be the main ground on which persons become reputed for "quickness" or for "originality"'. Hudson's work supports some such interpretation quite strongly; 'divergent' schoolboys, as compared with 'convergent' ones, are more fluent, make more errors on orthodox tests, are emotionally more forthcoming, are more sociable, and prefer 'arts' to 'science' subjects – all characteristics of extraverts as compared with introverts. There is, in fact (as Hudson acknowledges), no evidence to show that 'divergent' boys are more creative than 'convergent' ones; as he points out, one can be 'creative' in different ways. All that we seem to be dealing with in this distinction would seem to be a kind of response set or 'style'; it is, perhaps, unusual to apply this concept in relation to intelligence tests, but it applies here probably more than in relation to personality inventories.

The limitation of psychometry

These various ways in which personality and intelligence testing interact do not by any means exhaust the available evidence. Factor analysts usually assume, without proof, that groups which do not differ in performance on a group of tests will also not differ in factorial solution. Lienert (1963) showed that this assumption is, in fact, erroneous; children high and low on N, respectively, do not produce identical correlation matrices or factors, when administered sets of intelligence tests, nor do the two groups even agree in the number of factors produced. As Eysenck and White (1964) have shown in a re-analysis of the data, 'the stable group has a more clearly marked structure in the cognitive test field than has the labile group'. (It has also been found that students differing in intelligence do not have identical factor patterns on personality questionnaires; the evidence is presented by Shure and Rogers, 1963.) It is not unlikely that some of the observed differences in factor structure are connected with the intellectual response styles which we have found to be characteristic of different personality groups, but at present there is no evidence to indicate precisely how this may have come about. Much further work is clearly required before we can be sure of our facts in this complex field.

All that has been said in this paper is only suggestive, and I do not in any way believe that the hypotheses stated, and sometimes supported by experimental data, are at the moment anything but guideposts pointing in the direction of interesting and important factors which will almost certainly have a bearing on the proper measurement of intelligence. We have noted four stages in the development of intelligence tests; it is the main purpose of this paper to suggest the importance of starting out on a fifth stage of intelligence assessment, a new stage based on theoretical and experimental work, and not divorced from the main body of academic psychology. Psychometrics and factor analysis have important contributions to make, but they can do so only in conjunction with other disciplines, not by 'going it alone'. What is required is clearly an integration of intelligence testing with the main stream of academic psychology, and a more determined experimental and laboratory approach to the problems raised by the various theories of intellectual functioning. Some obvious suggestions emerge from the inevitably somewhat rambling and uncoordinated discussion of this paper:

1. Analysis of performance should always take into account individual items, rather than tests, i.e. averages taken over what may be, and usually are, non-homogeneous sets of items. Such analysis should be made in terms of latencies, i.e. speed of individual item solution, as well as of errors, persistence before abandoning items, and other similar differential indicators of response style.

2. Investigators should pay more attention to laboratory studies of learning and memory functions, of speed of information processing, and other experimental measures in the testing of specific hypotheses regarding the nature of intellectual functioning. Analysis of intelligence tests of the orthodox kind raises problems, but cannot in the nature of things go very far towards answering them.

3. Investigators should experiment with variations in experimental parameters, such as rest pauses, time from end of learning to recall, rate of presentation, degree of motivation, etc., in an effort to support or disprove specific theoretical predictions regarding the process of learning and problem solving.

4. Personality variables, such as stability–neuroticism and extraversion–introversion, should always be included in experimental studies of intellectual functioning, because of their proven value in mediating predictions and their interaction potential in all types of learning and performance tasks.

Vigorous research along these lines carries with it the promise that notions such as intelligence, IQ, ability and factor will cease to be regarded as poor relations, and will return to the eminent and successful status they held before the war; it also furnishes the only means of making these concepts scientifically meaningful, academically respectable, and practically more useful.

References

BARRON, F. (1963), *Creativity and Psychological Health*, Van Nostrand.
BENDIG, A. W. (1958), 'Extraversion, neuroticism and verbal ability measures', *J. consult. Psychol.*, vol. 22, p. 464.
BENDIG, A. W. (1960), 'Extraversion, neuroticism and student achievement in introductory psychology', *J. educ. Res.*, vol. 53, pp. 263–7.
BINET, A. and SIMON, R. (1905), 'Méthodes nouvelles pour le diagnostic du niveau intellectuel des anormaux', *L'Année Psychol.*, vol. 11, pp. 191–244.
CATTELL, J. MCK. (1890), 'Mental tests and measurements', *Mind*, vol. 15, pp. 373–80.
CATTELL, R. B. (1936), *Manual of Mental Tests*, University of London Press.
CATTELL, R. B. (1964). 'Fluid and crystallized abilities', in R. B. Cattell, *Personality and Social Psychology*, Knapp.
CHILD, D. (1964), 'The relationships between introversion, extraversion, neuroticism and performance in school examinations', *Brit. J. educ. Psychol.*, vol. 34, pp. 187–96.
DUNCANSON, J. P. (1964), *Intelligence and the Ability to Learn*, Princeton, Educational Testing Service.
EYSENCK, H. J. (1939), 'Primary mental abilities', *Brit. J. educ. Psychol.*, vol. 9, pp. 270–5.
EYSENCK, H. J. (1944), 'The effect of incentives on neurotics, and the variability of neurotics as compared with normals', *Brit. J. med. Psychol.*, vol. 20, pp. 100–103.
EYSENCK, H. J. (1947), *Dimensions of Personality*, Routledge & Kegan Paul.
EYSENCK, H. J. (1953), *Uses and Abuses of Psychology*, Penguin.
EYSENCK, H. J. (1957), *The Dynamics of Anxiety and Hysteria*, Routledge & Kegan Paul.
EYSENCK, H. J. (1959), 'Personality and problem solving', *Psychol. Rep.*, vol. 5, p. 592.
EYSENCK, H. J. (1960), *The Structure of Human Personality*, Methuen.
EYSENCK, H. J. (1963), 'The biological basis of personality', *Nature*, vol. 199, pp. 1031–34.
EYSENCK, H. J. (1966), 'Personality and experimental psychology', *Bull. Brit. psychol. Soc.*, vol. 62, pp. 1–28.
EYSENCK, H. J. (1967), *The Biological Basis of Personality*, New York, C. C. Thomas.
EYSENCK, H. J. and HALSTEAD, H. (1945), 'The memory function', *Amer. J. Psychiatry*, vol. 102, pp. 174–80.
EYSENCK, H. J. and WHITE, P. O. (1964), 'Personality and the measurement of intelligence', *Brit. J. educ. Psychol.*, vol. 34, pp. 197–202.
FARLEY, F. H. (1966), 'Individual differences in solution time in error-free problem solving', *Brit. J. Soc. clin. Psychol.*, vol. 5.
FRANK, H. (1963), 'Informations Psychologie and Nachrichtentechnik', in N. Weiner and J. P. Schade (eds.), *Progress in Brain Research*, vol. 2, *Nerve, Brain and Memory Models*, Elsevier Publishing, Amsterdam.
FURNEAUX, W. D. (1960), 'Intellectual abilities and problem solving behaviour', in H. J. Eysenck (ed.), *Handbook of Abnormal Psychology*, Pitman.

FURNEAUX, W. D. (1962), 'The psychologist and the university', *Univ. Quart.*, vol. 17, pp. 33–47.

GALTON, F. (1883), *Inquiries Into Human Faculty and its Development*, Macmillan.

GUILFORD, J. P. (1966), 'Intelligence: 1965 model', *Amer. Psychol.*, vol. 21, pp. 20–26.

HICK, W. (1952), 'On the rate of gain of information', *Quart. J. exp. Psychol.*, vol. 4, pp. 11–26.

HUDSON, L. (1966), *Contrary Imaginations*, Methuen, Penguin 1968.

HYMAN, R. (1953), 'Stimulus information as a determinant of reaction time', *J. exp. Psychol.*, vol. 45, pp. 188–96.

JENSEN, A. R. (1964), *Individual Differences in Learning: Interference Factors*, US Dept. of Health, Education and Welfare, Co-op. project no. 1867.

KLEINSMITH, L. J. and KAPLAN, S. (1963), 'Paired-associate learning as a function and interpolated interval' *J. exp. Psychol.*, vol. 65, pp. 190–93.

LIENERT, A. A. (1963), 'Die Faktorenstruktur der Intelligenz als Funktion des Neurotizismus', *Zhstr. F. Exp. Angew. Psychol.*, vol. 10, pp. 140–59.

LYNN, R., and GORDON, I. E. (1961), 'The relation of neuroticism and extraversion to intelligence and educational attainment', *Brit. J. educ. Psychol.*, vol. 31, pp. 194–203.

MCNEMAR, R. (1964), 'Lost: our intelligence? Why?', *Amer. Psychol.*, vol. 19, pp. 871–82.

MERKEL, J. (1885), 'Die zeitlichen Verhältnisse der Willenstätigkeit', *Philos. Studien*, vol. 2, pp. 73–127.

OTTO, W. (1965), 'Inhibition potential in good and poor achievers', *J. educ. Psychol.*, vol. 56, pp. 200–207.

OTTO, W. and FREDRICKS, R. C. (1963), 'Relationship of reactive inhibition to reading skill achievement', *Educ. Psychol.*, vol. 54, pp. 227–230.

PAYNE, R. W. (1960), 'Cognitive abnormalities', in H. J. Eysenck (ed.), *Handbook of Abnormal Psychology*, Pitman.

RANKING, F. (1963a), *Reading Test Performance of Introverts and Extraverts*, 12th Yearbook of Nat. Reading Conf., Milwaukee.

RANKING, F. (1963), 'Reading test reliability and validity as function of introversion: extraversion', *J. Devel. Reading*, vol. 6, pp. 106–17.

ROTH, E. (1964), 'Die Geschwirdigkeit der Verarbeitung von Information und ihr Zusammenhang mit Intelligenz', *Atschr F. Exp. Angew. Psychol.*, vol. 11, pp. 616–622.

SAVAGE, R. D. (1962), 'Personality factors and academic performance', *Brit. J. educ. Psychol.*, vol. 32, pp. 251–52.

SCHMIDTKE, H. (1961), 'Zur Frage der informationstheoretischen Analyze von Wahlreaktionsexperimenten', *Psychol. Forschung*, vol. 26, pp. 157–78.

SCHONFIELD, D. (1965), 'Memory changes with age', *Nature*, vol. 208, p. 918.

SHURE, G. H. and ROGERS, M. S. (1963), 'Personality factor stability for three ability levels', *J. Psychol.*, vol. 55, pp. 445–56.

SPEARMAN, C. (1904), '"General intelligence" objectively determined and measured', *Amer. J. Psychol.*, vol. 15, pp. 201–293.

SPEARMAN, C. (1926), *The Nature of 'Intelligence' and the Principles of Cognition*, Macmillan.

SPEARMAN, C. (1926), *The Abilities of Man*, Methuen.

SPENCE, K. W. (1964), 'Anxiety (drive) level and performance in eyelid conditioning', *Psychol. Bull.*, vol. 61, pp. 129–39.

STAKE, R. E. (1961), 'Learning parameters, aptitudes and achievements', *Psychometric Mon.*, no. 9.

TAYLOR, C. W., and BARROW, F. (eds.) (1963), *Scientific Creativity*, Wiley.

THORNDIKE, E. L. (1926), *The Measurement of Intelligence*, Teachers' College, Columbia University.

THURSTONE, L. L. (1926), *The Nature of Intelligence*, Harcourt, Brace & World.

VERNON, P. E. (1965), 'Ability factors and environmental influences', *Amer. Psychol.*, vol. 20, p. 273.

WOODROW, H. (1946) 'The ability to learn', *Psychol. Rev.*, vol. 53, pp. 147–58.

Part Five
Cross-Cultural Studies

Perhaps the most sensitive areas in education today are those of individual and group differences. When skills or abilities which seem associated with success in our Western industrialized society are said to be found differentially in groups, classes or races, then such statements are vociferously denounced. Stephen Wiseman was well aware of the sociopolitical implications of this important area of individual differences. He chose authors whose stature put them personally above the emotional arena, and from their writings he selected passages which comment generally on the differences between groups that have been found.

For my part, the debate, a flattering noun in retrospect, sparked off by Jensen's work, is as fascinating as his findings. One can appreciate the concern of professional and amateur politicians that their group is in no way inferior to another. Thankfully, as educators, we deal with individuals and the wide-ranging differences that face us in each classroom put the politicians' problem where it should be for us – an interesting academic discussion which, unfortunately, seems to be carried on in this context with noisy contributions from people without the training or inclination to weigh evidence as accurately as sociopolitical prejudice.

Our attitudes to differences between people appear to be governed more by ideological values than carefully acquired facts. There is the positive regard which implies that individual differences should be the essence of the educational system, which must adapt its materials, methods and administration to the individual needs of each child in the classroom. However, certain differences are more tolerable than others. No one blinks when John is said to be a better footballer or taller than Jim, nor is Jim seen as appreciably deprived by his lack of inches. Heated debate does not ensue as to the nature–nurture contribution to the difference in height. On the other hand, if one suggests differences in academic ability, or worse, its correlate, general ability, or worst, intelligence, then heated debate certainly ensues, variously involving the utility or even the existence of the concept of intelligence, and the nature–nurture wrangle is invoked with venom. After a short time recourse to emotive words occurs – such as 'compensatory', 'deprived', 'disadvantaged' (we do love to patronize) or 'selective', 'elitist' (we do not like other people to have advantages, or having utilized them for ourselves or our children, we wish to indicate how liberated we are by denying them to others). It does seem that we tolerate individual differences as long as they are not influential in the competition evoked by our Western industrialized society.

Another way of becoming less tolerant of individual differences is to associate them with groups. John may be taller than Jim, but to indicate that John, a Watusi, is taller than Jim, an Eskimo, elicits a new degree of sensitivity which can be heightened if you generalize that the Watusi as a race are taller than Eskimaux. The precarious situation is clearly seen in the accurate but nevertheless defensive statement that 'of course some Eskimaux are taller than some Watusi'.

For emotion to really run high though, you have to compound a difference that matters with large groups with political power. Everyone is encouraged to become an expert when statements are made alluding to differences between groups in an ability linked with success in society. Emotions are driven high, political capital is made both for the protagonists and the opponents of such statements. Social tension rises and the people least likely to gain are John and Jim. These are the types of statements outlined in this section. Evidence is presented that indicates that groups, classes and races of people differ in abilities which have been respected as hallmarks of success in our society. These authors have compounded the two sins and have drawn upon themselves the abuse of the anti-intellectual as well as the deserved criticism of their peers.

No experimental or survey study is perfect and it will always be possible to question parts or the whole of a study, in terms of its reliability, validity, interpretation and generalization. If infallibility was required of every part of a study, then no research would be undertaken and nothing learned by these methods. When reviewing research findings, it is usual to check atypical or 'unwanted' findings with a greater stringency than would be applied to results that fit with the hypothesis and previous known fact. If this additional stringency does challenge (or debunk) the atypical result, then in all honesty we should go back to the 'approved' findings and test them with the same stringency.

The passages that follow are taken from the writings of Jensen, Lesser, Feifer and Clark, and Vernon. These authors have suggested that inter-group, inter-class and inter-race differences on important educational variables have been found in their studies. In the current egalitarian ethos, these reports have, along with those of Eysenck, been put under great scrutiny. All the ifs, buts and maybes have been highlighted and any weaknesses in methodology criticized. The inevitable denunciation from emotional quarters has occurred, but sadly the equally thorough examination of the other side of the coin has not been undertaken. As Jensen says, 'a pre-ordained doctrinaire stance . . . hinders the achievement of a scientific understanding of the problem. To rule out of court . . . any reasonable hypotheses on purely ideological grounds is to argue that static ignorance is preferable to increasing our knowledge of reality.' To deny and denounce rather than dispute and disprove any evidence that ill-fits our picture of reality is evidence in itself of how insecure is our grasp of reality. This section should be read accordingly.

13 A. R. Jensen

How Much Can We Boost IQ and Scholastic Achievement?

Excerpt from 'How much can we boost IQ and scholastic achievement?', in
Environment, Heredity and Ability', Harvard Educational Review Reprint,
1969, series no. 2.

Race differences

The important distinction between the *individual* and the *population* must always be kept clearly in mind in any discussion of racial differences in mental abilities or any other behavioral characteristics. Whenever we select a person for some special educational purpose, whether for special instruction in a grade-school class for children with learning problems, or for a 'gifted' class with an advanced curriculum, or for college attendance, or for admission to graduate training or a professional school, we are selecting an *individual*, and we are selecting him and dealing with him as an individual for reasons of his individuality. Similarly, when we employ someone, or promote someone in his occupation, or give some special award or honor to someone for his accomplishments, we are doing this to an individual. The variables of social class, race, and national origin are correlated so imperfectly with any of the valid criteria on which the above decisions should depend, or for that matter, with any behavioral characteristic, that these background factors are irrelevant as a basis for dealing with individuals – as students, as employees, as neighbors. Furthermore, since, as far as we know, the full range of human talents is represented in all the major races of man and in all socioeconomic levels, it is unjust to allow the mere fact of an individual's racial or social background to affect the treatment accorded to him. All persons rightfully must be regarded on the basis of their individual qualities and merits, and all social, educational, and economic institutions must have built into them the mechanisms for insuring and maximizing the treatment of persons according to their individual behavior.

If a society completely believed and practised the ideal of treating every person as an individual, it would be hard to see why there should be any problems about 'race' *per se*. There might still be problems concerning poverty, unemployment, crime, and other social ills, and given the will, they could be tackled just as any other problems that require rational methods for solution. But if this philosophy prevailed in practice, there would not need to be a 'race problem'.

The question of *race* differences in intelligence comes up, not when we deal with individuals as individuals, but when certain identifiable *groups* or subcultures within the society are brought into comparison with one another *as groups or populations*. It is only when the groups are disproportionately represented in what are commonly perceived as the most desirable and the least desirable social and occupational roles in a society that the question arises concerning average differences among groups. Since much of the current thinking behind civil rights, fair employment, and equality of educational opportunity appeals to the fact that there is a disproportionate representation of different racial groups in the various levels of the educational, occupational, and socio-economic hierarchy, we are forced to examine all the possible reasons for this inequality among racial groups in the attainments and rewards generally valued by all groups within our society. To what extent can such inequalities be attributed to unfairness in society's multiple selection processes? ('Unfair' meaning that selection is influenced by intrinsically irrelevant criteria, such as skin color, racial or national origin, etc.) And to what extent are these inequalities attributable to really relevant selection criteria which apply equally to all individuals but at the same time select disproportionately between some racial groups because there exist, in fact, real average differences among the groups – differences in the population distributions of those characteristics which are indisputably relevant to educational and occupational performance? This is certainly one of the most important questions confronting our nation today. The answer, which can be found only through unfettered research, has enormous consequence for the welfare of all, particularly of minorities whose plight is now in the foreground of public attention. A preordained, doctrinaire stance with regard to this issue hinders the achievement of a scientific understanding of the problem. To rule out of court, so to speak, any reasonable hypotheses on purely ideological grounds is to argue that static ignorance is preferable to increasing our knowledge of reality. I strongly disagree with those who believe in searching for the truth by scientific means only under certain circumstances and eschew this course in favor of ignorance under other circumstances, or who believe that the results of inquiry on some subjects cannot be entrusted to the public but should be kept the guarded possession of a scientific élite. Such attitudes, in my opinion, represent a danger to free inquiry and, consequently, in the long run, work to the disadvantage of society's general welfare. 'No holds barred' is the best formula for scientific inquiry. One does not decree beforehand which phenomena cannot be studied or which questions cannot be answered.

Genetic aspects of racial differences

No one, to my knowledge, questions the role of environmental factors, including influences from past history, in determining at least some of the variance between racial groups in standard measures of intelligence, school performance, and occupational status. The current literature on the culturally disadvantaged abounds with discussion – some of it factual, some of it fanciful – of how a host of environmental factors depresses cognitive development and performance. I recently coedited a book which is largely concerned with the environmental aspects of disadvantaged minorities (Deutsch, Katz and Jensen, 1968). But the possible importance of genetic factors in racial behavioral differences has been greatly ignored, almost to the point of being a tabooed subject, just as were the topics of venereal disease and birth control a generation or so ago.

My discussions with a number of geneticists concerning the question of a genetic basis of differences among races in mental abilities have revealed to me a number of rather consistently agreed-upon points which can be summarized in general terms as follows: Any groups which have been geographically or socially isolated from one another for many generations are practically certain to differ in their gene pools, and consequently are likely to show differences in any phenotypic characteristics having high heritability. This is practically axiomatic, according to the geneticists with whom I have spoken. Races are said to be 'breeding populations', which is to say that matings within the group have a much higher probability than matings outside the group. Races are more technically viewed by geneticists as populations having different distributions of gene frequencies. These genetic differences are manifested in virtually every anatomical, physiological, and biochemical comparison one can make between representative samples of identifiable racial groups (Kuttner, 1967). There is no reason to suppose that the brain should be exempt from his generalization. (Racial differences in the relative frequencies of various blood constituents have probably been the most thoroughly studied so far.)

But what about behavior? If it can be measured and shown to have a genetic component, it would be regarded, from a genetic standpoint, as no different from other human characteristics. There seems to be little question that racial differences in genetically conditioned behavioral characteristics, such as mental abilities, should exist, just as physical differences. The real questions, geneticists tell me, are not whether there are or are not genetic racial differences that affect behavior, because there undoubtedly are. The proper questions to ask, from a scientific standpoint, are: What is the direction of the difference? What is the magnitude of the difference? And what is the significance of the difference – medically, socially, educationally, or from whatever standpoint that may be relevant to the characteristic in question? A difference is important only within a specific context. For example, one's blood type in the ABO system is unimportant until one needs a transfusion. And some genetic differences are apparently of no importance with respect to any context as far as anyone has been able to discover – for example, differences in the size and shape of ear lobes. The idea that all genetic differences have arisen or persisted only as a result of natural selection, by conferring some survival or adaptive benefit on their possessors, is no longer generally held. There appear to be many genetic differences, or polymorphisms, which confer no discernible advantages to survival.[1]

Negro intelligence and scholastic performance

Negroes in the United States are disproportionately represented among groups identified as culturally or educationally disadvantaged. This, plus the fact that Negroes constitute by far the largest racial minority in the United States, has for many years focused attention on Negro intelligence. It is a subject with a now vast literature which has been quite recently reviewed by Dreger and Miller (1960, 1968) and by Shuey (1966), whose 578-page review is the most comprehensive, covering 382 studies. The basic data are well known: on the average Negroes test about one standard deviation (fifteen IQ points) below the average of the

1. The most comprehensive and sophisticated discussion of the genetic behavior analysis of race differences that I have found is by Spuhler and Lindzey (1967).

white population in IQ, and this finding is fairly uniform across the eighty-one different tests of intellectual ability used in the studies reviewed by Shuey. This magnitude of difference gives a median overlap of 15 per cent, meaning that 15 per cent of the Negro population exceeds the white average. In terms of proportions of variance, if the numbers of Negroes and whites were equal, the differences *between* racial groups would account for 23 per cent of the total variance, but – an important point – the differences *within* groups would account for 77 per cent of the total variance. When gross socioeconomic level is controlled, the average difference reduces to about eleven IQ points (Shuey, 1966), which, it should be recalled, is about the same spread as the average difference between siblings in the same family. So-called 'culture-free' or 'culture-fair' tests tend to give Negroes slightly lower scores, on the average, than more conventional IQ tests such as the Stanford–Binet and Wechsler scales. Also, as a group, Negroes perform somewhat more poorly on those subtests which tap abstract abilities. The majority of studies show that Negroes perform relatively better on verbal than on non-verbal intelligence tests.

In tests of scholastic achievement, also, judging from the massive data of the Coleman study (Coleman *et al.*, 1966), Negroes score about one standard deviation (SD) below the average for whites and Orientals and considerably less than one SD below other disadvantaged minorities tested in the Coleman study – Puerto Rican, Mexican–American, and American Indian. The one SD decrement in Negro performance is fairly constant throughout the period from grades one through twelve.

Another aspect of the distribution of IQs in the Negro population is their lesser variance in comparison to the white distribution. This shows up in most of the studies reviewed by Shuey. The best single estimate is probably the estimate based on a large normative study of Stanford–Binet IQs of Negro school children in five south-eastern states, by Kennedy, Van De Riet and White (1963). They found the SD of Negro children's IQs to be 12·4, as compared with 16·4 in the white normative sample. The Negro distribution thus has only about 60 per cent as much variance (i.e. SD^2) as the white distribution.

There is an increasing realization among students of the psychology of the disadvantaged that the discrepancy in their average performance cannot be completely or directly attributed to discrimination or inequalities in education. It seems not unreasonable, in view of the fact that intelligence variation has a large genetic component, to hypothesize that genetic factors may play a part in this picture. But such an hypothesis is anathema to many social scientists. The idea that the lower average intelligence and scholastic performance of Negroes could involve, not only environmental, but also genetic, factors has indeed been strongly denounced (e.g. Pettigrew, 1964). But it has been neither contradicted nor discredited by evidence.

The fact that a reasonable hypothesis has not been rigorously proved does not mean that it should be summarily dismissed. It only means that we need more appropriate research for putting it to the test. I believe such definitive research is entirely possible but has not yet been done. So all we are left with are various lines of evidence, no one of which is definitive alone, but which, viewed all together, make it a not unreasonable hypothesis that genetic factors are strongly implicated in the average Negro–white intelligence difference. The preponderance of the evidence is, in my opinion, less consistent with a strictly environmental hypothesis than with a genetic hypothesis, which, of course, does not exclude the influence of environment or its interaction with genetic factors.

References

COLEMAN, J. S. *et al.* (1966), *Equality of Educational Opportunity*, US Department of Health, Education, and Welfare.

DEUTSCH, M., KATZ, I. and JENSEN, A. R. (eds.) (1968), *Social Class, Race, and Psychological Development*, Holt, Rinehart & Winston.

DREGER, R. M. and MILLER, K. S. (1960), 'Comparative psychological studies of Negroes and whites in the United States', *Psychol. Bull.*, vol. 57, pp. 361–402.

DREGER, R. M. and MILLER, K. S. (1968), 'Comparative psychological studies of Negroes and whites in the United States: 1959–1965', *Psychol. Bull.*, Monogr. Suppl., vol. 70, no. 3, part 2.

KENNEDY, W. A., VAN DE RIET, V. and WHITE, J. C., Jr. (1963), 'A normative sample of intelligence and achievement of Negro elementary school children in the Southeastern United States', *Monograph Soc. Res. Child Development*, vol. 28, no. 6.

KUTTNER, R. E. (1967), 'Biochemical anthropology' in R. E. Kuttner (ed.) *Race and Modern Science*, Social Science Press, pp. 197–222.

PETTIGREW, T. (1964), *A Profile of the Negro American*, Van Nostrand.

SHUEY, A. M. (1966), *The Testing of Negro Intelligence*, Social Science Press, 2nd edn.

SPUHLER, J. N., and LINDZEY, G. (1967), 'Racial differences in behavior' in J. Hirsch (ed.), *Behavior-Genetic Analysis*, McGraw-Hill.

14 G. S. Lesser, G. Feifer and D. H. Clark

Mental Abilities of Children from Different Social-Class and Cultural Groups

Excerpts from G. S. Lesser, G. Feifer and D. H. Clark, *Mental Abilities of Children from Different Social-Class and Cultural Groups*, Monographs of the Society for Research into Child Development, 1965.

The purpose of this study was to examine the patterns among various mental abilities in young children from different social-class and cultural backgrounds. The patterns among four mental abilities (verbal ability, reasoning, number facility, and space conceptualization) were studied in first-grade children from four cultural groups in New York City (Chinese, Jewish, Negro, and Puerto Rican), with each cultural group divided into middle-class and lower-class groups.

Until recent years, there has been little empirical study of differential mental abilities in young children. In contrast, much theoretical and methodological progress (e.g. Burt, 1939, 1941, 1944, 1949, 1954; Carroll, 1941; Clark, 1944; Garrett, 1946; Kelley, 1928; Meyer and Bendig, 1961; Swineford, 1948, 1949; Thurstone, 1948; Vernon, 1950) has been made in defining the organization of differentiated mental operations in adults and in children old enough to respond to group tests. Within the past decade, however, sufficient knowledge has accumulated (e.g. Davis, Lesser and French, 1960; Meyers and Dingman, 1960; Meyers, Orpet, Attwell and Dingman, 1962) to indicate that differentiated mental abilities can be identified in children who are too young to read and write.

Our purpose was to extend the general demonstration that differential mental abilities exist in young children by examining the variations in the *patterns* of these diverse abilities that are associated with variations in social-class and cultural conditions. While it has been established that group factors beyond a general-ability factor exist in young children, little has yet been discovered about the differences in *patterns* of intellectual expression related to the influences of different social classes and cultures.

General implications of the research

This research problem has several theoretical and practical implications. Certain of these implications are part of the growing discussions (e.g. Passow, 1963; Riessman, 1962) of the problems of the 'disadvantaged' or 'culturally deprived' children from 'depressed' areas. However, in the absence of clear, consensual definitions of these concepts and of substantial empirical evidence relevant to the opinions presented, it is difficult to formulate rigorous and testable propositions about the problems of disadvantaged children. When these problems are viewed within the contest of evolving theories of intelligence and analyses of the sociological forces associated with social-class and cultural influences, testable questions can be asked with greater scientific meaning and precision.

The attempt to establish similarities and differences between the structures of mental abilities of young children in different social-class and cultural groups is linked to several scientific issues. One such issue is the long history of investigation of trait organization and intra-individual variations in test performance. Social-class and cultural-group determinants of the structure of mental abilities are also related to the development of mathematical procedures for identifying the dimensions of human behavior and to a psychological issue with a most venerable background, the heredity *versus* environment controversy. Evidence concerning the environmental antecedents and correlates of diverse mental abilities is also central to theory construction in developmental psychology. Such evidence provides a clarification of the basic nature, function, and organization of the mental abilities themselves and of the characteristics of the environmental conditions that influence their development.

Implications for psychological assessment and educational procedures

Perhaps the most important implications of this research on patterns of mental ability in young children relate to the practical efforts to determine the optimum educational conditions and the most valid assessment instruments for children from diverse backgrounds. The loss of outstanding intellectual talent in groups labeled 'culturally deprived' has been a source of increasing concern. American society is dedicated to the development of intellectual ability wherever it is found. However, before talent can be developed, it must be located and identified. In the last few decades, intellectual ability has been located primarily with the aid of a few popular tests of intelligence (e.g. the Revised Stanford–Binet Intelligence Scale). For better or worse, we have, in practice, defined 'intelligence' in terms of the most popular tests that presume to measure it.

These intelligence tests have been frequently criticized for being too heavily loaded with verbal items that are both unfair to certain groups within our population and too narrow as assessments of intellectual functioning. A score based on a test that is heavily loaded with one factor can tell little about the quality and quantity of the various talents that an individual has. Perhaps because of such intelligence measures, or for reasons as yet undiscovered, we are failing conspicuously to discover outstanding talent in certain strata of our society. It is clear from the research literature that lower socioeconomic groups and certain cultural groups do not contribute their proportion of intellectually productive individuals.

Teachers must make both immediate and continuing educational decisions about children from different social-class and cultural backgrounds in order to provide effective classroom instruction. There is, however, a serious lack of valid information available regarding the abilities of these children. When a child is classified on the basis of a single, global score, such as a general-intelligence quotient (even if the test is appropriate and valid for his social-class and cultural group), much remains to be known about the range and operation of his abilities. However, if that single global score is not only too narrow but is also inappropriate and invalid for his group, the information available to the teacher becomes even more obscure and less useful.

The study of cultural differences in mental abilities attacks a fundamental, persistent problem for education and psychology: how do we provide valid psychological evaluation of children from widely dissimilar cultural groups? There is no doubt that one of the most pressing needs expressed by teachers and school administrators is for testing instruments that will provide fair, accurate, and broad assessment of the abilities of young children from cultural backgrounds other than those typical of our total school population.

School personnel in 'underprivileged areas' contend that their children cannot possibly perform well on the available psychological tests because the tasks required of them are either unimportant or alien. The claim has often been made that intelligence tests (such as the Stanford–Binet Intelligence Scale) were originally designed to measure those aspects of mental ability in which middle-class children excelled, ignoring those other aspects of mental ability in which the lower class, through its culture, encourages its children to perform favorably. This is understandable since intelligence tests were developed to answer the need for prediction of performance in school. As long as schools function to train children who are best able to understand and work within standards that are based on middle-class, white, urban values, such tests should do a reasonably good job of predicting those children of superior academic 'ability'.

We are no longer satisfied with such limited educational goals, however. We must educate children who can contribute to our changing society in ways that we may well not be able to anticipate today. This means we must broaden our definition of 'ability' or 'talent' to include behaviors based on values that, thus far, have not been prominent in middle-class culture. We must be able to identify relative intellectual strengths *within* an individual, and we must be able to identify his individual intellectual strengths, no matter what his social-class or cultural identity may be. Having done this psychological assessment job, we must develop educational techniques that will help the most talented children develop their talents fully, although radical departure from traditional educational procedures may be necessitated thereby.

Before the psychological assessment job can begin, however, information is needed on the possible variations in the *patterns* of diverse mental abilities as they relate to variations in social class and culture. In order to understand the relative strengths of an individual child's mental abilities, we must have information on how children of a particular background (e.g. middle-class Puerto Rican or lower-class Chinese) tend to express their intellectual abilities, in contrast to how the majority of the school population tends to express its intellectual abilities. Perhaps intelligence tests can then be developed that will yield intra-individual profiles of scores for the various mental abilities of children, with contrasting normative profiles for children of similar social-class and cultural identity and for children in the entire nation. [. . .]

Implications for educational practice

No effort to add to our knowledge about social-class and ethnic-group effects upon mental ability will have tangible or socially useful educational outcomes unless accompanied by simultaneous coordinated efforts to develop curricula, train teachers, modify school organization, and improve methods for establishing public policies for our schools. Each of the many educational efforts that affect children from culturally diverse groups – issues of measurement, curriculum, teacher training, school organization, etc. – has remained almost entirely divorced from the others. These studies seem to spin in their own orbits, each remaining theoretically or methodologically discrete, profiting little from each other's existence, and failing to feed any really useful information to the practitioner conducting daily classroom instruction. When innovations are attempted, they are introduced in one or another of these educational areas singly, with insufficient concern for how an attempted innovation in any one area will affect all the other parts of the educational system.

The present attempt to construct suitable testing procedures for studying children from culturally diverse groups has not yet departed from this traditional isolation of educational efforts. We have not yet incorporated considerations of curriculum development, teacher training, and school organization as essential aspects of our test development, and our results, consequently have little immediate, direct applicability to the solutions of these problems.

The present study, however, has taken the first step toward contributing to the solution of the broader educational problems: we have shown that several mental abilities are related to each other in ways that are culturally determined. We have been interested in identifying these abilities as distinct from the motivations, aspirations, and individual attitudes of the subjects. However, we have not yet attempted to relate these patterns of ability to school performance but have proposed, instead, that the identification of relative strengths and weaknesses of members of different cultural groups is a basic and vital prerequisite to making enlightened decisions affecting the educational process and aims. The attempt to apply the present findings to the building of new school programs and the adaptation of old school practices to fit the knowledge of the patterns of abilities in culturally diverse groups is the most compelling extension of this research.

Beyond the problem of incorporating these findings into broader educational plans and policies, the following other related issues seem promising and important:

1. Investigations of the sociocultural environments to determine which aspects of those environments are most salient for the

development of different patterns of abilities. The following variables provide a focus for such investigations:

(a) differential reinforcement
(b) natural selection
(c) adaptive solutions to minority group problems
(d) attention span
(e) availability of models
(f) cognitive style
(g) family interaction
(h) impulse control
(i) socialization methods
(j) independence training
(k) work methods
(l) self-concept

2. Case studies of individuals within a sociocultural group who show a marked adherence to or divergence from the norms of that group.

3. Investigations of diverse mental abilities designed to identify further and isolate such abilities, to determine the relations among them and their relative contributions to the child's intellectual functioning.

Additional specific questions for study follow:

1. Will the major finding of this study, that differential patterns of ability are related to ethnic-group differences, remain stable across age groups? That is, does ethnic-group membership continue to determine the pattern of abilities for children with increasing maturity and school experience? Do the relative strengths and weaknesses of the subjects represent different rates of learning that eventually level off to a more or less common mean for all groups, or do they indeed represent stable cognitive organizations?

2. Is there an optimal pattern among mental abilities that results in superior school performance? Or are different optimal patterns among mental abilities associated with superior school performance in different subject-matter areas? Can the child's abilities be differentially reinforced so that these optimal patterns can be produced? Or, conversely, should the educational program adjust itself to the relative strengths and weaknesses of the child?

3. Is the learning process for each of the diverse mental abilities the same or different? Are these abilities developed in different ways with differentially suitable reinforcements?

4. What is the effect of the development of one ability on that of another? Will an attempt to increase the level of one ability affect its relation with other abilities?

5. What effect does the presence of a tester of the same or different cultural group have on the test results for each child? In the present study, the use of a tester from the child's own cultural group may have served to maximize the responses most appropriate within the cultural group. Does the child adapt himself to a different set of expectations for different testers and is the child's cognitive functioning affected accordingly?

6. Are the kinds of reinforcements necessary to maintain the development of abilities, or to internalize long-term commitment to the application of these abilities, relevant to the cultural-group reinforcements that first determine the child's pattern of mental abilities? How can this knowledge be most profitably incorporated into educational procedures?

Summary

This study examined the patterns among various mental abilities in six- and seven-year-old children from different social-class and cultural backgrounds. The main intent was to extend the empirical analyses of the development of differential mental abilities in children, but the findings of this research also bear directly upon the problems of building valid and precise assessment instruments for children from different cultural groups.

Despite the considerable amount of work in the field of mental abilities in an attempt to create 'culture-free' or 'culture-fair' tests, little has been shown to yield consistent and valid results. The problem still remains of how to evaluate the intellectual potential of children whose backgrounds necessarily handicap them seriously on the usual tests of mental ability. This study focused on two major aspects of the problem: first, to devise tests that would be as free as possible of any direct class or cultural bias but still would be acceptable measures of intellectual traits and, second, to structure a testing situation that would enable each child to be evaluated under optimal conditions.

Hypotheses were tested regarding the effects of social-class and ethnic-group affiliation (and their interactions) upon both the level of each mental ability considered singly and the pattern among mental abilities considered in combination. Four mental abilities (Verbal Ability, Reasoning, Number Facility, and Space

Conceptualization) were studied in first-grade children from four ethnic groups (Chinese, Jewish, Negro, and Puerto Rican), with each ethnic group divided into middle- and lower-class groups.

The following specific predictions were made:

1. Significant differences will exist between the two *social-class* groups in the *level* of scores for each mental ability.

2. Significant differences will exist among the four *ethnic groups* in the *level* of scores for each mental ability.

3. *Social-class* and *ethnicity* will interact significantly in determining the *level* of scores for each mental ability.

Table 1 Analysis of variance of patterns of mental-ability scores for ethnic groups

Variable	Sum of squares	df	MS	F	p
Tests	1·509	3	0·50	0·13	
Ethnic groups	16,898·596	3	5,632·87	25·27	<0·001
Individuals	70,435·647	316	222·90		
Ethnic groups × Tests	5,913·575	9	657·06	17·32	<0·001
Residual	35,969·666	948	37·94		
Total	129,218·993	1279	101·03		

4. Significant differences will exist between the two *social-class* groups in the *pattern* of scores from the four mental-ability scales.

5. Significant differences will exist among the four *ethnic* groups in the *pattern* of scores from the four mental-ability scales.

6. *Social-class* and *ethnicity* will interact significantly in determining the *pattern* of scores from the four mental-ability scales.

To test these hypotheses, a $4 \times 2 \times 2$ analysis-of-covariance design (completely balanced randomized blocks) was used. The four ethnic groups (Chinese, Jewish, Negro, and Puerto Rican) were each divided into two social-class groups (middle and lower), each in turn divided into equal numbers of boys and girls. A total of 16 subgroups, each composed of 20 children, was represented. The total sample was thus composed of 320 first-grade children. Three test influences were controlled statistically in the analysis-of-covariance design: effort and persistence, persuasibility or responsiveness to the tester, and age of the subject.

The major findings were as follows:

1. Differences in *social-class* placement *do* produce significant differences in the absolute *level* of each mental ability but *do not* produce significant differences in the *patterns* among these abilities.

2. Differences in *ethnic-group* membership *do* produce significant differences in *both* the absolute *level* of each mental ability and the *patterns* among these abilities.

3. *Social-class* and *ethnicity do* interact to affect the absolute *level* of each mental ability but *do not* interact to affect the *patterns* among these abilities.

Thus, predictions 1, 2, 3, and 5 were strongly confirmed. No statistically significant support was found for predictions 4 and 6. The following other specific results were found:

1. Regarding social-class effects upon mental abilities, middle-class children are significantly superior to lower-class children on all scales and subtests.

2. Regarding ethnic-group effects upon mental abilities (*see* Figure 1 and Table 1):
(a) On Verbal Ability, Jewish children ranked first (being significantly better than all other ethnic groups), Negroes ranked second and Chinese third (both being significantly better than Puerto Ricans), and Puerto Ricans fourth.
(b) On Reasoning, the Chinese ranked first and Jews second (both being significantly better than Negroes and Puerto Ricans), Negroes third, and Puerto Ricans fourth.
(c) On Numerical Ability, Jews ranked first and Chinese second (both being significantly better than Puerto Ricans and Negroes), Puerto Ricans third, and Negroes fourth.
(d) On Space, Chinese ranked first (being significantly better than Puerto Ricans and Negroes), Jews second, Puerto Ricans third, and Negroes fourth.

3. Regarding sex differences, boys were significantly better than girls on the total Space scale, on the Picture Vocabulary subtest (but not on the total Verbal scale), and on the Jump Peg subtest (but not on the total Reasoning scale).

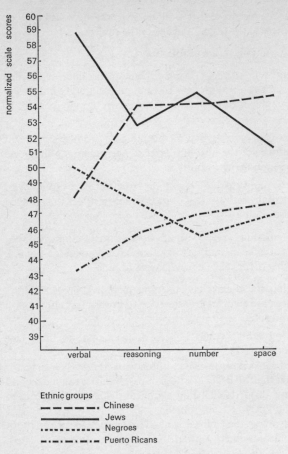

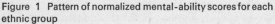

Figure 1 Pattern of normalized mental-ability scores for each
ethnic group

4. Regarding the interactions of social class and ethnicity, two
effects combined to produce the statistically significant interaction
effects upon each scale of mental ability:

(a) On each mental-ability scale, social-class position produced
more of a difference in the mental abilities of the Negro children
than in the other groups. That is, the middle-class Negro children
were more different in level of mental abilities from the lower-
class Negroes than, for example, the middle-class Chinese were
from the lower-class Chinese.

(b) On each mental-ability scale, the scores of the middle-class children from the various ethnic groups resembled each other to a greater extent than did the scores of the lower-class children from the various ethnic groups. That is, the middle-class Chinese, Jewish, Negro, and Puerto Rican children were more alike in their mental-ability scores than were the lower-class Chinese, Jewish, Negro, and Puerto Rican children.

5. Regarding the interactions of sex and ethnicity, the significant interactions for both Verbal and Space reflected the higher scores for boys than for girls in all ethnic groups, except for the Jewish children; Jewish girls were superior to Jewish boys for both Verbal and Space scales.

It was concluded that social-class and ethnic-group membership (and their interaction) have strong effects upon the level of each of four mental abilities (Verbal Ability, Reasoning, Numerical Facility, and Space Conceptualization).

Ethnic-group affiliation also affects strongly the pattern or organization of mental abilities, but once the pattern specific to the ethnic group emerges, social-class variations within the ethnic group do not alter this basic organization. Apparently, different mediators are associated with social-class and ethnic-group conditions. The mediating variables associated with ethnic-group conditions do affect strongly the organization of abilities, while social class status does not appear to modify further the basic pattern associated with ethnicity.

These findings allow a reassessment of the various proposed explanations of cultural influences upon intellectual performance. The importance of the mediators associated with ethnicity is to provide differential impacts upon the development of mental abilities, while the importance of the mediators associated with social class is to provide pervasive (and not differential) effects upon the various mental abilities. This conclusion allows selection among the several explanations offered to interpret cultural influences upon intellectual activity; the explanations based upon natural selection, differential reinforcement, motivation, problem-solving tactics, work habits, and so forth, were re-examined in the light of the present results.

In summary, the findings lend selective support to Anastasi's premise that 'groups differ in their relative standing on different functions. Each . . . fosters the development of a different *pattern* of abilities.' It seems true that social-class and ethnic groups do 'differ in their relative standing on different functions'. However, ethnic groups do 'foster the development of a different pattern of abilities', while social-class differences do not modify these basic organizations associated with ethnic-group conditions.

The present effort to construct suitable testing procedures for studying children from culturally diverse groups must now incorporate the broader educational considerations of curriculum development, teacher training, and school organization. We have shown that several mental abilities are related to each other in ways that are culturally determined. We propose that the identification of relative intellectual strengths and weaknesses of members of different cultural groups must now become a basic and vital prerequisite to making enlightened decisions about education in urban areas.

References

BURT, C. (1939), 'The relations of educational abilities', *Brit. J. educ. Psychol.*, vol. 9, pp. 45–71.

BURT, C. (1941), *The Factors of the Mind: An Introduction to Factor Analysis in Psychology*, Macmillan.

BURT, C. (1944), 'Mental abilities and mental factors', *Brit. J. educ. Psychol.*, vol. 14, pp. 85–9.

BURT, C. (1949), 'The structure of the mind: a review of the results of factor analysis', *Brit. J. educ. Psychol.*, vol. 19, pp. 176–99.

BURT, C. (1954), 'The differentiation of intellectual ability', *Brit. J. educ. Psychol.*, vol. 24, pp. 76–90.

CARROLL, J. B. (1941), 'A factor analysis of verbal abilities', *Psychometrika*, vol. 6, pp. 279–308.

CLARK, M. P. (1944), 'Change in primary mental abilities with age', *Arch. Psychol.*, no. 291.

DAVIS, F. B., LESSER, G. S., and FRENCH, E. (1960), 'Identification and classroom behavior of gifted elementary-school children', *Cooperative Res. Monogr.*, no. 2.

GARRETT, H. E. (1946), 'A developmental theory of intelligence', *Amer. Psychol.*, vol. 1, pp. 372–8.

KELLEY, T. L. (1928), *Crossroads in the Mind of Man: A Study of Differentiable Mental Abilities*, Stanford University Press.

MEYER, W. J., and BENDIG, A. W. (1961), 'A longitudinal study of the Primary Mental Abilities Test', *J. educ. Psychol.*, vol. 52, pp. 50–60.

MEYERS, C. E., and DINGMAN, H. F. (1960), 'The structure of abilities at the preschool ages: hypothesized domains', *Psychol. Bull.*, vol. 57, pp. 514–532.

MEYERS, C. E., ORPET, R. E., ATTWELL, A. A. and DINGMAN, H. F. (1962), 'Primary abilities at mental age six', *Soc. Res. Child Developm. Monogr.*, vol. 27, no. 1.

PASSOW, A. H. (ed.) (1963), *Education in Depressed Areas*, Teachers College Publications.

RIESMAN, Z. (1962), *The Culturally Deprived Child*, Harper.

SWINEFORD, F. (1948), 'A study in factor analysis: the nature of the general, verbal, and spatial bi-factors', *Suppl. Educ. Monogr.*, no. 67.

SWINEFORD, F. (1949), 'General, verbal, and spatial bi-factors after three years', *J. educ. Psychol.*, vol. 40, pp. 353–60.

THURSTONE, L. L. (1948), 'Psychological implications of factor analysis', *Amer. Psychol.*, vol. 3, pp. 402–8.

VERNON, P. E. (1950), *The Structure of Human Abilities*, Methuen.

15 P. E. Vernon

Types of Social Structure of Values

Excerpts from P. E. Vernon, *Intelligence and Cultural Environment*, Methuen, 1969, pp. 83–6, 213–21, 228–33.

If the values and aspirations of the different classes in Western society are so intimately bound up with children's intellectual development, how much greater must be their effects in non-Western ethnic groups? The trouble is, of course, that societies and their values are tremendously varied, and there is no generally accepted taxonomy, though several attempts have been made to distinguish contrasted types. Doob (1960), while admitting the uniqueness of each culture, makes a good case for classifying as it were on a unidimensional scale from 'more' to 'less civilized'. From anthropological evidence and from his own testing and interviewing in African countries, Jamaica and in American Indian reservations, he arrives at a generalized picture of the 'less civilized', which includes the following characteristics:

They tend to live in small communities, each of which is economically self-supporting. There is little trading or competition, and few contacts, between communities.

All members of the community have face-to-face contacts with all others, and tend to have common understandings of status and of the world in which they live. Social structure is rigidly prescribed, and there are strong pressures to conformity.

The society is essentially static and conservative, yielding only slowly to change when influenced by other cultures. (Most of Doob's book is concerned with the conditions under which such changes occur.) Their beliefs are characterized by absolutism: the order of the world was fixed from the beginning, their customs are hallowed by the experience of generations.

Life is relatively simple, since there are well-tried methods for coping with daily needs or emergencies. Though there may be specialization and an elaborate social structure, there is little compartmentalization of spheres of life: work, religion, the family, bringing up children, are all of one piece.

Since their activities are mainly centred around satisfying the biological needs, they live primarily in the present. And they are more concerned about continuity with the past, i.e. with the spirits of their ancestors, than with planning for the future. (However it would not be true to say that the principle of postponed gratification is lacking; clearly it operates when a nomadic people changes to an agricultural, though still uncivilized, mode of life.)

Note that there is not much resemblance between these attributes and the attributes of the lower working classes in a Western society. However when the 'uncivilized' become 'more civilized' they do tend to take on Western ideas and attitudes. Doob's (1960) data show that the better educated and more acculturated members of his samples scored more highly on most of his tests. In the course of his extensive studies of mine-workers in Sierra Leone, Dawson developed a questionnaire on traditional $v.$ Western beliefs, with questions on the place of women in society, superstitions about illness, etc. Not only did this correlate highly with scores on several aptitude tests but also gave, if anything, better predictions of work efficiency than did the tests.

In contrast, the American 'core culture', according to Kluckhohn (1950), is:

1. Active rather than passive. The environment does not have to be accepted, it can be manipulated.

2. Individualistic rather than collective. Man is responsible for what happens to himself and is judged by his own character and abilities.

3. Future rather than present oriented.

This epitomises the Western middle-class culture that we have already described [not reproduced here], though it is much less characteristic of poorer-class Western groups. It is also almost identical with Weber's analysis of the Puritan ethic, to which he attributed the rise of capitalism in Western Europe. Calvinistic Protestantism taught that man is his own saviour, and that evil resides in him, though it can be overcome by the building up of internal moral controls. Consonant with this asceticism is the view that work is a duty, a way to grace, and that man should strive to save for the future rather than enjoy the present. In Riesman's terminology, Western man is 'inner-directed', not 'tradition-directed' like less civilized peoples, and he is competitive rather than cooperative.

Weber's portrayal of Western middle-class values is extremely far-reaching: it contrasts not only Protestant with Catholic, and more with less civilized people, but also the higher with the lower social classes, and even industrial with rural. Zentner (1964) helps to clarify this by his threefold classification into the Pre-Neolithic ethic, the Feudalist–Agrarian and the Post-Industrial ethic, the latter being identical with Weber's Puritanism.

The Pre-Neolithic refers to the hunting economies of the American Indians, and is essentially individualistic, based on providing subsistence for the family or the small group. The world is there to be exploited and is regarded as fundamentally hostile.

The Feudalist–Agrarian or Catholic ethic derives from the Judaistic conception of a patriarchal supreme being, and is typical of the agricultural economies of the Middle Ages. It denies worldly values and accepts poverty and pain in the present life for the sake of salvation hereafter. It is collectivist, stressing dependence on the family, and is organized hierarchically (e.g. the village under the lord of the manor). Status is hereditarily determined rather than dependent on man's own efforts.

Other writers have drawn attention to the contrast between hunting and rural economies within less civilized groups. Particularly relevant is the attempt by Barry, Child and Bacon (1959) to delineate the 'modal personalities' and child-rearing practices of cultures which do or do not accumulate food. The latter, i.e. the hunting, fishing, food-gathering and nomadic peoples (like Zenter's Pre-Neolithics) stress more aggressive or resourceful traits, while the agricultural peoples favour conformity with the group docility. Berry's experimental study of Eskimos and Temne people provides further confirmation. Although Zentner's Catholic agrarians are obviously very different from, say, African agrarians, they do show some similar traits which are opposed both to those of hunting peoples and to Puritan, middle-class, industrialized, civilization.

We must stress again that not only do these types overlap in a confusing way, but that each one conceals a wide range of ethnic group differences. However the discussion suggests an interesting link-up with ability differences, which is crudely represented in Figure 1. It shows the Western middle class as high in intellectual ability or g factor and 'formal' language, and contrasted with the less civilized and with the Western working classes. Cutting across this dimension is the spatial-verbal which tends to differentiate hunting from agricultural peoples. Note that this does not imply that agriculturalists are necessarily high in verbal ability (unless they also have sufficient g), only that they are relatively better on this than on the spatial side. Witkin's dependence dimension (1962) is shown as oblique, since it combines elements of g and k, of middle classness and of resourcefulness.

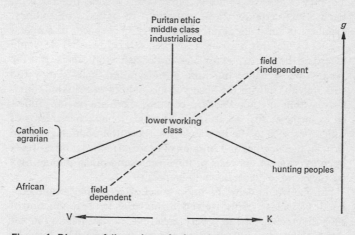

Figure 1 Diagram of dimensions of culture groups

The use of factorial concepts in classifying cultures is not new. Cattell, in 1949, collected measures of seventy-two demographic and other variables on sixty-nine nations, and showed that they could be resolved into some 10 meaningful dimensions. Much the largest general factor (before rotation) clearly corresponds to standards of living. Subsequent factors show no resemblance, however, to those which we have hypothesized, probably because the great majority of his nations were 'civilized'. The second largest factor appeared to represent the amount of educational and political acitivity, and the third the size of the country. But Cattell's notion of the 'syntality', i.e. the factor-pattern or syndrome of traits displayed by a nation or other ethnic group, would be well worth following up [. . .]

Summary and implications

This book has ranged widely over several countries of the world, and it has drawn on many psychological theories and investigations. Throughout, however, it has drawn attention to, and expressed concern over, the differences between peoples in their level of technological advance, of education and civilization or backwardness. Although the psychologist's tests are highly inadequate instruments for bringing out the full strengths and weaknesses of different groups or individuals, particularly when applied outside the cultural group for which they were constructed, they nevertheless tend to confirm our everyday observations. Each group certainly shows variations in patterns of abilities: members of an underdeveloped country may reach, or surpass, Western standards on some tests, and fall below what we would regard as the borderline for mental deficiency on others. But the average performance on quite a wide range of tests only too strikingly fits in with the observed inequalities of mankind. Similarly, within any one Western country, there are obvious differences in the status, vocational and educational achievements of subgroups such as the social classes, the coloured immigrants in Britain, the Negroes and Indians of North America; and however open to criticism our tests of intelligence and other abilities may be, they tend to reflect these differences.

No one would deny the importance of geographical and economic handicaps, of disease and malnutrition in the production of such differences. But to a very great extent man makes himself and fashions his own environment, and it is he who must be changed if he is to achieve a more prosperous and healthy existence. We suspect that his offspring fail to develop the high-level skills and mental abilities required for adaptation and progress in the modern world because of the way he brings them up in the home and community, and the schooling or training he provides. It is not only the poor circumstances of the parents but their backwardness and resistance to change which result in the underdevelopment of their children's capacities. However in every group there are the more and the less able; and many of the former do achieve good education and positions of leadership. They influence their own societies, sometimes dramatically, usually more gradually, and bring up their own children less disadvantageously. Changes are occurring too as groups and subgroups come in contact with and try to help one another, even if the influences they exert are often motivated by self-interest and political considerations.

These, however, are not matters for the scientific psychologist to dabble in. Yet he can make very real contributions by studying the present situation and trying to disentangle the main factors underlying the stimulation or retardation of intellectual growth, by clarifying the nature of the essential variables and developing and testing sound hypotheses, also by improving the diagnostic tools which he uses in his evaluations. He cannot, of course, claim to be wholly impartial or free from ethnocentrism and middle-class prejudice; inevitably he views other groups through the spectacles of the values and concepts of his own group. Indeed even these opening paragraphs sound as though the middle-class Western way of life was being held up as the ideal to which all inferior groups aspire. True, there is a kind of universal scale of economic prosperity and technological advance; and psychologically there is a scale ranging from the relatively simple to the more complex and powerful types of mental process, and the two are interlinked. But the writer has been at pains to point out that the complex intelligence of the Western middle class is not the only one, and that its development is accompanied by serious draw-backs; that over and above variations in position on these scales there are, and doubtless always will be, countless variations which promote the adjustment and stability of different cultures. Also that although most tests, including those used in the writer's researches, do reflect Western-type intelligence, there is no reason why psychological techniques should not be applied in studying the particular abilities and qualities of other groups, and the factors underlying their growth.

Part 1 shows first that much of the controversy regarding differences in abilities between ethnic groups and subgroups has arisen because the term 'intelligence' is ambiguous. It is used here to refer to the effective all-round cognitive abilities to comprehend, to grasp relations and reason (Intelligence B), which develops through the interaction between the genetic potential (Intelligence A) and stimulation provided by the environment. One must also distinguish constitutional equipment, that is, the potential as affected by pre-natal or other physiological conditions; and Intelligence C – the results obtained on various intelligence tests, which provide merely a limited sample of the Intelligence B displayed in behaviour and thinking at home, at school, at work. There is strong evidence that differences in Intelligence B and C between individuals within one culture are largely – certainly not wholly – genetically determined. But when environmental differences are more extreme, as between ethnic groups, their effects predominate. This does not mean that there are no innate racial differences in abilities, but they are probably small and we have no means of proving them. Differences between sub groups such as social classes are partly genetic, not wholly environmental.

Current conceptions of cognitive growth derive largely from the work of Piaget, Hebb and Bruner. From the initial sensory-motor reflexes of the newborn, a succession of more complex and adaptive schemata or skills are built up through the impact of environmental stimulation on the maturing nervous system and through the infant's active exploration and experiment. Thus a series of stages or successive reorganizations can be recognized in the child's perception, speech and thinking, through which different children progress at different rates. (Bruner's enactive, iconic and symbolic modes of coding differ in important respects from Piaget's sensory-motor, preoperational, concrete and formal stages, but both are useful in describing intellectual development.) Moreover more backward groups typically fail to progress as far as others along this scale, and though they may develop lower-order skills which are highly effective for survival, their reasoning capacities remain similar in many ways to those of younger children, or even regress through lack of appropriate stimulation. That is, they learn to be unintelligent, instead of acquiring the skills that constitute intelligence. An important implication is that man has by no means reached the limits of his mental powers; there is immense room for improvement at the lower end of the scale, and also the possibility of more effective 'techniques' at the top end.

General intelligence is merely the common element in a whole host of distinguishable, but overlapping, cognitive abilities. When dealing with homogeneous or highly selected populations, it is profitable to study different mental faculties and abilities along special lines, adopting the factorial models of Thurstone and Guilford. But with more heterogeneous populations, and particularly when considering different ethnic groups or sub-groups, the common element or g factor tends to dominate. And there are advantages in following the hierarchical or group-factor model, which successively subdivides more specialized types of ability. This implies that, while we should certainly try to study a wide variety of mental functions in contrasted ethnic groups or subgroups, we are most likely to discover conditions that affect general or all-round ability; then those that favour or inhibit verbal and educational as contrasted with perceptual, spatial and practical abilities, and later the smaller (but still quite broad) group factors such as number, memorizing, fluency or creativity, etc. Intelligence B cannot be precisely defined since it refers to the totality of our schemata, but its essence lies in the more generalized thinking skills, which can be applied to a wide variety of problems. An appendix to this chapter examines an alternative formulation of factors in intelligence, namely Cattell's theory of 'fluid' and 'crystallized' general ability.

What then do we mean by the potential ability of an underdeveloped group or individual? It is not Intelligence A or constitutional potential, since these cannot be assessed and are of use only in so far as previous environment has developed them. Equally the conventional expedient of contrasting achievement measures with intelligence test scores (verbal or non-verbal) is beset with fallacies. Abilities at different types of test often differ, and by surveying these patterns of abilities in the light of the individual's or group's physical and cultural background, education and motivation, the psychologist can often arrive at useful diagnoses and remedial proposals. If plausible reasons can be suggested either for general backwardness or for unevennesses in performance, and if the remedial measures at the disposal of the community can be shown to, or reasonably be expected to, work, then that person or group has potentiality.

Part 2 surveys the major environmental factors which have been found to influence the development of intellectual abilities, concentrating on recently published investigations. Most studies consist of cross-sectional comparisons of groups or individuals who differ in respect of many interacting conditions, and these do not readily demonstrate the effects of any particular condition. The methodologically superior experimental approach where one condition is changed and other factors are kept constant, and the longitudinal follow-up of a sample who undergo various conditions, have their own difficulties. Thus even in the case of relatively clear-cut conditions such as malnutrition during pregnancy or later, and debilitating diseases, our knowledge is scrappy and often indirect. The incidence of dietary deficiencies is worldwide especially in the low-income countries, and it is found that they can cause permanent impairment to the brain at the formative stage of pregnancy and early infancy, and seriously reduce later intellectual capacity. After this stage, poor health and nutrition or endemic diseases, though often associated with poor performance, do not seem to affect mental growth as such.

Particular stress is laid by most psychologists on the sensory stimulation, opportunities for activity, and the emotional relationships of the first year or two of life, as basic to later psychological development. But the evidence, apart from that of animal experiments, is unconvincing. While it is clear that extreme social deprivation has traumatic effects on human infants, probably the ordinary range of social and physical environments (even among relatively primitive groups) provides adequate stimulation. In other words, conceptual and linguistic deprivation during the period from about one-and-a-half years and throughout childhood, when children should be building up their concepts of objects and their relations, labels and thinking skills, may be more important than so-called sensory or perceptual deprivation. And while the preschool and early school periods are crucial, the modifiability of intellectual capacities by changed conditions even in adolescence has been underestimated.

Certain types of visual discrimination are strengthened in environments where they are important for survival. But the evidence for the effects of ecological environment (e.g. 'carpenteredness' v. rounded, and open-vista v. closely filled) on susceptibility to illusions is conflicting. Perceptual development seems to depend to a greater extent on social norms, education and acculturation. Clearly however many African peoples have difficulties with analytic perception of figures and pictures, and with three-dimensional interpretation. This deficiency is not found among other quite backward groups such as Eskimos. Its origins are obscure, and it may be remediable by appropriate training, but the main explanation would seem to lie in lack of visual-kinaesthetic experience and of encouragement of play and exploration throughout childhood.

The interactions of language with thinking are highly complex and controversial. But a child's language, which is wholly shaped by his cultural group, must be intimately involved in his perceptions and conceptualizations of the world. Hence his intellectual development is highly vulnerable to poverty of linguistic stimulation, and to the inadequacies of the mother-tongue – in many societies – as a medium for education. Bernstein's analysis of 'formal' and 'public' language codes (1961) describes the extremes of a continuum which is typical not only of the British socioeconomic classes, but applies in many respects to technological as against more primitive cultures. Bernstein brings out also the close connection between linguistic training and cultural values: the formal code is associated with internalized controls (superego formation), high educational aspirations and planning for the future; the public code with externally imposed discipline and with less purposeful attitudes to life.

Infant rearing practices and maternal deprivation may cause temporary emotional traumata, and seem to be associated with certain cultural traits. But their long-term effects on personality, and particularly on the development of abilities, are more dubious. A number of investigations indicate that socialization practices and the home 'climate' during preschool and school years are more influential. The 'democratic' but demanding home climate makes for better intellectual progress than the over-protective, the autocratic or the 'unconcerned' homes. The work in this area of Witkin and his colleagues provides important evidence that the encouragement of resourcefulness and independence in growing children leads to greater clarity and differentiation of perceptions and concepts, while maternal over-protection tends rather to favour verbal abilities. It is not clear whether it is general intelligence or spatial abilities which are chiefly affected, nor what parts are played in causation by social-class differences, by sex or temperament, or by masculine identification, etc. However Witkin's generalizations have fruitful applications to differences between cultural groups, e.g. Eskimos and certain African groups.

Turning then to intellectual progress at school: the major researches in the UK of Fraser (1959), Wiseman (1964, 1966, 1967), Warburton, and Douglas, are outlined. These show that, although the handicaps of poverty are much less marked than forty years ago, socioeconomic class and its associated conditions of child care, neighbourhood morale, and good or poor schooling, still make substantial differences to children's intelligence and achievement. Even between eight and eleven years the differential between the middle-class and lower-working-class child becomes progressively greater. But the most important factor of all appears to be the cultural level of the home and the parents' interest in and aspirations for their children's education. Hence the further improvements that we would desire in material conditions, social welfare and schooling will not of themselves eliminate the handicaps of the lower working and less educated classes.

Much the same factors are shown to be significant by research in the USA, though the major differences there are not so much between socioeconomic classes as between ethnic and linguistic groups, i.e. between whites and Negroes or recent immigrants. American Negroes tend to score in the low eighties on tests of intelligence and achievement, though there are considerable geographic variations, and differences on different types of test. Moreover younger children perform better and show a cumulative deficit at later ages. Negroes are at least as handicapped in non-verbal or spatial tests as in verbal abilities, though relatively better in simple number and rote learning tests; and this may be attributable to familial factors such as the frequent absence of masculine identification models for boys. The interpretation and implications of observed differences in abilities have given rise to even more heated controversy in the USA. At the same time there have been valuable positive efforts to reduce the handicaps of 'disadvantaged' children by compensatory or introductory schooling, or by integrating schools of different ethnic composition. It is too early to say how successful these measures are in improving general intellectual growth and scholastic performance, or whether the effects of home upbringing and of intergroup suspicions are too strong.

There is rather little evidence of the effects of different kinds of schooling, or of studying different subjects in different ways, on general mental growth. But it is clear that sheer amount of schooling, even – in backward countries – of low-quality education, helps to promote both school achievement and the kind of reasoning measured by non-verbal tests. Also if such schooling is unduly delayed, the possibilities of mental growth deteriorate. The acquisition of lower-order schemata opens up the way to higher-order thinking, but they can also become rigidified and block further progress. Likewise in Western countries the level of adult intelligence depends on the kind and amount of intellectual stimulation provided by the adolescent's secondary schooling and occupation. The notion of optimal or critical periods for learning probably has less applicability to conceptual than to sensory-motor functions, and greater importance should be attached to motivational factors – to the maintenance or repression of curiosity, and to the child's or young adult's aspirations and prospects of advancement. In this sense growth depends on the future as well as on the past.

Cultural groups and subgroups are exceedingly varied, and so also must be their effects on the intellectual growth of their members. A number of attempted classifications or typologies are examined, and it seems reasonable to regard the Puritan ethic of the Western middle class as producing the greatest development of intelligence, in contrast both to the Western lower class and to the 'less civilized' cultures. The two latter differ in important respects, but the less civilized can be subdivided into hunting and agricultural types, which coincide rather closely with Witkin's field-independent and dependent; i.e. they are to some extent linked with the major group-factors of spatial and verbal abilities.

The evidence in the preceding Part that Intelligence B is built up in response to environmental stimulation and is therefore affected in many ways by cultural differences does not mean that tests constructed in Western cultures are always worthless elsewhere. Despite the valuation of different skills in different ethnic groups, all groups have increasing need for complex, symbolic thinking. Researches in Africa and other countries in fact show that adaptations of Western tests possess promising validity in assessing educational aptitudes and work effectiveness, though this may be partly because they are measuring language skills required for advanced schooling in the former situation, or acculturation and cooperativeness with white employers in the latter. Correlations with job efficiency assessments (which tend to be unreliable) are low, but this is true in Western cultures also. However tests may often be inappropriate not so much because they do not measure useful abilities as because they are also greatly affected by unfamiliarity with the materials, or with the testing situation, or by other irrelevant 'extrinsic' factors.

Cross-cultural comparisons are unavoidable when members of different cultural groups or subgroups, who have very likely been reared under different conditions and are differently handicapped, are in competition for the same schooling or same jobs. Different regression equations, or different norms or cut-offs for acceptance, may be needed for such groups. Another legitimate cross-cultural application is for studying the effects of different background conditions on abilities, and this is the main aim in the present book.

Unsophisticated testees are handicapped in many ways by lack of relevant experience, failure to understand the instructions, and absence of the motivations and sets which sophisticated testees bring with them to the testing situation. However the distinction between these extrinsic factors, and intrinsic factors which affect the underlying ability, is only a relative one. Probably it is best defined in terms of how readily the handicap can be overcome, e.g. by better conditions of administration. A bimodal score distribution or the piling up of low scores among 'non-starters' is another useful indication of extrinsic difficulties. Also differences in the order of item difficulty may show that a test is measuring different things in different groups. However a number of investigations of practice effects among Africans indicate that these are not so large as is sometimes supposed, particularly when the testees have received some schooling. The results are comparable to those obtained with unsophisticated testees in the UK, and the same kind of measures used to familiarize British children with tests can be applied or extended. The suggestion that abilities should be judged from scores on several successive administrations, i.e. from learning curves, is technically unsound.

It is obviously far more difficult to transfer western-type tests to relatively unacculturated groups, with little or no schooling, and the psychologist may have to confine himself to individual testing with specially constructed materials, under informal conditions. However Biesheuvel's work (1949, 1952, 1959, 1966) shows that it is possible to get across performance tests to groups of linguistically heterogeneous and illiterate adults; and Schwartz has formulated a series of useful principles for giving group tests, e.g. to applicants for technical training, which amount to teaching the testees beforehand precisely what they have to do. For most purposes it would be better to construct new tests based on materials and conditions appropriate to the culture concerned, than to adapt Western ones, though this is difficult in view of the shortage of trained personnel. It is essential to validate old or new tests locally and to devise an appropriate system of norming.

In attempting to assess the educational potential of immigrant children, verbal tests are preferable to non-verbal or performance – either standard tests in English if they can communicate in it, or if not then similar tests in their own tongues. Alternatively a varied battery should be given and the results interpreted in the light of their educational, linguistic and social history, i.e. clinically. Objective tests of achievement are being produced in many developing countries and used on a large scale for secondary school selection. Less progress has been made with aptitude tests, e.g. for technical training, largely because, in the absence of suitable background experience, the skills needed for technical work are too undeveloped to provide a basis for worthwhile tests [. . .]

Implications

In summing up, it is desirable to stress once again that surveys of this kind are not very effective in pinning down the factors that underly any particular deficiency, or superiority, in an ability. In other words, our attributions are often speculative, though the fact that they are mostly based on the results of several tests, and on comparisons of several samples, gives them more substance. On the other hand, it should also be admitted that tests may measure rather different abilities in different groups, or be affected in different ways by what we have called extrinsic factors. Particularly non-verbal, spatial and perceptual tests are apt to show varied factor loadings (though this is no doubt partly due to the small sizes of the samples). Verbal and educational tests are more likely to measure the same thing in different contexts, since all our samples are being taught a similar body of knowledge and skills in English-medium schools. Hence, while our results on the whole justify quite widespread use of Western-type tests across cultures (provided these are not too widely dissimilar), they also indicate the need for more intensive studies of particular aspects of mental development with locally constructed tests within non-Western cultures.

Many psychologists might be inclined to banish further studies of 'intelligence' in non-Western cultures on the grounds that it has no precise meaning or uniform content. While admitting its difficulties, the writer would point out that the same objection applies to any other more specialized abilities, e.g. perceptual discrimination, ideational fluency, problem solving, etc., not to speak of the American psychometrist's factors; since the structure and content of these are likely to be equally variable. Even if an investigator talked only in terms of performance on particular tests, e.g. Progressive Matrices or Kohs Blocks, he would still not be measuring the same ability, since the tests have to be given in different ways to, and have different meanings to, North American whites and, say, Africans. 'Intelligence' is justifiable in so far as it has been shown that a general factor always emerges from a wide range of varied tests, though one must be aware that it is culturally loaded. What is important is that, in concentrating on abilities recognized by Western culture, psychologists should not neglect special talents that might be more highly developed in other cultures. For example, in the writer's researches, little opportunity was provided for Eskimos to demonstrate their artistic and mechanical abilities, and none at all for Ugandans to display their auditory and rhythmic skills.

In the light of our surveys of four seriously handicapped groups, and of the literature summarized in earlier chapters, what are the main factors underlying poor performance on tests either of general intelligence or of more specialized mental faculties and educational or other attainments? A summary list will be useful, not only in considering how to help underdeveloped nations, but also in trying to diagnose the underlying handicaps of disadvantaged children, particularly immigrants, in our own culture. They are classified below under three or four main headings to correspond to our distinction between Intelligences *A*, *B* and *C*.

C Extrinsic handicaps

1. Unfamiliarity of testees with any test situation, and lack of motivation.

2. Difficulties due to particular form of items or materials (e.g. pictures), and conditions of testing (e.g. working at speed).

3. Anxiety, excitement, suspicion of tester.

4. Linguistic difficulties in understanding instructions or communicating responses.

B Constitutional handicaps

5. Brain damage due to pre- or post-natal malnutrition, maternal stress, or disease. Birth injury; later brain pathology and deterioration.

Positive environmental factors

6. Reasonable satisfaction of biological and social needs, including exercise and curiosity.

7. Perceptual and kinaesthetic experience; varied stimulation, encouragement of exploration, experiment and play.

8. Linguistic stimulation encouraging a 'formal code' and clarity of concepts.

9. 'Demanding' but 'democratic' family climate, emphasizing internal controls, responsibility, and interest in education.

10. Conceptual stimulation by varied environment, books, television, travel, etc.

11. Absence of magical beliefs; tolerance of non-conformity in home and community.

12. Reinforcement of nos. 8 and 9 by school and peer group.

13. Regular and prolonged schooling, also demanding-democratic, emphasizing discovery rather than rote learning only.

14. Appropriate methods to overcome language problems.

15. Positive self-concepts with realistic vocational aspirations.

16. Broad and deep cultural and other leisure interests.

A Genetic factors

17. General plasticity.

18. Genes relevant to special aptitudes.

Naturally many other classifications are possible, and some of the factors listed (e.g. B 15 and 16) are less well attested than others. Note that socioeconomic status as such does not appear, though it is, of course, associated with nos. 6–13; nor does emotional security or maternal warmth, except under no. 6. Ecological and climatic conditions might merit inclusion, but are probably covered by no. 7.

What can be done to improve these conditions? Economic progress within the developing nations, and technical assistance from abroad, will obviously impinge at some points, particularly in reducing malnutrition and disease, building up the educational system, and providing worthwhile occupational prospects for much larger numbers. Likewise reduction of unemployment and better housing among immigrants in Britain should open the way to advance in many or most of the categories.

We would naturally expect the education system to provide the chief mode of attack on the syndrome of negative factors in a backward culture or subculture. Schooling is given by fairly small numbers of the more intelligent members of the population, who should be open to new ideas and who can be trained to follow new methods and aims; and they influence the minds of a large proportion or even the whole of the population over the period when concepts, skills and values are being built up. However the school is by no means as powerful an instrument in practice as in theory. Teachers are themselves so strongly imbued with the traditions of the old culture that they do not readily absorb or communicate the new; and the younger, more progressive, individuals cannot easily stand up to the entrenched beliefs of older, more conservative colleagues or of the community in which they work. And when they have charge of thirty to sixty and over, it is only the exceptional personality whose influence is sufficient to outweigh that of the home and the peer-group. They can get across 'peripheral' skills such as spelling and mechanical arithmetic fairly successfully, and therefore – in backward educational systems – tend to concentrate unduly on these. But it is far more difficult to develop logical reasoning, flexibility of mind, the use of 'formal' language, understanding of the world and society, initiative, responsibility, and democratic attitudes. The effects of peripheral training are easily forgotten and, of course, have scarcely any transfer to the daily life of ex-pupils or to the bringing up of their children more intelligently. Nevertheless one should not be too pessimistic. When even a few in each school generation are helped to be more intelligent, they leaven the community.

The greatest promise of quick advance lies in the field of language teaching, that is the spread of effective methods of acquiring a language which is suitable as a medium for advanced education, communication and thinking among children whose mother-tongue is ineffective for these purposes. This applies equally to dialect-speaking Africans, to Jamaicans in Jamaica or Britain, and to lower-working-class or deprived children in any Western nation whose natural speech is of the 'public' type. However it is not sufficient to teach the second language as a subject, i.e. peripherally. Our own results have shown that current techniques, not only in Jamaica and Uganda but even in Canada, produce some competence in written English tests but fail to develop English as a central tool of comprehension and thought. But linguistic and psychological research, together with the experiments under way in American introductory schools, in Kenya and elsewhere, offer prospects of a considerable breakthrough.

Whether it is realistic to advocate the extension of such methods to the complete populations of developing countries is a moot point, since the mother-tongues are adequate for the lives that the majority are going to live for generations to come, and much more useful types of education could be devised for them. But such a policy would involve a split between the minority educated in the foreign language and the rest; and even if this was not socially disastrous, how would the minority be chosen at a sufficiently early age?

Clearly the major barrier to the fuller realization of human intellectual potential lies in the realm of adult values and child-rearing practices, and we have scarcely any assured techniques of modifying these. Changes are occurring all the time, but seldom as planned by the administrators; and although anthropological and psychological studies have greatly increased our understanding of the dynamic forces of social change, we are hardly in a position yet to offer much practical advice. (Psychological theories of crime and delinquency, for example, do not seem to have done anything to reduce the amount of social deviancy.) And yet it is not impossible to plan and to carry through radical changes – an outstanding example being supplied by Soviet Russia. There can be no doubt that over the past fifty years the average level of Intelligence B of the Russian population has been raised tremendously. Ruthless techniques may indeed have been applied which other countries would be loath to adopt, and they have not always achieved their purpose. But to a large extent they have succeeded in transforming a country which was as economically weak, as educationally backward, and as culturally and linguistically heterogeneous as many underdeveloped nations of today.

Among the more humane approaches are community development schemes where local or foreign teams persuade a backward community to cooperate in improved agricultural techniques, in an industrial or housing project, in health or child-care measures, or in local government. Usually these are small-scale, trial and error, ventures, and frequently they fail or have no lasting effects. But they can be conducted in the people's own language, be shown to have direct value to the community, and be integrated with, rather than destroying, the existent culture. Where they do take roots they are likely to spread geographically, and to affect many cultural elements beside the particular practices worked on.

More sure, perhaps, but slower is the traditional method of educating the upper strata of the population to a high level and encouraging their contacts with outside cultural groups. If they thereby acquire good intelligence and adopt some of the attitudes associated with it, they are better able to bridge the gulf between the old and the new. In so far as they achieve prestige positions, their influence tends to percolate and they make possible greater progress in subsequent generations. Admittedly this mode of attack does not always work; it seems to have broken down among Canadian indigenes, and it is clearly failing to meet the needs of American Negroes. The more able and acculturated members of the relatively backward group often meet with rejection, either from their own or from the more advanced groups.

We return finally to the point that changes in material conditions, which the more favoured nations and subcultures are in a position to facilitate, are important, but not the whole answer. Even more important and vastly more difficult are changes in people's attitudes and ways of life. Developing nations often seem to be trying to bring about in a matter of years developments which, in Europe, took place over centuries. There are far more resources of technology, of communication, of intelligent and trained people anxious to help, in the world of today than ever before. But our knowledge of human individuals and societies and our control over our own prejudices and emotions are still so rudimentary that progress can only be fragmentary and disappointing.

References

BARRY, H., CHILD, I. and BACON, M. K. (1959), 'Relation of child training to subsistence economy', *Amer. Anthropol.*, vol. 61, pp. 51–63.

BERNSTEIN, B. B. (1961), 'Social class and linguistic development: A theory of social learning', in A. H. Halsey (ed.), *Education, Economy and Society*, The Free Press.

BERNSTEIN, B. B., and YOUNG, D. (1966), 'Some aspects of the relationships between communication and performance in tests', in J. E. Meade and A. S. Parkes, *Genetic and Environmental Factors in Human Ability*, Oliver & Boyd, pp. 15–23.

BIESHEUVEL, S. (1949), 'Psychological tests and their application to non-European peoples', *Yearbook Educ.*, Evans, pp. 87–126.

BIESHEUVEL, S. (1952), 'The study of African ability', *African Stud.*, vol. 11, pp. 45–58 and 105–17.

BIESHEUVEL, S. (1966), 'Some African acculturation problems with special reference to perceptual and psychomotor skills', *Burg-Wartenstein Symposium*, no. 33, Wenner-Gren Foundation for Anthropological Research, New York.

BIESHEUVEL, S. and LIDDICOAT, R. (1959), 'The effects of cultural factors on intelligence-test performance', *J. Nat. Inst. Personn. Res.*, vol. 8, pp. 3–14.

CATTELL, R. B. (1949), 'The dimensions of culture patterns by factorization of national characters', *J. abn. soc. Psychol.*, vol. 44, pp. 443–69.

DOOB, L. W. (1960), *Becoming More Civilized*, Yale University Press.

DOUGLAS, J. W. B. (1964), *The Home and the School*, MacGibbon & Kee.

FRASER, E. (1959), *Home Environment and the School*, University of London Press.

KLUCKHOHN, F. R. (1950), 'Dominant and substitute profiles of cultural orientations: their significance for the analysis of social stratification', *Soc. Forces*, vol. 28, pp. 376–93.

WISEMAN, S. (1964), *Education and Environment*, Manchester University Press.

WISEMAN, S. (1966), 'Environmental and innate factors and educational attainment', in J. E. Meade and A. S. Parkes (eds.), *Genetic and Environmental Factors in Human Ability*, Oliver & Boyd.

WISEMAN, S. (1967), 'The Macheto survey', Appendix 9, *Children and Their Primary Schools*, vol. 2, HMSO.

Part Six
Wider Implications

We come to the final section of this book, a section which, to some extent, tries to summarize some of the important gains in knowledge over the first half of this century in the cognitive field, and also tries to suggest ways forward.

The first paper, by Ferguson, a Canadian psychologist, is one of two which he wrote in the middle fifties: two important papers which received less attention than they deserved. Here he is pointing the way ahead, suggesting ways in which the theories of the factor analysts and the psychometricians might be allied to learning theory and the imaginative and stimulating work of Piaget. This seems a highly promising line of attack.

The other contribution in this section is an extract from Hunt's monumental work *Intelligence and Experience*. This is a remarkable book, notable for the width and catholicity of its survey, the incisiveness of its critical analysis, its scholarly treatment of unresolved problems and its wealth of explicit and implicit suggestions for further work. It forms a fitting conclusion to the sixteen other contributions, and in its form and content undoubtedly exemplifies man's intelligence, ability and aptitude.

16 G. A. Ferguson
Learning and Human Ability

G. A. Ferguson, 'On learning and human ability', *Canadian Journal of Psychology*, vol. 8, 1954, pp. 95–112.

My purpose is to present a generalized theory which draws together within a single conceptual framework the study of human learning and the study of human ability. Those concerned with the description and classification of man's abilities have usually adopted an individual difference approach. They have paid scant attention to problems of learning. The experimentalists, engrossed in the study of learning, have for various theoretical and practical reasons shown little interest in individual differences. They seem unaware that they too are students of man's abilities. This divergence between two fields of psychological endeavour has led to a constriction of thought and an experimental fastidiousness inimical to a bold attack on the problem of understanding human behaviour.

At present no systematic theory, capable of generating fruitful hypotheses about behaviour, lies behind the study of human ability. Current approaches arc largely empirical. Psychological test theory and factor theory, evolved as they were for the study of human ability, are largely technologies which do not presume to answer psychological questions *per se*, although they may aid in the answering of such questions once raised. The pioneers of factor analysis, Spearman (1927), Thomson (1946) and others, proposed theories of brain functioning, and resorted to factor analysis as a means of testing deductions from those theories. Few attempts are made today to correlate the descriptive parameters of behaviour identified by factorial methods with any structural or dynamic properties of a brain model. Many factorists, although accepting this as a legitimate problem, regard its exploration as beyond their province and possibly premature. Earlier factorists thought otherwise. Many physiological psychologists on the other hand still concern themselves with rather vague and global concepts of intelligence, and seem unaware that these concepts are regarded as obsolete by many students of human ability. The concept of intelligence, however it be framed, is no longer a useful scientific concept except as subsuming some defined set of clearly distinguishable abilities.

If the study of human ability lacks theoretical buttressing, the study of human learning most certainly does not. The physical bases of memory have been the subject of much speculation at least since the time of René Descartes. One of the postulates of a recent theory proposed by Hebb (1949) is identical in form with the postulate of Descartes. The extent and persistence of this class of theorizing are apparent in a recent extensive review by Bronislaw Gomulicki (1953). One recent line of speculation in this area has been advanced by the cyberneticists and by those concerned with the development of electronic calculators and related devices. Analogies have been drawn between the principles which govern the functioning of machines that 'learn' and 'remember' and the principles which govern the functioning of the human brain.

In the field of human learning there is clearly a plenitude of diverse theoretical constructs, together with an extensive accumulation of experimental data. In the field of human ability, although we suffer from a paucity of systematic theoretical constructs, we have an extensive technology, much data based on the study of individual differences, and formal ways of thinking about problems which are, I believe, foreign to many who work in the learning field. It follows that, if we can logically incorporate the two fields in a single conceptual framework, some mutual enrichment may occur.

Ability and overlearning

'Ability' is defined operationally by the performance of an individual in a specified situation. Thus Thurstone (1947) states that 'an ability is a trait which is defined by what an individual can do'. It follows, as Thurstone points out, that 'there are as many abilities as there are enumerable things that individuals can do'. Factor analysis, a classificatory technique, undertakes a parsimonious description of the multitudinous array of abilities in terms of a relatively small number of categories. It is clear that the term 'ability', in addition to its operational meaning, may be assigned a formal postulational meaning within a framework of theory.

'Learning', as conventionally used in experimental psychology, refers generally to changes, with repetition, in 'ability' to perform a specified task, the changes being regarded as functionally dependent on, or in part assignable to, repetition. Other assignable causes of change, such as fatigue, sensory adaptation, artifacts of measurement, and the like, are presumed to be controlled. This commonly accepted statement of what is meant by learning is inadequate and leads to logical pitfalls. It will, however, serve my immediate purpose. Note that I have introduced the term 'ability' into the definition of learning. It is seldom used in connection with learning experiments, although indices of performance used in such experiments are clearly measures of the ability of the subject at various stages in the learning process. Conventional learning curves are simply descriptions of changes in ability with repetition.

If we regard the term 'ability' as defined by an individual's performance, we may identify two broad classes of ability: a class which is more or less invariant with respect to repetition or its cessation, and a class which is not. Thus some of the things which individuals can do appear to have a fairly high degree of permanence, showing little change, either in the presence or in the absence of repetition. Other things individuals can do may exhibit gross improvement with repetition, or gross impairment following a period in which no repetition occurs.

The typical learning curve shows that in most learning situations a level of performance is attained with repetition beyond which no further improvement is observed. Moreover, in certain learning situations, particularly those demanding a high degree of overlearning, the subject when tested may exhibit no impairment in performance even after lengthy periods of time without repetition. It seems that in most learning situations the ability of the subject reaches a crude limit[1] beyond which no systematic improvement is likely to occur with repetition. Of course in some cases rapid improvement may occur following a 'plateau' in learning.

While the term 'ability' may be used generally to refer to performance on any type of task, whether or not it varies with repetition, many psychologists conventionally use the term, in the case of adults, to refer to performance which does not vary much over lengthy periods of time. Likewise it is assumed that the abilities of children are reasonably stable over short time intervals, although

1. The term 'limit' is used here in a very loose and imprecise sense to refer to a level beyond which no very gross and systematic change seems likely to occur. The term is not used in the rigorous sense in which it is understood in elementary mathematics or in the stochastic sense of probability theory.

they may show systematic improvement with age. For example, in Thurstone's classification of mental abilities (1938), reasoning ability, number ability, perceptual ability, spatial ability, and the like, are presumed, in the adult subject, to be reasonably stable attributes of behaviour over lengthy periods and, in the child, to have considerable stability at any given age level. It is not presumed that an individual's reasoning ability will be markedly changed by solving large numbers of verbal analogies or number series items, or that his spatial ability will show pronounced improvement with practice on paper form-board items or other spatial tasks. Although some improvement with practice will occur in many subjects, we do not expect such improvement to be gross.

These observations bring us to the first hypothesis of this discussion, namely, that in the adult subject in our culture, those more or less stable attributes of behaviour which we ordinarily speak of as abilities, and which are defined in terms of performance on psychological tests, refer to performance at a crude limit of learning. This is regarded as applying to all attributes in the Thurstone classification and to whatever is subsumed under the term 'intelligence'. The hypothesis implies that these abilities are overlearned acquisitions, and that the stability which characterizes them is the result of overlearning. It assigns to learning a central role in the study of human ability, and opens the way for the study of ability and learning within the same conceptual framework. It is proposed that any theory which implies that individual differences in ability are individual differences at some crude limit of performance reached by overlearning be referred to as a *limits of learning* theory of human ability.

The role of learning in human ability is well illustrated by number ability. Number ability is defined by the performance of individuals on certain simple arithmetical tasks involving addition, subtraction, multiplication, and division. Tests of number ability are usually highly speeded. In our culture the majority of educated adults are fairly facile at tasks entailing ordinary arithmetical operations. Arithmetical facility has for many individuals been so reinforced by innumerable repetitions over prolonged periods of time that a crude limit of learning has been attained. Although some might show improvement with systematic practice, this would probably not be great. It seems plausible, therefore, that in many adults individual differences in number ability refer to individual differences at some crude limit of performance.

The role of learning in perception is a controversial subject. Much evidence supporting the view that perception involves a prolonged period of learning has been marshalled by Hebb in *The Organization of Behavior* (1949). This evidence strongly suggests that various perceptual abilities represent performance at the limits of learning in perception. In the normal child the limits of learning in many perceptual tasks may be reached at a fairly early age.

The role of learning in reasoning – that is, in the type of ability required for the solution of number series items, verbal analogies, and so on – is far from obvious. But numerous arguments can be advanced to support the view that reasoning ability involves a prolonged period of learning.

The view that 'ability' has reference to performance at some crude limit of learning is not new. It is implicit in the theories of Hebb (1949) although not formulated by him in the above manner. In much of the work carried out in the animal laboratories at McGill the 'intelligence' of the rat or dog is defined in terms of performance on a maze test following a lengthy learning period. The animal performs in the test situation until his performance reaches a crude stability, or until a limit of performance is very roughly approximated, and this limit serves to define his 'intelligence'.

Gross individual differences in ability do exist. These differences are a complex result of the interaction of the biological propensities of the organism and the learning which occurs at particular stages of life. This topic has been discussed by Hebb (1949). His distinction between early and late learning is relevant here. It appears that the state of an organism at any given time and its ability to respond to any immediate situation is a complex function, not only of its biological propensities and previous learning, but also of the stage in life at which learning of various types has occurred. This implies that the stage of development at which learning of a particular class has occurred is one factor in determining the limit of overlearning at the adult stage. Thus, as Hebb observes, early learning or its lack may have a permanent and generalized effect in the adult.

Many of the abilities which psychologists have studied increase with age. Intelligence as defined by such tests as the Stanford–Binet increases until about the age of seventeen, when a limit of performance is reached. In our culture children are exposed to an environment that demands rapid learning of many things. They proceed as rapidly through the school system as their abilities at any stage will allow. It is probable that many children at any particular age are functioning fairly close to the limit of their potentiality with regard to certain classes of activity. It follows that some of the abilities measured by psychologists are, for many children, indices of performance at a crude limit of learning for the age in question. However, if a child's environment is restricted with respect to certain activities he may function well below the limit of his potentiality in those activities at varying ages, and a permanent impairment at the adult stage may result. Presumably children reared in different environments, which demand different types of learning at different ages, develop different patterns of ability.

Transfer

'Transfer' is frequently used in a general sense to refer to the effects of changes, resulting from repetition, in ability to perform a specified task, on the ability to perform either the same task under altered conditions or a different task. This is the meaning usually assigned to the term 'transfer' for laboratory experimentation. An implicit condition is that the prior task is in some respect different from the subsequent task. When the two tasks are presumed on the basis of superficial inspection to be similar, the term 'learning', and not 'transfer', is used to refer to the changes in ability that occur. It seems, therefore, that transfer is the general phenomenon and 'learning' is a particular *formal* case which may never occur either in laboratory experimentation or in real life situations. The notion of learning implies the identity of a sequence of learning situations.[2] The fact that learning is a par-

2. The inability of students of learning to deal appropriately with the problem of the identity of and difference between tasks has led to logical difficulties in our concepts of learning and transfer. To my mind these concepts require some revision. To say that an individual is repeating the same task, or that one task is different from another, demands a precise statement of what is meant by 'same' and 'different'. The referents of these terms in current thinking on learning are largely phenomenological; that is, they have to do with our immediate experience upon inspection of the tasks in question. Two ways out of this difficulty suggest themselves. First, the terms 'same' and 'different' are always with respect to some property or properties. In view of this, it may be possible to define operationally properties with respect to which tasks may differ, and to study the relationship of such differences to differences in transfer effects. Attempts have been made to do this. Second, 'same' and 'different' may be defined in terms of correlation. If the correlation of the performance of a group of individuals on two tasks

ticular formal case of the general phenomenon of transfer has been recognized by Cook (1944) who writes:

There is no separate problem of transfer of training. Or conversely, all learning (unless there exists a limiting case in which successive trials are identical on all counts) involves the problem posited in the transfer of training experiments: what identities and differences in successive trials affect what sort of learning?

With the possible exception of some learning which occurs very early in life, all learning occurs within the context of experience. We bring to bear on the learning of any task a mass of prior experience which may either facilitate or inhibit the learning of that task. On this point McGeoch (1946) writes:

After small amounts of learning early in the life of the individual every instance of learning is a function of the already learned organization of the subject; that is all learning is influenced by transfer . . . The learning of complex, abstract, meaningful materials and the solution of problems by means of ideas (reasoning) are to a great extent a function of transfer. Where the subject 'sees into' the fundamental relations of a problem or has insight, transfer seems to be a major contributing condition. It is, likewise, a basic factor in originality, the original and creative person having, among other things, unusual sensitivity to the applicability of the already known to new problem situations. Perceiving, at whatever complex level, is probably never free of its influence, and there is no complex psychological event which is not a function of it.

Hebb (1949) in discussing the same point writes:

If the learning we know and can study, in the mature animal, is heavily loaded with transfer effects, what are the properties of the original learning from which those effects come? How can it be possible even to consider making a theory of learning in general from the data of maturity alone? There must be a serious risk that what seems to be learning is really half transfer. We cannot assume that we know what learning transfers and what it does not: for our knowledge of the extent of transfer is also derived from behavior at maturity, and the transfer from infant experiences may be much greater and more generalized.

---

or on successive trials of what experientially is the same task, is roughly unity, error being taken into account, then the tasks may be said to be the same. If the correlation departs from unity then the tasks may be said to be in some degree different. We may be prepared to go beyond a strict operational statement of this kind and speak of tasks on successive trials as involving the same or different functions. This essentially is the rationale of factor analysis. This second approach in effect defines the stimulus in terms of the responses of the subjects.

If all adult learning is heavily loaded with transfer, what is the nature of the prior learning which transfers to the learning of new tasks, and how does it affect the learning of such new tasks? Two hypotheses are put forward.

The first is that, in many adult learning situations, the most important variables exerting transfer effects on subsequent learning are the 'abilities' – the prior acquisitions that have attained their limit of performance. This hypothesis has long been widely accepted and is deeply entrenched in our thinking. It is commonplace to say that 'bright' children learn more quickly in school than 'dull' children, where brightness and dullness are defined in terms of performance on an ability test. The validation of tests against training criteria implies that the abilities of man are significant variables in the learning process. Such a loose statement as 'intelligence is learning ability' reflects the important role frequently assigned to intelligence in learning situations. There are two reasons for emphasizing this hypothesis. First, it is formulated within a new theoretical framework which alters substantially our way of thinking about the role of human abilities in learning. The problem can now be regarded as a problem in transfer. Second, the role of human ability in human learning has always been a matter of major practical concern to the applied psychologist. Indeed, it may be the most important problem in the applied field. And yet this problem has received little attention from the theoreticians or the laboratory experimentalists. Experiments on transfer carried out under laboratory conditions are so distantly removed from learning as it occurs in real life situations that they provide few answers of the slightest usefulness in the field of applied psychology. Questions of what prior learned acquisitions, or abilities, transfer to what learning, and how, and under what conditions, remain largely unanswered.

The second hypothesis concerns the way in which overlearned acquisitions, or abilities, affect subsequent learning. It is that such abilities exert their effect differentially in any learning situation; that different abilities exert different effects at different stages of learning, and that the abilities which transfer and produce their effects at one stage of learning may be different from those which transfer and produce their effects at another stage. This means that individual differences in abilities which may be functionally related to individual differences in performance in the early stages of learning a task, may not be functionally related, or may be related in a different way, to performance in the later stages. An implication of this hypothesis is that an individual might possess the abilities to perform a given activity with a high degree of proficiency, but might lack the abilities to learn to perform the task under certain specified conditions of learning. Likewise an individual might possess the ability to improve rapidly in the early stages of learning, but might lack the abilities necessary to attain high proficiency at the stage of high habituation or overlearning. The learning of many motor activities probably belongs to this class.

This hypothesis, if experimentally confirmed, will have important educational implications. It implies, for example, that a slow learner under given learning conditions may have a capacity for ultimate performance in excess of the fast learner under the same training conditions. In the test validation field, where tests are frequently validated against training criteria, it becomes important to consider the stage of training to which the criterion relates, since tests with an acceptable degree of validity at one stage of training may have little or no validity at another stage.

A prior overlearned acquisition, an ability, may not only facilitate the learning of a new task but may also inhibit it. Thus we may consider both positive and negative transfer effects, and the simultaneous operation of such effects. Although the terms positive and negative transfer are used to refer to net effect of the operation of a variety of variables, experiments could readily be designed to separate out the positive and negative effects of different abilities on the same learning situations.

Experimental design

The experimental investigation of these hypotheses involves an individual difference approach. There have been a number of such approaches in the learning field (Simrall, 1949; Tilton, 1949; Woodrow, 1940 and 1949), but this line of attack has been relatively unpopular, owing to the practical difficulties of finding appropriate learning tasks which will provide reliable measures of performance and permit the collection of data on substantial numbers of subjects.

The type of experiment suggested by the hypotheses in this paper may be illustrated as follows. Say that we are concerned with the transfer of certain overlearned acquisitions, or abilities, to the learning of a motor task, that a number of learning periods are allowed, and that a measure of performance, or score, is obtained for each learning period for each subject. We may select and administer to our subjects a number of tests of abilities which *a priori* considerations have led us to believe may transfer either positively or negatively to the learning of the motor task. For any group of subjects the inter-correlations between all the variables may be calculated. The relationship between performance at various stages of learning is described by the correlation between scores on the learning task. The correlations between the ability tests and scores on the learning task are measures of the extent of transfer of the abilities to the learning situation at various stages of learning. The results obtained from such an experiment can probably best be handled by factorial methods, treating the tests of ability as criterion variables.

Experiments of this design will permit observation of the differential transfer of abilities at different stages of learning. The design may also be readily extended to cover forgetting, and the differential effects of transfer through a cycle of learning and forgetting. Further, the design permits the differentiation of the simultaneous operation of positive and negative transfer effects.

Culture and human ability

Extensive investigations have been carried out on the effects of various cultural factors on 'intelligence', as defined by the standard intelligence tests. The general conclusion is that a variety of cultural variables are related to 'intelligence' as so defined. Since this is so, the view is held by many investigators that existing intelligence tests when used in selection, classification, and the like are 'unfair' to certain sections of the population. This has resulted in attempts to develop types of test material which are more or less invariant with respect to certain cultural factors. Examples of this are the Culture-Free Tests developed by Cattell (1940 and 1941). A recent extensive investigation by Eells, Davis *et al.* (1951) attempted to isolate groups of test items which showed relatively small or negligible differences between individuals in various socioeconomic groups.

Many investigators concerned with this class of problem regard 'intelligence' as a basic underlying biological attribute. Methods of measuring it are, however, affected by cultural factors. How, then, can inferences be drawn regarding differences in cultural or racial groups in 'intelligence' viewed as a biological attribute? There is no obvious answer to this question. One way out is to accept the hypothesis (incapable, of course, of any experimental test by existing methods) that no difference exists between cultural and racial groups in 'intelligence', and that where such differences are found they are the result of cultural factors. If this hypothesis is accepted the next step is obvious.

Tests must be constructed which are invariant with respect to certain controllable cultural factors, and so are 'better' measures of the basic biological variable called 'intelligence'. As Turnbull (1951) has recently pointed out in criticizing this line of argument, a 'fair' or 'good' test is one which shows no differences. Thus, as Turnbull remarks, the process has gone full circle. The hypothesis is accepted that no differences exist between cultural groups in biological intelligence. Tests are constructed by the careful selection of items which show no differences between groups. These are then used as evidence that there *is* no real difference.

The position described above has been widely adopted, although its logical ramifications have seldom been explicitly stated. Its basic weakness lies in a naïve concept of 'intelligence', which leads to an experimental impasse avoidable only by the acceptance of an unverifiable hypothesis. Thus the existing position held by many investigators is logically untenable, and hence cannot lead to profitable research.

The theory presented in this paper enables us to regard these problems in a different light, and to formulate them in more meaningful terms. It states that the more or less stable attributes of behaviour, commonly referred to as abilities, represent performance at crude limits of learning, and that such limits are determined by the biological propensities of the individual and by cultural factors which prescribe what shall be learned and at what age. Therefore, questions raised about the role of cultural factors in human ability are essentially questions about the relationship between learning and human ability.

The obvious inference from this line of argument is that individuals reared in different cultures will develop different patterns of ability. It is substantiated by a mass of anthropological evidence. It must be so. It cannot be argued that, if no differences between cultural groups on a particular test are found, we are measuring a biological capacity in which no differences exist between groups. Nor, conversely, can it be argued that where differences are found they are the result of biological differences. Such arguments are ruled out of court in the above theoretical position. The initial problem becomes one of describing the patterns of ability which are characteristic of individuals reared in different cultural environments. The initial problem is not one of demonstrating that intercultural differences exist with respect to a particular ability, or that they do not, or of drawing inferences from such findings one way or another.

I regard the inferences drawn from many of the extensive investigations on racial differences in 'intelligence' as essentially invalid. Many of these studies sought differences in 'intelligence', biologically regarded, between racial groups; race being a biological concept. Hypotheses pertaining to this problem are unverifiable in terms of the present theory. Racial groups may exhibit different patterns of ability, as defined by performance on particular tests, but to argue from these data for or against the existence of biological differences is not meaningful.

In Canada during the war the Armed Services attempted to develop parallel tests for French- and English-speaking personnel. The hypothesis underlying the development of such tests was that no differences in the pattern of abilities existed (or should exist) between these groups, an hypothesis which was politically expedient regardless of its scientific validity. This resulted in statistical manipulation to ensure that the French and English forms, when applied to samples of the respective populations, gave the same means and variances. A practicable approach to this problem, which avoids such difficulties, is to develop tests, possibly quite different, for French and for English, and to validate them separately in French and English situations. If similar non-language tests are developed for French and for English, and these then show pronounced differences in the patterns of ability between French and English, the problem is not one of obscuring these differences by statistical manipulation, but of ascertaining the best use to which these differences can be put in the selection and classification of personnel.

As for isolated, underprivileged, and restricted[3] cultural com-

3. Implicit in the use of such terms as 'restricted', 'underprivileged', and the like to refer to cultural groups is the evaluation that because many cultures are different from our own they are in some vague sense 'not as good'. Even some of our better scientific thinkers seem incapable of observing a difference between cultures without implying a value judgement. Such terms have meaning only in relation to some particular criterion variable. If that variable is the availability of medical services or the number of refrigerators per 1000 population, then these terms may be assigned a precise meaning in relation to such variables. If, however, the criterion variable is a phenomenological one, such as 'happiness', then the terms are probably meaningless, because propositions relating to the relative 'happiness' of peoples in different cultures are unverifiable. Some observers infer that the Eskimos in Baffin Island are a very 'happy' people, whereas others seem prepared to

munities, the initial problem is again one of developing tests for describing adequately the abilities of the members of such communities. These tests should conform to the usual criteria of reliability, discriminatory capacity, and the like. In the Newfoundland outports, for example, many individuals display excellent skill in boat building, navigation, and fishing. On tests of the abstract thinking type developed for use in urbanized cultures, the members of such communities make low scores. The tests discriminate poorly. The abilities that develop among the members of such communities, and upon which their survival depends, are probably quite different from those that our urbanized culture fosters. The first step is to discover adequate ways and means for describing these abilities. Once this is done, an attack can be made on other problems.

Age and ability

There is a substantial body of experimental data on the relationship between test performance and age in different cultural groups, but it has not been adequately interpreted or carefully assessed in relation to a theory of mental ability. The theory proposed in this paper permits an interpretation of these data and leads to certain hypotheses which, if substantiated, may be of some practical consequence in the development of tests for different cultural groups.

Take the studies by Gordon (1923)[4] on canal-boat and gypsy children in England. The canal-boat children received a very limited education. The average school attendance was estimated at only 5 per cent of that in the ordinary elementary schools. Each family led a relatively isolated existence and had little contact with other canal-boat families. In a sample of seventy-six children the average IQ (Stanford–Binet) was 69·6. Notable was the sharp decline in IQ with age. The correlation between IQ and age was −0·755. The four- to six-year group had an average IQ of 90, whereas the oldest group averaged 60. In children of the same family a consistent drop from the youngest to the oldest was observed. The mental ages of children within a single family were similar, although chronological ages differed.

contend that the inhabitants of Manhattan Island are not. That Baffin Islanders are 'happier' than Manhattan Islanders still remains an unverifiable proposition.

4. My account of Gordon's work is taken from Anastasi and Foley (1949). I do not have access to the original source.

In the case of gypsy children the mean IQ in a sample of 82 was 74·5, and the correlation between age and IQ was −0·430. The school attendance of the gypsy children was about 35 per cent of possible school days. Although IQ was negatively correlated with age, it was positively correlated with school attendance. The increment of mental with chronological age was far below that which generally obtains.

Similar results have been found in studies of mountain children made by Hirsch (1928), Asher (1935), Sherman and Key (1932), and others. Studies on Eskimo children carried out by Anderson and Eells (1935) report the same findings. The Mean IQ on the Stanford–Binet at the 8-year age level was 99·6 and at the 18-year age level 66·8. On the Goodenough scale for 'drawing a man the corresponding average IQs were 100·0 and 87·2. Similar observations were made by Porteous (1931) in applying the Porteous Maze Test to Australian aborigines. Yerkes (Yerkes and Anderson, 1915) reported a similar result with respect to different socioeconomic groups, the increment of score with age being less for a low-status than for a high-status group. This finding, however, does not seem to have been clearly substantiated by later work.

Unequivocal interpretation of the above findings is not possible since the tests used at different age levels were somewhat different; but it seems reasonable to conclude that for any particular test the change in performance with age may vary markedly from one cultural group to another. In one the increment of test performance with age may be substantial, in another negligible. This must be mainly due to the demands of the cultural environment, which dictate what shall be learned and at what age.

If we accept this as the most plausible view, the inference may be drawn that those abilities that are of importance in a particular cultural environment, and that may be expected to correlate with performance in the important activities which the culture demands, are those which show a pronounced increment with age.[5]

5. This hypothesis assumes a direct relationship between the abilities that a particular form of education fosters in the child and the demands that the culture imposes at the adult level. In the history of education many cases of incongruity exist between éducation and the changing demands of a culture. Probably only in the most stable culture is a really high degree of congruence attained. Incongruity may enrich a culture, may destroy it, or may produce other effects. For example, if we impose our rather urbanized system of education, with its great emphasis on verbal abilities, on isolated Newfoundland communities, either these communities may be greatly enriched or extensive migration may occur. The latter alternative is more probable.

It is possible that the abilities which the ordinary intelligence test defines are fairly independent of the types of activity which make for success in, say, a canal-boat culture, provided possibly that some minimal level is attained. It is possible that other abilities, if they could be defined, might show a marked increment with age, and be expected to correlate with the important classes of activity which make for survival in that culture.

The usual tests of intelligence correlate with a wide variety of classes of activity in our 'more privileged' Western cultures. Such tests show substantial increase in performance with age until about the age of seventeen. We may speculate that tests which show a small age increment may correlate only with very specialized types of performance, and be of restricted usefulness.

If this line of inference could be substantiated, we would have available a criterion for the selection of tests which were likely to prove useful in a particular cultural environment. We would select those types of test material which had a high correlation with age and discard those which had a low one. Age would then be a general criterion for the validation of tests correlating with performance on important classes of activity demanded by a particular culture.

Culture and factor theory

There are implications for factor analysis in the theory proposed in this paper. The following observations are speculative and call for more elaboration and refinement than can be afforded here.

The hypothesis of differential transfer which has been proposed implies that the factors or underlying parameters which transfer, and either facilitate or inhibit performance of a task, are not invariant with respect to the stage of learning at which the task is performed. Although a task may appear on superficial inspection to be the 'same' at different stages of learning, operationally – in terms of factorial content – it may be different. Further, since the level of performance of a particular class of task may differ markedly from one culture to another, depending on the cultural dictum concerning what is learned and when, it follows that the factorial composition of tests may differ markedly from one culture to another. This simply means that, through learning, individuals in diverse cultures may bring different abilities to bear on the solution of an identical problem. Factorial invariance presumably applies only within the framework of a clearly defined cultural group, and has no broad cross-cultural implications. Were it technically feasible to construct a battery of tests which could be appropriately administered to a random sample of adult subjects both in Toronto and in the Newfoundland outports, I have no doubt that we should find marked differences between the two groups in the factorial composition of many of the tests used. What we know about factors has reference to our own highly urbanized culture, which fosters the acquisition of certain verbal and reasoning abilities; our knowledge should not be presumed to extend beyond this.

The problem of a general factor

Spearman (1927) strove to show that a general intellective factor operated in the performance of many mental tasks. Thurstone's (1938) attempt to disprove Spearman's theory was not conclusive, since most of the factors in his classificatory system are correlated factors. The concept of a general factor is still with us. In the light of present knowledge this concept derives from the fact that many abilities, identified factorially in some loosely defined domain of intellectual activity, are not independent of one another. As currently regarded, it does not imply that all the innumerable identifiable abilities within that domain are correlated. Limitations on the generality of a general factor are not clearly prescribed.

A scrutiny of the general factor problem suggests that we must consider two aspects of it. We must account not only for the fact that many abilities are in some degree positively correlated with one another, but also for the fact that they are in some degree differentiated from one another. A theory which accounts for one aspect of the problem does not necessarily account for the other. Thus a theoretical explanation may account for abilities being correlated, but it may not, if pressed to its ultimate conclusion, account for their not being perfectly correlated, or there not being one ability only. The theory of human ability proposed in this paper can account very simply for the former aspect of the problem. To account for the latter aspect is more difficult.

Let us accept the general proposition that all learning, with the exception of some which occurs very early in life, occurs in a context of prior experience. This means that an individual will learn more readily activities which are facilitated by prior acquisitions, and will learn less readily those activities which are not facilitated or are perhaps inhibited by prior learning. Since in the adult many abilities are regarded as overlearned acquisitions, it follows that in the development of distinctive abilities those abilities will tend to develop which are facilitated and not inhibited by each other. It follows, therefore, that the positive correlation between abilities, which gives rise to the notion of a general factor, can be accounted for in the present theory by the operation of positive transfer. Although this is undoubtedly an over-simplification, it does provide a simple and plausible explanation.

Can we account for the fact that many abilities, while correlated, are none the less clearly differentiated? In approaching this problem we may observe that any attempt to explain learning and the formation of abilities by transfer alone leads to an obvious absurdity, since it cannot explain how early learning can occur at all. To escape this difficulty I propose a two-factor theory of learning. This theory states that much learning, excluding some very early learning, involves not only transfer components which are common to prior learning and the learning of a new task, but also components which are specific to the new task. In terms of the factorial model, this means that variation in performance at various stages of a task can be accounted for in part by the variation in prior acquisitions, and in part by specific abilities that emerge and are formed during the process of learning the task itself. I should anticipate that, as the learning of certain classes of tasks continues through a series of stages, the variance attributable to general transfer components may decrease whereas the variance attributable to abilities specific to the task itself, or common only to the task, will increase. Further, it seems reasonable that variation in early learning can be accounted for much less by transfer than by other processes, since there are fewer prior acquisitions to transfer. In the adult, learning may be accounted for largely in terms of transfer and to a much lesser extent in terms of other processes.

In sum, it seems to me that what happens is this. Some early learning must occur which is independent of prior learned acquisitions. As the individual grows, learning is facilitated more and more by prior acquisitions. It is probable that transfer effects become continuously and increasingly more important with age. In the learning of a particular task, transfer effects are probably greater at the earlier than at the later stages of learning. Thus, as the learning of a particular task continues, the ability to perform it becomes gradually differentiated from, although not necessarily independent of, other abilities which facilitate its differentiation. Learning is clearly a process by which the abilities of man are differentiated from one another, but the process of differentiation is aided and abetted by the abilities which the individual already possesses.

In conclusion, therefore, we may account for a component general to many abilities in terms of the operation of positive transfer, and for the differentiation of abilities in terms of the learning process itself, which, according to the theory presented here, operates in such a way as to facilitate differentiation.

Summary

In an attempt to draw together crudely within the same scheme the study of learning and the study of human ability I have advanced the following views. Different environments result in the overlearning of certain patterns of behaviour, which, because they are overlearned, become more or less invariant with respect to repetition or cessation. A crude limit of performance is reached. What is spoken of as an ability, in conventional psychological usage, has reference to performance at some crude limit of learning. This applies to the abilities of the Thurstone system and to whatever is subsumed under the term 'intelligence'. Differences in ability are the results of the complex interaction of the biological propensities of the organism, prior learning, and the age at which prior learning occurs. The role of human ability in subsequent learning, for example, intelligence in relation to scholastic performance, can be viewed as a problem in transfer; the question is in what way prior overlearned acquisitions – the abilities – affect subsequent learning. Abilities may transfer differentially in any learning situation; that is, the abilities which transfer and produce their effects at one stage of learning may be different from those which transfer and produce their effects at a later stage of the same task. An individual may possess the necessary ability to perform a task adequately, but may lack the ability to learn to perform the task under particular learning conditions. The investigation of problems emerging from these lines of argument involves an individual difference approach and use of the methods of factorial analysis. The implications of the theory for problems of the role of cultural factors in human ability are elaborated. The line of theory developed leads to the inference that those abilities which are of importance in a particular culture, and which may be expected to correlate with performance in the important activities demanded for survival in the culture, are those which show a pronounced increment with age. This provides a basis for test validation of a certain type. The implications of the theory of human ability for factor theory are considered. The inference is drawn that ostensibly similar tests may have different factorial compositions in different cultures and in different strata of the same culture. The problem of a general factor is examined. A two-factor theory of learning is proposed. The correlation among abilities is explained in terms of positive transfer, and their differentiation by the development of abilities specific to particular learning situations.

References

ANASTASI, A., and FOLEY, J. P. (1949), *Differential Psychology*, Macmillan.

ANDERSON, H. D., and EELLS, W. C. (1935), *Alaska Natives: A Survey of Their Sociological and Educational Status*, Stanford University Press.

ASHER, E. J. (1935), 'The inadequacy of current intelligence tests for testing Kentucky Mountain children', *J. Genetic Psychol.*, vol. 46, pp. 480–86.

CATTELL, R. B. (1940), 'A culture-free intelligence test', *J. educ. Psychol.*, vol. 31, pp. 161–79.

CATTELL, R. B. (1941), 'A culture-free intelligence test: evaluation of cultural influences on test performance', *J. educ. Psychol.*, vol. 32, pp. 81–100.

COOK, T. W. (1944), 'Repetition and learning: I, stimulus and response', *Psychol. Rev.*, vol. 51, pp. 25–36.

EELLS, K., DAVIS, A. *et al.* (1951), *Intelligence and Cultural Differences*. University of Chicago Press.

GOMULICKI, R. BRONISLAW (1953), 'The development and present status of the trace theory of memory', *Brit. J. Psychol. Monogr. Suppl.*, vol. 29.

GORDON, H. (1923), *Mental and Scholastic Tests Among Retarded Children*. Educ. pamphlet no. 44, Board of Education, London.

HEBB, D. O. (1949), *The Organization of Behavior*, Wiley.

HIRSCH, N. D. M. (1928), 'An experimental study of East Kentucky mountaineers', *Genet. Psychol. Monogr.*, vol. 3, pp. 188–244.

McGEOCH, J. A. (1946), *The Psychology of Human Learning*, Longman, New York.

PORTEOUS, S. D. (1931), *The Psychology of a Primitive People*, Longman, New York.

SIMRALL, D. (1949), 'Intelligence and the ability to learn', *J. Psychol.*, vol. 23, pp. 27–43.

SHERMAN, M. and KEY, C. B. (1932), 'The intelligence of isolated mountain children', *Child Develop.*, vol. 3, pp. 279–90.

SPEARMAN, C. (1927), *The Abilities of Man: Their Nature and Measurement*, Macmillan.

THOMSON, G. H. (1946), *The Factorial Analysis of Human Ability*, 2nd edn, University of London Press.

THURSTONE, L. L. (1947), *Multiple Factor Analysis*, University of Chicago Press.

THURSTONE, L. L. (1938), *Primary Mental Abilities*, University of Chicago Press.

TILTON, J. W. (1949), 'Intelligence test scores as indicative of ability to learn' *Educ. Psychol. Measurement*, vol. 9, pp. 291–6.

TURNBULL, W. W. (1951), 'Socioeconomic status and predictive test scores', *Canad. J. Psychol.*, vol. 5, pp. 145–9.

WOODROW, H. (1940), 'Interrelations of measures of learning', *J. Psychol.*, vol. 10, pp. 49–73.

WOODROW, H. (1946), 'The ability to learn', *Psychol. Rev.*, vol. 53, pp. 147–58.

YERKES, R. M. and ANDERSON, H. (1915), 'The importance of social status as indicated by the results of the point-scale method of measuring mental capacity', *J. educ. Psychol.* vol. 6, pp. 137–50

17 J. McV. Hunt
Intelligence and Experience

Excerpts from J. McV. Hunt, *Intelligence and Experience*, Ronald Press, 1961, chapters 8 and 9, pp. 308–64.

Before recapitulation, it remains to look again at some of the old concepts and at some of the old facts which have been interpreted to support the assumptions of fixed intelligence and predetermined development. These old concepts and facts remain. Is their meaning altered by the conception of intelligence as central processes comprising strategies for processing information that develop in the course of the child's interacting with his environment? It remains also to re-examine the issue of the proportional contributions of heredity and environment to tested intelligence, to examine the predicted fall in the intelligence of future generations from the fact of differential fertility in the social-class structure, and to indicate the investigative, educational import of the theory and evidence reviewed here.

The meaning of intelligence test scores
Semantics and logic

Although the assumption of fixed intelligence has a basis in the history of thought, it is worth noting that it may have yet another basis in semantics and in the unwarranted generalization of certain conceptual sets. On the semantic side, intelligence has commonly been termed a *dimension* and has been seen as a dimension of a person. The tests of intelligence have been termed *scales* as if they were measuring a fixed dimension of the person or the person's behavior. Such terminology derives from the physical sciences where objects are constant, at least relatively so for most purposes, and where the systems of relationships among them are closed. Objects are constant, for instance, with respect to such dimensions as height, circumference, weight, volume, and shape, and this constancy is one of the concepts mediated by the central processes that grow with experience. The systems of relationship among them are closed in the sense that, with the relevant conditions specified, certain events involving their relations always occur, as in the case of the law of falling bodies.

The application of such terms as *dimension* and *scale* may at once tend to carry their meaning in the physical world over to the world of organismic behavior and to imply that the concept of constancy of dimensions is being generalized from static objects to non-static persons and their behavior. On the conceptual side, moreover, since persons change relatively slowly, especially in adulthood, it is easy to see how such conceptual sets as object-constancy, quantity-conservation, and number-conservation would readily be generalized from the world of static things to the world of changing organisms and persons. Once change has come to be conceived to be a matter of mere appearances behind which exists a constant essence, it is no easy matter to distinguish essences which are in fact static from essences which are in fact changing. It is probable that unwarranted generalization of conceptual constancy-sets is one factor behind the persistence of the belief in fixed intelligence. Fixed intelligence is a conception like the preformationistic notion that the bodily structure of a species is to be found within the egg or the sperm. Both rest upon such an ancient conceptual constancy-set as 'hair cannot come out of not-hair, nor flesh out of not-flesh' attributed to Anaxagoras of Clazomenae (Cornford, 1930) and which may be generalized as 'no essence can be derived from something which does not include that essence'. Once one has acquired such a conceptual constancy-set, the idea that an essence like intelligence can change tends to produce 'cognitive dissonance'. And one tends to build defenses against such emotional disturbance. In the light of such considerations, calling intelligence a *dimension* and speaking of tests as *scales* may be unfortunate. In so far as they may serve to reduce the dissonance that would come with recognizing the full implications of the epigenesis in the development of intelligence, they may also obscure reality.

In the light of such considerations, moreover, the assumption of predetermined development looks like a withdrawal from the untenable position of preformationism to the next redoubt. Exaggerating the degree of *predetermination* in development may gain one a defensive preservation of his constancy-set; he may thereby avoid the dissonance that would come from recognizing that organisms not only change but that the process of change is itself open-ended. In the words of Dobzhansky, the geneticist (1950), 'at any stage of development, the [phenotypic] outcome of the development depends on the genotype and on the succession of environments which the developing organism has encountered up to that stage'. But more than cognitive dissonance may be involved here. One implication of this idea that the development of organisms and persons is an open-ended process puts a logical limitation on the predictive validity[1] of tests of intelligence or on measures of any personal characteristic. Recognizing such a limitation would disturb anyone who aspired to predictions from tests which have the supposed support of logical necessity. Prediction in science, however, is always a matter of stating what will happen to given objects in a closed system for which the relevant conditions can be and are fully specified. It is this fact that makes scientific prediction an essential criterion for understanding and for the correctness of predictions as formulated. It may become possible to formulate laws which predict the characteristics that organisms with specified genetic constitutions will develop under specified programs of encounters with the environment. It would appear to be outside the realm of scientific possibility, however, to predict with precision the future characteristics or phenotypic fate of any organism from knowing merely its present characteristics, without being able to specify what any person's future encounters with his environment will be, attempting to predict his future behavior from test performances alone is at best a matter of statistical empiricism. At worst it smacks of occult prophecy. Although these considerations eliminate the support of logical necessity from all predictions of future behavior made from tests, either intelligence tests or tests of other characteristics, it avails nothing to deny these considerations except possibly to avoid some of the insecurity felt by some of those professionally concerned with predicting the behavior of people from their performances on tests. The tests have neither more nor less empirical usefulness in practical affairs because they lack the support of logical necessity for the empirical predictions derived from them.

1. By *predictive validity* is meant here the capacity of the test-scores of individuals from testing at one stage of development to predict either the test-scores or the criterion performances of those individuals at a later period of their lives. It should be noted that this is not always the definition given to *predictive validity*. Cronbach (1949), for instance, has used *predictive validity* in the sense that *criterion validity* is used here, namely, to refer to the capacity of the performance of persons on tests to predict such contemporary criteria as their school grades, their success in flight training, or the quality of their clerical work. For Cronbach's usage, the time between the two performances (test to test, or test to criterion) is not a matter of explicit consideration in the definition.

The nature of intelligence and of intelligence tests

The semantics of *dimension* and *scale* fit the procedures of testing less well than do the semantics of sampling behavior for evidence of the presence of such organizational structures as schemata, operations, and conceptions. Intelligence tests consist essentially of samplings of behavior. The vocabulary tests, for example, sample the subject's knowledge of the meaning of words; absurdities test sample recognitions of the logical relationships among various concepts, and most other tests sample the subject's grasp of various relationships or whether or not he does educe various relationships. In traditional tests, what is sampled is typically named in terms of such skill categories as verbal or arithmetic skill. The attempts by factor analysts, including Spearman's *g*, Thurstone's primary abilities, and Guilford's factor structures of intellect, to specify what is sampled yield what is probably best conceived as systems of coordinates which simplify the comparing of people in their test-performance and perhaps facilitate making predictions about the efficiency of people.[2] These systems of co-ordinates, regardless of the names given to them, may – yes, probably – have little or nothing to do with the natural structures, schemata, operations, and concepts organized within individuals that determine their problem-solving. It is the merit of Piaget to give attention to the natural structures of the central processes that mediate problem-solving. It is an intriguing paradox, more-over, that, if the temporal order of appearance of the landmarks diagnostic of the structures proves to be fixed, his work will have produced the first evidence to justify what might properly be called a natural scale of intelligence. That scale will be ordinal in nature, and it will be based upon sampling behavior to determine the presence or absence of the various hierarchically arranged structures with their logical characteristics.

Reliability and validity of tests

The semantics of sampling behavior for signs of such structures as sensorimotor schemata, operations, and conceptions do no violence to the facts concerning the reliability and validity of intelligence tests. Intelligence test-scores are reliable chiefly in the sense that the individual's rank in a group as determined by a

2. This is, of course, but one point of view, the one held also by Anastasi, Burt, Thomson, Vernon. Against this view are the arguments of Cattell, Guilford, Holzinger, Kelley, and Thurstone for the notion that the factors are genuine causal entities.

part of a test (split half) or by one test approximates his rank in that group or in another comparable group as determined in the same fashion. In so far as the central structures mediating intelligent behavior change only gradually, their presence at one time should indicate their presence again at another time if the two times are not too widely separated and no encounters with circumstances have intervened that force radical changes in them.

Validity is a term with various meanings. Two of these meanings are especially relevant. First, *criterion validity*: test-scores may be said to be valid in the sense that the rank of an individual in a group derived from his performance on an intelligence test approximates his rank in that group or a comparable one derived from such criteria as his performance in school or on a variety of jobs. Again the concept of the sampling of structures does no violence to the facts, for insofar as the structures of central processes that constitute or mediate intelligence generalize across situations, the persons who show them in the test situation should also show them in school or workaday situations.

Second, *predictive validity*: test-scores may also be said to be valid if the individual's rank in a group at one time as determined by his performance on tests approximates his rank in that group or a comparable one at a later time, as determined by his performance on tests. This is the kind of validity involved when an attempt is made to predict the final adult level of intelligence from tests given earlier in youth, childhood, or infancy (Bayley, 1954). The finding that the degree of correlation between the score at any testing and the score at age 18 drops off with the amount of time that separates the testing from the determination of the final level is not consonant with the assumptions of either fixed intelligence or predetermined development but it is precisely what one would expect from the conception of intelligence as central structures developed in the course of child environment interaction, with the role of heredity being that of setting limits.

Constancy and fluctuations of DQ and IQ

The DQ and IQ are rates of development, at least for children, if not for adults. They do not, however, describe the absolute rate of change in intelligence structures per unit of time. Rather, they are rates relative to age which provide chiefly a scale for the comparison of individuals. In any absolute sense, the rate of change in schemata and intelligence structures is largest during the early months of life, and it drops off thereafter. In this slowing process, the development of behavioral structures follows a course resembling that of the embryological development or morphological structures. The notion of fixed intelligence implies that individual differences in the relative rate should be constant. The curves of the IQ from successive testings of individual children, in such longitudinal studies as the Berkeley Growth Study, fail to show the constancy to be expected from the notion of fixed intelligence. While the developmental rate is high during the preschool years, great variability in scores from successive testings is not uncommon. An appreciable degree of constancy emerges only after about five when the developmental rate has slowed greatly and when going to school brings a relatively common program of environmental encounters into the lives of children.

While the fluctuations of DQs and IQs during the early years are highly embarrassing to the assumption of fixed intelligence, and also to that of predetermined development, unless one makes with Goodenough and Maurer (1942) the additional *ad hoc* assumption of predetermined patterns in rate of development, they are entirely consonant with the notion of intelligence as central processes developing as a function of the child's interactions with the environment. Moreover, in view of the fact that any pair of parents may have attitudes and child-rearing practices which foster very rapid rates of development at some stages and interfere with development at other stages, one might expect that a child would be quite advanced at one stage and retarded at another during these early months and years. Murphy (1944) has pointed out that there is a constant interaction between the mother's personality and the characteristics of the young infant and child. She has written, for example, that

in infancy, that protective mother may give the child a great deal of satisfaction (and we might add variety of stimulation) if she is the kind who is protective because she is fond of babies and gets a great deal of satisfaction from them. But at the age of expanding locomotion and exploration (when the child needs to throw things and to indulge in activities that might apparently be harmful both to himself and to valuable things), the over-protective mother becomes an inhibitor and deprives the child of opportunities which he needs to use his new abilities . . . the excessively scientific mother (on the other hand) who deprives the child of emotional satisfaction at the infancy level may, by contrast, give the child more approval and emotional satisfaction at the locomotor period, because she is pleased by the new signs of independence.

Such considerations suggest the possibility of discovering important relationships between the age at which Piaget's behavioral landmarks appear, if they do constitute a genuine ordinal scale, and the manner in which parents manage their children at various stages of development. It is just possible, for instance, that the negative correlation that Bayley (1954) has found between DQs and IQs in children of less than a year in age and the educational level of parents may result from the misinformation about child-rearing that has been communicated to those who read and can act upon what they learn by reading. If this line of reasoning is correct, it may be possible, from a knowledge of the parental attitudes toward the various phases of infantile development, to make roughly accurate predictions of the phases at which children in given families will be advanced or retarded.

Viewing intelligence as a sampling of schemata makes it sensible to use tests in early development as a method of assessing some of the consequences of parental practices and attitudes. Parental behaviors are very probably much more important determinants of rates of development than are such traditional indices of intellectual environment as level of parental education, socioeconomic level, number of books in the house, etc. In fact, these traditional indices of intellectual environment may be very poor indicators of the behaviors which are important determinants. Finally, inasmuch as developmental rates are most rapid, in absolute terms, during the early months and first couple of years, this is probably the period of most importance for maximizing intellectual potential. Such a verdict is completely contrary to what has been believed from assuming that intelligence is fixed and that development is predetermined and from assuming that experience, especially during the early years, is of no significance for future intellectual level.

The notion that intelligence tests are sampling schemata and intellectual structures helps to clarify the fact, pointed out by Anderson (1940), that the predictive invalidity of infant tests derives from the fact that they have few elements which are common to the successive age levels. This is no accident. It derives inevitably from the fact that the child at a year has absorbed almost all of the schemata observable at six months into a new set of structures, and the child at two years has absorbed those evident at a year into another new set. It derives inevitably and directly from the fact that the epigenesis of intellectual structures is very rapid in the preschool years.

On the other hand, it is quite incorrect to consider the infant tests invalid. Bayley has shown that the reliability of the infant tests is of the order of $+0.9$ so long as only a week or two elapses between tests. In the sense that the infant tests fail to predict the ultimate level of intelligence, they do lack predictive validity, but predictive validity could be expected only by assuming fixed intelligence and predetermined development. Otherwise, as already noted, prediction would be impossible without understanding fully all the influential factors in the child-environment interaction and without being able to specify completely the program of encounters that the child will have with the environment throughout the period between testing and the determination of final level. In so far as the infant tests indicate what the child can do at a given time, in so far as they indicate the structures which are present at a given time, they are entirely valid. Insofar as the DQ and IQ represent the appearance of genuine capacities relative to age, they are also valid. These structures should generalize from the testing situation to criterion situations, but unfortunately criterion situations have seldom been a consideration in the pre-school years. The meaning of validity has been limited to predictive validity. If they are seen as having criterion validity, the infant tests may also be seen as potentially sensitive indicators of the effects of various kinds of environments. On the other hand, for such purposes, it may be wiser to use such natural landmarks in behavior as Piaget has uncovered.

Heredity versus environment

Ever since Galton pioneered with the use of twins to compare the relative influence of heredity and environment in the causation of various traits efforts have been directed chiefly toward assessing the proportional importance of each. Thorndike attempted to answer this question with respect to intelligence in his classical application of correlational methods to the study of the differences in the intellectual achievement of twins. In 1913, moreover, he indicated that, while in one sense nothing in human nature is due either to heredity or to environment, 'in another sense, the most fundamental question of human education asks precisely that we assign separate shares in the causation of human behavior to man's original nature on the one hand and his environment on the other'. Some twenty years later, Shuttleworth (1935) saw the problem of selecting methods of improving the health, intelligence, and general welfare of mankind to be dependent upon an answer to this proportion question. In 1941, Woodworth echoed the same view in the introduction to his critical survey of the studies of twins and foster children. Very recently, Cattell (1958) and his collaborators have expressed this view again. Without doubting that both the genes and the series of encounters with the environment during development influence individual differences in tested intelligence, one can have grave doubts about both the method by which answers have been sought to this proportion question, about the answerability of the question, and about the strategy of asking this particular question.

Samplings of the traditional view

In a competent review of the studies which have attempted to answer this proportion question, Loevinger (1943) has credited Fisher with introducing the statistical model and technique for answering the proportion question. Using the correlations between relatives (identical twins, siblings, foster children, etc.), he assumed additive Mendelian factors as the hereditary causes of the physical traits in which he happened to be interested, and he assumed that the effects of the environment would be added to the effects of heredity. Fisher, moreover, used the ratio of variances, now familiar as F, to assess the proportional contributions. The proportion of variance attributable to heredity, for instance, is the ratio of the variance contributed by indicators of the hereditary factor to the variance in the trait concerned; here the trait is some measure of intelligence. Since the F-Ratio of the variance of the differences between pairs (of identical twins, foster children, etc.) in test-score or IQ to the variance for the whole sample of paired individuals is equal to twice the complement of the coefficient of correlation between the pairs (V_d/V sample $= 2(1-r)$, where d refers to the pair differences, and r refers to the correlation between the pairs), correlations can be used directly in such analyses. In some instances, moreover, the square of the coefficient of correlation, which states the variance common to the correlated variables, has been used to assess the variance attributed to the special factor the two have in common.

In one approach, which has yielded two of the most widely quoted answers to the proportion question, Burks (1928) and Leahy (1935) compared the correlations obtained from foster children and from biological children with various indicators of the inter-familial differences in the intellectual value of their homes. Using father's IQ, mother's IQ, material advantages of the home, cultural advantages of the home, and income (i.e. of foster parents, for foster children, and of biological parents for their children), Burks got multiple correlations of $+0.42$ for the foster children and $+0.61$ for the biological children. She wrote, 'the *square* of this (former) multiple (0.17) represents the variance of children in ordinary communities that is due to home environment'. Squaring the latter coefficient, she got 0.37 as the proportion of the variance which 'represents the combined effect of home environment and parental mental level . . .'. This latter proportion leaves 63 per cent of the variance not accounted for. Inasmuch as only one-half of the chromosomes of each parent are present in a child, however, Burks inferred that the correlation between the IQs of children and their parents would underestimate the true correlation between intelligence and heredity. She therefore considered that the major share of this residual variance would be due to genetic constitution, and so concluded that 'close to 75 or 80 per cent of the IQ variance is due to innate and heritable causes'. Leahy did not use multiple correlation, and the corresponding coefficients that she obtained were $+0.23$ (foster children with foster parents and homes) and $+0.53$. The same procedure yields estimates of 5 per cent of variance in IQ attributable to environment and over 90 per cent to heredity.

In a second approach, Wright devised the method of 'path coefficients' for this same purpose. His approach assumed that the variance in an effect variable is equal to the weighted sum of the variances in a set of causal variables. From the correlations between the effect variable and measures of several related factors he computed the weights that he called 'path coefficients'. The squares of these weights were then taken as the proportional contributions of the cause of the variance in the effect variable. After finding fault with Burks' (1928) analysis, Wright (1931) suggested as an alternative a procedure based on the fact that parents' intelligence is a variable correlated with the other variables in Burks' biological families but uncorrelated with heredity in the foster group. Using the two sets of correlations between child IQ and parent IQ to solve for the unknown correlations with the postulated 'heredity factor', Wright developed 'path coefficients' from which he concluded that home environment contributed approximately only 9 per cent of the variance in IQ, and he assumed that the residual 91 per cent should be attributed to error and to heredity, with error getting but a very minor share.

In a third widely quoted approach, Newman, Freeman and Holzinger (1937) explicitly limited their answer to the proportion question to fraternal twins reared together. Because the gene patterns of identical twins are identical, they assumed that any differences between the pairs must be attributed to environment. In essence they developed from the formula relating variance to correlation a method of subtracting the variance of the differences attributable to environment, between pairs of identical twins, from the variance of the differences between fraternal twins, and then determining the proportion that the remaining variance of the differences between pairs of fraternal twins was of the total variance among their sample of fraternal twins. This was achieved in their formula for h^2 ($h^2 = (_ir - _fr)/(1 - _fr)$) (where $_ir$ is the coefficient of correlation between identical twins, and where $_fr$ is the correlation between fraternal twins). For their sample, the proportions of variance thus attributed to heredity in fraternal twins reared together ranged from 0·65 for Binet mental age to 0·80 for Otis IQ.

From such types of evidence comes the commonly quoted statement that 80 per cent of the variance in tested intelligence can be attributed to heredity, only 20 per cent to the environment.

Recently efforts have been made to refine the analysis-of-variance model for answering the proportion question. Cattell (1958) designates four sources of individual differences: (1) between-family environmental differences, (2) between-family hereditary differences, (3) within-family environmental differences, and (4) within-family hereditary differences. He contends that it is these variances and their interactions that need to be taken into account in the predictions that the clinician and the educator must make.

Existing conditions versus potential conditions and the proportion question

So long as the goal is obtaining a general answer to the proportion question, efforts to refine the statistical model are irrelevant to the contention that various classes of hereditary and environmental variance are what need to be taken into account by the clinician and the educator. There is no general answer to the proportion question, and any educational or welfare policies formed on the basis of any given answer purporting to be general are likely to have unhappy consequences.

Although such geneticists as Hogben and Haldane and such investigators of the genetic factor in human intelligence as Schwesinger and Newman, Freeman and Holzinger (1937) have warned against seeking a general answer to the proportion question, the effort to find one seems never to die, and those answers available get implications attributed to them which they do not have. Although Woodworth (1941) made several still highly pertinent and useful suggestions for future research on the roles of heredity and environment, he, for instance, also included among the conclusions of his review of attempts to answer the proportion question from the studies of twins and foster children the statement that 'not over a fifth, apparently, of the variance of intelligence in the general population can be attributed to differences in homes and neighborhoods acting as environmental factors'. Following the assumptions underlying the sort of contentions about what needs to be taken into account by clinicians and educators attributed above to Cattell, this statement has been used to justify the estimate that no matter what might be done in the way of manipulating a child's encounters with the environment during the course of his development, one could not expect to modify his IQ appreciably, and certainly not by more than about 20 per cent of the variance in IQ to be found in the population. The available data provide no justification for such an estimate. Leaving aside the appropriateness of the analysis-of-variance model, so long as samplings are based on any given set of existing conditions, the answer to the proportion question obtained from them says nothing about what answer might be obtained from another set of conditions.

Inferring from existing answers to the proportion question no clinical or educational policy assumes that samples of the existing variation in the conditions of heredity and environment are statistically representative. They are probably not representative for heredity, and they definitely cannot be representative for the environment. The fact is that between-family and within-family variations in environment within the full range of the social classes in the culture of America constitute but a small part of the variation that has existed historically on the face of this earth. Moreover, if the assumptions that intelligence is largely fixed and that development is largely predetermined are discarded, and if behavior scientists devote themselves to the task of manipulating the encounters of children with their environments to maximize their potential for happy intellectual growth, who knows what the limits are? It is inconceivable that they are to be fixed by any given set of existing conditions.

In order to simplify this point, consider the potentialities for variance in Binet IQ attributable to environmental conditions in the case of identical twins, where heredity is held constant. From the work of Newman, Freeman and Holzinger (1937), one finds the correlation between the IQs of identical twins reared together to be +0.88. According to the formula for relating variance ratio to correlation presented above, the proportion of variance attributable to environment would be 24 per cent (i.e. 2(1−0.88)). From the same study, when the IQs of identical twins reared apart were correlated, the resulting coefficient was +0.67, and the variance attributable to environment became, by the same logic, 66 per cent. Now, suppose that one obtains a sample of identical twins in which one of each pair is reared in a family while the other is reared in an orphanage like the one Dennis (1960) found in Teheran, what will the proportion attributable to environment become? Any answer would be pure conjecture, but it could be expected to drop further. If the interaction between heredity and environment, a factor assumed to be omitted by the analysis-of-variance model, is not great across such a contrast in environments, considerable correlation might continue to be evident, and the main evidence of effect might show in that the difference between the pairs would drop considerably. Now again, suppose that one obtains yet another sample of identical twins in which one is reared in such an orphanage while the other is given an enriched program of encounters with the environment such as McGraw arranged for her trained twin, Johnny. What will the correlation between the IQs of these twins be?

It is obvious from such considerations that the answer to the proportion question depends upon the environmental conditions sampled, and that the potential range of variation in environmental conditions is limited only by the inventive genius of behavior scientists. Since such genius grows as it feeds upon the results of its efforts, the potential range is not specifiable. On these grounds alone, there is no general answer to the proportion question.

It is obvious also from such considerations that any policies concerning division of effort in the clinic or the classroom based on the commonly quoted answer of a 20/80 percentage split between environment and heredity would be quite wrong. Even if the figure has the meaning for the general population that Woodworth (1941) attributed to it, this does not mean that intellectual development is predetermined by the genes, but rather, given the existing culture of the subjects used in the studies of twins and foster children, children's encounters with the environment during their development is sufficiently similar in its growth-evoking capacity to yield this figure. On the side of reducing the variation of stimulation, it is clear from Dennis' observations of children in the orphanage in Teheran that the appearance of the walking schema can be delayed by at least from age two to age four, a DQ shift of 50 points. On the side of manipulating children's encounters with the environment from birth on to maximize intellectual growth, who knows what might be done? Various bits of evidence reviewed here indicate that substantial increases in intelligence as now measured may be possible. The important question for educational policy, the important question for the welfare of man now living in technological cultures that demand a higher proportion of people with high capacity for the manipulation of symbols in problem-solving, is to determine what the potential for increasing intellectual capacity may be. Answers to the proportion question based on an analysis of the variance within any sampling from the *status quo* have no bearing on this potential.

Critique of the analysis-of-variance model

But answers to the proportion question based on the analysis of the variance in tested intelligence attributable to heredity and environment are suspect also on the grounds that the analysis-of-variance model fits the data from the heredity–environment relationship too poorly to permit a meaningful answer. As Fisher constructed it, and as Dunlap and Cureton have pointed out, this model is based on the principle that the variances from heredity and environment are additive and without interaction. As Loevinger (1943) has put it, 'this principle states that *if* the score on the dependent variable is the sum of scores on a set of independent variables, then the variance on the dependent variable is the sum of variances on the set of independent variables'. How well does this principle fit what is known from various other sources about the operation of heredity and environment? Loevinger (1943) has answered this question, and the present writer believes correctly, by saying 'that (1) the additive assumption concerning the causation of intelligence is ambiguous in meaning, (2) is not supported by the known evidence, and (3) leads to no results capable of verification' (p. 746).[3]

The additive assumption is ambiguous in meaning, first, because neither heredity nor environment operates directly on behavior, and certainly not directly in the terms of the various scales by means of which they are assessed; and second, because it is unlikely that intelligence, heredity, or environment are properly regarded even as scales, not to say scales based upon family income, the vocabularies of father and mother, the Whittier scale, etc.

The genes must operate indirectly through a chain of mechanisms. Beadle has assembled evidence that appears to indicate that each of the various genes controls a biochemical step in metabolism. How many steps there may be in the chain of influence between biochemical steps in metabolism and mental age or the IQ no one knows. Even in the case of maximal directness, as in the case of phenylpyruvenic feeblemindedness where the gene concerned blocks the conversion of phenylaline to tyrosine so that it accumulates and is excreted in the urine, the remaining steps in the chain of influence are only partially clarified. The maze-brightness of Tryon's selectively bred rats appears to be based on cue-preferences and on emotionality, but how many links may exist in the chains of influence between these behavioral bases and the metabolic actions of various genes is not even a topic for responsible speculation. The IQ may have a genetic basis in something akin to Hebb's concept of the A/S ratio and also in something like the ease with which cerebral systems are modified by experience, because certain low-grade feebleminded human beings do not acquire learning sets much more readily than rats. But each of these hypothetical factors might be expected to go through an indirect chain of causal links of unknown number. It is commonly assumed that the influence of the genes through these many links will randomize after the fashion of the normal curve of probability, but how this justifies the additive assumption in the analysis-of-variance model is unclear.

3. It should be noted that this critique of the model does not condemn it for use as a method of testing the statistical significance of variance attributable to specific variations of either hereditary or environmental influences. Neither does it condemn its use as a way of estimating the relative proportions of the total variance in a given set of intelligence measures that can be attributed to specific variations of hereditary and environmental influences.

The environment also operates indirectly in forcing accommodations at the early stage of development in schemata which have little that is obviously in common with the performances tested. Considerable space was taken in chapter 7 [not reproduced here] to discuss the problem of matching a child's schemata with the environment that he encounters at each stage to maximize the rate of the child's intellectual development. Until this problem is solved, it is impossible even to rank environments meaningfully in terms of their capacity to foster intellectual growth. Moreover, Fuller and Scott have shown that one class of environmental encounters, wherein a standard is enforced, serves to reduce variance among either individuals or strains. Another class wherein each individual moves to a new level as soon as he has acquired the old one serves to expand individual differences. Just how two such disparate programs of environmental influence can be meaningfully put onto the same interval continuum is unclear. Furthermore, what relationship the effective encounters that children have with their environments may have to do with such matters as family income, father's vocabulary, mother's vocabulary, and scores on the Whittier scale for home grading it is impossible to specify.

In sum, to say that the additive assumption is ambiguous when applied to the influence of heredity and environment on the development of intelligence constitutes an understatement of large degree.

The absence of interaction between heredity and environment implied by the additive assumption is not supported by the available evidence. Absence of interaction would mean that any given heredity would have the same force in the production of the IQ regardless of the kind of environment, and vice versa. Ever since Johannsen, whom geneticists rank with Mendel as a progenitor of the science of genetics, did the classic work that led to the distinction between the *genotype* (referring to the constellation of genes in the organism) and the *phenotype* (referring to the organism's observable characteristics at any given time), evidences of interaction between the genotype and the organism's encounters with the environment have been accumulating. Hogben, for instance, cites the experiment of Krafka on the fruit-fly (*Drosophila*) showing that the curve which expresses the dependence of the number of eye-facets on the temperature at which the larvae are raised varies with the genotype. Thus, while increasing the temperature tends to reduce the number of facets, the reduction that occurs over temperatures ranging from 61° to 25°C is about five times as great in one genotype as in another. In another instance, Sinnot, Dunn and Dobzhansky cite Rappoport's discovery that when the larvae of typical brown vinegar flies (*Drosophila melanogaster*) are fed food containing silver salts, they develop into yellow flies which cannot be distinguished from a yellow mutant found by Morgan in 1910. When Morgan's yellow mutants are raised on food containing silver salts, they also become yellow flies anyway.

Even such a fundamental characteristic as sex can be altered by the conditions under which development occurs. At the University of Illinois, Horsfall has got phenotypic female mosquitoes from genotypic male larvae by exposing them continually to a temperature of 29° C. This transformation occurs in *Aedes stimulans*, a snow-pool mosquito common to northern latitudes. In temperatures up to 24° C, the larvae of genotypic males develop antennae, palpi, mouth parts, external genitalia, accessory glands, seminal vesicles, vasa deferentia, and testes that are normal in appearance and function. When the larvae of genotypic males are reared in a temperature of 29° C, they become like females in all respects except for slight differences in palpi. Internally, these genotypic males that have developed into phenotypic females have ovaries, oviducts, and spermathecae, and they lack testes, vasa deferentia, seminal vesicles, and bilobed accessory glands. Their ovaries have globular egg chambers indistinguishable from those of young genotypic females. Moreover, the fact that eggs have been observed in the process of development suggests that these genotypic male but phenotypic female parts may be functionally as well as morphologically transformed. Abnormally high temperatures have no effect on the development of genotypic females, and the degree of effect upon genotypic males is a function of the duration of exposure. Neither do such temperatures affect the genotypic males of species of mosquitoes that ordinarily develop in higher temperatures. Clearly, interaction between genotype and environment has been demonstrated in the case of a variety of characteristics, and even including such a fundamental one as sex.

In the case of intelligence, several of those who have used the statistical procedures based on the additive assumption have also argued, and inconsistently, that the influence of the environment may vary with the individual's genetic endowment. In this inconsistency, the argument appears to be more correct than the choice of statistical procedure, for wherever children are given an opportunity to proceed at their own speed in learning such a subject as mathematics, where each step builds upon earlier acquisitions, individual differences in achievements increase. Such has been the experience in the project of the University of Illinois Committee on School Mathematics.[4] In such an environment, those who lag soon drop out with feelings of failure. Contrariwise, when teaching proceeds by lock step, the bright may get bored, lose out from lack of motivation, and then get the feeling that they do not like and cannot do mathematics. This is a matter of the match between environmental encounters and central structures discussed in chapter 7. Inasmuch as such interaction between genotypes and environments in the production of phenotypes appears more likely to be the rule than absence of such interaction, it follows that there is an indefinite number of answers to the proportion question, and therefore, no answer.

Paradoxically, the way in which to maximize the role of heredity in the IQ would not be to standardize the environment; it would be to individualize the encounters that each child has with his environment in such a fashion as to maximize his potential for growth. The resulting variation in children's intelligence would then be completely a function of their genotypes. As already seen, it would tend to increase individual differences.

The verification of any proposition purporting to state generally the contribution of heredity or environment to the IQ demands, as Loevinger (1943) has pointed out, that it be possible to replicate the effective conditions of both heredity and environment. Replication, she notes, would mean that any two persons of a given age with heredity of, say, 0·7 standard deviations above the mean and environment of, say, 1·2 standard deviations above the mean would be alike not only in heredity but in environment and in interaction between the two. But since the indicators of heredity

4. This program is under the direction of Beberman. Even though the students in the program have been selected for both high academic ability and high academic interest, some have soon so outdistanced others that it has been necessary to divide the classes. Failure to divide groups on the basis of achievement sufficiently early traumatizes some with the feeling that they cannot do mathematics, and they give up, while the program fails to maintain the challenge of the subject-matter for others. The ablest achieve rapidly. One group of seven students has got ready for a rigorous course in calculus by the end of their junior year. Since most of these students have already done the seventh and eighth grades in one year, they are still but 15 years old. Thus, as 16-year-old high school seniors, they will be doing the level of mathematics that college students usually get to only when they are college juniors of 20.

and environment now used say so little about what elsewhere are conceived to be the effective aspects of either heredity, the constellation of genes, or environment, the child's encounters with the circumstances of his life in the course of development, it becomes impossible to replicate the effective conditions.

In sum, in spite of the recent efforts to improve the analysis-of-variance model, using it to get a general answer to the question about the proportions of variance in intelligence caused by heredity and environment is about like using a bulldozer to study the details of the topography of an area. Or, when one considers the matter of making policy decisions concerning education, child-rearing, and clinical work from such general answers, perhaps it is worse. Perhaps using the model for a general answer is more like attempting to ascertain the ideal topography of an area by going over the existing details with a bulldozer while giving no thought to what those details might become.

More appropriate questions

It appears that Thorndike's (1913) question about the proportionate shares of heredity and environment in the causation of intelligence is an unfortunate one. A more sensible strategy is to ask specific questions which are of significance either for programs of education, child-rearing, and human welfare in general, or for specific issues in the theory of human development and human nature.

To questions significant for educational planning and human welfare belongs the one about how much the intelligence of the feebleminded children can be elevated by such special programs of environmental encounters as come in nursery-school experience. Kirk (1958) has asked this question and obtained one answer in a carefully conducted study. This one answer, of course, is a function of the particular nursery-school experiences supplied. Some eighty-one retarded children, aged between three and six and with IQs between 45 and 80, were identified and studied over a period of years. A group of twenty-eight attended a special nursery-school in the community and were followed up with tests and observations from three to five years after leaving school. A second group of fifteen children, all of whom had been committed earlier to an institution for mental defectives, were enrolled in an institutional nursery-school, and these were followed up after discharge from the school either to the institutional primary school or to the community. A third group of twenty-six children, similar in age, IQ, and social status to those in the community group, remained in their community environments without attending nursery-school. A fourth group of twelve children, already committed to a second institution for mental defectives, remained in their institutional environment without attending nursery-school. Both of these latter two groups were tested at the same intervals as were those children who got the special nursery schooling, and they were also followed up after they entered primary schools at the age of six. The evidence was processed both as case studies of the various experimental children and in terms of statistical comparisons of the two groups that got nursery schooling with the two contrast-groups that got none. The overall effects of the nursery schooling on these retarded children were positive. Of the forty-three retarded children who received the nursery-school experience thirty (70 per cent) showed an acceleration in rates of intellectual growth ranging from 10 to 30 points in IQ. The overall average increase in IQ for the experimental groups was greater than that for the contrast groups ($p < 0.05$). Moreover, and this is an important item, the children retained the accelerated rates of growth established during the nursery-school experience during the follow-up period of from three to five years. Such findings indicate that society would not be wasting its time to supply nursery-school experience for retarded youngsters of the preschool age. For instance, six of the fifteen children in the institutional nursery-school gained enough to permit them to be placed in foster homes in the community with apparently good adjustments, whereas not one of the twelve contrast children could be placed. Inasmuch as the United States Public Health Service has estimated that committing a child to an institution for the retarded at an early age and keeping him there for life costs the state approximately $50,000, an institution could apparently save a state money simply by employing one nursery-school teacher for each five such children, even if only one instead of two out of five were placed after nursery-school experience of two or three years.[5] But this experiment also has some theoretical

5. The matter of weighing ability against cost can be applied more broadly. Graffam has made an interesting study in which he has compared the mean scores of large random samples of 18-year-old Navy recruits from the Northeastern, Western, Middle Western, and Southern regions of the US on the Navy's classification tests, with emphasis on tests of reading, arithmetic, reasoning, and spelling. The mean performance for each region appears to be a function of educational opportunity as indicated by the amount of money spent per child for education.

significance. It adds, for instance, another item of evidence against the notion that rates of growth are irrevocably fixed by inheritance or by the conditions of the organism at the time of testing. On the other hand, 30 per cent of the children failed to gain from the nursery-school experience. Would other approaches in nursery-school affect them? How are they limited?

Especially important for both educational practice and theory of human development and nature are questions, as Anastasi has pointed out, about *how* both the genotype and the environment operate to produce such phenotypical characteristics as intelligence. At the present stage of behavior science in this area, strategy still concerns what kinds of factors make a difference. Thus, on the environmental side, it is important that Pasamanick, Knobloch and Lilienfeld have found that various deficiencies of maternal diet associated with socioeconomic level can produce complications of both pregnancy and parturition which result in intellectual retardation and behavioral disorders in offspring. It is important that Harrell, Woodyard and Gates (1955) have found evidence that supplements for maternal nutrition in women whose diets were known to be deficient resulted in significantly higher IQs in their offspring at ages three and four than were found in the offspring of control mothers not given the supplement. It is important that Milner (1951) has found reading readiness in the first grade to be a function of opportunities for verbalization at home. On the genetic side, it is important that Jervis (1939) has traced some of the mechanisms whereby the gene that controls the enzyme which disposes of phenylpyruvic acid in cerebral metabolism causes feeblemindedness. It is important to look for the kinds of genetic factors that indirectly, as Dobzhansky puts it, set the 'norm' or, in the terminology of psychological statistics, the 'range of variation' within which environmental circumstances determine the eventual outcome. Hebb's A/S ratio may be one of these factors. Another may reside in biochemical conditions which limit the readiness with which cerebral firing-systems can be established and modified.

Much of the evidence reviewed in this work is concerned with showing that experience, and especially early experience, is of importance. In spite of all the information psychologists have gathered about learning, much of the conceptualizing is unfruitful, and so much remains to be learned about how encounters with the environment influence the rate of development that one can say only that beginnings of essential knowledge are available.

In asking how experience influences development, moreover, knowledge of *how much* comes inevitably, because amounts of change in such variables as tested intelligence or the age at which landmarks of intellectual development appear become the criteria by which answers to the question of *how* are to be recognized. For instance, Dennis finding that the conditions of development prevailing in a Teheran orphanage increase the age at which nearly all children learn to walk from a little less than two years to more than four years, a reduction in DQ of over 50 points, does not by itself say *how* the orphanage experience works, but a hint comes from the fact that Dennis found no delay in the age at which the walkingschema appeared in Hopi children reared for the first year on cradle-boards, even though the boards greatly hampered the use of their legs. It should be noted, in connection with the question *how*, that these Hopi children got a rich variety of visual and auditory experience while being carried about on the backs of their mothers. One may hypothesize, for the purpose of future testing, that it is relatively unimportant that the firing-systems established in those regions of the brain not immediately involved with either receptor inputs or motor outputs be based on use of legs. Hebb may be essentially correct in his emphasis on perceptual experience in primary learning. On the other hand, he may be missing the fact that both looking and listening involve motor outputs as well as receptor inputs, i.e. the fact that they are, as Piaget calls them, sensorimotor schemata. Perhaps it is true, nevertheless, that the visual and auditory schemata are of essential importance during the early months while the use of the limbs is not. Perhaps it is only later after these early cerebral firing-systems have been established and such schemata as walking are already established that motor activities become important for future development. But this is not the place to go into detail. The point to be made here concerns the fact that it is by determining *how much* rates of growth and the ages at which various behavioral landmarks appear are displaced by various programs of encounters with the environment that one learns *how* experience operates. Such questions, emerging from the view of development as continuous organism–environment interaction, are markedly different from the traditional proportion question, and they promise to be much more fruitful. The answers should bring the race to a new level of adaptability.

Summary and conclusion

The meaning of the old concepts and facts that have been interpreted to support the assumptions of fixed intelligence and predetermined development change in the light of the new conceptions of intelligence and the new evidence with respect to its development.

With respect to the assumption of fixed intelligence, it has been seen that the semantics of *dimension* and *scale* in the assessment of intelligence tend to lead to an over-generalization of the conceptual habit of seeing dimensions and scaled characteristics as fixed attributes of static objects so that dimensionalized intelligence and scaled traits tend also to be seen as fixed characteristics of persons and organisms. Because persons and organisms are open systems in which change will occur as a function of unspecifiable future conditions, such transfer is unwarranted and it probably constitutes one of the spurious semantic supports for the assumption of fixed intelligence. The alternative semantics of *sampling behavior for evidences of such organizational structure as schemata, operations, and concepts* have been seen to fit the actual procedures even of traditional intelligence-testing better than do the semantics of *dimension* and *scale*. Moreover, it has been argued that the semantics of sampling for evidences of such organizational structures also fit the facts of the predictive and the criterion validity of intelligence test-scores and also the facts of the inconstancy of the IQ early in life, when epigenesis is rapid, and the relative constancy of the IQ after epigenesis slows down and after schooling tends to introduce a relatively standard program of encounters with the environment.

With respect to the assumption of predetermined development, the finding that development of the swimming schema is independent of practice in swimming in the tadpoles of salamanders and frogs need not apply to the development of the central processes that mediate intelligent behavior in higher organisms. This lack of application results both from the fact that the swimming schema is one which requires little in the way of autonomous central processes and from the fact that the A/S ratio for the brains of salamanders and frogs is about minimal. Against the conclusion from Coghill's work that behavior unfolds automatically with anatomic maturation are not only these theoretical considerations but also the observations of Kuo on the development of behavior in the embryos of chickens. Kuo's work shows quite clearly that organism–environment interaction in the control of development extends back into the early embryonic phase of development. Against the early evidence that infantile deprivations and enrichments of experience have only very evanescent effects is the fact that when the duration of such experiences has been increased, the effects show considerable permanence. Also against the conclusion from the evanescent effects of infantile practice in the early studies is the consideration that the practice and its effects concerned the same performance. The investigators missed what is now a basic consideration in 'primary learning', namely, that the everyday experiences of their non-practised subjects may have had as much influence on the development of the central processes mediating the skills measured as did practice on those skills.

The question concerning the variance in IQ attributable to heredity and environment has been seen to have no general answer. First, there is no general answer because each answer obtained by way of analysis of the variance in the IQ for any given sample of individuals involves only an existing range of hereditary and environmental conditions. No such sample can be considered representative of all conditions so long as anyone is capable of inventing a new program of environmental encounters for children during their development. Second, there is no general answer because genotype and environment interact. Third, the answers available from the analysis-of-variance model are meaningless because this model fails to fit what is known about the interactive operation of heredity and environment in the course of development. Since no general answer can be got, and since the model upon which the commonly quoted answers are based is inappropriate, educational and child-rearing policies decided on the basis of the obtained answers are almost certain to be wrong. Differential fertility across the social-class structure has been re-interpreted to appear less dire in its consequences, at least for intelligence, than has been contended. In fact, the negative correlation between family size and intelligence, which has commonly been interpreted to be the most direct evidence of 'the galloping plunge toward intellectual bankruptcy', is probably more reasonably interpreted to be an environmental consequence based on the fact that infants in large and closely spaced families cannot get the same variety of stimulation that comes from individualized attention from adults as can infants in a small, widely spaced family unless there is the wealth with which to pay for nursemaids.

In view of the technological developments in Western culture during the past half-century, which demand that a higher and higher proportion of the population have a high level of ability to manipulate symbols in the solution of problems, probably the most unfortunate consequences of the assumptions of fixed intelligence and genetically predetermined development lie, first, in the encouragement they have given to the policy of leaving infants essentially alone during their early months so that they can grow undisturbed by excessive stimulation, and second, in the discouragement they have given to the investigation of the effects of various programs of child environment interaction during the full course of development from birth to maturity.

It is fairly clear from the evidence surveyed in these chapters that impoverishments of experience during the early months can slow down the development of intelligence. In terms of the traditional measurement of intelligence, this means reducing the IQ. Various bits of the evidence have strongly suggested that such slowed development is permanent, that it may result not only in a permanently reduced IQ but in a failure of the basic criterion capacities of individuals to develop to the degree that they might have developed under other, more varied programs of encounters with the environment which were appropriately matched to the intellectual structures developing within the child. But much remains to be learned about the degree of permanence in such failures to develop and about the conditions under which these failures become permanent.

But there is also a positive side to the picture. It is highly unlikely that any society has developed a system of child-rearing and education that maximizes the potential of the individuals which compose it. Probably no individual has ever lived whose full potential for happy intellectual interest and growth has been achieved. Various bits of the evidence reviewed hint that if the manner in which encounters with the environment foster the development of intellectual interest and capacity were more fully understood, it might be possible to increase the average level of intelligence within the population substantially. In view of the interaction between genotype and environment, it would be probable that individual differences would be increased, and that the biggest gains would occur in those genotypes with the highest hypothetical potential. There would be, of course, a long step between learning how to effect changes in child-rearing and getting them adopted by the culture, but learning how is the first step. The hope of increasing the average level of intelligence by proper manipulation of children's developmental encounters with their environments, a hope which becomes reasonable with the evidences surveyed here and with relinquishing the assumptions of fixed intelligence and predetermined development, provides a challenge of the first order. It has great implications for human welfare as the growth of technology in Western cultures demands a higher and higher percentage of people who can manipulate symbols and solve complex problems. In this challenge the theory of man's nature and the fate of his welfare are obviously intertwined.

Intelligence has been a topic of central concern for those seeking to understand human nature. Even though tests of intelligence and of the aptitudes derived therefrom have been of more practical help than tests of any other kind in selecting people for quality of performance in various situations, discussions of intelligence have typically been marked by polemics. These polemics have usually concerned two of the beliefs or assumptions about intelligence that have dominated thought on the topic from the turn of the twentieth century through World War II. According to these two dominant assumptions intelligence is fixed and immutable, and the development of the individual's basic repertoire of responses and capacities is predetermined by his heredity.

The implications of these two assumptions spilled over in various directions. Intelligence came to be defined as 'inherited capacity', and it was looked upon as a basic dimension of an individual person. The hope of improving man's lot was shifted from the euthenic strategy of improving his upbringing and education to the eugenic strategy of finding some way to select only the more intelligent for the propagation of the race. Differential fertility came to be viewed with alarm. Investigative effort concerning child nature and child development was directed toward the normative mode of measuring and individual characteristics and relating the measures to age. Individual characteristics were quantified and discussed in the language of *dimensions* and *scales* without ascertaining their developmental and neuro-psychological characteristics. Investigations of the effects of various kinds of experience at various ages on the development of intellectual capacity were discouraged. Practical educational efforts to cultivate intellectual capacity, particularly in the very young, were discouraged. With behavioral development conceived to be a process in which anatomic maturation automatically brought with it the response repertoire, experts warned parents not to overstimulate their infants but rather to leave them alone to grow. Finally, the assumptions of fixed intelligence and predetermined development may well have had something to do with what has probably been an over-emphasis on personnel selection and an under-emphasis on problems of both training and arranging the social climate of institutions to foster personal interest and growth.

Fixed intelligence

The assumption of fixed intelligence has historical roots in Darwin's theory that evolution occurs by way of the survival of those inherited chance variations which show their fitness by growing up and propagating. It was his cousin, Francis Galton, who launched the study of individual differences, developed some of the first anthropometric tests, and founded the eugenics movement. Although Binet, who with Simon developed the method of intelligence testing that survived, conceived of intelligence as a fundamental and complex faculty, he did not regard it as immutable. But it was Cattell, a student of Galton, who introduced the interest in measuring individual differences to America. Moreover, it was the students of G. Stanley Hall, the evolutionist who saw in the notion that 'ontogeny recapitulates phylogeny' an explanation of both individual differences and individual development, who translated Binet's tests into English and cultivated their use in America. In both instances, the testing movement came to America via people who believed in fixed intelligence, and at least partially for this reason the belief has tended to dominate the testing movement.

Evidence consonant with the notion of fixed intelligence came with the finding, artifactual though it was, that the mean IQ obtained from groups of differing ages is constant. Moreover, the scores for individual children showed considerable constancy for the years of later childhood and adolescence; and scores from various tests showed considerable correlation both with each other and with measures of such criterion performances as those in school and those on various types of jobs. Finally, direct evidence of hereditary influence came from the fact that the correlations among the test-scores of people closely related are higher than are those among the test-scores of people not closely related.

Evidence dissonant with the assumption of fixed intelligence came from the fact that the correlation between the IQs of identical twins reared apart is lower than that for the IQs of identical twins reared together. More of such evidence came from the fact that the IQs of infants, obtained at successive ages, show considerable variation, and also from the fact that the IQs of infants show little correlation with their IQs as adults. But the import of such facts was largely explained away by assuming that the infant tests lacked validity, without, however, distinguishing between what has here been termed criterion validity and predictive validity. Still more such evidence came from the fact that orphanage-reared children score lower on tests than do children reared in foster homes, but this fact was explained away by assuming that the children who got into orphanages are so selected as to be innately inferior to the children who got placed in foster homes. Finally, the finding of improvement in IQ with nursery-school experience was explained away in terms of defects in the designs of the investigations in which they appeared, and also in terms of validity for the changes in tested intelligence. Some of the urgency of the effort to explain away these bits of dissonant evidence may well have derived not only from the historical sources but from generalizing the conceptual set of seeing the dimensions of objects as immutable to seeing the characteristics of organisms and persons as also immutable.

Predetermined development

Historically, the belief in predetermined development replaced the belief in preformationism when, in the latter half of the eighteenth century, C. F. Wolff marshaled effectively both the evidence and the arguments for an epigenesis of body structures in the embryological development of the chicken egg. This belief got further support from Darwin's theory of natural selection and from that notion that 'ontogeny recapitulates phylogeny'. G. Stanley Hall communicated both of these beliefs to his students and to the child-study associations emerging in America. They tended, therefore, to become accepted as 'common sense' beliefs. Indirect conceptual support came historically from a complex development in comparative psychology. Darwin and Romanes attempted to show that the faculties of mind, such as emotion, for instance, and intelligence, were continuous between animals and man. The loose analogical reasoning about mental faculties in these studies led Lloyd Morgan to extirpate them with Ockham's razor of parsimony and to substitute the concept of 'trial and error'. Loeb's utilization and development of the concept of forced movements or tropisms as the fundamental units of behavior set the stage for the emphasis on peripheral factors in the place of central factors in behavior. Thorndike's law of effect made response survival, like variation or mutation survival, a matter of the fitness of the response, and the stage was set for what has been called the 'empty organism'. From this standpoint, development consisted of two essentially distinct processes, maturation and learning. The basic response units were conceived to come automatically with the maturation of the anatomical structures upon which they were presumed to depend. These response units were then conceived to be hooked up into various combinations by means of stimulus–response bonds. Such a conceptual schema got a good deal of support from the conception of the brain as a kind of static switchboard. Although this conceptual schema was probably somewhat dissonant with the notion of intelligence as a dimension, little was made of this because the investigators concerned with this picture of behavioral development composed a group which had little communication with the group concerned with measuring individual differences and especially individual differences in intelligence. Moreover, the general notion that behavioral development is an automatic aspect of anatomic maturation could also lend indirect support to the assumption of fixed intelligence. Although the Gestalt psychologists composed yet another group, and one opposed to the notion of elementary units of behavior being hooked up into various more complex systems, the physical *Gestalten* of the brain were also conceived to come automatically with anatomic maturation. Thus, their emphasis on 'insight' in problem solving as restructuring of these physical *Gestalten* offered no corrective for the notion of predetermined development.

Evidence apparently consonant with the notion of predetermined development came from several sources. Coghill found the head-to-tail and center-outward orders of anatomical maturation to hold for the development of the swimming reaction in the tadpoles of salamanders (*Amblystoma*). Carmichael found that the tadpoles of frogs and salamanders that had developed without any opportunity for behavior while anesthetized with chloretone wam as well as others that had developed normally in unadulterated water, and he took this to be a demonstration of the existence of 'unlearned behavior'. When Shirley found not only the head-tailward order of behavioral development in human children but also a marked degree of consistency in the order in which various responses appear in children, her findings were conceived to indicate that principles induced from observing the behavioral development of the lowly salamander generalize to man, and she herself argued that the consistency in order favored the notion of predetermined maturation. The early experiments in which various kinds of experience were either subtracted or added seemed to have little permanent effect on behavior. Chicks reared in darkness for a few days actually learned to peck accurately with a greater rate of improvement than did chicks that had every opportunity to practise pecking. Children who were given special practice in such skills as tower-building, stair-climbing, cutting with scissors, etc., showed improvement, but children who were not given such special practice appeared to achieve the same degree of mastery of these skills with much less practice at a later age. Dennis found that the Hopi Indian children who were reared on cradle-boards, which prevented their using their legs, learned to walk at the same average age as Hopi children who were reared with full use of their legs.

Bits of evidence clearly dissonant with the conception that development is entirely predetermined also appeared. Altering developmental experience was found to interfere with the development of instinctive patterns. For instance, Birch found that the maternal behavior of female rats reared with collars to prevent them licking their own genitalia was to eat their young at parturition instead of retrieving them and licking them. Moreover, Riess found that rats reared in cages devoid of nesting materials failed to build nests at parturition even though proper materials were available. Apropos the Gestalt principles of perception and thinking, it was observed that when people deprived of visual experiences from birth by congenital cataracts were operated on to restore their vision, they might immediately distinguish between figure and ground and be able to say whether two impressions were the same or different, but they could not recognize objects without months of visual experience. Moreover, various investigators found that insightful responses tended to appear only in those monkeys and chimpanzees who had been observed to play with the tools to be used insightfully.

A new emphasis on central processes

Very shortly after Morgan had extirpated the mental faculties with Ockham's razor of parsimony and Loeb, Thorndike and Watson had attempted to explain all complex behavior in terms of stimulus–response chaining, Lashley destroyed the explanatory value of such chaining for complex behavior by pointing out that time would not permit such a sequence of central–peripheral synaptic connections in the case, for example, of a pianist playing a rapid cadenza on the piano. Then stimulus–response method, as distinguished from stimulus–response theory, began producing evidence that motivated re-furnishing the empty organism with conceptualized processes intervening between stimulus and response. There resulted the symbolic processes of Hunter, the intervening variables of Tolman, the 'pure stimulus acts' of Hull, the response-produced drives and cues of Dollard and Miller, and the mediational responses of Osgood. In the case of these, however, an attempt was made to tie the intervening variable to both its roots in past experience and to its manifestations in overt behavior.

Recently, however, emphasis on central processes has been greatly increased by developments in several areas with important implications for the theory of intelligence. In neuropsychology, Hebb, prompted by noting that behavior is to a considerable degree independent of receptor inputs and failing to find intellectual deficits on standard tests of intelligence following removal of upwards of 20 per cent of the mass of the cerebrum in adults while noting that cerebral lesions in infancy produce feeble-mindedness, led off with his attempts to conceptualize the semi-autonomous central processes that intervene between receptor inputs and motor outputs. His notions of cell-assemblies and phase-sequences, established within the associative regions of the cerebral cortex by primary learning, which he conceived to be largely perceptual in nature, set a new trend. His concept of the A/S ratio, i.e. ratio of association areas to areas concerned directly with either receptor inputs or motor outputs, appears to have considerable explanatory power.

Intelligence as central processes and as strategies for the processing of information

Hebb's conceptions led to a substantial revision in the conception of intelligence. His notion of the important role of autonomous central processes in behavior suggested that intelligence would probably be a function of the variegation and mobility of the cell-assemblies established through primary learning within those regions of the brain not immediately concerned with receptor inputs or motor outputs. This conception suggested further that adult intelligence should vary with opportunities for perceptual and perhaps even motor experience in which a variety of inputs with appropriate degrees of redundancy are available. It also stimulated a number of studies of the effects of infantile experience on later learning and problem-solving. These studies have shown that rats reared with ample opportunities for a variety of perceptual experience do learn mazes more readily than rats reared with minimal opportunities for a variety of such experience. Pet-reared rats with a background of highly varied experience have been found to perform with more facility on the Hebb–Williams test of intelligence than do cage-reared rats with a background of little variation in experience. Similarly, Thompson and Heron have shown that in a wide variety of situations pet-reared dogs behave in a fashion much more intelligent than their littermates who were cage-reared for the first eight months of their lives. The fact that the effects of such differences in early experience on adult intelligence appear to be considerably greater in dogs than in rats is consonant with the expectation that the importance of infantile experience for later intelligence is a function of the size of the A/S ratio in the species concerned. In yet another example of the effects of infantile experience, this time on perception, Riesen has found that chimpanzees kept in darkness for the first months of their lives lack object-recognition and the various responses which depend upon such recognition. Moreover, even the anatomic development of the visual apparatus appears to be hampered by lack of visual stimulation.

Combined with Hebb's theorizing and the work stimulated by it in this new emphasis on central processes and their dependence upon experience are other developments. The people who program electronic computers for the solving of problems have begun to systematize the conception of the requirements of problem-solving in terms of strategies for the processing of information. These strategies resemble the logical operations of the logical calculus as described by Boole. The strategies are arranged hierarchically for access and application. From studies of animal problem-solving, Harlow has shown that by repeatedly learning the solution to any given type of problem, monkeys develop learning sets which give them the capacity to solve that type of problem almost immediately with the information derived from perception of the situation. These 'learning sets' look fairly analogous to the strategies for the processing of information that programmers wire into their electronic computers. The thought that the computer and the brain have similarities of operation has prompted a re-examination of the theory of brain function. Although von Neumann has warned that the mathematics of the brain in operation fail to correspond to mathematics as now conceived, such neuropsychologists as Pribram have pointed to approximate counterparts of the hierarchies of strategies for processing information and executing action within the brain. Pribram conceives these to be stored in those regions of the brain that receive no receptor inputs and have no direct access to musculature. These include the anterior and posterior nuclei of the thalamus with their tract-connections, respectively, with the frontal lobe and with the parietal and temporal lobes. These are termed intrinsic mechanisms and are conceived to have a function similar to Hebb's association areas. Hierarchical systems of memories for the redundant aspects of past perceptions are conceived to be stored in the posterior intrinsic mechanism, while the anterior mechanism is conceived to contain the hierarchical arrangement of intentions which are based on an organization of the homeostatic mechanisms localized in the reticular core around the midline ventricles. Damage to the tracts under the cortex of the parietal and temporal lobes may not interfere with such reflexive acts as catching a fly on the wing, but it does interfere with perceptual recognition. Damage to the tracts under the frontal lobe may not interfere with perceptual recognition, but it does interfere with the execution of sequential systems of action. The unit of response is conceived to be one of 'test-operate-test-exist' (TOTE). Intelligence, from the standpoint of such a conceptual scheme, would appear to be a matter of the number of strategies for processing information that have been differentiated and have achieved the mobility which permits them to be available in a variety of situations.

Piaget's observations of the development of intelligence

The conception of intelligence deriving from Piaget's observations of the development of adaptive ability in children resembles so much that which derives from considering the computer and the brain and from the work of Hebb and Harlow that his observations may be considered to lend further empirical support to this new conception of intelligence. A basis for the hierarchical arrangement of the central processes that mediate intelligence appears in Piaget's descriptions of behavioral development wherein the sensorimotor organizations of each stage became incorporated, in the course of the child's assimilations of both food and the modifications in his sensorimotor schemata deriving from his psychological interactions with the environment, into the more complex sensorimotor organizations of the next stage. Things heard become things to look at; things seen become things to grasp; things grasped become things to suck, etc. In the course of such coordinations, inputs from the distance receptors, and especially the eyes, acquire control over motor activities. Intentions emerge, means are distinguished from ends, interest in activities and in objects develops, and behavior becomes more and more variable and adaptive. All this happens presumably as central processes become both coordinated and re-differentiated. The sensorimotor period ends when the child is about eighteen months old and the sensorimotor schemata and imitations begin to become internalized as images. During this same sensorimotor period of eighteen months, objects acquire permanence, while causality, space, and time become objective.

During the preconceptual phase from about eighteen months to four years of a second major period (from eighteen months to twelve years) images accumulate to form intuitions. Intuitions are grouped at about seven years to form the first of the mobile equilibrii. These are the concrete operations with the logical properties of reversibility, associativity, transitivity, identity, and tautology. They arrive as the child begins to think generally with concrete objects and as he acquires the capacity to conserve quantity and number and the capacity to order objects serially by such properties as length. These concrete operations are further elaborated at about age nine or ten when the child acquires the capacity to conserve weight and to order objects serially by the property of weight. At age eleven or twelve, he acquires the still higher level of capacity to conserve volume and to order objects serially by the property of volume. Inhelder and Piaget have also reported that conservation of volume always includes the capacities to conserve weight and quantity, and that the conservation of weight always includes the capacity to conserve quantity and number. Such findings suggest that Piaget's landmarks of transition in the development of intelligence and thought represent a natural ordinal scale of intelligence. During these successive elaborations of the concrete operations, parallel transformations are occurring in the child's conceptions of causality, space, and time.

Finally, during a third major period beginning at about age eleven or twelve the concrete operations are re-grouped into formal operations as the young pre-adolescent acquires the proportionality schema that permits him to conserve volume. At this landmark of transition, he also acquires the capacity to deal with propositions as he has hitherto been able to deal only with concrete objects. It is thus that he achieves the level of formal reasoning. At this transition, instead of observation directing thought as it has in the period of concrete operations, the adolescent's thought directs his observing. He thereby acquires the essential intellectual capacity for the scientific method. Moreover, inasmuch as the observed conditions of society can now be seen in comparison with imagined ideal conditions of society, the adolescent also acquires the capacity required for social reform. These formal operations of the adolescent Piaget describes in terms of their logico-mathematical properties which include the proportionality schema, the INRC group structure, and the 16 binary operations of the Boolean logical calculus. In fact, Inhelder and Piaget find that it is these logico-mathematical schemata operating implicitly in the thought of adolescents that direct their observing in science-like problem-solving.

Piaget's theory: implications and validity

Five main themes dominate Piaget's theoretical formulations. The first concerns the continual and progressive change, or epigenesis, in the structures of behavior and thought in the developing child. This theme serves as a corrective for the preformationism that still lurks in both epistemology and psychology. The second theme concerns the fixed nature of the order in which the successive structures make their appearance. If this order is corroborated by other investigators, in view of the hierarchical organization indicated, it may indeed supply the basis for a natural ordinal scale of intelligence. Furthermore, the existence of such a natural ordinal scale would suggest the investigative method of measuring the effects of various kinds of experience on the rate of development in terms of the time elapsing between the successive landmarks of transition.

Piaget's third theme concerns the invariant functions of accommodation (adaptive change to outer circumstances) and of assimilation (incorporation of the external into the inner organization with transfer or generalization to new circumstances) that operate in the child's continuous interaction with the environment. The nature of accommodation suggests that the rate of development is to a considerable degree a function of the child's encounters with the environment. Piaget formulates a principle to account for such a relationship between intelligence and experience in essentially motivational terms: the more an infant has seen and heard, the more he later wants to see and hear. This principle gets empirical support from the studies of the dependence of intelligence upon early experience in animals, which studies were generated by Hebb's theorizing. The principle also gets support from the retarding effects of the relatively unchanging stimulation in various orphanages. As recently reported by Dennis, in some instances this retardation, even of such functions as sitting alone and walking alone, can be great. While such evidence clearly supports the principle that the rate of development depends upon the nature of the child's encounters with the environment, it does not say how irreversible such retardation may be, and neither does it indicate the degree to which the adult level of intelligence is ultimately reduced. On the other hand, the fact that Thompson and Heron have found that dogs pet-reared for the first eight months of their lives do show a substantially higher level of intelligence at eighteen months of age than do dogs cage-reared for their first eight months suggests considerable permanence for these effects of early experience.

Within the domain of Piaget's third theme, the nature of accommodation implies great importance for the match between the kind of external circumstances encountered and the kind of internal organization already present in determining the nature and degree of effect of any given encounter. This match is still poorly understood, but it is the appropriateness of the match between the circumstances that the child encounters as he develops and the nature of his own intellectual organizations at the time of the encounters that appears to determine in very large part his rate of intellectual development. Put another way, the richness of an environment for intellectual growth is a function of the appropriateness of this match between inner organizations and external circumstances in a child's succession of encounters with his environment. While it is highly unlikely that even the 'best' of contemporary child-rearing and education comes near maximizing the potential of children, any attempt to facilitate intellectual development with improvements in child-rearing and education demands a markedly increased understanding of this matter of the match. Piaget's description of the stages in the development of intelligence in children, which receives empirical support from the study of behavioral development in animals by such investigators as Fuller and Scott, helps to take some of the guess-work out of such matching.

Within this third theme of Piaget's, one also finds a number of parallels with the theorizing of Hebb which are relevant to this problem of the match. Both Piaget and Hebb see behavior and intelligence determined by central processes. Both see these central processes changing with experience. Both see early experience as of probably crucial importance in determining both the rate and the final level of ability. Some of the parallels concern motivation, but Piaget makes little of his observations and pronouncements about motivation while Hebb has motivation near the center of his concern. Both see a basis for pleasure in discrepancies between the existing central processes that mediate anticipations and the receptor inputs from environmental circumstances. Pleasure occurs if this discrepancy is of a proper degree. Both also see a basis for fear and distress in such discrepancies when they are too great to be accommodated. While this line of theorizing is still vague in its implications for experimental operations, it has the happy implication that with proper control of the match between the internal structure of a child's central processes and the circumstances that he encounters, maximizing his rate of intellectual growth should also be a source of exciting interest and pleasure.

Piaget's fourth theme concerns the relation of thought processes to action. Thought processes are conceived to originate through a process of internalizing actions, which is essentially like the short-circuiting principle offered by Hebb, Osgood, and many others. Piaget also conceives that intelligence increases as thought processes are loosened from their bases in perception and action and thereby become reversible, transitive, associative, etc. This conception, in turn, implies that intelligence develops as central neural processes become increasingly autonomous. The fact that Max has found a negative correlation between tested intelligence and amount of education, on the one hand, and, on the other, the frequency of muscular action potentials in deaf-mutes asked to solve problems mentally, tends to lend empirical support to such a conception of the relation between intelligence and the autonomy of central neural processes and action. In this theme, Piaget's theory makes a considerably greater place for action than does Hebb's, but since looking and listening are conceived by Piaget to be reflexive schemata with both sensory and motor aspects, whereas Hebb conceives of them largely as receptors, the difference may be more apparent and verbal than operational.

Piaget's fifth theme concerns the logical properties of thought processes. He sees these properties to be products of a mobile equilibrium in which all the virtual transformations compatible with the relationships of the system compensate each other. The reversibility of thought operations account for the Gestalt-like quality of thought. The laws of the mobile equilibrium account for the intersubjectivity of reasoning.

Factor-analytic studies of intelligence pose some problems for the conception of intelligence that derives from this fifth theme of Piaget's theory. The grouping of images and intuitions into concrete operations at about seven or eight and the regrouping of concrete operations into formal operations at about eleven or twelve with each having such apparently far-reaching consequences in intellectual functioning, imply a homogeneity of intelligence that appears to be dissonant with the heterogeneity of intelligence found in the factor–analytic studies of intelligence. The notion that the successive landmarks of transition in the development of intelligent behavior and thought may constitute a natural ordinal scale of intelligence also implies a homogeneity of intelligence that is dissonant with the heterogeneity found in the factor studies. This dissonance is diminished, however, by considering that heterogeneity of abilities is relatively slight in childhood, which constitutes the period when most of Piaget's observations have been made. This dissonance is further diminished by considering that a hierarchical factor structure, with Spearman's g at the apex as the English factor analysts have tended to conceive of intelligence, is precisely what would be expected from considering abilities as the accumulative effects of the transfer of training or learning in varied situations. It has been the merit of G. A. Ferguson to make these points in a pair of highly provocative theoretical papers. The dissonance between the implications of Piaget's conceptions and the results of factor-analysis studies is essentially eradicated by considering that Piaget's conception of accommodation corresponds to the change in function that occurs with training or learning and that Piaget's conception of assimilation corresponds to the notion of transfer of training.

A factor analyst might also raise the question as to why, if the concrete operations and the formal operations are intellectual structures of such importance, the factor-analytic investigations of intelligence have not uncovered them. Several reasons can be found. Perhaps most important is the fact that most factor studies have been cross-sectional in nature. They have used subjects varying little in age. In consequence, all of the subjects used in each such investigation share these basic intellectual operations, and they can therefore appear in the factor studies only as the basis for the fact that abilities are regularly positively correlated in any sample of individuals. In fact, these intellectual structures of Piaget might be seen as an explanation of Spearman's *g*. Moreover, support for such a view comes from Hofstaetter's factorization of the repeated longitudinal testings of children in the Berkeley Growth Study, for the finding of a large factor of 'intellection' on which the loadings on age increase especially rapidly between the ages of four and eight is almost exactly what one would be led to expect.

Although Piaget's work has led him to a concern with both the strategies for information processing utilized in programming computers and with the neural basis of operational thought, the fact that a major share of his observations antedate these later developments and are yet consonant with them is very interesting.

Some reinterpretations

In the light of this newer conception of intelligence, which puts its neural basis in autonomous central neural processes located largely in the intrinsic regions of the brain and which explicitly gives its roots in the child's encounters with his environment, the old evidence once considered disturbing is what would be expected. Moreover, the old evidence once conceived to support the assumptions of fixed intelligence and predetermined development can readily be reinterpreted to be consonant with the newer conception.

The semantics of *dimension* and *scale* for tests of intelligence actually fit the procedures of testing less well than would a semantics of sampling behavior for evidence of the presence of such organizational structures as schemata, operations, and conceptions. The validity of tests can be divided into at least two kinds, *predictive validity*, or the capacity of a score from a testing at one time to predict the score from a testing at a later time in the individual's life, and *criterion validity*, or the capacity of performance on tests to predict performances at the same stage of development in various types of life situation. The fact that the scores from repeated testing in infancy, when the rate of change in the intellectual structures is greatest, fluctuate radically and the fact that such scores show poor predictive validity are precisely what would be expected if intellectual capacity depends to a considerable degree upon the child's encounters with his environment, but such fluctuations are highly embarrassing to the assumptions of fixed intelligence and predetermined development. Lack of predictive validity, so long as the child's encounters with his environment are not controlled, would be expected, but lack of predictive validity need not imply that the infant tests lack criterion validity.

In view of the low A/S ratio in the brains of frogs and salamanders, and since the effects of experience appear to increase with the size of the A/S ratio, Coghill's finding that behavioral development follows the head-tailward and proximo-distal orders found for anatomical development need not imply that the behavioral development of organisms with higher A/S ratios is largely a function of anatomical maturation. In fact, the work of Kuo indicates that the embryo chick's interaction with its environment in the egg has much to do with its behavioral development and later abilities. Similarly, the fact that Carmichael found swimming movements coming without opportunity for practice in the chloretoned frog and salamander tadpoles, with their low A/S ratios, need not imply that encounters with the environment are unimportant for behavioral development in higher organisms. The apparent evanescence of the effects of either subtracting or adding experience in the development of various organisms was apparently to some degree a function of the short duration of the subtraction or the addition. When frogs were kept in chloretoned water longer than Carmichael kept them there, they failed to learn to swim properly. When chicks were kept in the dark longer than Cruze kept them there, they lost the pecking response. Although the advantage got from a few weeks of special early practice in tower-building, stair-climbing, buttoning, and scissoring quickly disappeared when the controls, who started later, got to practising these same skills, when Myrtle McGraw gave her trained twin, Johnny, nearly a year's experience at roller-skating, the untrained twin, Jimmy, was not able to catch up quickly. In fact, where Johnny had had little trouble learning to roller-skate at eleven months of age, Jimmy could not learn the skill at all at twenty-two months of age.

In view of the Hebbian distinction between primary learning and later learning, moreover, it is hardly surprising that the special practice on such activities as tower-building, stair-climbing, buttoning, scissoring, etc., produced but evanescent superiority in these skills because, presumably, the incidental activities of the control children in these experiments might have been expected to have produced as much development in the central processes mediating these activities as would the direct practice on them, and perhaps even more.

Although the fact that change in the intellectual structures is most rapid during the early months and years suggests that the effects of environmental encounters during the early period should perhaps be most potent, it remains to be determined in crucial fashion how great and how permanent such effects can be.

Probably the question concerning the relative proportion of the variance in intelligence attributable to heredity and to environment, which is the one most frequently asked, has been unfortunate. No general answer to this question is possible. This impossibility has long been recognized by geneticists, for only the phenotype can be measured, and how much any genotype can be altered by experience can be ascertained only by submitting that genotype to all possible life programs of encounters with the environment. Much more pertinent are specific questions relevant to either problems of educational and welfare practice or to the theory of human intelligence and its development. Inasmuch as Dennis has very recently found that in orphanage environments where the variety of stimulation is minimal, only 42 per cent of the children sit alone at two years of age, and only 15 per cent walk alone at four years of age, it appears to be quite clear that the rate of development is not predetermined by the genes. On the other hand, although it is unlikely that any person has ever achieved his full potential for intellectual development, it is not known how much various procedures for improving the match between circumstances and level of behavioral development to foster the accommodative modification of central structures might increase the rate and the final level of intellectual capacity over the rate and level common under existing circumstances. No general answer can be made to questions of this sort, but a variety of such investigations might be expected to lead to generalizations about the nature of environments rich or poor in their capacity to promote intellectual development.

Many investigators have been concerned about the supposed loss of intelligence associated with differential fertility. They point to the negative correlation between number of siblings and tested intelligence as perhaps the most direct evidence for this loss. Inasmuch as about the same degree of inferiority appears for twins and for doubles born close together as appears for those in large families, and inasmuch as this negative correlation disappears among the well-to-do who can afford to have help in the care of their infants during the early months, it is quite as logical to see this negative correlation as evidence of intelligence failing to develop from lack of the stimulation that comes from young infants having ample adult contact as it is to see it as evidence that those genetically inferior are supplying more than their share of the next generation.

Conclusion and the challenge

In view of the conceptual developments and the evidence coming from animals learning to learn, from neuropsychology, from the programming of electronic computers to solve problems, and from the development of intelligence in children, it would appear that intelligence should be conceived as intellectual capacities based on central processes hierarchically arranged within the intrinsic portions of the cerebrum. These central processes are approximately analogous to the strategies for information processing and action with which electronic computers are programmed. With such a conception of intelligence, the assumptions that intelligence is fixed and that its development is predetermined by the genes are no longer tenable.

In the light of these considerations, it appears that the counsel from experts on child-rearing during the third and much of the fourth decades of the twentieth century to let children be while they grow and to avoid excessive stimulation was highly unfortunate. It was suggested in the text above that perhaps the negative correlations found between intelligence test-scores for the first two years and the late adolescent level of intelligence may possibly be attributable to such counsel, inasmuch as it would be those educated people at the higher levels of tested intelligence who read and can act in terms of what they read who would have been most likely to follow this advice. The problem for the management of child development is to find out how to govern the encounters that children have with their environments to foster both an optimally rapid rate of intellectual development and a satisfying life.

Further in the light of these theoretical considerations and the evidence concerning the effects of early experience on adult problem-solving in animals, it is no longer unreasonable to consider that it might be feasible to discover ways to govern the encounters that children have with their environments, especially during the early years of their development, to achieve a substantially higher adult level of intellectual capacity. Moreover, inasmuch as the optimum rate of intellectual development would mean also self-directing interest and curiosity and genuine pleasure in intellectual activity, promoting intellectual development properly need imply nothing like the grim urgency which has been associated with 'pushing' children. Furthermore, these procedures, in so far as they tended to maximize each child's potential for intellectual development, would not decrease individual differences in intellectual capacity as assessed by tests but would increase them. The discovery of the ways to govern the encounters children have with their environments for this purpose would require a great deal of expensive and difficult investigation of the effects of various kinds of early experience on later intellectual capacity. Even after the discovery of the ways, if they can be found, the task of effecting the necessary changes within the culture in child-rearing practices and in educational procedures would be Herculean. Nevertheless, ours is a technological culture of increasing complexity. Its development continually demands an ever larger proportion of the population with intellectual capacity at the higher levels. It calls also for intellectual giants to solve the problems that become increasingly complex. The fact that it is reasonable to hope to find ways of raising the level of intellectual capacity in a majority of the population makes it a challenge to do the necessary research. It is one of the major challenges of our times. It is a challenge, moreover, where the chances are fairly good that the behavioral sciences can make a contribution of great social, as well as theoretical, significance.

References

ANDERSON, J. E. (1940), 'The prediction of terminal intelligence from infant and pre-school tests', *Yearbook Nat. Soc. Stud. Educ.*, vol. 39, no. 1 pp. 385–403.

BAYLEY, N. (1954), 'Some increasing parent–child similarities during the growth of children', *J. educ. Psychol.*, vol. 45, pp. 1–21.

BURKS, B. S. (1928), 'The relative influence of nature and nurture upon mental development', *Yearbook Nat. Soc. Stud. Educ.* vol. 27, no. 1, pp. 219–316.

CATTELL, R. B. (1958), 'Variance analysis equations and solutions for nature–nurture research', *Psychol. Rev.*, vol. 67, pp. 353–72.

CORNFORD, F. M. (1930), 'Embryology and the homeomereity of Anaxagoras', *Classical Quart.*, vol. 24, pp. 14–24.

CRONBACH, L. J. (1949), *Essentials of Psychological Testing*, Harper & Row.

DENNIS, W. (1960), 'Causes of retardation among institutional children', *J. genet. Psychol.*

DOBZHANSKY, TH. (1950), 'Hereditary, environment and evolution', *Science*, vol. 111, pp. 161–6.

GOODENOUGH, F. L., and MAURER, K. M. (1942), *The Mental Growth of Children From Two to Fourteen Years*, University of Minnesota Press.

HARRELL, R. F., WOODYARD, E. and GATES, A. I. (1955), *The Effect of Mothers' Diets on the Intelligence of the Offspring*, Bur. Publ. Teach. Coll., Columbia University Press.

JERVIS, G. A. (1939), 'A contribution to the study of the influence of heredity on mental deficiency', *Proc. Amer. Assoc. Stud. ment. Def.*, vol. 44, pp. 13–24.

KIRK, S. A. (1958), *Early Education of the Mentally Retarded*, University of Illinois Press.

LEAHY, A. M. (1935), 'Nature–nurture and intelligence', *Genet. Psychol. Monogr.*, vol. 17, pp. 235–308.

LOEVINGER, J. (1943), 'On the proportional contributions of differences in nature and nurture to differences in intelligence', *Psych. Bull.*, vol. 40, pp. 725–56.

MILNER, E. A. (1951), 'A study of the relationships between reading readiness in grade one school children and patterns of parent–child interaction', *Child Develop.*, vol. 22, pp. 95–112.

MURPHY, L. B. (1944), 'Childhood experience in relation to personality', in J. McV. Hunt (ed.), *Personality and the Behavior Disorders*, Ronald.

NEWMAN, H. H., FREEMAN, F. N., and HOLZINGER, K. J. (1937), *Twins: A Study of Heredity and Environment*, University of Chicago Press.

SHUTTLEWORTH, F. K. (1935), 'The nature – nurture problem', *J. educ. Psychol.*, vol. 26, pp. 561–78 and 655–81.

THORNDIKE, E. L. (1913), *The Original Nature of Man*, Columbia University Press.

WOODWORTH, R. S. (1941), 'Heredity and environment: a critical survey of recently published material on twins and foster children', *Soc. Sci. Res. Coun. Bull.*, no. 47, pp. 324–8.

WRIGHT, S. (1931), 'Statistical methods in biology', *J. Amer. statis. Ass. Suppl.*, vol. 26, pp. 155–63.

Acknowledgements

Permission to reproduce the Readings in this volume is acknowledged to the following sources:

1 Macmillan Co.
2 *American Journal of Psychology*
3 Stanford University Press
4 T & A Constable Limited for the University Press of Edinburgh
5 Methuen and Co. Limited
6 *British Journal of Educational Psychology*
7 *American Psychologist*
8 John Wiley & Sons Inc.
9 *British Journal of Educational Psychology*
10 *British Journal of Educational Psychology*
11 *Journal of Special Education*
12 *British Journal of Educational Psychology*
13 *Harvard Educational Review*
14 Society for Research in Child Development Inc.
15 Methuen and Co. Limited
16 *Canadian Journal of Psychology*
17 Ronald Press Co.

Author Index

Alderson, E., 28
d'Alembert, J. le R., 193
Anastasi, A., 107, 109, 289, 325,
   336, 353
Anderson, H. D., 326
Anderson, J. E., 339
Aristotle, 184, 197
Asher, E. J., 180, 326
Attlee, C. R., 149
Attwell, A. A., 279

Bacon, M. K., 294
Bagley, W. C., 96, 97
Bain, J., 188
Balinsky, B., 108
Ballard, P. B., 191
Barron, F., 262
Barry, C., 28
Barry, H., 294
Bayley, N., 337, 339, 340
Beadle, G. W., 347
Beberman, M., 350n.
Benda, J., 94, 95
Bendig, A. W., 256, 279
Berger, P., 259, 260, 261
Bernoulli, J., 126
Bernstein, B., 300
Bickersteth, M., 125
Biesheuvel, S., 304
Binet, A., 10, 12, 120, 123, 141, 169,
   185, 187, 244, 245, 359
Birch, H. G., 362
Bloom, B. S., 240
Boole, G., 364
Boswell, J., 187
Bouillaud, J. B., 125
Bramwell, B. J., 126
Broca, P., 125
Brown, W., 87, 190
Brugmans, H. J. T. W., 80
Bryant, S., 115
Bulley, M., 133
Bunyan, J., 193
Burks, B. S., 341, 342
Burt, C., 10, 11, 15, 16, 22, 99, 103,
   113, 117, 118, 120, 124, 125, 131,
   132, 133, 163, 189, 190, 195, 230,
   231, 245, 279, 336
Butler, G., 28

Cancardas, 133
Carey, N., 124
Carlyle, T., 187, 193
Carmichael, L., 361, 372
Carroll, J. B., 279
Cattell, J. McK., 244
Cattell, R. B., 111, 133, 137, 138,
   209, 221, 224, 226, 227, 253, 262,
   295, 299, 322, 336, 341, 343, 344,
   359
Child, D., 256
Child, I., 294
Christal, R. E., 148
Churchill, W. S., 149
Cicero, Marcus Tullius, 184
Claparède, E., 185
Clark, M. P., 107
Coghill, G. E., 355, 361, 372
Coleman, J. S., 277
Collar, D. J., 126
Cook, T. W., 319
Corkhill, T. J., 130
Cornford, F. M., 334
Cox, D., 193
Crane, F., 133
Cromwell, T., 193
Cronbach, L. J., 335
Cruze, W. W., 372
Cureton, E. E., 346

Darwin, C., 185, 186, 359, 360
Davey, C. M., 77, 78
Davies, J. A., 124
Davis, A., 322
Davis, F. B., 279
Defoe, D., 193
Dennis, W., 345, 346, 354, 362, 373
Descartes, R., 314
Deutsch, M., 275
De Vries, H. A., 198
Dewar, H., 133
Dingman, H. F., 279
Dobzhansky, T., 334, 349, 353
Dodgson, C., 130
Doll, E. A., 171
Dollard, J., 363
Doob, L. W., 292, 293
Doppelt, J. E., 107
Douglas, J. W. B., 301
Dreger, R. M., 235, 276

Duncanson, J. P., 251
Dunlap, J. W., 346
Dunn, L. C., 349

Eckland, B. K., 231
Eells, K., 322
Eells, W. C., 326
El Koussy, A. A. H., 129
Ellis, H., 193
Emmett, W. G., 108
Erlenmeyer-Kimling, L., 161
Eysenck, H. J., 111, 117, 119, 133,
    137, 138, 245, 248, 251, 254, 256,
    258, 259, 260, 261, 262, 263

Faraday, M., 193
Farley, F. H., 255, 258
Ferguson, G. A., 370
Fisher, R., 199, 341, 346
Flugel, J. C., 121, 136
Foley, J. P., 325
Frank, H., 250
Franklin, B., 193
Fraser, E., 301
Fredricks, R. C., 256
Freeman, F. N., 343, 344, 345
Fry, R., 133
Fuller, J. L., 348, 369
Furneaux, W. D., 247, 248, 249,
    250, 253, 256

Galton, F., 10, 12, 17, 21, 22, 115,
    123, 124, 126, 137, 161, 186, 187,
    188, 192, 340, 359
Garnett, J. C. M., 66, 67, 80
Garrett, H. E., 107, 129, 279
Gates, A. I., 353
Gauss, J. K. F., 126, 193
Gibson, J. B., 231
Gomulicki, R. B., 314
Goodenough, E. L., 338
Gordon, H., 15, 180, 325
Gordon, I. E., 256, 258
Goulburn, H., 28
Graffam, D. T., 352
Gray, J. L., 90
Guilford, J. P., 100, 105, 144, 156,
    184, 207, 235, 245, 246, 248, 298,
    336

Haldane, J. B. S., 344
Hall, G. S., 359, 360
Halstead, H., 251
Hargreaves, H. L., 123
Harlow, H. F., 364, 365
Harrell, R. F., 353
Head, A., 126

Hebb, D. O., 162, 169, 176, 210,
    298, 314, 316, 319, 347, 354, 363,
    364, 365, 368, 369
Henning, H., 119
Heron, W., 364, 368
Hewlett, E. T., 126
Heymans, G., 80
Hick, W., 250
Higgins, C., 234
Hirsch, N. D. M., 326
Hofstaetter, P. R., 371
Hogben, L., 344, 348
Holzinger, K. J., 72, 73, 129, 245,
    336, 343, 344
Honzik, M. P., 231
Horn, J. L., 210, 215, 218, 221, 224
Horsfall, W. R., 349
Hotelling, H., 103
Howard, M., 199
Hsu, E. H., 119
Hudson, L., 195, 262
Hull, C. L., 363
Hunter, W. S., 363
Hyman, R., 250
Hymovitch, B., 176

Jackson, H., 185
Jarvik, L. F., 161
Jensen, A. R., 231, 232, 234, 252,
    254, 258, 268, 271, 275
Jervis, G. A., 353
Johannsen, W., 348
Johnson, Dr Samuel, 186, 187
Jones, W., 80
Jung, C. G., 70, 120

Kant, I., 193
Kaplan, A., 254, 255
Karlin, J. E., 118
Katz, I., 275
Kaye, Bishop, 28
Kelley, T. L., 22, 77, 88, 103, 279,
    336
Kennedy, W. A., 234, 277
Kepler, J., 193
Key, C. B., 326
Kirk, S. A., 351
Kleinsmith, L. J., 254, 255
Kluckhohn, F. R., 293
Knobloch, H., 353
Knox, J., 193
Kuo, Z. Y., 355, 372
Kuttner, R. E., 275

Lacey, J. I., 105
Lake, C. H., 115
Lambert, N. M., 231, 235

Lankes, W., 79, 80
Lansdell, H., 176
Laplace, P., 193
Lashley, K. S., 186, 362
Lawley, D. N., 103
Lawrence, E. M., 231
Leahy, A. M., 231, 341, 342
Lesser, G. S., 279
Lienert, A. A., 263
Lilienfeld, A. M., 353
Lincoln, A., 193
Lindzey, G., 276
Loeb, J., 360, 362
Loevinger, J., 341, 346, 350
Ludlow, H. G., 231, 235
Luther, M., 193
Lyndhurst, Lord Chancellor, 28
Lynn, R., 256, 258

Macaulay, A., 28
McBride, K. E., 169
McDougall, W., 103, 117, 122, 135, 136, 137
McFarlane Smith, M., 81
McGeoch, J. A., 319
McGurk, M. C., 235
McGraw, M. B., 345, 372
McLaughlin, H. L., 254
McNemar, Q., 107, 108, 246
Maddox, H., 195
Marlowe, C., 193
Maurer, K. M., 338
Maurras, C., 95
Max, L. W., 369
Melcher, R. T., 171
Mendel, G., 185, 197, 348
Merkel, J., 250
Meumann, I., 122, 136
Meyer, W., 279
Meyers, C. E., 279
Mill, J. S., 183, 193
Miller, K. S., 235, 276
Miller, N. E., 363
Milner, E. A., 353
Moebius, 59
Moore, R. C., 120, 123, 124, 130, 131, 136
Morgan, C. L., 185, 349, 360, 362
Moshinsky, P., 90
Muller, G. E., 70
Murphy, L. B., 338

Neff, W. S., 179, 180
Newman, H. H., 195, 343, 344, 345
Newton, I., 192, 193

Opie, J., 193
Orpet, R. E., 279
Osgood, C. E., 363, 369
Otto, W., 256

Pasamanick, B., 353
Passow, A. H., 280
Pastore, N., 16
Payne, R. W., 258
Pearson, K., 21, 117, 182, 189, 198
Pelling, V. G., 133
Pettigrew, T., 278
Phelps, W. M., 171
Piaget, J., 185, 298, 311, 336, 354, 365, 366, 367, 368, 369, 370
Plato, 92, 95, 97, 183
Porson, R., 28
Porteous, S. D., 326
Pribram, K. H., 365

Quételet, M., 31, 32

Rankin, G. F., 256
Rapier, J. L., 232
Reichard, S., 107
Reymert, M. L., 138
Riesen, A. H., 364
Riesman, Z., 280, 293
Riess, B. F., 362
Roe, A., 169
Rogers, M. S., 263
Rohwer, W. D., 232
Romanes, G. J., 360
Roth, E., 251, 252
Russell, B., 131

Sadler, M., 88
Savage, R. D., 256
Scheinfeld, A., 195
Schmidtke, H., 250
Schonfield, D., 253
Schwesinger, G. C., 344
Scott, J. P., 348, 369
Sherman, M., 326
Sherrington, C. S., 116, 185
Shirley, M. M., 361
Sholl, D. A., 185, 186
Shuey, A. M., 276
Shuke, G. H., 263
Shuttleworth, F. K., 340
Simon, T., 11, 244, 359
Simrall, D., 321
Sinnot, E. W., 349
Sivers, C., 234
Slocombe, C. S., 77
Smith, I. M., 129, 134

Smith, M., 122
Spearman, C., 10, 14, 22, 67, 69, 70, 71–81, 87, 88, 104, 105, 112, 115, 117, 119, 121, 123, 135, 138, 182, 188, 189, 190, 191, 206, 209, 244, 251, 262, 313, 328, 336, 370
Spence, K. W., 255
Spencer, H., 184, 185, 186, 188
Sperrazzo, G., 235
Spuhler, J. N., 276
Stake, R. E., 251
Stephenson, W., 133, 190
Stewart, W., 69
Stoddard, G. D., 174, 180
Sully, J., 184, 189, 190
Swineford, F., 107, 279
Symmes, E. F., 69

Taylor, C. W., 262
Terman, L. M., 13, 81, 94, 111, 141, 193
Thompson, W. R., 364, 368
Thomson, G. H., 10, 22, 87, 103, 107, 109, 110, 112, 188, 190, 245, 313, 336
Thorndike, E. L., 116, 117, 121, 248, 351, 361, 362
Thurstone, L. L., 16, 88, 103, 105, 112, 116, 117, 129, 138, 141, 144, 154, 190, 209, 215, 218, 244, 245, 279, 298, 314, 316, 328, 336
Tieck, J. L., 193
Tilton, J. W., 321
Tolman, E. C., 363
Tryon, R. C., 347
Turnbull, W. W., 323
Tyler, L. A., 231

Van De Riet, V., 234, 277
Vernon, M. D., 120

Vernon, P. E., 10, 16, 99, 100, 117, 134, 137, 205, 245, 279, 336
Von Neumann, J., 365

Walker, J. F., 69
Warburton, G. B., 301
Ward, W., 117, 135, 137, 138, 188, 189, 190
Watson, J. B., 124, 362
Watt, J., 193
Webb, E., 66, 67, 80
Wechsler, D., 252
Weisenburg, T., 169
Wellman, B. L., 174, 180
Werner, H., 170
Whewell, W., 193
White, J. C., 234, 277
White, P. O., 263
Wiersma, E., 80
Wilkins, W. L., 235
Williams, E. D., 133
Williams, H. S., 108
Winckelmann, J. J., 193
Wing, H. D., 118, 133
Wiseman, S., 15, 268, 301
Wissler, C., 38, 134, 135
Witkin, H., 295, 301
Wolff, C. F., 360
Wolfle, D., 121, 122, 135
Wolsey, T., 193
Woodrow, H., 244, 251, 321
Woodworth, R. S., 341, 344, 346
Woodyard, E., 353
Wright, S., 342
Wundt, W., 37, 118, 135

Yerkes, R. M., 326
Young, J. Z., 122
Young, M., 231

Zentner, P., 294
Zwingli, H., 193

Subject Index

Abstraction, 130
Aesthetic processes, 132
Age, differentiation of abilities with, 107, 117, 325
Animals, researches on, 175
Aphasia, 165
Apprehension of relations
  analytic v. synthetic, 131
  combination of relations, 132
  content factors v. formal factors, 131
Aptitudes, 16
Arithmetical ability, 126
Army Alpha test, 11, 78, 97
Association, 121, 123
Assortative mating, 199
Attainment tests, 12–15
Attention, 135

Brain damage, 168–72

Californian Growth Study, 371
Cattell – Peterson factors, 212, 216–17, 221
Classics, 58
Cognitive ability, 143, 145
Comprehensive education, 92
Consolidation process, 254
Convergent thinking, 143, 152
Correlation, 21, 38, 43–9
Creativity see Originality
Cybernetics, 314

Development Quotient, 337
Diet deficiencies, 353
Digit span, 234, 236, 237, 252
Direct learning tests, 231–4
Divergent thinking, 148
  tests, 262

Educational opportunity, 90, 273
Educational selection, 84
  academic v. practical types, 113–15
  motives for, 88–93
Emotion, 136
Environment
  class differences, 201
  effects on bright children, 201
  effects on genetic factors, 69
  infantile deprivation, 356

intrauterine, 195
  maximizing potential, 350, 357
  parental behaviour, 339
  school effects, 83, 112, 200, 351–2
Ethnic groups, 286, 287
  interactions of social class and ethnicity, 288, 290
Eugenics, 97, 98
Evaluative abilities, 154
Examination marks, 27

Factor analysis
  effect of age on, 329
    culture on, 327
    range of ability on, 106
    temperamental influences on, 111
    training on, 109
  group factors, 104, 106
  limitations of, 246
  principal components, 117
  psychological nature of factors, 109
  second-order factors, 190
  speed factor, 134
  $v:ed$ and $k:m$, 101, 106, 110, 112, 113
  verbal factor, 130, 209, 218, 285, 298
Factorial separability, 210
Fluency, 123, 149
Furneaux model, 247

Generalization, 130
Genes, 69
Genetics and race, 275
Greek civilization, 93
Gypsy children, 325

Heritability estimates, 235
Historical personality factors, 225 ff.
Hopi children, 354

Imagery, 124
Imagination, 123
Intelligence
  character and, 95, 112
  crime and, 97
  dispersion of, 30, 89, 317
  education and, 96, 97, 158

experience and, 333
factor analysis of, 12, 74
  bipolar factors, 103
  British *v.* American methods, 87,
    104
  centroid method, 103, 117
  group factors, 16, 101
  primary abilities, 16, 105
  Spearman's *g*, 50, 71, 87, 116, 228
  specific factors, 76
  Thomson's sampling theory, 109,
    112
  heredity and environment and, 14,
    69, 78
  analysis of variance model, 344,
    346, 356
  and early learning, 177, 356
  and educational planning, 351
  different cultures, 174, 322
  hereditary genius, 192
  innate potential *v.* level of
    functioning, 173
  interaction of, 348
  Mendelian hypothesis, 185, 197,
    341
  'path coefficients', 342
  relative influence of, 199, 344, 373
measurement of, 41, 86
  culture-fair tests, 178, 213, 231,
    285, 322
  errors of sampling, 73, 339
  error variance, 104
  examples of item-difficulty,
    general population, 165–8
  mental age, 10, 87
  practice effects, 77
  teachers' gradings, 42, 189
  tests, 76, 124
  units of, 87
memory and, 121
national need for, 91
nature of, 56, 84, 336
  and character, 95
  as mental energy, 79, 191
  as strategies for processing
    information, 363, 374
    definition of, Burt's, 187
    Cicero's usage, 184
    Hebb's A and B, 162, 173, 365
    Thurstone's classification, 316
  intelligent behaviour, 85
  1921 Symposium, 183
  unitarian doctrine, 138
personality and, 111
politics and, 98
social differences and, 93
Interests, 113, 114, 138

Introversion–extraversion, 70, 120,
  258, 264
IQ
  assumption of constancy of, 14, 97,
    174, 359
  fluctuation of, 337
  infant *v.* adult, 180
  interaction between mother and
    child, 338
  and learning, 251
  lowering of, 318
  reliability and validity of, 336, 340,
    371
  Stanford–Binet, 106, 125, 141,
    169, 230, 234, 277, 281, 317
Irrationalism, 97

Learning
  and ability, 314
  and intelligence, 251, 253
  limits of, 316
  overlearning, 320
  role in perception, 317
  transfer, 318

McLaughlin–Eysenck experiment,
  260
Mathematical ability, 27–8, 56–8
Maxplane, 215, 219, 224
Maturation *see* Predetermined
  development
Mechanical ability, 81, 101, 129
Memory, 28, 71, 81, 105, 121, 143
  general factor, 122
  memory types, 123
  symbolic and semantic, 148
Mental speed function, 249, 251,
  259
  and intelligence, 250
Moray House tests, 190
Morrisby Compound Series test,
  261
Motor abilities, 120
Multifactorial inheritance, 198
Multiple correlation, 105
Musical ability, 57–9

Negro intelligence, 276–8
Nervous system, 116, 185
Norwood Report, 112
Nursery schools, 351

Originality, 151
Oscillation, 74, 80

Patterns, 279, 282
Perceptual processes
  general sense perception, 119

motor capacity, 120
visual perception, 128
Performance tests, 127
Perseveration, 70–71, 74, 80
Persistence, 80
Phenylpyruvenic feeble-mindedness, 347
Piaget
  accommodation, 368
  behavioural landmarks, 339
  on the development of intelligence, 365
  schemata, 336, 354
Practical ability, 127
  v. educational verbal ability, 227
Pragmatism, 95
Pre-determined development, 355, 360;
Primary mental abilities, 16, 105, 107, 248
  see also IQ
Progressive Matrices, 234, 237, 240

Reasoning, 130, 147
Rotoplot, 215, 219, 224

Scholastic achievement, 78, 83, 105, 112
Scree test, 219, 220, 222–4
Sensory processes, 118
  hearing, 118
  kinaesthesis, 119
  sight, 118
  smell, 119

Short-term memory, 237
Social class, 163, 201, 279, 280, 286
  class differences, 235
Socioeconomic status (SES), 230–41
Spatial ability, 71, 101, 128, 132
Structure of abilities, 101, 115
  broad and narrow group factors, 104
  compensation theories, 112
  Guilford's operational classes, 143, 156, 245, 248
  hierarchical structure, 106, 110, 115
  principal components, 117
  receptive *v.* executive functions, 134
  second order factors, 190
  special talents, 114

Temperament, 137, 191
Terman–Merrill test, 106
Test-sophistication, 167
Tetrad differences, 67, 72
Thurstone's Primary Factors, 245
Transfer *see* Learning
Twins, 161, 179, 195, 343

Verbal ability, 71, 77, 101, 124
Vocabulary, 171, 256

Wechsler scale, 230, 277
  test, 252

Yerkes–Dodson Law, 255, 258, 260